From Environmental Action to Ecoterrorism?

From Environmental Action to Ecoterrorism?

Towards a Process Theory of Environmental and Animal Rights Oriented Political Violence

Gerry Nagtzaam

Associate Professor, Faculty of Law, Monash University, Australia

Edward Elgar
PUBLISHING

Cheltenham, UK • Northampton, MA, USA

Published by
Edward Elgar Publishing Limited
The Lypiatts
15 Lansdown Road
Cheltenham
Glos GL50 2JA
UK

Edward Elgar Publishing, Inc.
William Pratt House
9 Dewey Court
Northampton
Massachusetts 01060
USA

A catalogue record for this book
is available from the British Library

Library of Congress Control Number: 2016949938

This book is available electronically in the **Elgar**online
Social and Political Science subject collection
DOI 10.4337/9781785367359

Printed on elemental chlorine free (ECF)
recycled paper containing 30% Post-Consumer Waste

ISBN 978 1 84980 119 5 (cased)
ISBN 978 1 78536 735 9 (eBook)

Typeset by Columns Design XML Ltd, Reading
Printed and bound in the USA

Parts of this book have already been published as:

Gerry Nagtzaam and Pete Lentini (2008) 'Vigilantes on the high seas?: The Sea Shepherds and political violence', *Terrorism and Political Violence*, **20**, pp. 110–33.

Gerry Nagtzaam (2014) 'Gaia's Navy: the Sea Shepherd Conservation Society's battle to stay afloat and international law', *William & Mary Environmental Law & Policy Review*, **38** (3), pp. 613–96.

Gerry Nagtzaam (2014) 'End of the line? Paul Watson and the future of the Sea Shepherd Conservation Society', *Journal of Arts and Humanities*, **3** (2), pp. 9–20.

Gerry Nagtzaam (2014) 'Righting the ship?: Australia, New Zealand and Japan at the ICJ and the barbed issue of "scientific whaling"', *Australian Journal of Environmental Law*, **1**, pp. 71–95.

Contents

Acknowledgements

This book is dedicated to Jason Sherlock, of the Gunnadoos, the best captain I ever played under. Until we both can take block together again.

I would sincerely like to thank a number of people without which this book would never have been completed. Firstly my thanks go to my friend and colleague Pete Lentini without whom this book project would never have even begun. Your willingness to help me never ceases to amaze me. Secondly my thanks go out to my able research assistant Sarah for patiently researching and compiling the huge reams of information a book like this takes. Lastly my gratitude and thanks to Kim for all her help with the proofreading, and patience as I worked far too many weekends and evenings on this book.

Abbreviations

AEPA	Animal Enterprise Protection Act
ALF	Animal Liberation Front
ALFSG	Animal Liberation Front Supporters' Group
ARM	Animal Rights Militia
ARNI	Animal Rights National Index
EF!	Earth First!
ELF	Earth Liberation Front
EMETIC	Evan Mecham Eco Terrorism International Conspiracy
ENGO	environmental non-governmental organization
FBI	Federal Bureau of Investigation
HLS	Huntingdon Life Sciences
ICR	Institute of Cetacean Research
ICRW	International Convention for the Regulation of Whaling
IWC	International Whaling Commission
JARPA II	Japanese Whale Research Program under Special Permit in the Antarctic II
JD	Justice Department
NAALPO	North American Animal Liberation Press Office
NETCU	National Extremism Tactical Coordination Unit
NGO	non-governmental organization
PETA	People for the Ethical Treatment of Animals
RARE II	Roadless Area Review Evaluation
RCMP	Royal Canadian Mounted Police
RSPCA	Royal Society for the Prevention of Cruelty to Animals
SHAC	Stop Huntingdon Animal Cruelty
SSCS	Sea Shepherd Conservation Society
SUA	United Nations Convention for the Suppression of Unlawful Acts Against the Safety of Maritime Navigation
UNCLOS	United Nations Convention on the Law of the Sea

Introduction

The introduction of modern environmental activism in the 1960s also saw the eventual emergence of a strain of radical environmentalism, which believed that the damage being done to the planet by actors like states and corporations required a more robust response than mere protesting. These environmentally minded individuals and groups are concerned that the pace of change is not occurring fast enough or in a direction they deem appropriate through mainstream political avenues.[1] The central question here is, to paraphrase Mohammed Hafez and Creighton Mullins, why and how, and to what extent do environmental activists in democratic and affluent societies come to embody radical ideologies to the point where they are willing to commit political violence in the furtherance of their cause?[2] The aim of this book is to provide some answers to this question.

To their opponents such actors are 'ecoterrorists';[3] to others, who applaud their behaviour, they are ecowarriors committing ecotage on behalf of Mother Earth.[4] Indeed, like in other political movements, there have been instances in which a small minority of environmental activists engaged in political violence to attempt to advance their agendas. Environmental-oriented political violence may also be considered to be associated with a form of identity politics. In these circumstances, the terrorists view humans and non-human species as equals. Hence, the identity politics espoused here is one that could be considered to be more of a non-hierarchical, non-anthropomorphic nature.

Radical environmentalists perceive themselves as 'entrenched' in a battle for environmental and animal liberation 'against the social order'.[5] H.H.A. Cooper argues that terrorists come to believe that maintenance of the status quo is far worse than the violence they perpetrate.[6] Radical environmental groups can fit this mould, arguing that acts such as scientific experimentation on animals and the destruction of habitat are the true crimes.[7] Acts that to outsiders may be considered terrorism are considered by these groups to be just revenge for these social evils, or a lesser evil than that perpetrated by governments or corporations. Thus 'terrorism' is perceived as the only recourse available to provide redress or end actions considered evil.[8]

However, given that this book seeks to understand whether environmental groups have radicalized to the point of utilizing violence it is important to use nomenclature correctly. While their opponents may decry them as terrorists this has not been demonstrated as accurate. One purpose of this book is to determine the veracity of such claims. Consequently, it will not utilize the term 'ecoterrorism' to apply to their actions at this stage (unless a quote or criticism) but will refer to 'radical environmental groups'.[9]

It is important initially to note that, from a research perspective, the accuracy of the number and severity of any purported action remains uncertain. The questionable nature of any public information on environmental protest and incidents occurs because: first, any individual and any action may be taken on as the responsibility of one of the organizations. This means that hundreds of individuals partaking in a single action increases significantly the appearance of the group's activity level.

Second, a member of the public can perform an action and claim it on behalf of the organization (through an online communiqué or a simple vandal tagging at the scene of the action), and it is impossible to know how many activists are core, repeat offenders or fed-up citizens taking part in a single, frustrated action. Third, not only is there the potential for groups to take credit for random acts of defiance and destruction, but it is just as likely that shop owners do not report every act of destruction – for a myriad of reasons, including fear of further retaliation, a potential increase to their insurance or even the attempt to reopen their business as quickly as possible. Lastly, collaborations between radical environmental groups are quite common, allowing the illusion of a more active and larger movement.

According to Bandow, 'ecoterrorism' as a phenomenon first manifested in the early 1970s. One of the first known cases involved an individual known as 'the Fox', engaged in a campaign of ecosabotage against Chicago-area firms during that time period. In 1972 a group calling itself 'Environmental Action' published the self-help guide *Ecotage!*.[10] According to Long, the 1970s provided an increase in the number of acts of environmental sabotage across the USA, including the destruction of mining equipment on Black Mesa in the Desert Southwest by the Arizona Phantom.[11] Former activists, despairing at the state of the environment and the glacial pace of change in humanity's attitude towards nature, in the decade after the modern environmental movement was born went on to form groups such as the Animal Liberation Front (1971), the Sea Shepherd Conservation Society (1977), Earth First! (1979) and its spinoff group the Earth Liberation Front, all of which are the subject of inquiry here.[12]

While these groups (at least initially) swore off targeting individuals for violence there have been examples where individuals have utilized physical violence in pursuit of environmental goals. Theodore Kaczynski (the Unabomber) is a prominent example of such radical eco-activism, who in 1978 undertook an 18-year individual bombing campaign against what he considered to be the environmentally destructive 'industrial-technological' system. His bombings were responsible for the deaths of three people and injuries to a further 23.[13]

Young further argues that by the 1980s, 'a few groups had started to engage in similar activities' – including the 'Bolt Weevils' in Minnesota, the 'Ecoraiders' in Arizona, the 'Billboard Bandits' in Michigan and the 'Eco-Commandoes' in Florida.[14] The damage caused by these groups, and others, has been significant in the UK, Canada and the USA. The increasing radical activities of environmental organizations in this period caused concern for 'political and industry leaders' and intelligence services, particularly in Western democracies where such groups were most prevalent. Groups such as the Earth Liberation Front and the Animal Liberation Front have been accused of utilizing intimidation and violence against both property and persons to bring about environmental change.[15]

Despite the concern by governments and security forces there has been a surprising paucity of academic writings analysing the overall phenomenon in a cogent and overarching way. As Eagan notes, 'little scholarly attention has been paid to the phenomenon of eco-terrorism'.[16] Further, few recently published books on the occurrence of terrorism mention ecoterrorism. Those publications that mention ecoterrorism only do so 'in a paragraph or a page or two at best. In these short descriptions, these authors also generally fail to provide a definition of eco-terrorism that lends itself to empirical research.'[17]

Thus despite the plethora of works on environmentalism and terrorism the phenomenon of 'ecoterrorism' remains relatively unstudied and undertheorized.[18] According to Taylor, there appears to be major and problematic differences between activist empirical accounts of their activities, which tend to be hagiographic, and outsider or academic accounts of the historical growth of such groups that tend to focus on one group operating in isolation.[19] Further, academic research in this area has not tended to examine such entities as part of a continuing *process* as is customary in terrorism studies. As such, Taylor concludes, 'these phenomena deserved much closer scrutiny than most had heretofore received'.[20] Relative to the issue there has been little academic empirical work that systematically documents the ongoing activities of these groups.[21] Rather the scholarly 'gap' has tended to be filled by government institutions monitoring such groups, in particular the Federal Bureau of Investigation (FBI).[22]

Although there are works that address environmental and animal rights actors, outside of a handful of contributions to scholarly journals such as *Terrorism and Political Violence* and *Studies in Conflict & Terrorism* there are few that are not either alarmist, implying that all environmental and animal rights actors intend to derail contemporary civilization, or that uncritically glorify all the acts they take, regardless of whether they destroy property or actually or potentially place people in harm's way, including circumstances that could have lethal consequences.

Commentators have also tended to understand this concept through the prism of their particular political bias when analysing this phenomenon. The term 'ecoterrorism' is utilized by proponents and opponents alike uncritically, particularly in public discourse – notwithstanding some insightful analyses from various academic researchers. However, to date no book has sought to engage with this topic that is neither hagiography nor a polemic screed against ecowarriors or ecoterrorists.

Environmental-oriented and animal rights-motivated violence constitutes significant scholarly and security concerns for two main reasons, and deserves more in-depth analysis. First, the environment is increasingly becoming the main global political issue. Indeed, it is one matter in which it is plausible to state that all humans are stakeholders. However, governments and others have not been able, often due to financial and other pressures, to deliver policies that may satisfy those individuals who had voted for them in the hope of seeing substantial change in environmental legislation and practices. In these respects, they may face a credibility gap amongst some of their most ardent supporters.

Within the context of political violence this is indeed significant as there is research which suggests that terrorism is often caused not by feelings of powerlessness and destitution, but by the feeling that progress was being made on a set of issues and that it was abruptly ended. In these respects terrorism occurs as a response to dashed expectations.[23] Therefore, governments' failure to address environmental issues in full may be a cause for concern for sporadic or premeditated violence from a small minority of environmental-oriented actors.

Second, the argument has been made by some researchers and opponents of radical environmentalism that violence by some radical environmental groups has occurred more frequently and has escalated in intensity.[24] Monaghan argues that, at least applied to the example of animal rights terrorism, incidents in the UK have in fact been reduced due to a sophisticated policing and judicial response.[25]

Adopting a historical narrative approach will enable a determination as to whether the selected radical environmental groups are carrying out operations in greater numbers and with ever-increasing political violence. Thus, there is a need to develop a more enhanced understanding of environmental and animal rights-oriented actors, and their actual and potential use of political violence – and, more importantly, to identify what features may have been factors in influencing them to revert to the use of political violence, including terrorism. Such an initiative would sit well with the emerging literature on radicalization.[26]

This book further seeks to understand and identify what, if any, are the various trigger points for moving from one stage of radicalism to the next. It examines the issue of targeting carried out by such groups with their emphasis on ecotage (or ecosabotage) that privileges attacks on property rather than humans.[27] It considers whether we can observe an escalation in environmental political action, as the breeding pool for such activists is becoming much larger as ecological consciousness becomes widespread within the global community. Given that issues such as global warming are receiving such widespread attention, can we expect to see an upsurge in environmental political action as individuals/groups become concerned that the pace of reform is not fast enough to deal with what they consider to be an imminent threat to the planet?

Although global in scope, the book concentrates mainly on organizations and groups from three countries: the USA, the UK and Australia, but other examples are included where relevant. These three countries are significant for understanding these movements for several key reasons. First, animal rights activism has its origins in the UK (Hunt Saboteurs, Animal Liberation Front), and some of its most active groups (Stop Huntingdon Animal Cruelty) operate there. Further, the Environmental Liberation Front was also born there in 1992. The USA also has a very strong tradition of environmental activism ranging from groups such as the Sierra Club, and was the initial home for Earth First!. Australia also has a strong environmental-oriented culture. It has members of the Green Party sitting in federal and various state parliaments. There have also been acts of environmental-oriented violence conducted in Australia. Recently, the Earth Liberation Front threatened the director of a major Australian power plant.[28] Additionally, the Sea Shepherds often use Australian ports to begin their campaigns to disrupt Japanese whaling.

This book further seeks to rigorously examine the growth of radical environmental groups operating on a global scale, how they form, their principles, philosophies and their history. Specifically, it seeks to generate understandings on how or whether such groups evolve from activists to militants to ecoterrorists and argues that such a progression is a process that can be explained. For the purposes of this book an ecoterrorist group is one that uses or threatens the use of violence of a criminal nature against innocent victims or property by an environmental-oriented group for environmental–political reasons, or violence aimed at an audience beyond the target, often of a symbolic nature.[29]

It has been argued that the primary objective of ecoterror is to preserve the environment. Such activity is starkly distinct from 'normal environmentalism' in the belief of 'doing whatever they consider necessary to disrupt any activity or project that they determine is detrimental or a threat to the environment'.[30] The belief of many radical environmental groups is that, 'through fear and economic damage, environmental "violators" will cease their behavior'.[31]

Given the scope of this book, not all radical environmental groups can be examined. Thus it critically examines the key radical environmental groups, both historically and currently active in such activities, including Earth First!, the Earth Liberation Front, the Animal Liberation Front and the Sea Shepherd Conservation Society. Further, it examines questions of how such groups perceive their actions, and addresses questions of whether they see themselves as vigilantes, upholding a higher law on behalf of the environment or whether they view themselves outside of any law.[32] It further seeks to understand the group's motivations, history and objectives in a broader thematic context. In particular, it is concerned with how these groups adopted violence as a tactic within their overall strategies to effect social change on behalf of the biosphere.

The proposed study contains several novel features:

- First, unlike most current books on 'ecoterrorism' that concentrate on an uncritical narrative, this book seeks to establish an historical understanding of *why* groups advocate and conduct political violence on behalf of the environment, by critically examining the history and actions of these groups.
- Second, it compares and contrasts the selected groups, highlighting their similarities and differences as regards their use of political violence and pathways of radicalization.
- Third, it attempts to fuse existing theoretical approaches to group radicalization – but with some focus on identifying the type of individual who becomes involved with radical environmentalism – and apply them as a model to current global radical environmental groups to determine their efficaciousness.

However, before we can proceed to examine potential political radicalization of environmental groups there is a need to understand key terms that will be utilized in this text.

UNPACKING THE TERM: TERRORISM

Whilst terrorism has been a mode of political violence for almost two millennia it has been amongst the most debated terms in political science and public discourse.[33] Defining the term 'terrorism' has proven fraught for researchers given the different perspectives and rationales advanced for the concept. There are numerous definitions of 'terrorism' that can be observed. Quillen correctly observes, 'far too many trees have been slain and far too much ink spilled debating the exact definition of terrorism' and that there 'are as many definitions of terrorism as there are acts of terrorism'. Establishing an agreed-upon definition has proven difficult.[34] The term 'terrorism' first emerged in the Oxford English Dictionary (1795) as, 'a government policy intended to strike with terror those against whom it was adopted'.[35] However, according to O'Lear, attempting to define terrorism is, 'like aiming at a moving target since the meaning of the word changes over time'.[36] Edward Said believes:

> The use of the word terrorism is usually unfocused, it usually has all kinds of implicit validations of one's own brand of violence, it's highly selective. If you accept this as the norm, then it becomes so universally applicable that it loses any force whatsoever. I think it is better to drop it.[37]

Griset and Mahan further argue that it is difficult to define since there are multiple types of terrorism, ranging from guerilla warfare and conventional warfare to criminal activity. The use of the term is always subjective and invariably utilized for partisan purposes.[38] Alex Schmid argues that thus there cannot possibly be one true definition of terrorism because it is an abstract concept that no single definition can encompass.[39]

A detailed engagement with the debate over the definition of terrorism is beyond the scope of this book and the term is and will remain an essentially contested concept. For the purposes of this inquiry, however, it is not necessary to resolve this epistemological fight. Schmid offers us a way forward. He notes that most leading definitions of the concept include two characteristics: 'someone is terrorized, and the meaning of the term is derived from terrorists' targets and victims'.[40] Building on this Monaghan argues that, while a definition cannot be agreed upon, scholars and governments have agreed to the following as 'core characteristics' of the phenomenon:

1. The use or threat of violence;
2. The existence of a political motive;
3. The targets selected are representative of a target category;
4. The aim is to terrorize, or create fear;
5. The goal is to modify behaviour;
6. The method employed may be extreme or unusual;
7. The act of terrorism is an act of communication.[41]

Features that are required to label the movement as 'terrorist' include:

> The distinguishing characteristic of the terrorist ... is a deliberate decision to abandon [conventional moral] restraints or to refuse to accept as binding the prevailing moral distinctions between belligerents and neutrals, combatants and non-combatants, appropriate and inappropriate targets, legitimate and illegitimate methods. The terrorist *knows* that others will regard his actions as shocking or as atrocities, and this is one reason why he acts as he does, for his object in using terror ... is to create a 'new consciousness' by methods which provoke extreme emotional reactions – panic, horror, revulsion, outrage, and sympathy ... The nature of the act, not the status of the persons who commit it, is the critical feature.[42]

Lentini proffers that most scholarly and state definitions define terrorism as: 'non-state actors using or threatening to use violence against civilians, non-violence and property in order to effect political change to achieve political goals by establishing a state of fear'.[43] Thus, building on the aforementioned definitions for the purposes of this inquiry it can broadly be defined as using or threatening to use violence against innocent people or non-combatants – or even property – to effect political change and achieve political goals by creating an atmosphere of fear.[44]

Left Wing/Right Wing/Special Interest Terrorism

While the term 'ecoterrorism' has thus been adopted to cover a range of different environmentally radical actions there have been attempts both to categorize and understand the phenomenon. There is some debate amongst researchers and government agencies as to how to classify accurately 'ecoterrorist' activities. One possibility is considering them to be left-wing terrorists as opposed to right-wing terrorism.[45] According to the FBI, such groups tend to 'profess a revolutionary socialist doctrine and view themselves as protectors of the people against the dehumanizing effects of capitalism and imperialism'.[46]

The objective of left-wing groups is to 'bring change in the U.S. and they believe this change will be realized through revolution rather than through the established political process'.[47] Smith's study found that 'it may very well be that animal rights and ecologists are politically leftist', though it is important to note that he was unable to come to a definite conclusion.[48]

However, the US government considers that 'ecoterrorism' should be understood as a type of *special interest* extremism.[49] Accordingly it should be distinguished from both traditional right-wing and left-wing extremism in that proponents seek to resolve specific issues (in this case ending the ongoing destruction of the environment) rather than seek to effect overarching political change through a revolution. Examples of such groups include anti-abortion groups, animal rights advocates and radical environmental activists.[50] Single-issue campaigns such as those focused on animal rights or protecting the global environment have seen adherents utilize political violence. Despite, however, some groups adopting tactics more usually associated with terrorism there has been a reluctance to label them as such since it is argued they pose no existential threat to the state.[51]

This book will also seek to determine which classification is correct. Are radical environmental groups influenced by revolutionary socialist doctrine that considers the root cause of environmental degradation to be capitalism? Or are they a special interest that focuses merely on one specific issue, which if resolved would mean that for such groups their *raison d'être* for existence would cease to be and they would disband? Or should they be understood as an amalgam of both approaches, requiring a new classification?

Etymology and Defining 'Ecoterrorism'

The labelling of environmental activism as terrorist can be traced back to its usage by private security companies in 1988 to describe these activities.[52] On top of various private security firms, public relations offices have also been responsible for the spread of such a label. In 1991 a leaked memo written by the public relations firm Ketchum, representing Clorox, exposed that there was a crisis management plan targeting Greenpeace for its chlorine phase-out campaign, concerned it would target private households and their use of bleach and thus impact profits.[53]

The plan, set out by Ketchum, recommended labelling the non-governmental organization as 'terrorists' and accusing the group of violence and conducting 'spurious research'. It further relied on separate industry associations to promote a 'Stop Environmental Terrorism' campaign, which would demand Greenpeace and the media to 'be more responsible and less irrational in their approach'.[54] According to Rowell the plan was devised by Ketchum and Clorox in order to bring about a paradigm shift in the public's perception of the group's activities: that they were in fact violent.[55]

A second example of such labelling is evidenced in the release of a false memo purportedly written by Earth First!, which called for 'acts of violence' against forestry workers that was sent to the *San Francisco Examiner* but was actually drafted and distributed by public relations firms representing the forestry industry in order to discredit the environmental movement.[56]

If groups like Greenpeace, which publicly advocates only 'bearing witness' to environmental damage, are accused of 'ecoterrorism' it can be observed that the actions for which groups like Earth First!, the ELF and Sea Shepherd have been held responsible have easily been labelled as 'ecoterrorism' or 'environmental terrorism'. By the mid-1990s the term was used to label any act of sabotage committed by these groups. It became the preferred term utilized not only by their opponents but also the mainstream news media, law enforcement and politicians.[57]

Radical environmental activists maintain, however, that the use of labels such as 'ecoterrorism' and 'environmental terrorism' unfairly 'spread blame to all who care about protecting the Earth'.[58] Some activists argue that: 'simply debating the term eco-terrorism gives it legitimacy' and allows law enforcement to clamp down on their activities since they are 'terrorist' in nature.[59] On the other hand, environmentalists have also been known to use exaggeration and overstatement in their use of the term and attempt to pin the label on their opponents. Dick Russell, an environmentalist, argues that, 'the real eco-terrorism is being committed every day by corporate America'.[60]

It is important when examining the phenomenon of 'ecoterrorism' to keep in mind that simply using the term does not 'provide much clarity or precision, confusing acts of terrorism with acts of civil disobedience, pollution and journalism'.[61] Further, some commentators such as Karasick are critical of using such a wide approach of defining the concept, arguing that, 'broadly defined ecoterror may include legitimate activity and attach to that activity the stigma of being labeled "terrorism"'.[62]

'Ecoterrorism', like terrorism, remains an essentially contested term: a plethora of researchers from various disciplines have generated multiple definitions and understandings. Schwartz argues that many North American academics have, at least within the North American domestic arena, uncritically accepted the concept.[63] Karasick maintains that the concept (and definitions) of 'ecoterror' involves the 'use of fear-inducing coercive tactics to the end of either protecting the environment or influencing those who may be affecting the environment to protect the environment (or at least cease affecting the environment)'.[64] Chalecki defines it as: 'the violent destruction of property perpetrated by the radical fringes of environmental groups in the name of saving the environment from further human encroachment and destruction'.[65]

According to Vlahos, 'ecoterrorism' is best understood as the 'violent destruction of property perpetrated most often by the radical fringes of environmental groups in the name of saving the environment from further human encroachment and destruction'.[66] Eagan states that the term is 'used to denote the use or threatened use of violence of a criminal nature against innocent victims or property by an environmentally oriented subnational group for environmental-political reasons, aimed at an audience beyond the target, and often of a symbolic nature'.[67] Eagan argues that the aim of an 'ecoterrorist' is to 'slow or halt the exploitation of natural resources and to bring public attention to environmental issues such as unsustainable logging or wildlife habitat loss through development'.[68]

Similar to labelling an individual a 'terrorist', labelling an entity as an 'ecoterrorist' organization can be considered a categorical assessment of their illegitimacy.[69] Some argue that: 'use of the term implies a degree of illegitimacy, and questions of legitimacy are inherently subjective'. As Richard E. Rubenstein points out:

> To call an act of political violence terrorist is not merely to describe it but to judge it ... Descriptively, 'terrorism' suggests violent action by individuals or small groups. Judgmentally, it implies illegitimacy ... To the defenders of a particular regime or social order, any politically motivated disobedience (even mass resistance) smacks of terrorism ... And on the other hand, a regime in power is considered terrorist by those who deny its legitimacy even if they are but a handful and their opponents legions. Nobody wants to be called a terrorist; terrorism is what the *other* side is up to.[70]

One potential problem involves a state establishing a definition that includes as many different activities as possible. For example, in the proposed US Stop Terrorism Property Act of 2003, the Act defined 'ecoterror' as implicating anyone who 'intentionally damages the property of another with the intent to influence the public with regard to conduct the offender considers harmful to the environment'.[71]

Chief Jarboe of the US Federal Bureau of Investigation Counterterrorism Division provided a more useful and the most cited definition in testimony before the US Congress in 2002, when he defined 'ecoterrorism' as:

> [T]he use or threatened use of violence of a criminal nature against innocent victims or property by an environmentally-oriented, sub-national group for environmental-political reasons, or aimed at an audience beyond the target, often of a symbolic nature.[72]

There are several problems with this definition. First, it does not account for the global reach of some of these groups. Radical environmental groups are now supranational in nature – with a worldwide following on the internet and cells scattered worldwide. Second, Chief Jarboe's FBI definition related to domestic groups does not apply to groups such as Sea Shepherd that act primarily on the high seas, generally outside of state jurisdiction. Third, there is an ongoing dispute amongst activists and researchers as to whether property damage should be considered violence so as to constitute ecoterrorism.

Is Ecotage (Destroying Property) Violence or a Terrorist Act?

Should the destruction of property alone be considered 'violent' or a 'terrorist' act or is it 'an unwarranted extension of the term that distorts its meaning?'[73] Some argue that such radical activities as these do not represent 'terrorism', as no human life is threatened by such activities. Weinberg and Davis maintain that terrorism is not the same as 'the sabotage of public or private property'.[74] Others, however, like Shackley, contend that we do a disservice if we dismiss these acts as mere pranks.[75] Further, Wiktorowicz argues that arson, vandalism and theft, being the preferred tactics of such groups, all fit into the FBI's definition of terrorism.[76]

It is important to highlight that the FBI definition, as espoused by Jarboe, removed the concept that an act should only harm persons in order to be classified terrorism, broadening it to include attacks on property.[77] The then FBI Director Louis French, appearing before Congress in May 2001, cited the propensity for environmental special interest extremists from the animal rights and environmental movements to increasingly use violence to advance their causes. This, he argued, meant that terrorism needed to be redefined to include attacks on property and such acts to be classified as 'ecoterrorism'.[78]

However, many question whether ecotage (that is, violence against inanimate objects rather than persons) should be classified as terrorism at all. For many activists who advocate destruction of property for a political purpose, such as Dave Foreman of Earth First!, the targeting of property for action is not considered a 'violent act'. However, legal codes invariably consider a crime of violence to include the use, or attempted use, of physical force against property.[79]

Such activists deem property's meaning to be socially constructed and, thus, any action against property must be examined in a historical/political context that allows for such actions, given the greater good that such actions may bring about.[80] As Vanderheiden points out, ecotage is not 'mindless, erratic vandalism'. Rather it is a calculated strategy against property that is environmentally destructive, for example bulldozers or logging equipment.[81] It is not targeted at life.[82] As Foreman explains, they pick their targets judiciously since vandalism is both counterproductive to their aims and immoral.[83]

A potential problem for ecotage adherents is that within its philosophy lies a conundrum that can derail any campaign or violate their stated principles in that they might well, in pursuit of their goals, cause inadvertent harm to humans, or their group could be taken over by those who are willing for humans to be killed or injured to further their cause.[84] Recklessness or negligence when committing ecotage that brings about an injury to humans may well constitute terrorism in the eyes of the law.

While there is debate regarding whether or not property damage should be considered as violent, arson and extensive vandalism are generally considered violent acts and crimes. What differentiates it from criminal acts for personal gain is the political motivation element. Ecotage also has victim-target differentiation, so it can be considered a form of terrorism.[85] Many environmental extremists, including Barbarash, insist that they are 'far from being terrorists' and that their actions focus on property not human life.[86] Given this ongoing debate, what needs to be considered is whether the acts of ecotage committed by these groups rise to the level of 'terrorism'.

POLITICAL RADICALIZATION

Historically, the literature on terrorism has tended to focus more on the last step, the 'transition to terrorism', rather than initial forms of protest or action. However, since the 9/11 attacks there has been greater focus on the earlier forms of activism and actions that can, in some cases, precede the use of political violence.[87]

Traditional sociological explanations of how *people* become terrorists focused on aspects such as political repression, socioeconomic marginalization and on indoctrination, but such factors have proved lacking in both theoretical parsimony and in predictive value.[88] Academics have further disproved the theory that radical individuals commit violent acts because they have a psychological disorder. The evidence shows that the rate of mental illness amongst terrorists is the same as among the general population.[89]

However problematically, like terrorism the concept of radicalism in the literature remains contested, but at its essence radicalism can be understood as diametrically opposed to political moderation and, critically to our understanding, it occurs on a continuum of action.[90] A terrorist is presumed to be a radical but a radical is not yet a terrorist.[91] A lengthy trajectory of radicalization and low-level violence almost invariably precedes the killing of civilians. A terrorist becomes 'mentally ready' to use lethal force only over time and when they have reached a stage when they have effectively dehumanized their perceived enemy.[92]

However, when examining the process of radicalization, what needs to be borne in mind is that while being a radical means rejecting the status quo it does not mean that all radicals engage in political violence.[93] This book therefore focuses on a subset of potential radicalization processes, namely that of violent radicalization, 'a process in which radical ideas are accompanied by the development of a willingness to directly support or engage in violent acts'.[94]

It is clear that some, but not all, activists do engage in political violence and can become terrorists.[95] However, as Moskalenko and McCauley point out, there is little systematic evidence provided in the literature as to how peaceful political action begets political violence in some cases.[96] Further, radicalization is underwritten by a 'syndrome of beliefs' about the current state of the world. Radicals believe that: 'We are a special or chosen group (superiority) who have been unfairly treated and betrayed (injustice), no one else cares about us or will help us (distrust) and the situation is dire – our group and our cause are in danger of extinction (vulnerability).'[97]

For the purposes of this book radicalization is defined as:

> [a] process in which individuals develop, adopt and embrace political attitudes and modes of behaviour which diverge substantially from those of any or all of the established and legitimate political, social, economic, cultural, and religious values, attitudes, institutions and behaviours which exist in a given society. Radicalization also involves advocating either replacing and/or attempting to replace the status quo by transgressing legitimate or accepted modes of political pursuits (electoral means, civil society organizations, sanctioned protests and strikes, and non-violent civil disobedience), using or condoning the use of violence against property or persons – whether private citizens or state employees – in order to implement new structures, values, leaders and elites which will usher in a new order or new society. Regardless

> whether they personally use, condone or encourage the use of violence by those other than themselves – or even disavow using violence entirely – radicals advocate significantly disrupting, dislocating and ultimately destroying existing political, economic, social and cultural norms and structures. The result of this process is an eponymous radical departure from that which they seek to overturn.[98]

The question that needs be asked is how does such radicalization occur? How do radical environmental groups that are prepared to utilize political violence move towards conflict and violence in attempting to achieve their goals? Understanding how environmental and animal rights groups radicalize from legal and socially sanctioned forms of protest to violent activity is an imperative for scholarly, counterterrorism and even environmental and animal rights activist stakeholders. This proposed volume seeks to provide such an analysis. First though we need to examine some of the prevailing theoretical models that seek to understand the process of radicalization.

The Process of Radicalization: Theoretical Models

There is contention amongst analysts over what fuels terrorism. Left-wing scholars and representatives from the developing world insist that poverty and destitution produce despair and foster conditions that force individuals to resort to violence to end what they perceive as unjust political, social, cultural, economic and even religious conditions.[99] Nevertheless, many terrorists, particularly their leaders, are drawn from the ranks of the middle class and are tertiary educated. Other theorists, usually of the centre-right orientations, associate terrorism with the presence of poor governance, corruption and lack of democratic institutions.[100]

Despite the upswing in scholarly interest in radicalization post-9/11 there is still no consensus as to the appropriate model to adopt when examining the process as to how individuals, or groups, become terrorists.[101] There tends to be greater agreement, however, that terrorism evolves as a process.[102] Radicalization when it occurs is not an overnight process, nor is there one single influence that brings it about. Most of the major academic models of radicalization (Sprinzak's 'delegitimization' stages, Moghadam's 'staircase' or Baran's 'conveyor belt') engender within them the idea that there is a progression over time involving different facets and an interplay of dynamics. While they may differ as to length and complexity of the process they all maintain that becoming a terrorist is a process and that the examination of radicalization entails discovering the nature of that process.[103]

When examining the literature on radicalization it is apparent that there are two levels of abstraction that can be focused on: first, the individual terrorist and how they became radicalized; second, focusing primarily on how groups radicalize to the point that they are willing to embrace political violence. This next section examines the current theories pertaining to both approaches.

Daalgard-Nielsen notes there are a number of strands of radical theorizing that can be utilized when examining ongoing radicalization of individuals. Gilles Kepel, Farhad Khosrokhavar and Olivier Roy argue that radicalization can best be understood as the individual trying to 'reconstruct a lost identity in a perceived hostile and confusing world'.[104] Their work focuses on how westernized Muslims in Europe attempt to create identities within an occasional unwelcoming Western society. Militant Islam can offer an answer to the search, providing a fixed values system, sense of community and an outlet from everyday frustrations such as ongoing racism. By blaming Western decadence for their exclusion individuals can rationalize their exclusion not as a personal failing but as a part of a Western systemic failure.[105]

Wiktorowicz utilizes framing theory that 'focuses on the social production and dissemination of meaning and on how individuals come to conceptualize themselves as a collectivity. A frame is an individual's worldview, consisting of values (notions about right and wrong) and beliefs (assumptions about the world, attributes of things, and mechanisms of causation).'[106] The main point is that frames are competing to become the dominant interpretation of social reality. How successful a group or movement is depends on its ability to make its version of reality resonate (frame alignment) with potential recruits.[107]

Framing, like the international relations theory of constructivism emphasizes the importance of social and intersubjective processes in establishing motivation when seeking to determine how activists become terrorists. How do 'normal' activists evolve into terrorists? Framing theory emphasizes how social and intersubjective processes create the motivation. Radical members are socialized through 'a constructed reality or worldview, which frames problems as not just misfortunes, but injustices, attributes responsibility for these injustices, and constructs an argument for the efficacy and/or moral justification of using violence against civilians to right the perceived wrongs'.[108]

Wiktorowicz maintains that being aggrieved does not inevitably lead to individuals undertaking political violence. Rather, for an individual to get to that point is best understood as a social process resulting from interactions both with and within a radical organization. As part of the process a person becomes convinced over time that due to injustices they can observe they must respond with physical violence.[109] Wiktorowicz never references the term radicalization in his article, preferring to focus on four processes he argues that can lead to someone joining an Islamic terrorist group: cognitive opening, religious seeking, frame alignment and socialization.[110]

Borum proposes a four-step approach to the emergence of the 'terrorist mindset' in individuals. The process begins with the 'framing of some unsatisfactory event, condition or grievance (It's not right) as being unjust (It's not fair). The injustice is blamed on a target policy, person or nation (It's your fault). The responsible party is then vilified – often demonized – (You're Evil) which facilitates justification or impetus for aggression.'[111] At the last stage negative stereotypes are perpetuated about group outsiders, with violence becoming legitimated towards the evil 'outgroup' that is held to be responsible for all apparent injustices.[112]

Similarly, Moghaddam's six-stage 'staircase' terrorism model begins with individuals having a 'desire to alleviate adversity and improve their situation. Unsuccessful attempts, however, lead to frustration, producing feelings of aggression, which are displaced onto some perceived causal agent (who is then regarded as the enemy). As their anger towards the enemy builds, some become increasingly sympathetic towards violent, extremist ideology and to the terrorist groups that act against them. Some of these sympathizers eventually join an extremist group, organization, or movement that advocates for, and perhaps engages in terrorist violence.'[113] Moghaddam argues that specific factors at each level can lead an individual deeper into radicalization and towards committing terrorist acts.[114]

WHAT TYPES OF INDIVIDUALS ARE ATTRACTED TO 'ECOTERRORISM'?

Given the focus of the above models on individuals undergoing radicalization, the key question to be considered is what kind of person is drawn to or willing to commit violent acts on behalf of the environment? Liddick argues: 'one of the most intriguing aspects of so-called eco-terrorism and animal liberation criminality is the mind-set and beliefs of the persons involved'.[115] Sprinzak argues that members of terrorist groups are generally an elite group led by young, well-educated middle- or upper-middle-class individuals.[116] Similarly, according to Eagan, the majority of environmental extremists are middle-class individuals who believe that: 'human beings are just an ordinary member of the biological community, no more important than, say, a bear or a whale'.[117] However, Scarce argues that a key distinguishing feature of many radical environmentalists is that they are 'poor to the point of destitution'. However, he does clarify this, arguing: 'this is by choice. They possess an array of talents, and most have at least some college education.'[118] Under this framework, cells tend to swing into action, not because of directives from above, but from a group of young men spending time with each other and spurring each other on.[119] Once a group has violent views they reach out to others that can connect them – in the case he examined, Al Qaeda. Or, alternatively, they act on their own recognizance inspired by ideology.[120]

Bakker's work also backs up a number of other studies which note that at least when applied to terrorists operating in Europe they vary widely in terms of age, socioeconomic background, education levels, occupation, family status and previous criminal record. Further, in terms of population and age they are 'normal' in terms of analysed socioeconomic factors.[121]

According to Nilson and Burke, 'it is hard to profile these terrorists' personalities in that they are perfectly normal, mentally healthy, educated and established individuals who have opted to engage in only this kind of deviant behavior'.[122] However, it has been argued that many terrorists begin with a troubled home and personal life. While this is not concluding that every troubled child will inevitably become a terrorist, 'studies of terrorist organizations have found a high incidence of fragmented families and violent childhoods, and the lives of many terrorists studied "demonstrated a pattern of failure both educationally and vocationally"'.[123] What needs to be considered is whether this holds true for people who have engaged in violent radical environmental action.

Liddick argues that the dedication of these activists should not be questioned, as they are what sociologist Eric Hoffer called 'true believers', and they wish to dedicate their lives to changing the world for the (perceived) better.[124] Eagan maintains that most terrorists (including environmental extremists) have an affinity with the philosophy of the cause to which they are dedicated.[125] When discussing the process of a non-violent animal/environmental activist developing into an ecoterrorist, Young argues that they are 'at least partly driven by the rising and falling fortunes for their cause'.[126]

Liddick argues that the role of women in the radical environmental and animal rights movements should not be downplayed. According to Ingrid Newkirk, 'the founder of ALF in the United States was a woman',[127] and the history of Earth First! tells us that women have always played an important role, sometimes assuming leadership or iconic positions, as in the cases of Judi Bari and Julia Hill.[128]

Within Einwohler's fieldwork she reports that many activists 'described themselves and their activism in terms of either emotional attachments to animals or emotional reactions to animal abuse and exploitation'.[129] Bartlett and Miller argue that four often overlooked factors can also influence how radicals can become terrorists: they may do so due to the emotional 'pull' they experience when confronted with injustice; for the thrill or 'coolness' of undertaking such activities; for the status conferred or because of an internal code of honour in place; or act due to peer pressure.[130]

McBride argues that a more sophisticated way to understand why terrorists engage in their activities is that the carrying out of terrorist acts can assuage existential anxiety. She proposes a theoretical model, an 'existential-terroristic feedback loop', for understanding terrorist ideologies. The feedback loop theory postulates that: 'existential anxiety compels individuals to seek meaning; for some individuals, support of a terrorist ideology functions as an anxiety-reducing, meaning-giving construct; these terrorist ideologies often result in acts of terrorist violence; terrorist violence ultimately exacerbates existential anxiety, compelling terrorists to defend their ideologies and returning them to the very state the ideologies were meant to relieve.'[131] For those individuals who commit political violence in the service of a radicalized terrorist ideology, the 'organization, ideology, religious themes, and combat environment all serve to mitigate existential anxiety'.[132]

Cottee and Hayward argue that engaging in terrorism for some adherents can be 'profoundly thrilling, empowering and spiritually intoxicating' and, while other motivations can be in play, it can be a crucial factor in understanding individual drives to commit such acts. The study of terrorism requires an understanding of how such adherents 'behave, how they think and ... *how they feel*'.[133] For some who engage in terrorism there can be three core existential motives, amongst other motivational drives, for doing so: (1) the desire for excitement; (2) the desire for ultimate meaning; and (3) the desire for glory. The carrying out of terrorist action for some allows for the manifestation of these existential desires.[134]

Cottee and Hayward, similarly to McBride, theorize that carrying out terrorism can relieve existential frustration at the boredom, banality or meaningless of life. Joining a terrorist organization furnishes members with 'an all-embracing cause and bonds of great intimacy and solidarity; they also open up a world of exhilarating action, violence, intrigue and drama'.[135]

Groups Evolving Towards Terrorism

The conducting of terrorism is both a political and collective activity; it is usually carried out by individuals acting in the context of a group identity. Thus understanding the nature and dynamics of terrorist groups should be considered essential by the researcher.[136] Writing in the early 1990s Sprinzak argued that the problem with terrorism research at that time was that it focused on explaining terrorists as opposed to terrorism – and current research reveals the same biases by most researchers in the area.[137] Problematically, individual cases of radicalization remain impossible to predict or determine with any certainty the factors that bring about individual radicalization.[138]

Rather, understanding the group process dynamic and its developmental stages is far more important than seeking to understand individual members' personal psychology motivations. Since the group identity overtakes much of the individual identity of adherents, and their actual behaviour can best be clarified by examining the psychology of the larger collective, there is a need to focus on this level of analysis.[139]

The most long-standing, and perhaps most respected, process theory of how groups embrace terrorism is Sprinzak's delegitimization perspective. Sprinzak argues that terrorism is best understood in political terms since it is an extension of opposition politics in a democracy. Sprinzak contends that political activists do not just suddenly decide to engage in terrorism. It almost always begins with non-violence by a group and, he argues, they proceed through a rather lengthy process that is involved with the delegitimization of the state.[140]

Sprinzak maintains that such a process 'involves a group of true believers who challenge authority long before they become terrorists, recruit followers, clash with the public agencies of law enforcement from a position of weakness, obtain a distinct collective world view, and, in time, radicalize within the organization to the point of becoming terroristic'.[141] Under such frameworks, the group believes that the state can no longer protect the interests of the identity group in the name that the terrorists are supposedly acting, in this case the environment. Sprinzak's model postulates that activists usually begin by engaging in protests using peaceful and lawful means, through such activities as strikes, demonstrations and other means of direct action and symbolic resistance actions to influence either the ballot box or civil society. Sprinzak calls this the 'crisis of confidence' phase.[142]

This crisis of confidence stage implies a conflict with the government and policies but the group is not seeking to challenge the foundations of the established political system. Rather the protesters assert that the government have misguided policies, rather than believing that the political system is fundamentally flawed. However, the group experiences a 'profound disenchantment' with the government that is beyond the typical political opposition on offer.[143] It can be observed at this stage that the distinctly different ideological group challenging the establishment will refuse 'to play according to the established rules of the game' but will not engage in illegal activity. If anything, its actions will be countercultural in nature.[144]

In the second phase, the conflict of legitimacy, the group begin to get more militant, as they view purely non-violent political or confrontational politics of limited success.[145] Further, the group is willing to question the legitimacy of the current political system and will seek to transform the system because of its flaws. The current system and its norms is thus delegitimated in favour of a new ideological and cultural system, which can be characterized as a break from the current political order. The stage is usually precipitated by a 'great disappointment' occurring with the previous stage. The former 'moderate' radicals are either frustrated by the government's responses to their demands/actions or from their failure to succeed in their endeavour, so they channel their frustration into more radical forms of protest.[146] They see themselves as 'soldiers in a just war' and their actions will create the required revolutionary conditions that will encourage a mass movement to develop.[147]

Thus an upswing in intense political action – running the gamut from angry protests (demonstrations, confrontations and vandalism) to acts of small-scale violence carried out against the state – can be observed. The group also undergoes intense radicalization and closes ranks, its members under great emotional change and 'totally consumed by the great moments' they are experiencing. The language and rhetoric enunciated by the group is both revolutionary and filled with exhortations of 'slanders and desecrations' against their enemy.[148] The conflict of legitimacy stage presupposes the emergence of an alternative ideological and cultural system that delegitimates the current regime and its code of social norms in the name of some better ones.[149]

In the final stage, the crisis of legitimacy, the activists make a complete transformation. Having failed to accept the rules of the game in which broader society rejects their initiatives (as exemplified by their inability to achieve political change through legal channels), a minority of individuals choose violence to attempt to achieve their political goals and to publicize their cause. During this crisis of legitimacy phase, these individuals consider anyone they define as associated with the regime to be an enemy, and they become willing to use violence against them.[150] At this level the formation of a small, isolated terror underground that engages in political violence against the regime and its allies can be observed. The group creates its own reality and strictly imposes on its adherents a new set of behavioural and moral standards.[151]

For Sprinzak this culminating stage has the terrorist group considering all people associated with the suspect political order to be depersonalized, dehumanized and virtually subhuman, allowing members to commit heinous actions up to and including murder.[152] To the members of the group the world becomes Manicheistic in nature, with the 'sons of light' (themselves) warring with the 'sons of darkness' (their opponents) – enabling a 'fantasy war' of the former versus the latter as fully legitimate. The first external sign of this stage is linguistic and symbolic in nature. Expressions of political delegitimation are 'no longer limited to political terms or social concepts but are extended to a language of objects, animals, or "human" animals'. The state and/or their lackeys are labelled as 'things', 'dogs', 'pigs', 'Nazis' or 'terrorists', enabling them to be killed because they are not legitimate members of the community and not human by default.[153] The group at this point often rejects conventional morality and believes itself free to engage in forms of criminality, or non-conventional sexual activity.[154] However, most radical groups stay the crisis of confidence or conflict of legitimacy levels rather than proceed to level three.[155]

Sprinzak argues that if terrorist activity is determined primarily by group identity two variables hold great explanatory value:

1. the changing symbolic behaviour of the activists involved – the ways in which they talk, categorize, theorize and stigmatize the world, both their own and that of the enemy;
2. the changing political and legal behaviour of the activists involved – the ways in which they interact with the prevailing political and legal system.

By examining how these two factors interconnect Sprinzak maintains that the researcher can determine the general facets of the three stages of the process of delegitimation.[156] Sprinzak's work is applicable in different contexts. Sprinzak utilized this model when examining the left-wing Weathermen group,[157] and with right-wing groups in which he modified his original thesis to accommodate what he calls 'split delegitimization'. Under this rubric, right-wing terrorists attack the state because they view it as 'the hostage' or the puppet of special groups. Hence, here the terrorists fail to see the distinctions between the state and the group against whom they are actively opposed.[158]

Examining the history of the 'ecoterrorist' groups demonstrates how a 'collective psychopolitical process can turn "some young, educated, sensitive human beings into tough revolutionaries and brutal killers"'.[159] The Weathermen leaders, politically socialized by violent confrontations, went through a 'psychopolitical crisis of legitimacy' process comprising four components: '(1) a political language of delegitimation of the regime, (2) rhetoric and symbols of depersonalization and dehumanization of individuals belonging to the system, (3) intended and planned violence, and (4) terrorism'.[160]

Wiktorowicz and Sageman, using network theory, argue that radicalization is more a case of who you know within your social network. Violent radicalization occurs within smaller groups where factors such as bonding, peer pressure and indoctrination can come into play, altering an individual's worldview gradually and changing the individual's view of the world.[161]

Sageman, also influenced by the social movement theory, emphasizes the importance of social bonds and networks bound together by a common ideology and by usage of the internet to create a community. Sageman notes that those who join a cell invariably know at least one member. Recruitment is a bottom-up process and there are a number of stages. It starts with a sense of moral outrage at violence or personal discrimination and leads to the conclusion that there is – as in Sageman's case study – a 'war against Islam'. Gradually the rhetoric escalates, with men encouraging each other that a violent response is necessary.[162]

The cell members or 'affinity cells' tend to reinforce each other towards performing acts of terrorist violence in what Sageman calls the 'bunch of guys' theory. Under this framework, cells tend to swing into action not because of directives from above, but from a group of young men spending time with each other and spurring each other on.[163] Once a group has violent views they reach out to others that can connect them – in the case he examined, Al Qaeda. Or alternatively they act on their own recognizance inspired by ideology.[164] Bakker's work builds on Sageman's with the emphasis on networks and personal bonds but adds that most people become radicalized in their domiciled state and that they tend to be of approximately the same age and from the same locale.[165]

Neumann and Rogers's work has also supported the importance of social networks and personal bonds in the radicalization process.[166] They note that groups provided these individuals with a community they can belong to and be accepted within and which provides both a mission and sense of superiority. They also examine how social pressures apply to the individual members of the groups and that this can increase group conformity over time.[167]

An approach that postulates a continuum linking activists to militants and militants to terrorists remains to date an undertheorized concept.[168] This book argues that becoming an ecoterrorist is a process of radicalization and what needs to be understood is what factors contribute to a group feeling compelled or, just as importantly not compelled, to engage in violence. The group theoretical models addressed here constitute broad political dynamics and constitute macro-level radicalization factors that this book will focus on. As it has been established that peer group influence greatly impacts upon radicalization, including pressure to conduct terrorist acts,[169] the volume also addresses what collective processes may be involved in influencing environmental and animal rights actors to progress from protest to more militant and violent forms of political expression.

This book intends to test the above theories empirically by applying them to the selected radical environmental group case studies. It adopts primarily the Sprinzak analysis – due to its long-standing nature and similarity to the group stage theories – to determine whether activists are indeed progressing towards violence. Sprinzak's process theory is also applicable in other circumstances and to other types of radical groups, regardless of their political belief structures, but is it fully applicable to the 'ecoterrorist' groups examined here.[170] His model is an appropriate starting point for analysing possible breakdowns in radical environmental groups' perceived legitimacy towards the liberal-democratic state or institutional order and the history and activities the examined groups operate in, but it remains to be seen if it holds great explanatory power when applied to potential 'ecoterrorist' groups.

To further assist our understanding of group radicalization this volume will adopt Wright-Neville's approach that we can observe a progression from activist to militant to terrorist, which corresponds respectively with Sprinzak's crisis of confidence, conflict of legitimacy and crisis of legitimacy phases.[171] The analysis intends to synthesize Sprinzak's approach with Wright-Neville's tripartite model of categorizing such actions in order to critically examine the selected radical environmental group case studies to determine if these approaches can yield some insights as to purported 'ecoterrorist'.

Wright-Neville defines an activist group that, while 'dedicated to altering or replacing the political hierarchy and its policies … they do not seek to change the principles that underpin existing political and/or democratic frame-works. Activists prefer to work "with the system", agitating within existing legal and political norms even though these might be manifestly biased against them and militate against the successful realization of their goals.'[172]

In certain circumstances, activists who experience 'accumulated frustration' combined with a sense of political impotence can be tempted to adopt more militant actions.[173] This stage maps neatly with Sprinzak's 'conflict of legitimacy' stage that tends to be preceded by a 'great disappointment' with earlier forms of protest and activism that have not generated expected results.[174] For Wright-Neville, terrorists exhibit dehumanizing behaviour towards their opponents that cannot be observed in the behaviour of activists or militants.[175]

So a key question becomes: can we observe amongst these radical environmental groups an 'accumulated frustration' with the prevailing political and social status quo that has led some activists to become militants and then some militants to progress to terrorism?[176] Other subsidiary research questions include: are these groups terrorist according to traditional analysis? Is the inspiration of fear through their actions their main goal? Do they claim they want their opponents to fear them?

However, the other theoretical approaches (both group and individual) to radicalization raise some interesting questions that should be tested empirically and can be mapped on to the primary approach adopted. Can we observe, as per Wiktorowicz and Sageman's approach, that radicalization only occurs in small groups and that bonding, peer pressure and indoctrination are key factors in altering individuals to adopt the group view of the world? As Sageman notes, how important has the internet been in creating a like-minded community?

Do members of radical environmental groups invariably know other cell members before they join? To what extent is Sageman wrong when he argues that most radicalization occurs amongst groups of young men? Are members primarily recruited from their own locale? Are Neumann and Rogers correct that radicalizing can provide people with a mission in life and a sense of superiority over others? As per Einwohler's research, are the type of people who join radical environmental groups doing so because of emotional attachments to animals and/or their abuse or because of a felt close connection to the Earth?

Bartlett and Miller argue that radicals can become terrorists do to the emotional 'pull' they experience from perceived injustice or from the thrill or 'coolness' of undertaking actions on behalf of the environment. Can we observe this in the case of radical environmental group members? Or, alternatively, do people become involved – as McBride, Cottee and Hayward contend – because it provides meaning in a person's life and mitigates existential anxiety, boredom or frustration?

Are such groups becoming more violent?

History teaches that radical groups' violence tends to escalate if their applied strategies and tactics are unsuccessful in achieving their goals.[177] According to Enders and Sandler, transnational terrorism will become more violent over time even if the number of attacks decreases.[178] Therefore, according to Beck, if radicalization is a universal process of all militant groups then such analysis should be applicable to the case of 'ecoterrorism'.[179]

This book will thus also examine whether environmental radical groups are on a continuum of violence: are they becoming more violent over time as the literature suggests? There appears to be two schools of thought. Some writers contend that recent evidence has suggested that some radical environmental organizations (including both the Animal Liberation Front and the Earth Liberation Front) are becoming more willing to pursue aggressive and violent tactics. Gary Ackerman (Monterey Institute for International Studies) observes that: 'a shift in [more violent] propaganda is considered to be the key indicator of an increase in an organization's propensity to use violence'.[180]

However, Taylor argues that such groups have internal dynamics and characteristics that mitigate against an increase in violence. He argues that such groups' anti-hierarchical structures provide venues for inter-movement debate and foster a culture of discourse that can have an ameliorating effect, which can prevent momentum towards utilizing violence. These include: open lines of communication – particularly via the internet – that reduce insularity; and the lack of a charismatic leader who dominates a movement and could, by sheer force of will, push a group towards violence. Additionally, environmental radicals tend not to sever ties with their families or communities (many terrorist groups demand a cutting off of all outside influences). They also tend to engage face-to-face with their opposition thus tending to humanize them. Moreover, such groups understand that committing acts of violence will draw the attention of law enforcement and they are not willing to run that risk. Finally, such groups tend to ascribe to deep ecological beliefs and hold life to be sacred, preventing the development of a type of ideology that allows for physical violence against individuals.[181]

Ackerman's analysis of the Earth Liberation Front and why they are unlikely to resort to more aggressive forms of violence also builds on Taylor's observations. He claims that many activists are young and relatively poor and the movements tend not to have generous benefactors and thus are not able to fund large-scale operations.[182] Taylor postulates that the greater threat is from a lone wolf activist like the 'Unabomber' who is isolated form the movements and their ameliorating effects regarding the use of physical violence.[183]

Thus, as Howard Ehrlich maintains, it is not unusual for radical-minded groups to resort to violence if they believe they have no other options and that their government or society is unresponsive to their brand of political activism.[184] Can we observe this occurring for the radical environmental groups being examined here? Do they perceive they have no choice but to operate outside the democratic political system, using violence to achieve their goals?

Thus a further series of research questions need to be interrogated: are attacks by 'ecoterrorists' becoming more frequent or more violent (either in overall attacks or attacks on sentient beings)? Have the groups' geographical reach expanded over time? According to Scarce, radical environmentalists recognize that their cause is a global one. Issues such as biodiversity loss and climate change demonstrate that the problems they rail against have a global dimension that needs to be tackled at that level.[185] It has become apparent that the movement has also spread geographically. Arslan argues that previously most actions undertaken were in industrialized, modern states (the UK, Italy, France, the USA) but there is now a shift in focus with actions committed in less-developed states such as Greece, Turkey and Eastern Europe.[186]

Can we further observe an uptick in attacks against purported environmental opponents as activists become more frustrated at the lack of progress relating to such issues as climate change or the perception that global environmental stocks are ever rapidly decreasing? Are lone-wolf operators a greater threat? Have these groups' political influence or ability to project political violence waned? As a potential mass movement (as groups such as Earth First!, Animal Liberation Front and Earth Liberation Front wish to become), have they been successful in building their group into a mass movement to achieve their objective? Lastly, are the various examined organizations merging into one entity with a single unified aim or are they still distinct groups with their own philosophies and differing types of actions?

AIM AND STRUCTURE

To recapitulate: what this book seeks to do is critically examine if or how the radical environmental groups selected (Earth First!, Earth Liberation Front, Animal Liberation Front and Sea Shepherd Conservation Society) progress from activists to militants to terrorists as the literature on political violence suggests. To answer the proposed research questions this book will historically trace the evolution of these groups, their strategies, tactics and philosophies as well as critically examining the biographies of key personnel.

The book is divided into several research themes. The first is introductory in scope. The second provides an overarching view of the radical environmental groups chosen. Part I examines the growth of groups dedicated to protecting animal welfare and rights such as the Animal Liberation Front, Animal Rights Militia and Stop Huntingdon Animal Cruelty. Part II examines Earth First! and the schism over the use of violence as a strategy that spawned the birth of the Earth Liberation Front. Part III considers the Sea Shepherd Conservation Society, and how and to what extent they have become radicalized. The book is set out as follows:

Chapter 1 scrutinizes the case study of the primary 'ecoterrorist' group protecting animals: the Animal Liberation Front (ALF). It sets out a brief history of animal welfare groups, the Hunt Saboteur protest group and the radical environmental group Band of Mercy that predated the ALF, as well as a biography of the group's charismatic leader, Ronnie Lee. The chapter describes the birth of the ALF both in the UK and the USA. It goes on to critically analyse both the ALF's underlying philosophy and the development of a radical animal rights philosophy that underpinned ALF actions.

Chapter 2 focuses on the ALF's organizational structure and financing, the reasons people have joined the group, its relationship with mainstream environmental groups and the strategy and tactics utilized to attempt to achieve its goals. The chapter also provides a history of the actions carried out by the ALF. It further critically examines the ALF's attitude to political violence and explores the reasons why it has proven to be the most violent of the 'ecoterrorist' groups, willing to proffer physical violence against those it designated to be an enemy. It provides a history of their campaigns and actions undertaken.

Chapter 3 critically examines the rise of purported 'offshoot' groups – the Animal Rights Militia, Justice Department and Stop Huntingdon Animal Cruelty – and their campaigns to end animal cruelty by targeting humans. The final section applies the previously outlined prevailing theories of radical group and individual evolution, and charts the ALF's (and their purported offshoots) members growth from activists to militants to terrorists willing to commit large-scale arson and attacks on humans to further their goals to end animal suffering.

Chapter 4 provides a critical examination of the group Earth First!, focusing on key proponents, its history, the conditions that brought it about and its philosophy. It examines the role played by Edward Abbey and the impact of his 1975 novel *The Monkey Wrench Gang* on radical environmentalism. It also examines the birth of Earth First!, their campaigns and the role played by Dave Foreman in creating this group dedicated to protecting the biosphere. It analyses their strategies and tactics, operating philosophy and campaigns, and seeks to explain their demise as a functioning group and why it never progressed towards more radical violent action.

Chapter 5 examines the Earth Liberation Front (ELF) and charts its development of a philosophy of property violence – or ecotage – as opposed to violence against humans. The group's evolution, as well as distinction, from the group it sprang from, Earth First! is also critically evaluated. The strategies, tactics and appeal of the group are critically examined as well as its successes and failures. The chapter evaluates how ELF has spread from its beginnings in England in 1992 to having autonomous cells globally. It examines this cell structure with its emphasis, in the case of ELF, on 'affinity groups', which are usually autonomous and self-funded, and asks if they can be considered examples of leaderless resistance. This chapter also provides a history of the various militant acts carried out by ELF. It considers whether these groups are vigilantes, militants or terrorists. Lastly it questions how effective ELF has been in achieving its stated goals. It further examines the group's evolution using prevailing radicalization theories and considers whether – given their actions – they should be considered terrorists or militants.

Chapter 6 sets out to explore the history and evolution of the Sea Shepherd Conservation Society (SSCS). It details the background of the group's totemic leader, Paul Watson, and his childhood influences that led him to want to work to save oceanic creatures. It describes his oft-times fiery relationship with the environmental non-governmental organization Greenpeace and his rancorous exit from that organization. It then critically examines the formation of Earthforce, the stillborn antecedent group to the SSCS, and the creation in 1977 of the SSCS. It goes on to critically analyse the group's ethos; its attraction to its members; its organizational structure, the strategy and tactics; its use of diplomacy; and the global media and militant direct action to achieve its goals. It further examines SSCS's attitude to violence carried out in the service of its mission, and its distinction between violence against humans and property damage, which the group argues should not be considered a violent act.

Chapter 7 provides a history of the various militant acts done by the SSCS since its inception. It focuses in particular on the ongoing annual confrontation between the SSCS and Japanese whalers in Antarctic waters. It further asks how effective the SSCS has been in their stated goals to end Japanese whaling and whether the methods are counterproductive to their stated goals. The chapter also critically examines the recent domestic state attempts to charge Watson and the SSCS for their actions. The chapter concludes by examining the implications of the arrest of the group's totemic leader on future campaigns. Lastly, its opponents – in particular the Japanese government – has labelled the SSCS as 'pirates' (a label the group wears proudly) and/or vigilantes or terrorists.

Chapter 8 analyses the various claims to legitimacy made by the SSCS. It demonstrates how the unwieldiness of modern international oceanic law has enabled the SSCS to evade legal punishment for their actions. Lastly it considers how successful the SSCS has been and whether such success will continue on in the future and, utilizing the previously examined radicalization theories, questions whether the SSCS is an ecoterrorist group or should be better understood as a vigilante group willing to use political violence to achieve its goals.

Conclusion – here the case studies and the theoretical analysis are drawn together to recapitulate the central findings as to whether we can observe a process in the examined groups from activist to militant to terrorist. In particular, we will determine whether there are distinctive radicalization patterns within particular groups, particular movements and tendencies (environmental or animal rights), and country-specific trends. In addition, the conclusion addresses other relevant questions about these groups: are the examined groups counterproductive to the aims of the broader environmental movement or a necessary 'evil' that enables more moderate groups to have success? Have the examined radical environmental groups flourished or grown weaker over time and what factors account for their relative strengths or weaknesses? Lastly, have they developed into a mass movement to realize their political goal of changing how humans interact with the environment?

NOTES

1. Steve Vanderheiden, 'Eco-terrorism or justified resistance? Radical environmentalism and the "war on terror"', *Politics and Society*, **33** (3), p. 445.
2. Mohammed Hafez and Creighton Mullins (2015) 'The radicalization puzzle: a theoretical synthesis of empirical approaches to homegrown extremism', *Studies in Conflict and Terrorism*, **38** (11), pp. 958–75, p. 959.
3. The first use of the term 'ecoterrorist' is claimed by Ron Arnold from the Center for the Defense of Free Enterprise: http://www.sourcewatch.org/index.php?title=Eco-terrorism. The term is further analysed and defined later in this introduction.
4. See the section on ecotage for further analysis, but at its simplest ecotage can be defined as illegal, non-public acts, motivated by environmental concerns that aim to retard or

prevent acts considered harmful to the environment. Steve Vanderheiden (2008) 'Radical environmentalism in the age of antiterrorism,' *Environmental Politics*, 17,(2), p. 301. It should be considered a tactic rather than a strategy. Vanderheiden, 'Radical environmentalism in the age of antiterrorism', p. 306.

5. Horacio R. Trujillo (2005) 'The radical environmentalist movement', *Aptitude for Destruction*, **2**, pp. 141–78, p. 146.
6. Donald R. Liddick (2006) *Eco-Terrorism: Radical Environmental and Animal Liberation Movements* (Westport, Connecticut: Praeger), p. 91; H.H.A. Cooper (1977) 'What is a terrorist: a psychological perspective', *Legal Medical Quarterly*, **1**, in Jonathan R. White (1998) *Terrorism: An Introduction*, 2nd edn (Elmont, CA: West/Wadsworth), p. 23.
7. Liddick, *Eco-Terrorism: Radical Environmental and Animal Liberation Movements*, p. 91.
8. Liddick, *Eco-Terrorism: Radical Environmental and Animal Liberation Movements*, p. 91; White, *Terrorism: An Introduction*, p. 22.
9. At its simplest, the consensus view amongst those studying radicalization appears to be that it is: '(1) a gradual "process" that entails socialization into an (2) extremist belief system that sets the stage for (3) violence even if it does not make it inevitable', Hafez and Mullins, 'The radicalization puzzle: a theoretical synthesis of empirical approaches to homegrown extremism', pp. 958–75, p. 964. See the radicalization section for a more comprehensive assessment of the term.
10. Hasan T. Arslan (2008) 'The social and operational intersections of environmental extremism in North America and Europe' (PhD dissertation, Sam Houston State University, Huntsville, TX), p. 23; D. Bandow (2003) 'American terrorism, environment-style', *Human Events*, **59** (33), p. 27.
11. Douglas Long, *Ecoterrorism: Library in a Book* (New York: Facts on File Inc.), p. 4.
12. Arslan, 'The social and operational intersections of environmental extremism in North America and Europe', p. 23; R. Young (2004) 'A time series analysis of eco-terrorist violence in the United States: 1993–2003' (PhD dissertation, Sam Houston State University, TX), *Dissertation and Abstracts International*, **65** (8), p. 56.
13. Ibid.
14. Arslan, 'The social and operational intersections of environmental extremism in North America and Europe', p. 23; Young, 'A time series analysis of eco-terrorist violence in the United States: 1993–2003', p. 56.
15. Michael Penders and William Thomas (2002) 'Ecoterror: rethinking environmental security after September 11', *Natural Resources and Environment*, **16**, pp. 159–207, p. 160.
16. Sean P. Eagan (1996) 'From spikes to bombs: the rise of ecoterrorism', *Studies in Conflict and Terrorism*, **19** (1), pp. 1–18, p. 2. According to Eagan (p. 2) only four citations on terrorism between 1980 and 1993 consider environmental terrorism.
17. Young, 'A time series analysis of eco-terrorist violence in the United States: 1993–2003', p. 17.
18. In recent years terrorism has become for many countries a significant, if not the most significant, political and security issue on their political agendas. Scholars are therefore rightly devoting attention to developing more nuanced understandings of this form of political violence. Indeed, it has been reported that since the 9/11 attacks there has been on average one book published on terrorism every six hours. Pete Lentini (2008) 'Understanding and combating terrorism: definitions, origins and strategies', *Australian Journal of Political Science*, **43** (1) pp. 133. However, there are other forms of terrorist and radical threats that are present and also deserve attention from researchers.
19. Bron Taylor (1995) 'Earth First! and global narratives of popular ecological resistance' in Bron Taylor (ed.) *Ecological Resistance Movements: The Global Emergence of Radical and Popular Environmentalism* (Albany, NY: State University of New York Press), p. 25.
20. Ibid.
21. Jennifer Varriale Carson et al. (2012) 'Terrorist and non-terrorist criminal attacks by radical environmental and animal rights groups in the United States, 1970–2007', *Terrorism and Political Violence*, 24 (2), pp. 295–319, p. 299.

22. Young, 'A time series analysis of eco-terrorist violence in the United States: 1993–2003', p. 138. However, even here there was an initial informational shortfall since the FBI was only granted permission by the US Attorney General in 1990 to consider the ALF and the ELF as domestic terrorist organizations: see Young, 'A time series analysis of eco-terrorist violence in the United States: 1993–2003', p. 143; Hooley, 'Plans for eco-terrorism legislation' *The Associated Press* (7 July 2001).
23. David Wright-Neville (2006) 'Terrorism as the politics of dashed expectations', *Dialogue*, **25** (3), pp. 11–24, p. 12.
24. Gerry Nagtzaam and Pete Lentini (2008) 'Vigilantes on the high seas?: The Sea Shepherds and political violence', *Terrorism and Political Violence*, **20**, pp. 110–33, 124–6. For example, the Sea Shepherd Conservation Society's recent annual campaign against Japanese whaling in the Southern Ocean constitutes the most significant example of animal rights violence escalating. Since 2000, the contest between the Sea Shepherds and the whalers has moved from one in which the former's members have attempted to get between the whalers and whales to prevent harpoons being shot into the cetaceans, to illegally boarding ships that carried particularly life-threatening consequences at international maritime law. For many years both sides have ratcheted up the means with which they confront each other. This has resulted in the emergence of increasing political violence.
25. Rachel Monaghan (2013) 'Not quite terrorism: animal rights extremism in the United Kingdom', *Studies in Conflict and Terrorism*, **36** (11), pp. 933–51, p. 945.
26. See for example M. Sageman (2004) *Understanding Terror Networks* (Philadelphia: University of Pennsylvania Press); John Horgan (2008) 'From profiles to *pathways* and roots to *routes*: perspectives from psychology on radicalization into terrorism', *The Annals of the American Academy of Political and Social Science*, 618.1, pp. 80–94; Mitchell D. Silber et al. (2007) *Radicalization in the West: The Homegrown Threat* (New York: Police Department); Clark McCauley and Sophia Moskalenko (2008) 'Mechanisms of political radicalization: pathways toward terrorism', *Terrorism and Political Violence*, **20** (3), pp. 415–33; Bertjan Doosje et al. (2013) 'Determinants of radicalization of Islamic youth in the Netherlands: personal uncertainty, perceived injustice, and perceived group threat', *Journal of Social Issues*, 69 (3), pp. 586–604; F.M. Moghaddam (2005) 'The staircase to terrorism: a psychological exploration', *American Psychologist*, **60**, pp. 161–9; and Marc Sageman (2008) 'A strategy for fighting international Islamist terrorists', *The Annals of the American Academy of Political and Social Science*, 618.1, pp. 223–31.
27. Ecotage, at its simplest, is defined as, 'the practice of damaging property to prevent ecological damage', Teale Phelps Bondaroff (2008) Throwing a wrench into things: the strategy of radical environmentalism, *Journal of Military and Strategic Studies*, **10** (4), p. 5. See section on ecotage and violence for a more complete analysis of the term.
28. 'Activists threaten power plant CEO', ABC News, http://www.abc.net.au/news/2009-06-15/activists-threaten-power-plants-ceo/1713308.
29. Nagtzaam and Lentini, 'Vigilantes on the high seas?: The Sea Shepherds and political violence', p. 115.
30. Paul J. Karasick (2009) 'Curb your ecoterrorism: identifying the nexus between state criminalization of ecoterror and environmental protection policy', *Environmental Law and Policy Review*, **33** (2) (Winter), p. 585; Joshua K. Marquis and Danielle M. Weiss (2005) 'Eco-terror: special interest terrorism', *Prosecutor*, (Jan–Feb), p. 32.
31. Karasick, 'Curb your ecoterrorism: identifying the nexus between state criminalization of ecoterror and environmental protection policy', p. 585; Chrystal Mancuso-Smith (2006) 'From monkeywrenching to mass destruction: eco-sabotage and the American West', *Journal of Land Resources and Environmental Law*, **26**, p. 322.
32. According to Ehud Sprinzak: 'Vigilante movements rarely perceive themselves involved in conflict with the government and the prevailing concept of law. They are neither revolutionary nor interested in the destruction of authority. Rather, what characterizes the vigilante mind is the profound conviction that the government and its agencies have failed

to enforce the law or establish order in a particular area... They believe they are acting legally against criminal elements because the authorities are either too weak to enforce the law or negligent in their duties.' Ehud Sprinzak (1995) 'Right-wing terrorism in comparative perspective: the case of split delegitimatization' in Tore Bjørgo (ed.), *Terror From the Extreme Right* (London: Frank Cass & Co. Ltd), pp. 17–43, p. 29. Rather they believe that the government is failing to create or enforce their laws requiring them to take on that role to effect justice. Ehud Sprinzak (1987) 'From messianic pioneering to vigilante terrorism: the case of the gush emunim underground', *Journal of Strategic Studies*, **10** (4), pp. 194–216, p. 211.

33. Pete Lentini (2013) *Neojihadism* (Cheltenham, UK and Northampton, MA, USA: Edward Elgar Publishing), p. 9.
34. Young, 'A time series analysis of eco-terrorist violence in the United States: 1993–2003', p. 4; C. Quillen (2002) 'A historical analysis of mass casualty bombers', *Studies in Conflict and Terrorism*, **25**, p. 281; H.W. Kushner (1998) *The Future of Terrorism: Violence in the New Millennium* (Thousand Oaks, CA: Sage Publications); E.L. Chalecki (2002) 'A new vigilance: identifying and reducing the risks of environmental terrorism', *Global Environmental Politics*, **2** (1), pp. 46–64.
35. Chalecki, 'A new vigilance: identifying and reducing the risks of environmental terrorism', pp. 47–8.
36. Shannon O'Lear (2003) Environmental terrorism: a critique, *Geopolitics*, **8** (3), pp. 127–50, p. 131.
37. Ibid., p. 132; Michael Gold-Biss (1994) *The Discourse on Terrorism: Political Violence and the Subcommittee on Security and Terrorism 1981–1986* (New York: Peter Lang), p. 11.
38. Young, 'A time series analysis of eco-terrorist violence in the United States: 1993–2003', pp. 4–5; Robert Young (1996) '"Monkeywrenching" and the processes of democracy', in Freya Mathews (ed.) *Ecology and Democracy* (London and Portland: OR: Frank Cass), p. 202; Pamala L. Griset and Sue Mahan (2013) *Terrorism in Perspective*, (3rd edn) (London: Sage Publications), p. 15.
39. Young, 'A time series analysis of eco-terrorist violence in the United States: 1993–2003', p. 11.
40. Ibid.
41. Young, 'A time series analysis of eco-terrorist violence in the United States: 1993–2003', p. 5; Rachel Monaghan (2000) 'Single-issue terrorism: a neglected phenomenon?', *Studies in Conflict and Terrorism*, **23**, pp. 255–65, p. 256.
42. Bron Taylor (1998) 'Religion, violence and radical environmentalism: from Earth First! to the Unabomber to the Earth Liberation Front', *Terrorism and Political Violence*, **10** (4), p. 25.
43. Lentini, *Neojihadism*, pp. 1–42, p. 9.
44. Pete Lentini (2003) 'Terrorism and its (re)sources: a review article', *The Australian and New Zealand Journal of Criminology*, **36** (3), pp. 368–78, p. 368. Similar definitions abound worldwide. For example, according to the United States Federal Bureau of Investigation, terrorism is defined as, 'the unlawful use of force or violence against persons or property to intimidate or coerce a government, the civilian population, or any segment thereof, in furtherance of political or social objectives'. See Young, 'A time series analysis of eco-terrorist violence in the United States: 1993–2003', p. 7; Federal Bureau of Investigation (2002) 'Terrorism in the United States: 1999', http://www.fbi.gov/publish/terror/terrusa.html.
45. According to Young, right-wing terrorist groups often, 'adhere to principles of racial supremacy and embrace antigovernment and anti-regulatory beliefs'. Such organizations often involve themselves in actions that are covered and protected by 'constitutional guarantees of free speech and assembly'. Examples of these groups include the World Church of the Creator and the Aryan Nations. See Young, 'A time series analysis of eco-terrorist violence in the United States: 1993–2003', p. 14.
46. Ibid., p. 15; Federal Bureau of Investigation, 'Terrorism in the United States: 1999'.

47. Ibid.
48. Ron Arnold (1995) *Ecoterror: The Violent Agenda to Save Nature, The World of the Unabomber* (Washington: Free Enterprise Press), p. 104; Brent L. Smith (1994) *Terrorism in America: Pipe Bombs and Pipe Dreams* (Albany, NY: University of New York Press), p. 125.
49. The concept of 'extremism' is also considered a nebulous term within political science circles. Lentini argues extremism can be characterized by an outlook that rejects ambiguity and considers opponents' 'answers' to be not merely wrong but evil. In an extremist's worldview, the world is Manichean with no shades of grey and compromise is both a sign of weakness and a betrayal. Extremists believe that their morally superior state of mind entitles them not to be bound by the prevailing strictures of the political order and thus are free to utilize violence against the state, corporations or individuals to achieve their goals. See Lentini, *Neojihadism*, p, 11.
50. Long, *Ecoterrorism: Library in a Book*, p. 4.
51. Monaghan, 'Not quite terrorism: animal rights extremism in the United Kingdom', pp. 933-4.
52. Andrew Rowell (1996) *Green Backlash: Global Subversion of the Environment Movement* (London, New York: Routledge), p. 150; C. Bertlet (1991) 'Hunting the "green menace"', *The Humanist*, July/August, p. 31.
53. Rowell, *Green Backlash: Global Subversion of the Environment Movement*, p. 150. It is important to note that industry has often sought to brand environmental activists as 'environmental terrorists'. For example, when Clorox became concerned that Greenpeace might launch a major public relations campaign against the company's household bleach, it hired Ketchum Public Relations to handle the spin control. The Ketchum 'Crisis Management Plan' laid out suggestions for Clorox that included, 'dealing with the environmentalists and any "unalterably" green journalists by accusing them of "environmental terrorism"'. See Eagan (1991) 'From spikes to bombs: the rise of ecoterrorism', p. 2; Charles Campbell, 'Crisis Plan's leak smudges Clorox', *Los Angeles Times*, 2 June, D8.
54. Andrew Rowell, *Green Backlash: Global Subversion of the Environment Movement*, p. 150; Ketchum, 'Crisis Management Plan for the Clorox Company', p. 3, 18; Greenpeace (1991) 'Clorox Company's public relations 'Crisis Management Plan' leaked to Greenpeace', Press Release, 10 May.
55. Rowell, *Green Backlash: Global Subversion of the Environment Movement*, p. 150.
56. Ibid., p. 151.
57. Craig Rosebraugh (2004) *Burning Rage of a Dying Planet: Speaking for the Earth Liberation Front* (New York: Lantern Books), p. 236.
58. Bryan Denson and James Long (1999) 'Eco-terrorism sweeps the American West', *The Oregonian*, 26 September.
59. Nick Harding (2010) 'Eco-anarchists: the new breed of terrorist', *The Independent (UK)*, 18 May.
60. Sean P. Eagan, 'From spikes to bombs: the rise of ecoterrorism', p. 2; Dick Russell (1989) 'Earth Last! Earth First! Members arrest case', *The Nation*, 17 July, p. 77.
61. Eagan, 'From spikes to bombs: the rise of ecoterrorism', p. 2. For example, during his testimony in front of Congress, Ron Arnold tended to conflate all environmentalists with terrorism, even considering situations where workers lost their jobs because of environmental activist lawsuits to be a kind of 'economic terrorism'. Steve Vanderheiden (2008) 'Radical environmentalism in an age of antiterrorism', *Environmental Politics*, **17** (2), pp. 299–318, p. 303.
62. Karasick, 'Curb your ecoterrorism: identifying the nexus between state criminalization of ecoterror and environmental protection policy', p. 583.
63. Daniel M. Schwartz (1998) 'Environmental terrorism: analyzing the concept', *Journal of Peace Research*, **35** (4), p. 484.
64. Karasick, 'Curb your ecoterrorism: identifying the nexus between state criminalization of ecoterror and environmental protection policy', p. 584; Alyson B. Walker (2007) 'A field

of failed dreams: problems passing effective ecoterrorism legislation', *Villanova Environmental Law Journal*, **18**, p. 104.
65. Chalecki, 'A new vigilance: identifying and reducing the risks of environmental terrorism', p. 4.
66. Young, 'A time series analysis of eco-terrorist violence in the United States: 1993–2003', p. 1; B. Vlahos (2002) 'They're green, they're anarchists and they're coming to your town', *Fox News*, 3 August, http://foxnews.com/story/0,2933,59476,00.html.
67. Eagan, 'From spikes to bombs: the rise of ecoterrorism', p. 2.
68. Young, 'A time series analysis of eco-terrorist violence in the United States: 1993–2003', p. 2; Eagan, 'From spikes to bombs: the rise of eco-terrorism', pp. 1–18.
69. O'Lear, 'Environmental terrorism: a critique', p. 139.
70. Eagan, 'From spikes to bombs: the rise of ecoterrorism', pp. 1-2; Richard E. Rubenstein (1988) *Alchemists of Revolution: Terrorism in the Modern World* (New York: Basic Books), pp. 17–18.
71. Karasick, 'Curb your ecoterrorism: identifying the nexus between state criminalization of ecoterror and environmental protection policy', p. 583. It is also interesting to note that the Stop Terrorism Property Act of 2003 provides a similar definition to the stated primary objective of the ELF, to 'inflict economic damage on those profitting [sic] from the destruction and exploitation of the natural environment', in Karasick, 'curb your ecoterrorism: identifying the nexus between state criminalization of ecoterror and environmental protection policy', p. 583.
72. Randall Amster (2006) 'Perspectives on ecoterrorism: catalysts, conflations, and casualties', *Contemporary Justice Review*, 9, September, pp. 287–301, p. 289.
73. Steven Best and Anthony Nocella (2004) 'Behind the mask: uncovering the Animal Liberation Front' in Steven Best and Anthony Nocella (eds), *Terrorists or Freedom Fighters: Reflections on the Liberation of Animals* (New York: Lantern Books), p. 30.
74. Eagan, 'From spikes to bombs: the rise of ecoterrorism', p. 9; Leonard B. Weinberg and Paul B. Davis (1989) *Introduction to Political Terrorism* (New York: McGraw-Hill), p. 7.
75. Eagan, 'From spikes to bombs: the rise of ecoterrorism', p. 9; Theodore G. Shackley (1990) 'Enviroterrorism', *Chief Executive*, July/August), p. 60.
76. Trujillo, 'The radical environmentalist movement', pp. 141–78, p. 144.
77. Amster, Perspective on ecoterrorism: catalysts, conflations, and casualties, p. 289.
78. Vanderheiden (2008) Radical environmentalism in an age of antiterrorism, p. 305.
79. For example in the USA the term 'crime of violence' means: (1) an offence that has as an element of the use, attempted use or threatened use of physical force against the person or property of another, or (2) any other offence that is a felony and that, by its nature, involves a substantial risk that physical force against the person or property of another may be used in the course of committing the offence. See US Code, Title 18, Part 1, Chapter 1, s 16, https://www.law.cornell.edu/uscode/text/18/16#.
80. Amster, 'Perspectives on ecoterrorism: catalysts, conflations, and casualties', p. 289. It has been further argued by some in the environmental movement that the aims of such movements will only be supported by 'elites in government and media' if their actions are non-violent. As a result, the majority of radical activists, including those involved in the animal rights movement, favour a non-violent approach. See Lyle Munro (2005) *Confronting Cruelty: Moral Orthodoxy and the Challenge of the Animal Rights Movement* (Boston, Leiden: Brill), p. 133.
81. Steve Vanderheiden (2005), Eco-terrorism or justified resistance? Radical environmentalism and the "war on terror"', *Politics and Society*, **33** (3), p. 432.
82. Dave Foreman (1985) Ecodefense: a field guide to monkeywrenching, reproduced at http://www.omnipresence.mahost.org/ch1txt.htm.
83. Ibid.
84. Vanderheiden, 'Eco-terrorism or justified resistance? Radical environmentalism and the "war on terror"', p. 445.
85. Colin Beck (2007), 'On the radical cusp: ecoterrorism in the United States, 1998–2005', *Mobilization: An International Quarterly Review*, **2** (2), p. 163.

86. Young, 'A time series analysis of eco-terrorist violence in the United States: 1993–2003', pp. 42–3.
87. Sophia Moskalenko and Clark McCauley (2009) 'Measuring political mobilization: the distinction between activism and radicalism', *Terrorism and Political Violence*, **21** (2), pp. 239–60, 239-40.
88. Anja Dalgaard-Nielsen (2010) 'Violent radicalization in Europe: what we know and what we do not know', *Studies in Conflict & Terrorism*, **33** (9), pp. 797–814, p. 799.
89. Randy Borum (2004) *Psychology of Terrorism* (Tampa: University of South Florida), p. 3; Ehud Sprinzak (1998) 'The psychopolitical formation of extreme left terrorism in a democracy: the case of the Weathermen', in W Reich (ed.), *Origins of Terror* (Baltimore, M.A.: John Hopkins University Press), p. 11.
90. Dalgaard-Nielsen, 'Violent radicalization in Europe: what we know and what we do not know', p. 798; Mark Sedgwick (2010) 'The concept of radicalization as a source of confusion', *Terrorism and Political Violence*, **22** (4), pp. 479–94, p. 481.
91. Sedgwick, 'The concept of radicalization as a source of confusion', pp. 479–94, p. 483.
92. Ehud Sprinzak (1998) 'The great superterrorism scare', *Foreign Policy*, **112**, Autumn, pp. 111–24, p. 113.
93. Jamie Bartlett and Carl Miller (2012) 'The edge of violence: towards telling the difference between violence and non-violent radicalization', *Terrorism and Political Violence*, **24** (1), pp. 1–21, p. 2.
94. Dalgaard-Nielsen, 'Violent radicalization in Europe: what we know and what we do not know', p. 798.
95. For example, the Weather Underground, which was born out of the anti-Vietnam war group Students for a Democratic Society in the 1960s, underwent such a progression. See Sprinzak, 'The psychopolitical formation of extreme left terrorism in a democracy: the case of the Weathermen', p. 11.
96. Moskalenko and McCauley, 'Measuring political mobilization: the distinction between activism and radicalism', p. 240.
97. McCauley and Moskalenko, 'Mechanisms of political radicalization: pathways towards terrorism', pp. 415–33, p. 416.
98. Pete Lentini (2009) 'The transference of Neojihadism: towards a process theory of transnational radicalisation', in Sayed Khatab, Muhammad Bakashmar and Ela Ogru (eds), 'Radicalisation crossing borders: new directions in Islamist and Jihadist political, intellectual and theological thought in practice, refereed proceedings from the International Conference, 26–7 November 2008, Parliament House, Melbourne Victoria (Caulfield: Global Terrorism Research Centre), pp. 1–32, http://artsonline.monash.edu.au/gtrec/files/2012/08/gtrec-proceedings-2008-01-pete-lentini.pdf. While again definitions of extremism are varied and there is no agreement among researchers as to a definitive classification, here we adopt the definition proposed by Manus Midlarsky where: 'Political extremism is defined as the will to power by a social movement in the service of a political program typically at variance with that supported by existing state authorities, and for which individual liberties are to be curtailed in the name of collective goals, including the mass murder of those who would actually or potentially disagree with the program. Restrictions on individual freedom in the interests of the collectivity and the willingness to kill massively are central to this definition.' Manus Midlarsky (2011) *Origins of Political Extremism: Mass Violence in the Twentieth Century and Beyond* (Cambridge UK: Cambridge University Press), p. 7. Extremists can be distinguished from radicals in that, 'Extremists strive to create a homogenous society based on rigid, dogmatic ideological tenets; they seek to make society conformist by suppressing all opposition and subjugating minorities. That distinguishes them from mere radicals who accept diversity and believe in the power of reason rather than dogma.' Alex P. Schmid (2013) 'Radicalisation, de-radicalisation, counter-radicalisation: a conceptual discussion and literature review, ICCT research paper, March, p. 8. None of the groups examined in this book rise to the level of extremists but fit comfortably within the rubric of radicalism.

99. Reaching Critical Will (2001) 'References to the definition of terrorism and the United Nations General Assembly Debate "Measures to Eliminate International Terrorism", 1 October to 5 October 5 2001, United Nations, New York', http://www.reachingcriticalwill.org/political/1com/terror.html.
100. Nagtzaam and Lentini, 'Vigilantes on the high seas?: The Sea Shepherds and political violence', p. 118. See also Larry Diamond (2002) 'Winning the new cold war on terrorism: the democratic-governance imperative', *Institute for Global Democracy Policy Paper No. 1* (March); Mark Lynch (2003) 'Taking Arabs seriously', *Foreign Affairs*, **82** (5) (September/October).
101. Hafez and Mullins, 'The radicalization puzzle: a theoretical synthesis of empirical approaches to homegrown extremism', p. 959.
102. Sageman, *Understanding Terror Networks*, p. 108.
103. Peter R. Neumann (2013) 'The trouble with radicalization', *International Affairs*, **89** (4), pp. 873–93, p. 874.
104. Dalgaard-Nielsen, 'Violent radicalization in Europe: what we know and what we do not know', p. 799.
105. Ibid., p. 800.
106. David Snow et al. (1986) 'Frame alignment processes, micromobilization, and movement participation', *American Sociological Review*, **51**, pp. 461–81, p. 464.
107. Ibid.
108. Dalgaard-Nielsen, 'Violent radicalization in Europe: what we know and what we do not know', pp. 801–2.
109. Ibid., p. 802.
110. Michael King and Donald M. Taylor (2011) 'The radicalization of homegrown Jihadists: a review of theoretical models and social psychological evidence', *Terrorism and Political Violence*, **23** (4), pp. 602–22, p. 605.
111. Randy Borum (2011) 'Radicalization into violent extremis II: a review of conceptual models and empirical research', *Journal of Strategic Security*, **4** (4), pp. 37–62, p. 39.
112. King and Taylor, 'The radicalization of homegrown Jihadists: a review of theoretical models and social psychological evidence', p. 602.
113. Borum, 'Radicalization into violent extremis II: a review of conceptual models and empirical research', p. 40.
114. King and Taylor, 'The radicalization of homegrown Jihadists: a review of theoretical models and social psychological evidence', p. 606.
115. Liddick, *Eco-terrorism: radical environmental and animal liberation movements*, p. 90.
116. Sprinzak, 'The psychopolitical formation of extreme left terrorism in a democracy: the case of the Weathermen', p. 79.
117. Young, 'A time series analysis of eco-terrorist violence in the United States: 1993–2003', p. 18; Eagan, 'From spikes to bombs: the rise of eco-terrorism', p. 3.
118. Rik Scarce (2006) Eco-warriors: understanding the radical environmental movement (updated edn) (CA: Left Coast Press), p. 6.
119. Sageman, *Understanding Terror Networks* p. 108.
120. Dalgaard-Nielsen, 'Violent radicalization in Europe: what we know and what we do not know', p. 804.
121. Dalgaard-Nielsen, 'Violent radicalization in Europe: what we know and what we do not know', p. 805.
122. Young, 'A time series analysis of eco-terrorist violence in the United States: 1993–2003' p. 19; C. Nilson and T. Burke (2002) 'Environmental extremists and the eco-terrorism movement', *Academy of Criminal Justice Sciences*, **24** (5), p. 3.
123. Eagan, 'From spikes to bombs: the rise of ecoterrorism', p. 12; Jager et al., as cited in Post's 'Terrorist psycho-logic: terrorist behavior as a product of psychological forces', in Walter Reich (ed.) (1990) *Origins of Terrorism: Psychologies, Ideologies, Theologies, States of Mind* (New York: Woodrow Wilson International Center for Scholars), p. 28.
124. Liddick, *Eco-Terrorism: Radical Environmental and Animal Liberation Movements*, p. 90.

125. Young, 'A time series analysis of eco-terrorist violence in the United States: 1993–2003', p. 19.
126. Ibid., p. 20; B. Barcott (2002) 'From tree-hugger to terrorist', *The New York Times Magazine*, 7 April, pp. 56–9.
127. Liddick, *Eco-Terrorism: Radical Environmental and Animal Liberation Movements*, p. 83; Ingrid Newkirk (1992) *Free the Animals! The Amazing True Story of the Animal Liberation Movement* (Chicago: The Noble Free Press, Inc).
128. Liddick, *Eco-Terrorism: Radical Environmental and Animal Liberation Movements*, p. 83.
129. Rachel L. Einwohler (2002) 'Bringing the outsiders in: opponents' claims and the construction of animal rights activists' identity', *Mobilization: An International Journal*, **7** (3), p. 261.
130. Jamie Bartlett and Carl Miller (2012) 'The edge of violence: towards telling the difference between violence and non-violent radicalization', *Terrorism and Political Violence*, **24** (1), pp. 1–21, 13–16.
131. Megan K. McBride (2011) 'The logic of terrorism: existential anxiety, the search for meaning, and terrorist ideologies,' *Terrorism & Political Violence*, **23** (4), pp. 560–81, p. 561.
132. Ibid., p. 567.
133. Simon Cottee and Keith Hayward (2011) 'Terrorist (e)motives: the existential attractions of terrorism', *Studies in Conflict & Terrorism*, **34** (12), pp. 963–86, p. 965.
134. Ibid., p. 966.
135. Ibid., pp. 978–9.
136. Ibid., p. 966.
137. Ehud Sprinzak (1991) 'The process of delegitization: towards a linkage theory of political terrorism,' *Terrorism & Political Violence*, pp. 50–68, p. 68.
138. Marieke Slootman and Jean Tillie (2006) *Processes of Radicalisation: Why some Amsterdam Muslims become Radicals*, (Amsterdam: Institute for Migration and Ethnic Studies, University of Amsterdam), p. 9.
139. Sprinzak, 'The psychopolitical formation of extreme left terrorism in a democracy: the case of the Weathermen', p. 79.
140. Ibid., p. 78.
141. Ibid., p. 79.
142. Nagtzaam and Lentini, 'Vigilantes on the high seas?: the Sea Shepherds and political violence', p. 118; Sprinzak, 'The psychopolitical formation of extreme left terrorism in a democracy: the case of the Weathermen', pp. 80–81.
143. Sprinzak, 'The process of delegitimation: towards a linkage theory of political terrorism,' p. 54.
144. Sprinzak, 'The process of delegitimation: towards a linkage theory of political terrorism,' p. 54.
145. Nagtzaam and Lentini, 'Vigilantes on the high seas?: the Sea Shepherds and political violence', p. 118.
146. Sprinzak, 'The psychopolitical formation of extreme left terrorism in a democracy: the case of the Weathermen', p. 81; Sprinzak, 'The process of delegitization: towards a linkage theory of political terrorism,' p. 55.
147. Sprinzak, 'The process of delegitimation: towards a linkage theory of political terrorism,' pp. 56–7.
148. Sprinzak, 'The psychopolitical formation of extreme left terrorism in a democracy: the case of the Weathermen', pp. 81–2.
149. Sprinzak, 'The process of delegitimation: towards a linkage theory of political terrorism,' p. 55.
150. Nagtzaam and Lentini, 'Vigilantes on the high seas?: the Sea Shepherds and political violence', p. 118.
151. Sprinzak, 'The psychopolitical formation of extreme left terrorism in a democracy: the case of the Weathermen', p. 83.

152. Ibid., p. 82. Similarly the well-respected National Extremism Tactical Coordination Unit (NETCU) has a radicalization model that broadly follows Sprinzak's approach. The first phase their model postulates is where radical activists pursue lawful protest including boycotts or demonstrations. The NETCU paradigm further maintains that if such an approach does not yield results then harsher tactics are enacted such as a coordinated intimidation or harassment campaign that targets organizations, individuals and businesses (trespass into offices, threatening letters, intelligence gathering on targets). In this second phase, if adherents become disillusioned with results they can turn to more radical action, with the line between peaceful yet passionate protest and the use of force becoming hazy for protesters. At this level activists consider campaigns of property damage, vandalism, theft or liberation operations as legitimate exercises. See Arslan, 'The social and operational intersections of environmental extremism in North America and Europe', pp. 155–8; National Extremism Tactical Coordination Unit, http://www.netcu.org.uk/protection/domesticextremisttactics.jsp.
153. Sprinzak, 'The psychopolitical formation of extreme left terrorism in a democracy: the case of the Weathermen', p. 82.
154. Ibid., p. 83.
155. Ibid., p. 85.
156. Ibid., p. 80.
157. For instance in his classic study of the Weathermen, Sprinzak demonstrated that this group emerged from the Students for a Democratic Society, who largely engaged in non-violent protest actions (crisis of confidence). Not being able to have influenced policies enough through these actions, various groups became more militant and took over campus buildings. Their activities culminated in the Days of Rage at the Democratic Convention in Chicago in 1968 (conflict of legitimacy). Following this crackdown, the Weathermen split off from the main protest groups and began their campaign of terrorist bombings throughout the USA (crisis of legitimacy). See Sprinzak, 'The psychopolitical formation of extreme left terrorism in a democracy: the case of the Weathermen' pp. 65–85.
158. Sprinzak, 'The psychopolitical formation of extreme left terrorism in a democracy: the case of the Weathermen' pp. 65–85; Sprinzak, 'The process of delegitimization: towards a linkage theory of political terrorism', pp. 50–68.
159. Sprinzak, 'The psychopolitical formation of extreme left terrorism in a democracy: the case of the Weathermen', p. 72.
160. Ibid., p. 77.
161. Sageman, *Understanding Terror Networks*, p. 158; Quintan Wiktorowicz (2004) 'Introduction: Islamic activism and social movement theory', in Q. Wiktorowicz (ed.), *Islamic Activism: A Social Movement Theory Approach* (Bloomington, In.: Indiana University Press), p. 16.
162. Dalgaard-Nielsen, 'Violent radicalization in Europe: what we know and what we do not know', p. 804; Nagtzaam and Lentini, 'Vigilantes on the high seas?: the Sea Shepherds and political violence', p. 118; Sageman, *Understanding Terror Networks*, p. 108.
163. Sageman, *Understanding Terror Networks*, p. 108.
164. Dalgaard-Nielsen, 'Violent radicalization in Europe: what we know and what we do not know', p. 804.
165. Edwin Bakker (2006) *Jihad Terrorists in Europe* (The Hague: Cliengendael), p. 52.
166. Peter R. Neumann and Brooke Rogers (2007) *Recruitment and Mobilisation for the Islamist Militant Movement in Europe* (London: Kings College, University of London), p, 16.
167. Dalgaard-Nielsen, 'Violent radicalization in Europe: what we know and what we do not know', p. 808. Neumann and Rogers, *Recruitment and Mobilisation for the Islamist Militant Movement in Europe*, p, 71.
168. Wright-Neville, 'Dangerous dynamics: activists, militants and terrorists in Southeast Asia', pp. 39–40.
169. See, for example, Sageman, *Understanding Terror Networks*.

170. For example, the anti-abortion terrorists proceeded through similar stages during the 1990s. Various interest groups performed as activists such as Operation Rescue, and so on. However, not being able in their opinion to win complete bans on abortions, the anti-abortion activists began demonstrating and blockading access to abortion clinics. As a result of this the pro-choice Clinton Administration introduced the Freedom of Access to Clinic Entrances (FACE) legislation. Thereafter, with one of their prime means of protest removed from them, the terrorists began engaging in acts of violence against abortion clinic workers. Indeed, as Christopher Hewitt observes, anti-abortion clinic terrorism, especially bombings and shootings, became deadly under President Clinton. Christopher Hewitt (2003) *Understanding Terrorism in America: From the Klan to Al Qaeda* (London: Routledge), pp. 38–41.
171. Wright-Neville, 'Dangerous dynamics: activists, militants and terrorists in Southeast Asia', p. 42.
172. Ibid., p. 32.
173. Ibid., p. 35.
174. Sprinzak (1990) 'The psychopolitical formation of extreme left terrorism in a democracy: the case of the Weathermen', p. 81.
175. Wright-Neville, 'Dangerous dynamics: activists, militants and terrorists in Southeast Asia', p. 40.
176. Ibid., p. 42.
177. M. Mobley (2002) The new wave of radical environmentalism: America's inaction and reaction to domestic ecoterrorism, *Appalachian Journal of Law*, **1**, p. 19, p. 29; Kevin Grubs (2010) 'Saving lives or spreading fear: the terroristic nature of eco-extremism', *Animal Law*, **16**, p. 366.
178. Beck, 'On the radical cusp: ecoterrorism in the United States, 1998–2005', p. 170. See also W. Enders and T. Sandler (2000) 'Is transnational terrorism: becoming more threatening? A time-series investigation', *Journal of Conflict Resolution*, **44** (3), pp. 307–32; Donatella Porta and Dieter Rucht (1995) 'The dynamics of environmental campaigns', *Mobilization*, **7** (1), pp. 1–14; Rudd Koopmans (1993) 'The dynamics of protest waves: West Germany, 1965–1989', *American Sociological Review*, **58** (5), pp. 637–58.
179. Beck, 'On the radical cusp: ecoterrorism in the United States, 1998–2005', p. 170.
180. Trujillo, 'The radical environmentalist movement', p. 164.
181. Taylor, 'Religion, violence and radical environmentalism: from Earth First! to the Unabomber to the Earth Liberation Front, p. 10; Trujillo, 'The radical environmentalist movement', pp. 141–78, pp. 168–9; Gary Ackerman (2003) 'Beyond arson? A threat assessment of the Earth Liberation Front', *Terrorism and Political Violence*, **15** (4), pp. 145–50.
182. Ackerman, 'Beyond arson? A threat assessment of the Earth Liberation Front', pp. 145–50.
183. Taylor, 'Religion, violence and radical environmentalism: from Earth First! to the Unabomber to the Earth Liberation Front', p. 11; Trujillo, 'The radical environmentalist movement', pp. 141–78, p. 169; Mark Button et al. (2002) 'New challenges in public order policing: the professionalisation of environmental protest and the emergence of the militant environmental activist', *International Journal of the Sociology of Law*, **30**, p. 21.
184. Arslan, 'The social and operational intersections of environmental extremism in North America and Europe', pp. 150–51.
185. Scarce, *Eco-Warriors: Understanding the Radical Environmental Movement*, p. 272; Jim Flynn (2005) 'Dear shit fer brains letters to the editors', *Earth First! Journal*, **25** (3), 1 March, p. 3.
186. Arslan, 'The social and operational intersections of environmental extremism in North America and Europe', p. 151.

PART I

1. Cage fighting: the Animal Liberation Front

> Despite the combined efforts of all the wretched industries we abhor, the ALF is alive and well and growing. If people want to stop the ALF it is simple: *stop doing unspeakable acts to other-than-human beings!* There will be an ALF for as long as tiny chicks feel the pain of that searing wire on their beaks and chained pigs dig hopelessly into the hard cement with their hooves ... as long as there are terrorized animal victims of human injustice and callousness.
>
> Valerie, an ALF activist[1]

INTRODUCTION

Of the radical environmental groups examined the Animal Liberation Front (ALF) is the oldest and still holds enormous sway today. It is also the most violent group in that they have been willing to directly target their human opponents at certain points in their history. In 1987 the FBI first categorized the ALF as a terrorist group.[2] Arslan's research demonstrates that the ALF is still the most dominant radical environmental group with its adherents committing almost half (43.8 per cent) of recorded radical environmental actions.[3]

To its adherents and its supporters, though, the ALF and its more violent *nom de guerres* – the Animal Rights Militia, the Justice Department and Stop Huntingdon Animal Cruelty – are willing to put their freedom on the line to defend animals against the 'vast industries [that] have built up around what Animal Liberators see as the "exploitation" of non-human animals'.[4] According to Best and Nocella, 'there are two faces of the ALF – the "benign" one that breaks into prisons to release and rescue animals, and the "malign" one that smashes windows, wrecks equipment, and torches buildings'.[5]

The ALF and its smaller antecedent group the Band of Mercy grew out of a concern that activist actions in trying to prevent ongoing hunting in the UK were not enough and that militant action was needed. Inspired by law student Ronnie Lee the group, drawing on the writings of animal liberationists such as Peter Singer and Tom Regan, began carrying out liberation raids to free animals before progressing quickly to arson against its perceived opponents. However, despite a public stance against physical violence by the early 1980s, as the Sprinzak delegitimation model suggests, some cells began to carry out car bombings and physical threats and attacks against their 'enemies'. In an effort to still maintain their public stance of non-violence, ALF members went as far as to create new 'groups', which publicly proclaimed they were distant from ALF cells but in reality were populated with ALF members determined to protect animals by virtually any means.

This chapter examines the historical roots of animal welfare groups that influenced the ALF philosophies and goals. It examines the role played by the Hunt Saboteurs Association and the perceived failure of its direct action approach on Ronnie Lee, the key founder of the ALF, which prompted him to create the Band of Mercy, a predecessor group to the ALF. The chapter further critically examines the birth of the ALF out of the ashes of the Band of Mercy in the UK and its subsequent spreading to the USA, where radical animal rights proponents enthusiastically embraced its approach to animal liberation. Lastly it focuses on the development of the philosophy of the ALF and its use to permit radical action that allowed, in the minds of some adherents, for a more radical approach that targeted humans in defence of animals.

A BRIEF HISTORY OF ANIMAL WELFARE GROUPS

The animal liberation movement can be traced back to the nineteenth century, with the establishment of the UK's Society for the Prevention of Cruelty to Animals (1824, the current 'Royal' prefix was attached in 1840). The organization was created to 'police the first animal welfare legislation' that had been passed two years earlier. By the end of the nineteenth century, several anti-vivisection groups had also emerged (including the National Anti-Vivisection Society and the British Union for the Abolition of Vivisection). By the end of the Second World War a further 16 similar national organizations were created in the UK. However, since 1960 there has been a plethora of new animal rights groups established.[6]

In the nineteenth century, the lack of moral status afforded to animals changed to a 'new position of moral orthodoxy, whereby animals were accorded a moral status but an inferior one to that of humans'. While humans had a responsibility to avoid 'unnecessary suffering' on animals, they were 'entitled to use them for their own benefit (e.g. food, clothing and to experiment upon)'.[7] The late 1970s and early 1980s saw the emergence of a distinct animal rights movement that 'retained the animal welfare tradition's concern for animals as sentient beings that should be protected from unnecessary cruelty' but added 'a new language' of 'rights' as the foundation that called for the end of societal animal exploitation.[8]

According to Finsen and Finsen, the traditional animal welfare/humane movement can be explicitly distinguished from the animal rights movement in the following way:

> The humane movement promoted kindness and the elimination of cruelty without challenging the assumption of human superiority or the institutions that reflect that assumption. The animal rights movement, on the other hand, does not seek human reforms but challenges the assumption of human superiority and demands abolition of institutions it considers exploitative. Rather than asking for a greater (and optional) charity toward animals, the animal rights movement demands justice, equality, fairness, and rights.[9]

However, it is important to establish that the animal rights view does not necessarily believe that animals and humans should hold identical rights, but that animals 'certainly have the right to life and to freedom from bodily interference'.[10] Garner notes that animal rights activists perceive that: 'the growth of mass activism is clearly linked to the belief, derived from an animal rights perspective, that since so much more is wrong with our treatment of animals than was previously thought, only permanent and sustained activism will help put things right'.[11]

The animal rights movement has subsequently spread throughout Western countries and beyond. The aim of such organizations however, 'has never been eliminating the institutions that exploit animals, but rather reducing or ameliorating animal suffering within such violent and repressive structures'.[12] Such organizations initially focused on 'anti-cruelty campaigns', including pets, working animals and animals killed in blood sports, with many 'traditional groups' still actively campaigning against these issues. However, over time animal scientific experimentation and vivisection, hunting and trapping, animals in entertainment, factory farming, the transshipment of animals and preventing fur-wearing have become important campaigns globally.[13]

The animal liberation movement currently operates on a global level, 'from the UK, US and Germany to France, Norway, and Russia'.[14] According to Best, the 'modern animal "rights" movement' is relatively new (he argues a few decades). However, in a relatively small amount of time it has clearly developed an outsized presence.[15]

Hunt Saboteurs Association

One of the animal rights groups established in the 1960s, this group ended up playing a seminal role in the creation of ALF. The Hunt Saboteurs Association (HSA) was established in 1963 in the UK, when 'antivivisectionists melded with class-conscious protesters to harass fox hunters, seen as conspicuous symbols of the rich "landed gentry" torturing an innocent creature for sport'.[16] It is important to note that many believe that the establishment of the HSA was due to the more traditional anti-hunting group, the League Against Cruel Sports with members being unwilling to engage in direct action, which some anti-hunting advocates were drawn to.[17]

The HSA traces its roots back to 1824 when Catherine Smithies established the 'Band of Mercy', a 'youth wing of Britain's Royal Society for the Prevention of Cruelty to Animals, which attempted to disrupt stag hunts and fox hunts in which the quarry was run down by dogs'.[18] John Prestige, a young freelance journalist, founded and served as the first chairman of the HSA. According to *The Guardian*, 'he picked the first of his supporters on 15 December 1963 … he is the founder of the Hunt Saboteurs Association … which has the support of the LACS, whose chairman, Raymond Rawley, says is willing to make available all the latest know-how on how to sabotage a hunt'.[19] The group was a highly visible one in the 1960s since it was willing to both openly criticize animal rights violations and, unusual for the time, was willing to employ confrontational tactics.[20]

The HSA's first action occurred on 26 December 1963. The first action was a rousing success that led to the cancelling of the targeted hunt. The group fed 50 lbs of meat to the hunting dogs to distract them and used hunting horns to create a cacophonous chaos. Even the local police, it was recorded, were bemused by the direct action tactics.[21] As their campaign to disrupt hunting continued the hunters and 'sabs', as they came to be known, began to recognize one another and 'call each other by first names, and trade insults and animosity'.[22]

The early result of these actions saw hunters financially and physically impeded from not only carrying out hunts but even prevented from being able to attend meets. Initially, members had not been convinced that such tactics would be effective but, over time, as new members were drawn to the group because of their willingness to engage in direct actions, the new approach was embraced.[23] The idea also spread to the USA. From 1987 to 1990, Hunt Saboteurs America targeted large game hunters and 'launched regular annual campaigns to stop the hunting of rare desert bighorn sheep and tule elk'.[24]

During each campaign, the sabs made their commitment to non-violence well known. According to Arnold, 'on the rare occasions when they were slugged by an angry fox hunter, they never struck back'.[25] As Kuipers points out, 'face to face confrontations with hunters who had drawn expensive, once-in-a-lifetime licenses to hunt these beasts had the potential to go down very badly'. Arguably, the only reason their campaigns went so well and drew on public support was the widespread knowledge that the HSA was committed to non-violence.[26]

However, such commitment to non-violence changed with the enlistment of a young law student, Ronnie Lee. He established a branch of the HSA in Luton, England in 1971 and adhered to 'their nonviolent tactics despite misgivings' as to their efficacy.[27]

Ronnie Lee biography

Surprisingly little is available on the personal details of Ronnie Lee, as opposed to his political writings. Ronnie Lee was born on 1 January 1951 and is a British activist who describes himself as a 'socialist animal liberationist'.[28] Lee is a veteran of the animal liberation movement and even his fiercest critics, such as journalist David Henshaw, describe him as charismatic and influential.[29]

Lee was a meat eater until the age of 19 when he was inspired by his sister's boyfriend back in the 1960s to become a vegetarian.[30] His sister's boyfriend was athletic, very fit and threw javelin for his county – he was also a vegetarian, and Ronnie Lee was kept awake at night trying to find an excuse for his meat eating. He couldn't and he became a vegetarian and eventually, by the 1970s, a vegan.[31] He felt it made sense to be one, so as to do something for the animals and to represent his cause honestly. At that time, most vegans were not associated with any animal rights movement or vivisection protests and were merely regarded as an eccentric minority.[32]

Lee's official involvement with animal rights began when he founded a new hunt sab group in Luton, an offshoot of the Hunt Saboteurs Association.[33] At its inception, the group began by meeting in a basement cafe in London, most of the attendees at that point having had experience as hunt saboteurs.[34]

Before his first experience of 'sabbing', Lee was studying to become a solicitor at a London law college.[35] According to Henshaw, 'Lee's political background was informed by anarchistic philosophies which he never renounced'.[36] However, animal liberation was not Lee's only focus, as he was also involved in the movement 'opposing the presence of troops in Northern Ireland'.[37] His environmental beliefs were a mix of anti-technological, anti-capitalist, anti-democracy and reduced-population philosophies. According to Lee:

> True freedom for all the Earth's creatures demands a decentralized non-hierarchical society with much lower levels of technology and a massive cut in the human population – as well as the ending of the more obvious abuses such as vivisection, factory farming etc.[38]

For Lee, animal cruelty was mostly brought about by the pursuit of profit, without which the incentives to treat animals badly would be minimized.[39] Lee was equally dismissive of democracy, stating; 'my main aim isn't to toady to the public. What we're trying to do is to actually sabotage the industries of animal abuse.'[40] He believed that: 'it is time for us to destroy the old world and to build the new in the only way possible – by our own direct action. It is time to dispense with all politicians, be they of the right or of the left.'[41] Lee perceived animal liberationists as the 'enlightened ones' – puritanical, self-abnegating and selfless in their cause.[42]

According to Henshaw, Lee and another member (and friend), Cliff Goodman, quickly became disillusioned with the HSA's refusal to 'return violence against violence'. As Henshaw further observes, there were other more puissant examples of how to prevent hunting and the newspapers 'were full of the doings of a shadowy group calling themselves the "Angry Brigade"'.[43] The following year, Goodman sustained an eye injury during the campaign and the event served to convince Lee that a 'different, more violent direction was called for, one that went beyond annoying the upper class to target any part of individual civilization that, in his view, abused animals'. As a result of this decision, Lee and Goodman created the Band of Mercy in 1972.[44]

The Band of Mercy

In Lee's opinion, the flaw with hunt sabotage was twofold. It focused only on a single issue, effectively ignoring other aspects of animal use, and such a strategy was confined to stopping hunters once they were actually engaged on the field. Lee believed that the hunts could be 'sabotaged far more effectively, and foxes saved much more efficiently, if the hunt never reached the field in the first place'.[45] Lee decided that there was a need to create a new organization, the Band of Mercy. The name of the organization was taken from the 'children's wing of the nineteenth century RSPCA'. The group initially comprised six members, including Lee.[46] The disillusionment with the HSA and its non-violent philosophy, strategy and tactics, and Lee's creation of a new group, fits neatly within Sprinzak's crisis of confidence stage.

The Band of Mercy combined 'the nineteenth century tradition of animal rights, which was most cogently voiced by Henry Salt ("Animals' Rights Considered in Relation to Social Progress" (1980), London), with a late 1960s assurance in the necessity and obligation of liberation struggles'.[47] While superficially it appeared on the surface to be similar to other animal welfare organizations, 'beneath this sanitary image lay a [new] radical attitude towards direct action for animal liberation'.[48]

The Band of Mercy also believed in the necessity of animal rights and that the group's morality allowed for greater scope of actions to prevent cruelty towards animals.[49] In 1973, the Band of Mercy destroyed kennel vehicles and, following these attacks, Lee and Goodman began to consider arson as a possible tactic.[50] By November 1973, the tactics used by the Band of Mercy had shifted from petty vandalism and the destruction of hunt vehicles to arson attacks (which they now perceived as an acceptable tactic) and destruction of butchers and purveyors of farm equipment. It was the opinion of the small organization that such actions were justifiable, 'in view of the cruelties and disrespect that it identified with the current lot of animals'.[51]

In less than a year, the group was responsible for two arsons at a pharmaceutical plant, causing £46,000 in damages.[52] After one arson attack at the Hoechst building the organization's communiqué to the media maintained:

> The building was set fire in an attempt to prevent the torture and murder of our animal brothers and sisters by evil experiments. We are a non-violent guerrilla organisation dedicated to the liberation of animals from all forms of cruelty and persecution at the hands of mankind. Our actions will continue until our aims are achieved.[53]

The only liberation raid conducted by the organization caused the targeted farm to close down for fear of a return visit. However, just six guinea pigs were rescued in this raid.[54] The Band of Mercy were unapologetic for their actions and tactics and concentrated on a strategy of economic damage, with the aim of rendering animal abuse unprofitable.[55] According to Molland, the group when carrying out an action always 'left a message to the hunters explaining the reasons behind their actions and the logic of animal liberation'. Arguably, this also served to confirm that these actions had not been planned and undertaken due to any personal animosity against a single individual.[56]

The activists successfully completed other direct actions until 1975, when Lee and Goodman (and another man, Robin Howard) were caught and arrested as they returned to the scene of a break-in.[57] The men were arrested as they prepared to set a fire at the Oxford Laboratory Animal Colonies near Bicester for a second time.[58] The activists were charged with 14 counts, including causing £57,000 in damage to several locations. The arrests caused public sympathy and support for their actions, including from Lee's MP, the Free Church Minister Ivor Clemiston.[59]

Lee and Goodman, as the leaders of the action, were each given a three-year prison sentence after admitting the charges. Howard was given a 12-month suspended sentence and a £500 fine. Significantly, the judge accepted that they were men of sincerity and integrity and not 'common criminals'.[60] Lee was sent to Winchester prison and Goodman was sent to Oxford prison.[61] Maintaining a vegan diet and lifestyle proved challenging in prison.[62] Lee's treatment by the prison drove him to hold a hunger strike at the Winchester prison that caused media attention.[63] In prison, he was offered only a vegetarian diet and decided to go on a strike to secure vegan food and clothing. During one of his campaigns for vegan rights, he resorted to eating only vegetable protein burgers for three months.[64]

It appears that Sprinzak's second phase, the conflict of legitimacy, occurred in November 1973, when the Band of Mercy took up property damage and arson, as opposed to liberation raids, as an approach to achieve their ends. They grew more militant, as they viewed purely non-violent political or confrontational politics as having limited value.[65] They had begun to question the legitimacy of the current political system and sought to transform the system because of its treatment of animals. The current system and its norms was thus delegitimated in favour of a new ideological and cultural system, which can be characterized as a break from the current political order. Sprinzak's idea of a 'great disappointment' needing to occur also appears to be linked to the failure of the HSA to achieve its goals.

THE BIRTH OF THE ANIMAL LIBERATION FRONT

Establishing the ALF in England

The militant approach employed by the Band of Mercy also became a foundational tenet of the ALF. Both Lee and Goodman were paroled in 1976 after serving 12 months, only one-third of their sentence.[66] Goodman came out of prison with only one purpose, not to go back. His career as an animal rights revolutionary was over and, whilst he remained a believer in animal rights, carrying out picketing, letter writing and attending demonstrations, he was determined not to break the law by his actions. He was critical of Lee's approach that he believed condoned violence, going so far as to describe his old comrade as a 'lunatic'.[67] Goodman would go down in history as the movement's first traitor or 'grass' (police informer) when he gave up the group's radio communication methods to the police.[68]

On the other hand, Lee left prison as the 'undisputed leader of the movement'. While his organization, the Band of Mercy, had disbanded by Lee's release in the spring of 1976, there were still a core of about 30 animal rights activists who were prepared to carry out actions and perceived Lee as their mentor.[69]

On his release Lee found that many regarded him as a martyr for being willing to go to prison for his beliefs.[70] He had used his time in prison to create a 'battle plan'. He believed that the best approach by activists was to incorporate hit-and-run tactics and a diffuse cells structure. Any raid carried out would be publicized through the mass media, trying to demonstrate ongoing animal abuse to shock society and to generate support for their cause. The proposed model could also be easily duplicated.[71]

The organization emphasized direct action as an economic strategy, with the overarching goal of inflicting economic loss on animal enterprises. According to Lee:

> If you go and damage a laboratory they have to pay to put it right and to install extra security measures (because often they won't get insurance unless they put in extra security). This money often comes out of their research budget and would be spent on experimentation. A lot of people criticize the fact that damage is done, saying that property is sacred. I think it is important to point out that damage to property does save animals.[72]

Lee wrote later, 'we saw the situation as a guerilla campaign and those participating in it were very much in the front line'.[73] Lee wanted to declare war on industrial society and was looking for a new vehicle for his ambitions.[74] While the British police had been able to stop many members of the Band of Mercy, Lee (also known as 'Captain Kirk') and the 30 remaining activists created what became ALF-UK in June 1976.[75] For many activists the ALF was born out of frustration. David Barbarash (former press officer for ALF) argues: 'many activists do not understand the revolutionary nature of this movement. We are fighting a major war, defending animals and our very planet from human greed and destruction.'[76] According to Kim Stallwood, the ALF was created because 'nothing was happening' to stop vivisection and other animal abuses'. Stallwood further maintains:

> It was a drastic situation and we needed a drastic course of action. No one was thinking about it, no one was concerned about it, no one knew anything about it. The illegal activity brought it out and gave it immediate attention ... There had been centuries of legal activity that had come to nothing. I don't think it is that unusual, because when you look at any movement for social change there has always been this combination of legal and illegal activities.[77]

While the Band of Mercy had focused primarily on the issues of hunting and animal experimentation, the nascent ALF also was concerned over the issue of animals in food production. The method adopted by the ALF was to use direct action to 'liberate animals from what is held to be their violent speciesist oppression'.[78]

With regards to naming this new operation, Mann explains, 'the Band of Mercy wasn't considered to be a sufficiently forceful name to represent the vanguard of the revolution that was envisaged, so it was ditched and the new (in)famous title – the Animal Liberation Front – was adopted in its place'.[79] According to Schnurer, three factors made the new organization a unique threat to the ongoing system of animal oppression:

1. The ALF documents a world hidden from view. Photographing and videotaping animals trapped in the most intense states of cruelty provides an immediate ethical challenge to an audience.
2. The ALF communicates a direct sense of warning to all those who participate in animal oppression. The actions of the ALF resonate in the minds of those who profit from animal abuse. This combined with financial cost can make industries unwilling to defend particularly high-profile animal abusers.
3. The actions of the ALF send a message to all who might encounter, or consider taking part in, animal oppression, that they must be aware of the stakes of the issue. The ALF encourages reflection on the part of anyone considering animal experimentation or any other form of exploitation.[80]

It did not take long for the ALF to become well established in the UK. In 1977, a small number of activists freed over 200 animals from laboratory supply companies.[81] The ALF has become increasingly 'radical and violent' since it was formed.[82] Within the UK, the ALF has long been considered the most radical ecogroup, with its paramilitary outfits and willingness to use violence to achieve its goals.[83] By the 1980s the group had been classified by Scotland Yard as a terrorist organization akin to the Irish Republican Army and the Palestine Liberation Organization.[84]

Establishing the ALF in the USA

The idea of an ALF was within a few years embraced by animal activists in the USA. The idea of so-called animal rights terrorism was once an alien concept to most Americans but over the last few decades has increased in both frequency and violence.[85] The first action attributable to the ALF remains contested. Some allege that the ALF's first action in the USA was in 1977, when it freed two dolphins from the University of Hawaii.[86]

An activist named 'Valerie' has also been credited with establishing the first US branch of the ALF. She was the architect in establishing numerous ALF cells throughout the USA and personally led numerous raids and provided logistical support for many more.[87] One early claim of ALF action was in 1981 when 17 macaque monkeys that had initially been removed by police from the lab of a Dr Edward Taub in Silver City, Maryland, were later stolen by ALF members from police custody and taken to Florida.[88]

However, others date its first action as December 1983 when 12 research dogs were taken from a medical laboratory in Torrance, California. The $50,000 theft ruined years of research on heart pacemakers. Several further break-ins occurred with the ALF claiming responsibility for each act.[89]

What is clear is that the name 'ALF' and its cause entered into the US political and social consciousness following an action in 1984 in which members went into a head-injury lab at the University of Pennsylvania. The activists caused $70,000 worth of damage but, more importantly, took videotapes made by the researchers themselves. The tapes showed the lab technicians laughing as severe head trauma was inflicted on conscious baboons.[90]

While the lab claimed to be following all standards imposed by the National Institute of Health, the public outrage was immense. In the wake of the public outcry the facility was closed, the head veterinarian's employment was terminated, and the university itself placed on probation.[91] Further, for the first time the Secretary of the Department of Health and Human Services suspended public funding to a laboratory, an unprecedented event.[92] These repercussions shocked the biomedical research community but were lauded by many environmentalists and animal rights activists as a righteous action since such footage could not have been obtained legally.[93]

Philosophical Underpinnings

Humanity's consideration of the role and moral worthiness of animals has a long history. Some argue that the animal liberation movement was created because of 'Judeo-Christian writings'.[94] However, the traditional attitude towards animals is best summed up in the book of Genesis (Gen. 1:27–28):

> So God created man in his own image, in the image of God he created him; male and female he created them. And God blessed them, and God said to them, 'Be fruitful and multiply, and fill the earth and subdue it; and have dominion over the fish of the sea and over the birds of the air and over every living thing that moves upon the earth.[95]

For many, however, Jeremy Bentham's writing encapsulated the founding idea of the entire animal liberation movement. At a time when France had just liberated its black slaves but the British continued the practice, Bentham stated:

> The day *may* come when the rest of the animal creation may acquire those rights which never could have been withholden from them but by their hand of tyranny. The French have already discovered that the blackness of the skin is no reason why a human being should be abandoned without redress to the caprice of a tormentor. It may one day come to be recognized that the number of legs, the villosity of the skin, or the termination of the *os sacrum* are reasons equally insufficient for abandoning a sensitive being to the same fate. What else is it that should trace the insuperable line? Is it the faculty of reason, or perhaps the faculty of discourse? But a full-grown horse or dog is beyond comparison a more rational, as well as a more conversable animal, than an infant of a day or week or even a month old. But suppose they were otherwise, what would it avail? The question is not, Can they *reason*? nor Can they *talk*? but, Can they *suffer*?[96]

Incorporating ideas from Jeremy Bentham and Henry Salt, Peter Singer suggested that 'racism, sexism, and specieism are the same breed of human behavior, and that slavery, the Jewish Holocaust, the subjugation of women, factory farming, and vivisection all reflect unjustified discrimination'.[97] Peter Singer's work, *Animal Liberation*, published in 1975, is commonly referred to as a turning point for the animal rights movement. For some the text gave the emerging radical movement a cohesive moral and philosophical perspective.[98] Singer suggested that animals should be given the same moral consideration as humans. Anything less was specieism, which should be fought in the same way that racism or sexism should be.[99] His seminal text provided a large amount of evidence that modern agribusiness practices inflicted suffering on animals that far outweighed the benefits accruing to humans.[100]

Singer argued that morality means 'that *all* creatures who are capable of suffering demand consideration of their interests'. He wrote: 'If a being suffers there can be no moral justification for refusing to take that suffering into consideration'.[101]

It is important to understand that Singer is not supporting animal rights per se, but rather demanding an end to prejudice and a right to equal consideration for all animals.[102] He wrote that, 'all sentient beings are entitled to equal consideration of their interests. A being possesses interests if it is capable of suffering and enjoyment; this capacity is the *fundamental* prerequisite for having interests at all. Equal interests must be equally respected, without regard to the species of beings whose interests they are.'[103] To that end he believes that the 'clearest and most dramatic form that testimony can take is vegetarianism'.[104]

Some argue that the work has been a 'bible' for activists interested in direct action.[105] However, it is important to note that Singer was unhappy with how his work has been utilized to justify radical action. He openly denounced the use of violence in the movement, stating, 'by violence, I mean any action which causes direct physical harm … and I would go beyond physical harm to acts which cause psychological harm like fear or terror'.[106]

While, arguably, Peter Singer's work had an intense influence on the radical animal movement, there has been 'a marked preference for action as opposed to boning up on correct theory'.[107] Henshaw argues that Singer had simply been 'overtaken by the revolution he had helped to begin'.[108] According to Best and Nocella, while Singer attempted to 'appeal to the "minds of the reasonable people"', the ALF 'believes that far too many are unreasonable and closed-minded, rendering force of reason and persuasion insufficient'.[109]

A third key philosopher has been Tom Regan. In 1983, his *The Case For Animal Rights* further developed Singer's initial findings, and 'laid the ideological groundwork for liberating animals from human oppression'.[110] Regan maintained that, 'animals have intrinsic rights … certain animals at least, especially mammals, have consciousness. Mammalian animals have beliefs and desires upon which they act.'[111] Regan further contended that:

> We are each of us experiencing subjects of a life, a conscious creature having an individual welfare that has importance to us whatever our usefulness to others. We want and prefer things, believe and feel things, recall and expect things. And all these dimensions of our life, including our pleasure and pain,

> our enjoyment and suffering, our satisfaction and frustration, our continued existence or our untimely death – all make a difference to the quality of our life as lived, as experienced, by us as individuals.[112]

As such, he concludes, arguments that 'only humans have rights because they are the only animals that have reason and language, besides being factually wrong, are completely irrelevant as sentience is a necessary and sufficient condition for having rights'.[113]

Tom Regan disagreed with many of the ideas espoused by Singer. Regan 'attacked Singer from a different philosophical position, while still sharing the same position on animal cruelty'. Regan argued that, 'Singer's utilitarianism supports animal's research for human purposes, even if it means that most of these animals will experience pain and harm',[114] and further insists that 'all animals are equal to humans in their right not to be harmed arbitrarily'.[115]

Shift to Radical Philosophy

Garner argues that although concern for the plight of animals in an organizational setting first emerged in the nineteenth century, since the birth of the ALF the animal protection movement has become radicalized.[116] Building on the philosophical underpinnings of Bentham, Singer and Regan the radical approach of the ALF has 'abolitionist objectives', with the aim to end all types of animal exploitation, whether for food, clothing, consumer safety, scientific advance or entertainment. Such activists argue that animals are 'bearers of rights – and particularly the right to life – we are not entitled to use them'.[117]

Since the 1970s, the 'radical philosophy has fed upon a much more receptive social climate and, in turn, this has encouraged further interest at the theoretical level'. However, this statement does not necessarily mean that 'activists are aware of the complex philosophizing that characterizes the leading radical works'. Obvious exceptions include Regan, Singer and Linzey (all of whom are leading academics and well-known activists). Such academic work has given the 'radical wing of the movement academic respectability in addition to a clearer set of objectives'.[118]

As Hall points out the ALF, building on the philosophical insights of Bentham and Singer, is concerned with the prevention of suffering.[119] Both the ALF (and, lately, the Justice Department, an offshoot animal liberation group) claim that, 'contemporary ways of treating animals are an infringement of the non-negotiable and absolute higher law of the truth of animals'.[120] According to David Barbarash (the former spokesman for the ALF): 'we're very dangerous philosophically. Part of the danger is that we don't buy into the illusion that property is worth more than life … we bring that insane priority into the light, which is something the system cannot survive.'[121]

Steven Best maintains that the struggle for animal rights should be seen as 'intimately connected' to the ongoing struggle for humanity.[122] However, while, arguably the basic philosophy behind the ALF is that of animal rights, there must be a distinction made between animal rights and animal liberation. According to Best and Nocella, 'whereas animal rights often is a legal fight without direct action, animal liberation is an immediate confrontation with exploiters'.[123] For ALF members:

> The implications of the new philosophy were rather more urgent than traditional and rather cosy notions of welfare. These were groups that were going to get things done, groups for activists who wanted more out of the membership than demonstrations of de-infestation techniques and the annual charity social.[124]

There are elements of millenarian philosophy in much of the movement. According to Henshaw, ALF members perceive humanity as such an ongoing evil that violence was inevitable.[125] For example, in 1984, Ronnie Lee wrote:

> Animal Liberation is a fierce struggle that demands total commitment … There will be injuries and possible deaths on both sides … This is sad but certain … true animal liberation will not come merely through the destruction of the Dachaus and Buchenwalds but demands nothing more than the driving back of the human species to its pre invasion boundaries.[126]

Many times the movement's writings, and the activists themselves, have spoken of their desire to return to a place where humanity can live in a state of grace with animals, nature is not restrained and human society is deindustrialized.[127]

Members of the ALF argue that many laws pertaining to animals exist only to protect animal exploiters and such laws that permit ongoing suffering are inherently corrupt.[128] In 1984 Lee stated in *The Guardian* newspaper: 'the law in this country offers little or no protection to animals so it is necessary for people to break the law to protect animals'.[129] Thus, as Henshaw explains, disobeying the law was an inevitable consequence of those beliefs but it was acceptable since activists did not believe they were 'real' laws. Members would argue that they were not breaking what they described as 'moral laws' but rather merely a 'legal law'. Breaking such a conception of the law was justified to do the 'right thing' in protecting animals from human exploitation.[130]

NOTES

1. Ingrid Newkirk (2000) *Free the Animals: The Amazing True Story of the Animal Liberation Front* (New York: Lantern), pp. 371–2.
2. Russell Lee Young (2004) 'A time series analysis of eco-terrorist violence in the United States: 1993–2003' (PhD dissertation, Sam Houston State University, Huntsville, TX), p. 42; C. Nilson and T. Burke (2002) 'Environmental extremists and the eco-terrorism movement', *Academy of Criminal Justice Sciences*, **24** (5), p. 4.
3. Hasan T. Arslan (2008) 'The social and operational intersections of environmental extremism in North America and Europe' (PhD dissertation, Sam Houston State University, Huntsville, TX), p. 106.
4. Rik Scarce (2006) *Eco-Warriors: Understanding the Radical Environmental Movement* (updated edn), (CA: Left Coast Press), p. 116.
5. Steven Best and Anthony Nocella, 'Behind the mask: uncovering the Animal Liberation Front' in Steven Best and Anthony Nocella (eds), *Terrorists or Freedom Fighters: Reflections on the Liberation of Animals* (New York: Lantern Books), p. 47.
6. Robert Garner (1993) 'Political animals: a survey of the animal protection movement in Britain', *Parliamentary Affairs*, **46** (3), p. 334.
7. Rachel Monaghan (1997) 'Animal rights and violent protest', *Terrorism and Political Violence*, **9** (4), p. 107.
8. Denise Case (2002) 'The USA Patriot Act: adding bite to the fight against animal rights terrorism?', *Rutgers Law Journal*, **187**, Fall, p. 191.
9. Lawrence Finsen and Susan Finsen (1994) *The Animal Rights Movement in America: From Compassion to Respect* (New York: Twayne Publishers), p. 3.
10. Donald R. Liddick (2006) *Eco-Terrorism: Radical Environmental and Animal Liberation Movements*, (Westport, Connecticut: Praeger), p. 26.
11. Monaghan, 'Animal rights and violent protest', pp. 108–9.
12. Steven Best (2006) 'Rethinking the revolution: animal liberation, human liberation, and the future of the left', *International Journal of Inclusive Democracy*, **2** (3), pp. 5–6. For example, in Britain – 'there are hundreds of pro-animal groups', including the Royal Society for the Prevention of Cruelty to Animals (that has approximately 500,000 supporters). In the USA there are the 'traditional groups' including the Humane Society, the Anti-Vivisection League and the Society for the Prevention of Cruelty to Animals (SPCA) and 'new groups' including the People for the Ethical Treatment of Animals (PETA, with approximately 300,000 supporters), the Gorilla Foundation, the Human Farming Association, Farm Animal Reform, Alliance for Animals, Citizens to End Animal Suffering and Exploitation (CEASE), Trans-Special Unlimited and the Digit Fund. Similar groups are also present in the Philippines, South Korea, Ukraine, Czech Republic, Mexico, India and Russia (among others). Jody Emel and Jennifer Wolch (1998) 'Witnessing the animal moment', in Woch and Emel (eds), *Animal Geographies: Places, Politics and Identity in the Nature-Culture Borderlands* (London and New York: Verso), p. 520.
13. Emel and Wolch, 'Witnessing the animal moment', p. 118.
14. Best, 'Rethinking the revolution: animal liberation, human liberation, and the future of the left', p. 2.
15. Steven Best (2010) 'War against animals: time to stop playing nice', *The Scavenger*, blog, 10 July.
16. Ron Arnold (1995) *Ecoterror: The Violent Agenda to Save Nature, The World of the Unabomber* (Washington: Free Enterprise Press), p. 207.

17. Keith Mann (2008) *From Dusk 'til Dawn: An Insider's View of the Growth of the Animal Liberation Movement* (US: Voice of the Voiceless), p. 45.
18. Dean Kuipers (2009) *Operation Bite Back: Rod Coronado's War to Save the American Wilderness* (New York: Bloomsbury), p. 35.
19. Mann, *From Dusk 'til Dawn: An Insider's View of the Growth of the Animal Liberation Movement*, p. 45.
20. Arslan, 'The social and operational intersections of environmental extremism in North America and Europe', p. 31; Finsen and Finsen, *The Animal Rights Movement in America – From Compassion to Respect*, p. 55.
21. Mann, *From Dusk 'til Dawn: An Insider's View of the Growth of the Animal Liberation Movement*, p. 46.
22. Arnold, *Ecoterror: The Violent Agenda to Save Nature, The World of the Unabomber*, p. 208; Frankel (1992) 'Fox hunting: clash of the classes – English animal rights groups, preservers of country life face off', *The Washington Post*, 1 March, p. A22.
23. Mann, *From Dusk 'til Dawn: An Insider's View of the Growth of the Animal Liberation* Movement, p. 50.
24. Kuipers, *Operation Bite Back: Rod Coronado's War to Save the American Wilderness*, p. 35.
25. Arnold, *Ecoterror: The Violent Agenda to Save Nature, The World of the Unabomber*, p. 208.
26. Kuipers, *Operation Bite Back: Rod Coronado's War to Save the American Wilderness*, p. 35.
27. Arnold, *Ecoterror: The Violent Agenda to Save Nature, The World of the Unabomber*, p. 208.
28. http://www.spokeo.com/Ronnie+Lee+1.
29. Carolyn Bailey (2010) 'Transcript of Ronnie Lee's ARZone Live Guest Chat', 27 March at: 7 p.m. Eastern DST, 11 p.m. UK time; and 28 March 2010 at 9 a.m. Australian Eastern Standard Time, http://arzone.ning.com/profiles/blogs/transcript-of-ronnie-lees-live
30. Noel Molland, 'Thirty years of direct action', *No Compromise*, **18**, http://www.nocompromise.org/issues/18thirty_years.html; http://www.animalliberationfront.com/ALFront/Premise_History/30yearsofDirectAction.htm.
31. Bailey, 'Transcript of Ronnie Lee's ARZone Live Guest Chat'.
32. Claudette Vaughan, 'Animal soldiers – a rare exclusive interview with Ronnie Lee' https://carmen4thepets.wordpress.com/2010/03/22/animal-soldiers-a-rare-and-exclusive-interview-with-ronnie-lee/; http://www.abolitionist-online.com/?f.
33. Molland, 'Thirty years of direct action'.
34. Vaughan, 'Animal soldiers – a rare exclusive interview with Ronnie Lee'.
35. David Henshaw (1989) *Animal Warfare: The Story of the Animal Liberation Front* (London: Fontana), p. 12.
36. Ibid., pp. 11, 50.
37. Keith Tester and John Walls (1996) 'The ideology and current activities of the Animal Liberation Front', *Contemporary Politics*, **2** (2), p. 80.
38. Henshaw, *Animal Warfare: The Story of the Animal Liberation Front*, p. 196.
39. Tester and Walls, 'The Ideology and Current Activities of the Animal Liberation Front', p. 82.
40. David Henshaw, *Animal Warfare: The Story of the Animal Liberation Front*, p. 34.
41. Ibid., p. 196.
42. Ibid., p. 56.
43. Ibid., p. 13.
44. Arnold, *Ecoterror: The Violent Agenda to Save Nature, The World of the Unabomber*, p. 208.
45. Tester and Walls, 'The ideology and current activities of the Animal Liberation Front', p. 79.
46. Bailey, 'Transcript of Ronnie Lee's ARZone Live Guest Chat'.

47. Tester and Walls, 'The ideology and current activities of the Animal Liberation Front', p. 80.
48. Mann, *From Dusk 'til Dawn: An Insider's View of the Growth of the Animal Liberation Movement*, p. 39.
49. Tester and Walls, 'The ideology and current activities of the Animal Liberation Front', p. 80.
50. Henshaw, *Animal Warfare: The Story of the Animal Liberation Front*, p. 14.
51. Tester and Walls, 'The ideology and current activities of the Animal Liberation Front', p. 80.
52. Arnold, *Ecoterror: The Violent Agenda to Save Nature, The World of the Unabomber*, p. 208.
53. Mann, *From Dusk 'til Dawn: An Insider's View of the Growth of the Animal Liberation*, p. 51.
54. Ibid., p. 52.
55. Ibid.
56. Molland, 'Thirty years of direct action', p. 69.
57. Arnold, *Ecoterror: The Violent Agenda to Save Nature, The World of the Unabomber*, p. 208.
58. Mann, *From Dusk 'til Dawn: An Insider's View of the Growth of the Animal Liberation*, p. 52.
59. Ibid.
60. Ibid., p. 53.
61. Vaughan, 'Animal soldiers – a rare exclusive interview with Ronnie Lee'.
62. http://www.spokeo.com/Ronnie+Lee+1.
63. Ibid.
64. Vaughan, 'Animal soldiers – a rare exclusive interview with Ronnie Lee'; Molland, 'Thirty years of direct action'.
65. Gerry Nagtzaam and Pete Lentini (2008) 'Vigilantes on the high seas?: the Sea Shepherds and political violence', *Terrorism and Political Violence*, **1**, p. 118.
66. http://www.spokeo.com/Ronnie+Lee+1.
67. Henshaw, *Animal Warfare: The Story of the Animal Liberation Front* , p. 18.
68. Vaughan, 'Animal soldiers – a rare exclusive interview with Ronnie Lee'.
69. Henshaw, *Animal Warfare: The Story of the Animal Liberation Front*, p. 19.
70. Arnold, *Ecoterror: The Violent Agenda to Save Nature, The World of the Unabomber*, p. 209.
71. Ibid., p. 208.
72. Derek Wall (2000) 'Snowballs, elves and skimmingtons?: genealogies of environmental direct action' in B. Seel et al. (eds), *Direct Action in British Environmentalism* (London and New York: Routledge), p. 86; Ronnie Lee (1983) 'Free the 4,344,843', *Peace News*, **2201**.
73. Henshaw, *Animal Warfare: The Story of the Animal Liberation Front*, p. 19.
74. Arnold, *Ecoterror: The Violent Agenda to Save Nature, The World of the Unabomber*, p. 209.
75. Arslan, 'The social and operational intersections of environmental extremism in North America and Europe', p. 37; Finsen and Finsen, *The Animal Rights Movement in America – From Compassion to* Respect, p. 100; Tester and Walls, 'The ideology and current activities of the Animal Liberation Front', p. 81.
76. Best, 'Rethinking the revolution: animal liberation, human liberation and the future of the left', p. 27.
77. Scarce, Eco-warriors: understanding the radical environmental movement, p. 140; Kim Stallwood interviewed by Rik Scarce, Rockville, Maryland (30 October 1989).
78. Tester and Walls, 'The ideology and current activities of the Animal Liberation Front', p. 81.
79. Mann, *From Dusk 'til Dawn: An Insider's View of the Growth of the Animal Liberation Movement*, p. 60.

80. Maxwell Schnurer (2004) 'At the gates of hell: the ALF and the legacy of Holocaust resistance', in Steven Best and Anthony Nocella (eds), *Terrorists or Freedom Fighters: Reflections on the Liberation of Animals* (New York: Lantern Books), p. 114.
81. Mann, *From Dusk 'til Dawn: An Insider's View of the Growth of the Animal Liberation Movement*, p. 62.
82. Stefan Leader and Peter Probst (2003) 'The Earth Liberation Front and environmental terrorism', *Terrorism and Political Violence*, **15** (4), p. 38.
83. Nick Harding (2010) 'Killing in the name of earth forms new breed of terrorist', *New Zealand Herald*, 23 May.
84. Arslan, 'The social and operational intersections of environmental extremism in North America and Europe', p. 37; Donald R. Liddick (2006) *Eco-Terrorism: Radical Environmental and Animal Liberation Movements* (Westport, CT: Praeger Publication), p. 41.
85. Young, 'A time series analysis of eco-terrorist violence in the United States: 1993–2003', p. 29.
86. Case, 'The USA Patriot Act: adding bite to the fight against animal rights terrorism?', p. 191; 'Animal Research Facility Protection: hearing before the House Subcommittee on Department Opinions, Research and Foreign Agriculture and the Subcommittee on Livestock, Dairy and Poultry, of the Committee on Agriculture', 101st Congress, url: http://www.animaliberationfront.com/ALFront/alfusa.htm); Joy A. Mench and Mark Bekoff (1998) *Encyclopedia of Animal Rights and Animal Welfare* (London: Greenwood Press), p. 51. Following this incident, the number and destruction of activities attributed to the organization steadily increased (http://www.animalliberationfront.com/ ALFront/ alfusa.htm).
87. Best and Nocella, 'Behind the mask: uncovering the Animal Liberation Front', p. 21.
88. Kuipers, *Operation Bite Back: Rod Coronado's War to Save the American Wilderness*, p. 44.
89. Bryan Denson and James Long (1999) 'Eco-terrorism sweeps the American West', *The Oregonian*, 26 September.
90. Kuipers, *Operation Bite Back: Rod Coronado's War to Save the American Wilderness*, p. 44.
91. Ibid.
92. Corwin Kruse, 'The movement and the media: framing the debate over animal experimentation', *Political Communication*, **18** (2001), p. 71.
93. Kuipers, *Operation Bite Back: Rod Coronado's War to Save the American Wilderness*, p. 44.
94. Case, 'The USA Patriot Act: adding bite to the fight against animal rights terrorism?', p. 190.
95. Cited in Monaghan, 'Animal rights and violent protest', p. 106.
96. Luc Ferry (1995) 'Animal liberation' or the rights of creatures', Chapter 2 in Luc Ferry (ed.) *The New Ecological Order* (Chicago and London: The University of Chicago Press), p. 27.
97. Liddick, *Eco-Terrorism: Radical Environmental and Animal Liberation Movements*, p. 36.
98. Susan Sperling (1988) *Animal Liberators: Research and Morality* (Berkeley: University of California Press), p. 82.
99. Kruse, 'The movement and the media: framing the debate over animal experimentation', p. 70.
100. Liddick, *Eco-Terrorism: Radical Environmental and Animal Liberation Movements*, pp. 36–7; Peter Singer (1990) *Animal Liberation* (New York: Random House).
101. Tester and Walls, 'The ideology and current activities of the Animal Liberation Front', p. 80.
102. Monaghan, 'Animal rights and violent protest', p. 107.
103. Ibid.
104. Tester and Walls, 'The ideology and current activities of the Animal Liberation Front', p. 80.

105. Arslan, 'The social and operational intersections of environmental extremism in North America and Europe', p. 48.
106. Henshaw, *Animal Warfare: The Story of the Animal Liberation Front*, p. 201.
107. Ibid., p. 32.
108. Ibid., p. 201.
109. Best and Nocella, 'Behind the Mask: Uncovering the Animal Liberation Front', p. 29.
110. Liddick, *Eco-Terrorism: Radical Environmental and Animal Liberation Movements*, p. 37.
111. Monaghan, 'Animal rights and violent protest', p. 107.
112. Tom Regan (1989) 'The case for animal rights', in Tom Regan and Peter Singer (eds), *Animal Rights and Human Obligations*, 2nd edn (New Jersey: Prentice Hall), pp. 111–12.
113. Best, 'Rethinking the revolution: animal liberation, human liberation, and the future of the left', pp. 7–8.
114. Arslan, 'The social and operational intersections of environmental extremism in North America and Europe', p. 48; E. Sundquist (2002) 'Nonhuman rights: are animals ours to eat, to wear, to experiment on?', *The Atlanta Journal Constitution*, 25 August, p. 1Q.
115. Arslan, 'The social and operational intersections of environmental extremism in North America and Europe', p. 48.
116. Robert Garner (1995) 'The politics of animal protection: a research agenda', *Society and Animals*, **3** (1), p. 43.
117. Ibid., p. 337.
118. Ibid.
119. Lee Hall (2006) *Capers in the Churchyard: Animal Rights Advocacy in the Age of Terror* (Darien, Connecticut: Nectar Bat Press), p. 71.
120. Tester and Walls, 'The Ideology and Current Activities of the Animal Liberation Front', p. 84.
121. Best, 'Rethinking the revolution: animal liberation, human liberation and the future of the left', p. 11.
122. Horacio R. Trujillo (2005) 'The radical environmentalist movement', *Aptitude for Destruction 2*, pp. 141–78, p. 160.
123. Best and Nocella, 'Behind the mask: uncovering the Animal Liberation Front', p. 27.
124. Monaghan, 'Animal rights and violent protest', p. 109.
125. Henshaw, *Animal Warfare: The Story of the Animal Liberation Front*, p. 26.
126. Tester and Walls, 'The Ideology and Current Activities of the Animal Liberation Front', p. 83.
127. Henshaw, *Animal Warfare: The Story of the Animal Liberation Front*, p. 33.
128. Tester and Walls, 'The ideology of current activities of the Animal Liberation Front', p. 84.
129. Ibid.
130. Henshaw, *Animal Warfare: The Story of the Animal Liberation Front*, p. 31.

2. Rattling the cages: Animal Liberation Front actions

We are fighting until every cage is empty, not until every cage is comfortable.

Danny Brady, ALF email

INTRODUCTION

The more radical philosophical approach by the ALF, which in the eyes of some adherents allowed for more forceful radical feats than direct action, underpinned a new kind of radical environmental group structure based on the Irish Republican Army's decentralized, non-hierarchical approach. This chapter critically examines the organizational structure that was created as well as the group's objectives, strategies and tactics that were developed to meet its overarching goals of ending animal suffering and exploitation. It further seeks to understand the relationship between the ALF and more mainstream animal rights groups, which in many cases have provided funding and whose personnel have also engaged in extra-curricular activities on behalf of the ALF. It charts the growth of the ALF as a global force and, lastly, examines the ALF's almost schizophrenic attitude to violence against humans to achieve its stated goals, which publicly argued against violence against humans while condoning it in many cases as a legitimate tactic.

ALF ORGANIZATIONAL STRUCTURE

According to Mann, the ALF is not so much an organization, but a banner. He observes that the entity is less a group and more 'a title, an umbrella name, or a state of mind if you like – under which individuals and groups of people claim responsibility for illegal actions'.[1] Liddick argues that while in prison, Ronnie Lee adopted the Irish Republican Army structural approach of decentralized, small, autonomous cells.[2] Thus while lacking a centralized authority structure it was also a non-hierarchical organization with no central command.[3]

However Lee's influence on this non-hierarchical structure was ever-present. He remained the group's 'press officer', meaning he was 'the contact who dealt with press and television, supplying information, explaining actions and managing to distance himself from any direct responsibility'.[4] Further, as both the number of cells and members increased, Lee stepped into the role of 'central co-ordinator', helped by trusted confidantes such as Vivian Smith who shared his anarchist beliefs.[5] Since the ALF is made up of a 'network of individual cells' the group can be perceived to be an ideology rather than an organization.[6]

To this day activists operate in autonomous cells and choose their own targets and methods to achieve their own goals.[7] Thus each ALF group is essentially independent. As Henshaw explains, 'everyone knew who the targets were, so there seemed little point in having all operations directed from headquarters'.[8] An anonymous activist once said, 'you get a call from someone you trust, about an activity which needs to be undertaken. If you trust them, you go out and do it and don't ask many questions. It's much more effective, run on a cell-based structure like that.'[9] Due to the structure (or lack thereof) of this organization, the ALF thus has 'little or no control over its activists' and if an individual cell decides a particular action then there is not much leading ALF members can do.[10]

Groups generally hold six or seven members and fragment if membership becomes any higher. Further, as Henshaw writes, 'you didn't "join" the ALF in any strict sense of the word: there were no membership forms or blood-rituals, or oaths of allegiance sworn on the collected works of such luminaries as Peter Singer and Hans Ruesch'.[11] ALF cells have proliferated over the world and follow the same organizational structure and operational freedom.[12]

It is important to note that a leaderless structure provides the organization with two pivotal advantages:

1. The group members have the comfort and luxury to move around and make decisions by themselves without any time constraints.
2. This being a 'lone wolf' structure also leads to a greater benefit for the members, which is anonymity, and this makes it difficult for the law enforcement community to carry out effective surveillance of those actively engaged in planning or carrying out direct actions.[13]

As already noted, some argue that the ALF began with a mere 30 activists. It is important to understand that there are no official membership lists and that an activist 'does not join the ALF'. In the 1990s, the organization claimed to have approximately 2,500 activists with an estimated 100 'dedicated activists' who were willing to utilize explosives and incendiary devices in pursuit of the group's objectives.[14] However, a 1993 Justice Department study put the number of hard-core members in the USA and the UK at less than 100, though they acknowledged there were many members willing to commit lesser acts of vandalism and animal liberation.[15]

According to an ALF publication, interested parties become members of the ALF by partaking in ALF actions. As such, if an individual announces their destructive actions as being done on behalf of the ALF, the person will be cheered and accepted as a 'member'. Formal ties are unnecessary. Lee once stated that: 'the ALF is not an organization; it's a state of mind'.[16] An article published in *Rolling Stone* describes the membership of these groups thus: 'the animal liberation front is so loosely knit that no one and everyone belongs. There's no membership list, no dues, no uniform. You undertake an "action", you slap the name ALF on it; you're an ALF-er.'[17]

FINANCING THE ANIMAL LIBERATION FRONT

Finance for the organization has been provided by the Animal Liberation Front Supporters' Group, (ALFSG), which has published a newsletter that 'combines philosophical debate with press cuttings and tactical hints and, more recently, letters and essays written by ALF activists in prison' who are described as 'Prisoners of War'.[18] The bulletin was also a forum for discussion and debate regarding the direction of the movement and the various tactics that should be used.[19]

Police forces have noted that the ALF can be likened organizationally to a series of concentric rings where thousands of supporters donate tiny amounts of money or man booths to a second layer of members willing to commit trespass and break into labs, to a third ring of leaders of cells, to the final layer of those willing to commit bombings.[20]

Within ten years of existence the ALF had grown to a movement of perhaps 1,500 activists.[21] In the mid 1980s, each supporter paid the ALFSG approximately £2 per month. In 1984 the group's newsletter was provided to 1,200 subscribers, generating an estimated annual income of around £29,000 (excluding fund-raising).[22]

By 1989 approximately 2,000 individuals contributed money or other resources to the ALF.[23] The ALF also suggests that there are a number of ways that individual affinity cells can personally fund their operations.[24] One London stall in Oxford Street raised £80,000 a year that went to support ALF activities.[25] Sources within the organization have stated that in 1995 the ALFSG had a membership of about 700 and the bulletin had a print run of 1,000–2,000 copies.[26] The ALFSG also paid individual members. According to Henshaw, the group paid David Nicholls, who had previously been a British Movement organizer before joining the ALF in 1982, £50,000 a year for his role with the group.[27]

People can also become members of the North American ALF Supporters' Group for US $20–30, with the money raised being used to support animal liberation and imprisoned members. The group publishes a newsletter, *Underground*, designs and promotes merchandise and organizes fund-raising events.[28] Ingrid Newkirk, president of People for the Ethical Treatment of Animals (PETA), has also admitted financially supporting the ALF periodical *No Compromise*, which publishes underground communiqués and calls to arms from ALF leaders.[29]

The activist group PETA also has been known to both hire ALF members and in some cases fund the legal defence of accused ALF members.[30] For example, PETA paid $27,000 for the legal defence of Roger Troen who was accused in October 1986 of burglary and arson at the University of Oregon. It gave $7,500 to Fran Stephanie Trutt, who allegedly tried to kill the chief executive of a medical laboratory. PETA also gave $45,200 to Rod Coronado's 'support committee' to fund his legal defence.[31] In all it is alleged that PETA gave Coronado more than $70,000 in grants.[32]

MEMBERS OF THE ANIMAL LIBERATION FRONT

So what type of person becomes a member of the ALF? The answer appears to be almost anyone. According to McClellan, 'they are farmers, lawyers, professionals, students, labourers, retirees, and teachers. They do not, for the most part, have prior criminal records. Most have normal homes and no personal profit motive.'[33] The ALF also successfully attracts 'middle class professionals' to its cause.[34]

Many activists are simply community individuals whose actions and identities are untraceable.[35] For example, Alex Pacheco became enamoured of the ALF in 1979 and the *Washington Post Magazine* ran a brief biography of the newest recruit, describing him as:

> [T]he son of a doctor, he'd grown up first in Mexico and then Ohio, where he graduated from high school and entered Ohio State, planning to become a Catholic priest. One summer in the mid-70s, while visiting a friend in Toronto, Pacheco took a tour of the slaughterhouse. It was the turning point in his life.[36]

According to Robin Webb (who at one point ran the ALF press office): 'That is why the ALF cannot be smashed; it cannot be effectively infiltrated; it cannot be stopped. You, each and every one of you: you are ALF.'[37]

Einwohler reports within her fieldwork that many activists described their activism as either emotional attachments to animals or emotional reactions to perceived animal abuse and exploitation. As one woman, Kelli, explained: 'I'm an animal lover, but not an animal user. The relationship is one of mutual interest. I just want to see animal suffering minimized as much as possible, because it just breaks my heart.'[38]

Einwohler concluded that her fieldwork demonstrated that activists tended to define themselves in comparison with others. The animal rights activists often described themselves as people who are 'aware' of the various cruelties against animals and therefore distinct from those who are either 'unaware' or unwilling to recognize these cruelties.[39] The activists tended to be dismissive of those not part of the movement, referring to the non-animal-right-activist public as 'the lunkheads', 'those dead heads', 'the meat eaters', or simply 'slime'. Members saw themselves as different from the 'mainstream public' understanding of the worthiness of animals, and that those differences were important to their own self-understanding.[40]

According to Best and Nocella, activists involved with the ALF perceive themselves as freedom fighters similar to those in Nazi Germany 'who liberated war prisoners and Holocaust victims and destroyed equipment – such as weapons, railway, and gas ovens – that the Nazis used to torture and kill their victims'.[41]

It is important to note that many activists who are caught and prosecuted do not seem to care, believing they are doing such important work that the risks are worthwhile. According to Laurent, 'most feel that not taking action is much worse than going to jail for a while'.[42] Tim Daley (Foreman's 'Commander-in-Chief') once said:

> You don't have to like animals to be in the movement: you have to be angry about the injustice of animals being abused in the laboratories and in the hunting field. You don't actually have to like the individual creatures to be against injustice.[43]

Further, the ALF's appeal was particularly strong amongst the young. Henshaw argues: 'it had the sort of emotional strength to pull in people who were otherwise indifferent to or disenchanted by conventional politics'.[44] Many activists view this movement as a cosmic struggle, with good fighting evil and needing to be willing to do anything to win the struggle.[45] Furthermore, according to Hall, radical activism draws in individuals seeking an identity and 'offers a ready-made enemy and a ready-made group of friends – who, like the animals, become victims to avenge'.[46] Scarce argues, however, that the West Coast/anarchist animal liberators were less educated, preferring only to work part-time or take menial jobs, freeing them to more fully dedicate their time to their crusade.[47] Yet intriguingly Henshaw argues that: 'most activists will use the terminology invented by the theoreticians of animal liberation, without necessarily having read the books'.[48]

One can observe how early members became radicalized. An interviewee (who had previously been involved in 'radical animal rights actions' in the 1980s) remembers:

> At the time the ALF were still rescuing animals mainly, but they were also getting involved with damaging stuff as well ... and then there was another strand of direct action which was based on daylight raids involving hundreds of people and they were called the Liberation League ... and these were responsible really for kind of smashing their way into a laboratory for example, but with minimum force and then nicking the documents and then photocopying them and giving them back or dumping them on a journalist because part of the legislation of vivisection is that you are not allowed to let anybody in to monitor ... so this was like exposé-type stuff. A few people got jobs (in labs) and there was a bit of tension between the ideology of the daylight big break-ins and the night-time small break-ins in the sense that some people would say, well, if you're going to all the trouble of getting in there you should at least smash the torture equipment up, and you can imagine the kind of thing you break into a set of dungeons and there's all the shackles there, do you leave them or do you take them that sort of thing, and so you can see where that tension was coming from' ('Phil' (2000) – interview, name has been changed).[49]

Rowan points out that many activists were 'frustrated and disaffected individuals who are tired of the slow change effected through dialogue, conciliation, and compromise'.[50] For many activists the pace of change was so slow that members began to feel that publicized civil disobedience was the only way truly to effect change.[51]

THE RELATIONSHIP BETWEEN EXTREMISM AND MAINSTREAM ORGANIZATIONS

The vast majority of ALF activists have some background or history involving the mainstream movement. According to Mann, 'it isn't that the Hunt Saboteurs Association has deliberately recruited for the ALF, or that

ALF leaders scout sab vans for talent, as the usual suspects have suggested. On the contrary, I for one was assisted in my transition by the behaviour of hunts and their supporters and police to go for the more direct, less confrontational approach. Oh, and because it worked.'[52]

Some radical environmentalists, in the past, have chosen to link or combine with the animal liberation movement, who have been represented by 'above ground' groups, such as PETA. Some argue that the two movements are merely 'different expressions of the same underlying ideology'.[53]

According to Paris, the link between PETA and the ALF goes back to early times when PETA, a Norfolk, Virginia-based animal rights organization, was publicized by the organization.[54] It is important to note that, while many mainstream organizations (such as Sierra Club and Wilderness Society, the American Society for Prevention of Cruelty to Animals (ASPCA) and the Humane Society) have renounced and condemned certain tactics, others (including PETA) have 'applauded ALF's actions while insisting their organization takes no part in them'.[55]

PETA attempts to explain the use of 'terrorist-like tactics', saying: 'One of the central beliefs shared by more animal rights activists is that we should not harm any animal – human or otherwise. All large movements, however, have factions that believe in the use of force.'[56] PETA has defended ALF actions by arguing: 'that the ALF only tries to bomb *empty* buildings, and it notes that ALF raids and attacks often reveal legitimate violations of federal animal welfare laws that might otherwise have gone unexposed'. The PETA website goes on to equate the ALF to the Second World War French Resistance and the Underground Slavery Railroad that operated in the USA in the nineteenth century. While PETA's founder, Ingrid Newkirk, maintains that the ALF is morally justified in committing their illegal direct actions, she insists that her organization has never been involved. However, PETA has been 'criticized for helping pay the legal fees of ALF members, a practice Newkirk defends by saying PETA merely wants to ensure that ALF members get fair trials'.[57]

AIMS OF THE ANIMAL LIBERATION FRONT

The ALF's aims are both short term and long term. In the short term the goal is to rescue animals that are suffering and to inflict economic hardship on those who profit from the exploitation of animals, by disrupting the practice.[58] The long-term strategy is to end all animal suffering by (1) forcing 'animal abuse' corporations and individuals out of business; and (2) to abolish institutionalized animal exploitation that treats animals akin to property.[59] ALF members are trying to change the belief that animals are merely objects that humans can exploit but rather should be treated at the same level as humans.[60] To that end, ALF raids not only hurt exploiting businesses economically but seek to shine a public spotlight on animal cruelty.[61] The Animal Liberation Front Guidelines reflect these goals, stating that members should aim:

1. To liberate animals from places of abuse (laboratories, factory farms, fur farms and so on) and place them in good homes where they may live out their natural lives, free from suffering.
2. To inflict economic damage to those who profit from the misery and exploitation of animals.
3. To reveal the horror and atrocities committed against animals behind locked doors, by performing non-violent direct action and liberations.
4. To take all necessary precautions against harming any animal, human and non-human.
5. To analyse the ramifications of any proposed action and never apply generalizations (as in all xxx are evil) when specific information is available.[62]

The overarching goal of the ALF is not just the liberation of individual animals but rather a call to arms to bring about revolutionary change in how societies both treat and interact with animals. For members their struggle can be analogized to that of ending human slavery. They are attacking an entire institutional framework with a view to altering the 'domineering values, mindset, identities, and worldviews of the human species'.[63]

ANIMAL LIBERATION FRONT TACTICS

The ALF uses a variety of tactics to achieve its strategy. The organization uses methods of direct action, using property damage and arson attacks.[64] For ALF members only direct action has any ethical or pragmatic worth since the use of direct action is an assertion of 'personal conviction and moral obligation: if you care about the animals it is no good hoping that someone else will carry out the required action – for, if everybody did that, there would be no direct action at all!'[65]

The tactics and actions of the ALF thus go much further than protests and demonstrations against their opponents, as more mainstream environmental groups advocate. Rather such groups as the ALF are for those who: 'feel compelled to take immediate action, to directly free as many prisoners as possible, and to break any security system or law that stands between them and a suffering animal they can help'.[66] In the words of David Barbarash:

> We need to be smart about how we move forward, and not discard any tactics. We shouldn't overlook the legal avenues to change, nor should we dismiss illegal means just because our society, at this moment in its history, has deemed these actions illegal (while sanctioning the horrendous pain and suffering inflicted on animals). I believe the most successful way forward to animal liberation is multi-pronged attack on all fronts by different people: while one group is lobbying government representatives for changes to legislation, another group is protesting and blockading the labs, and at another time the ALF will enter those labs to rescue the animals and destroy the implements of torture. If we all work together in solidarity and respect each other's paths we will move forward much quicker.[67]

The FBI has stated their belief that the organization gathers intelligence prior to an attack against potential targets, including reviewing open source (such as trade magazines and photographic/video surveillance of potential opponents, going so far as to post details on the internet for other members to utilize).[68] ALF members are known for gaining inside access to their targets, sometimes by taking menial positions within their targets or striking up relationships with employees, the aim being to gather intelligence and incriminating evidence to show the general public.[69] According to the FBI, most of the time the ALF does make an effort to hone in on a specific target, rather than broad attacks. For example, when targeting a university carrying out animal research they work to locate the specific laboratory to attack.[70]

Tactics have tended to fluctuate over time as they evolved or proponents of a certain approach left a cell. Until the early 1980s, the ALF's tactic was the use of 'impersonal attacks' against corporations. However, this began to change as targeting began to 'include personal threats to and on individuals'. This change in tactics was highly contentious within ALF circles, was not supported by all activists and some members left the ALF and formed animal liberation leagues. Such organizations believed that the more appropriate response was to gather video evidence and publicity rather than damaging property.[71] In the mid-1980s there were highly coordinated lab raids that evolved into a surge of small-scale property damage of the mid-1990s, then a further surge of fur-farm raids, followed by the return of the lab raid, the wave of Huntingdon Life Sciences (HLS) campaign actions, and then in the 2000s less numerous, yet higher-impact actions.[72]

Inspired by international movements, ALF activists have been willing to use force against their opponents.[73] When asked about why arson is such a common tactic within the movement, Rodney Coronado responded by saying: 'it is simply because after years of rescuing animals from laboratories, it was heartbreaking to see those buildings and those cages refilled within the following days. And for that reason, arson became a necessary tool.'[74] In an article published in the *Sunday Herald* (Scotland), a press officer for the British ALF baldly stated that sympathy for the use of violence to achieve their goals is growing. He wrote:

> When you look at other struggles, there comes a point when non-violent action no longer works. If activists become fed up with non-violent protest then they will take another road and adopt an armed struggle. When you have right on your side, it's easy to keep going. It really is.[75]

The process of radicalization has seen a shift in tactics, however. While many organizations denounce the use or threat of violence, others have embraced such actions. To accomplish such destruction, anarchists are more likely to use arson as a tactic. 'Mel' further states: 'along with liberating animals and creating an atmosphere wherein animals' rights will be discussed in the media, the anarchists' purposes in carrying out any activity are to inflict economic damage on the target and to discourage people form entering into professions which involve the use of animals'.[76]

As well as arson some members were willing to use bombs as tactics. Between 1982 and 1988, methods of the ALF shifted and the group chose to use 'letter bombs, product contamination threats and car bombs' in an attempt to realize their goals. During this time, the Animal Rights Militia (ARM) also emerged, willing to use violence against people to further the movement, including the infamous letter bombs sent to the British Parliament. The ARM later stated they had six minor bomb attacks at scientists' homes in 1985 and four car bombs in January 1986.[77] In 1988 Fran Trutt was arrested for placing a bomb outside the US Surgical Corporation.[78]

The use of such tactics is often discouraged and rebuffed by the broader animal rights community.[79] Many animal rights groups distanced themselves from these actions, fearing the use of violence undermines the entire movement and makes it easy for opponents to claim that all animal rights activists are terrorists.[80]

This apparent tactical shift from liberation to sabotage has seen a decrease in the ALF being portrayed in the media (especially in any positive light). Some further observe the shift, noting a move from a positive 'Robin Hood' label as seeking to realize a higher good, to being portrayed as violent extremists and terrorists.[81]

ACTIONS UNDERTAKEN

Kuipers argues that the ALF was formed to frighten its opponents and its rhetoric, while not always its tactics, took on the characteristics of a guerilla military faction, particularly in the UK. For example, Tim Daly (British ALF spokesman) told a BBC interviewer in 1987 that:

> In a war you have to take up arms and people will get killed, and I can support that kind of action by petrol bombing and bombs under cars, and probably at a later stage, the shooting of vivisectors on their doorsteps. It's a war and there's no other way you can stop vivisectors.[82]

It is difficult to get a complete picture of ALF actions since not all actions are publicly reported, but what is clear is that the scope of actions undertaken since its inception has been immense. Since 1976, the National Institute of Health (NIH) has created and maintained a summary of actions taken by animal rights activists in the USA. The 1990 issue detailed 260 events from 1976 to 1990 and showed that the number of incidents increased dramatically during that period. The NIH figures demonstrate that from 1976 to 1980 an average of 1.4 incidents occurred each year; in the time period 1981–5 the average rose to 16.4 incidents a year; and in 1986–90 the average jumped to 31.8 incidents a year.[83] This trend has continued past 1990.[84] Between 2000 and 2015 the ALF claimed responsibility for 2,847 actions, with the majority taking place in Europe, followed by the UK and North America.[85]

The success of the movement in the past 40 years is evident, with over 1,353 'actions' undertaken. Of the 4,934 animals rescued from labs, 128,314 released from fur farms, thousands of other animals liberated, and the unquantifiable effects of sabotage actions, fewer than 30 activists have been arrested. Of those, only a few served any substantial amount of prison time.[86]

Further, the costs imposed on businesses by their actions continue to grow yearly. Again, figures are difficult to quantify but, for example, the National Association for Biomedical Research estimates the cost to the fur industry and medical research losses as over US $45 million.[87] A study by Karolyi and Martell concluded that the overall economic impact of ALF attacks in the USA in terms of stock market losses exceeded $2.4 billion.[88]

It must be understood that the number of reported acts is only a portion of the acts that have actually been committed.[89] Further, that there is necessarily some confusion over which action was the first committed. The first recorded liberation raid conducted by the ALF occurred at a laboratory of the drug company Pfizer (at Sandwich in Kent) to rescue pregnant beagles. The activists used a stolen boat to navigate a river and avoid security guards.[90] The ALF's first successful campaign involving economic sabotage occurred when members broke into the Consultox lab in north London and caused £80,000 worth of damage to the facility, helping to bankrupt it.[91]

Ron Arnold cites that the ALF's first publicized action was against the Charles River Laboratories with activists causing several thousand pounds worth of damage. In just its first year the ALF did £250,000 worth of damage in the UK. They targeted butcher shops (particularly Halal), furriers, animal breeders, animal farmers, fast-food outlets and horse-racing tracks.[92] According to Arnold, the ALF in January 1977 set out to shock the public about the issue of animal mistreatment when three activists desecrated the grave of John Peel, a legendary huntsman, by breaking his headstone and digging up the grave.[93] At this point in the group's evolution, few activists encouraged or supported targeting individuals' homes, as opposed to the large 'centres of abuse'.

ESCALATION OF VIOLENCE

For Sprinzak the culminating crisis of legitimacy stage has a terrorist group that considers all people associated with the suspect political order to be depersonalized, dehumanized and virtually subhuman, allowing members to commit heinous actions, up to and including murder. Such a disposition can be first observed in the language that the group's members use towards others, such as referring to them as 'dogs' or 'things', and second, their outward acceptance of inflicting harm on them.[94] It would appear that this did happen with the ALF in the 1980s. Humans that the group considered to be enemies were targeted for physical harm. The group also created new organizations to carry out these acts while providing public deniability for the actions.

In the early 1980s the tactics of the group changed and the use of threats to use violence became accepted.[95] For much of the 1980s their primary tactic was the use of bombs. According to Henshaw, the purpose of such a tactic was twofold: such incendiary devices produced widespread economic harm and, second, personalized terror directed at specific individuals.[96] Hall maintains that those willing to commit violence on behalf of animals, mostly young persons and untutored in political history, can demonstrate their willingness to 'sacrifice comfort and freedom' and 'pay their dues' to the ALF.[97]

From 1980 onwards the ALF started targeting humans via threats. For example, that year group members targeted the home of an employee of a pharmaceutical company and drew graffiti at his home. The next year there were 40 similar attacks on one night against those accused of carrying out animal experimentation.[98]

The ALF also began targeting department stores selling fur products, by placing small incendiary devices on the premises but designed to ignite after-hours, timed to go off when the stores were closed. Their design was meant to mostly trigger the in-store sprinkler systems, with the principal aim of causing water as opposed to fire damage. This occurred at a Sheffield department store; but in two attacks at Luton and Plymouth the sprinkler systems failed to put out the fires and the premises were destroyed, costing £9 million in damages.[99]

The next year ALF members claimed they carried out 100 attacks, including two serious car bombs placed under alleged animal experimenter's cars. They also sent six letter bombs to livestock transportation corporations.[100]

In 1984, the debate regarding the use of violence against people and property boiled over. By now, the ALFSG Bulletin was in its pages openly calling for violent actions against targeted opponents. Their putative leader Ronnie Lee scornfully denounced non-violent options, going so far as to denounce Gandhian pacifist solutions arguing: 'the best way to deal with bullies is to give them a damn good hiding'.[101] That call was heard and by the end of 1987 at least 17 vivisectionists had been targeted with petrol- or car-bomb attacks. The majority of such violent actions were organized and carried out by the Animal Rights Militia, although, according to Henshaw, such groups taking responsibility for attacks were merely cover for the hard core of ALF 'planners'. Previously, Lee had 'openly called for the invention of new names to take notional responsibility for acts too violent to accord with the ALF's public stance of pacifism'.[102]

Molotov cocktails and car bombs soon replaced letter bombs. The ALF, for the most part publicly, kept their distance. However, it is important to note that the group in 1985 claimed responsibility for the petrol-bombing attack on two scientists' homes in Kent. They also threatened the UK Home Office Minister David Mellor for his support of a new and more stringent bill on vivisection through Parliament. Reportedly, the communiqué provided Mellor with the following warning: 'His time will come … he can expect drastic personal attention.'[103] Generally such attacks were preceded by warnings. However, in April 1986 a potential car bombing evidenced a shift in tactics, with the ALF stating there would be no more warnings before such assaults.[104]

In January 1987, Lee was found guilty at Sheffield Crown Court of the crimes of conspiracy to commit arson, commit criminal damage and incite others to commit criminal damage and was jailed for ten years.[105] Lee was never actually accused of setting the devices that caused the damage. In contrast, the individuals who actually committed the acts were only sentenced to a four-year prison term. Ronnie Lee served six years and eight months in total and he was released from prison in 1992, when he was 41 years of age.[106]

Actions undertaken in the UK during the 1990s were predominantly protests for animal rights and anti-roads. While, arguably, the majority of these activists were militant as opposed to violent, 'the representation of the activism in the mass media was of violence and extremism'.[107] There were attacks including a brick lobbed through a truck window during a demonstration.[108]

Ingrid Newkirk's book, *Free the Animals! The Amazing True Story of the Animal Liberation Movement* (1992) provides a more complete account of the emergence and actions attributed to the ALF in the USA. Newkirk argues, however, that the first raid conducted by the ALF in the USA occurred in late 1982, with a raid at Howard University laboratory to rescue 24 cats whose rear legs were being crippled as an experiment.[109] In 1981, Alex Pacheco (who co-founded PETA) famously infiltrated the Institute for Behavioral Research in Silver Spring, Maryland. While there he gathered video evidence of sadistic tests carried out on monkeys and eventually rescued 17 primates.[110]

Following the 9/11 attacks in 2001, acts by animal liberationists did not decrease. Examples include firebombing a federal corral for wild horses in north-eastern California; a fire at a primate research centre in New Mexico; and liberation of a fur farm to release more than 1,000 minks.[111] The number of activities did not decrease with the arrest and subsequent imprisonment of Rod Coronado on arson offences. In fact, the number of attacks attributed to the ALF over the years 'have increased in frequency and intensity'. This trend is supported by a Diary of Actions tallied in *Bite Back Magazine* that demonstrated that ALF attacks ranging from petty vandalism to incendiary attacks occurred daily across the world.[112]

Attacks continued with adherents targeting Darley Oaks Farm in Newchurch; the University of Oxford; and Huntingdon Life Sciences based in Cambridgeshire. The attacks on Darley Oaks Farm, owned by the Hall family, started in 1999 with the above liberation campaign and attacks including arson; death threats; hoax bomb threats; criminal damage; the body of Christopher Hall's mother-in-law, Gladys Hammond, stolen from her grave; and allegations of paedophilia.[113]

In May 1999 there was an attack on a fleet of refrigerated meat trucks in which nine explosive devices were planted on the trucks. There were also attacks on shops, bookmakers, factories, dairies, farms and laboratories, and ALF members were harassing individuals such as Oxford academic Professor Colin Blakemore whose research on vision necessitated experiments on cats. He received two letter bombs, was sent razor blades in the post, had his car damaged and his house vandalized. On World Day for Laboratory Animals in 1997, Professor Blackmore's house, in an attempt to intimidate him, was surrounded by 300 activists wearing balaclavas.[114]

The University of Oxford was also targeted because it was building a new biomedical sciences building, which would rehouse research animals. Animal rights group SPEAK was formed after the Stop Primate Experiments at Cambridge (SPEAC) group prevented the University of Cambridge from constructing Europe's largest primate research centre in 2003. Initially SPEAK asked members to focus on legal protests (demonstrations and letter writing) and publicly renounced violence as a tactic. However, co-founder Mel Broughton was arrested in 2007 after firebombs were placed at the university. An ALF communiqué posted on the Bite Back website following an arson attack on Hertford College's boat house warned:

> Oxford University's holdings now own the contract to build the South Parks lab, as far as the ALF are concerned this means that Oxford University as a whole must accept the consequences. From here on nothing you own, rent or have dealings with is off limits until the project is scrapped. To warn builders and suppliers that they are going to get some, even if their involvement comes to light years later we will not let you off the hook![115]

Two homes belonging to researchers at the University of California, Santa Cruz were firebombed in 2008.[116] According to an anonymous communiqué (received by the ALF Press Office website), the ALF claimed to have placed an incendiary device in the vehicle of vivisector Howard S. Fox of Scripps Research Institute, who became infamous for addicting primates to methamphetamines, infecting them with Simian

Immunodeficiency Virus (SIV) allegedly to imitate the effects of AIDS, and then euthanizing them.[117]

To make an accurate assessment even more difficult, every year many actions are committed and go unclaimed. Often, the police are unable to determine a motive behind the attacks. For example, in 2004, the University of Iowa 'kept silent about activists raiding the Spence psychology laboratories – referring to the break-in as unspecified apolitical vandalism, despite animal liberation slogans being painted on walls'. The lab later admitted that some animals had been released, once the ALF released a communiqué and it became impossible to deny the act.[118] Only 'those behind these incidents know whether the goal was animal liberation, or for some other motive such as criminal gains.'[119]

THE ANIMAL LIBERATION FRONT – GOING GLOBAL

The ALF has become a widespread organization with cells active in the UK, Canada, France, Germany, the Netherlands, Spain, Sweden, Norway, Russia, Croatia, Italy, Australia, New Zealand, Iceland, Finland, Denmark, Ireland, Austria, Belgium, Switzerland and the USA.[120] For example, in Spain, the 'El Front d'Alliberament Animal' attacked bullfighting.[121] According to *Le Progrès*, a French newspaper, a fire on 12 December destroyed two floors of the BioMatech administration building. Three activists, Costantino Ragusa, Silvia Guerini and Luca Bernasconi, were arrested in Switzerland on 15 April 2010 for 'planning to bomb an IBM nanotechnology/biotechnology research facility near Zurich'.[122]

This ALF communiqué was anonymously reported (in Germany):

> In the night of 30 November 2010 the ALF visited Christian Stiewe, Vice President at Fortress, Elisabethstrasse 28, 32756 Detmold, Germany. Paint was thrown over the steps in front of his apartment building and graffiti saying C. Stiewe Animal Abuser was spray-painted on the wall. Fortress needs to stop dealing with Huntingdon Life Sciences (HLS) and retract the 70 million dollar loan. This loan is HLS's lifeline right now and without it they will go bankrupt. – Animal Liberation Front.[123]

Numerous examples abound of the global reach of the ALF. There have been actions publicized in Venezuela where doves were bought to prevent them from being sold for Santeria (witchcraft) sacrifices;[124] in Chile where two pigs were liberated;[125] and in Mexico where a Kentucky Fried Chicken in the commercial area of Coacalco in Mexico State was destroyed using butane gas cylinders in the name of Frente de Liberacion Animal (Animal Liberation Front).[126]

It is believed that there is widespread training and organizing taking place between different radical environmental groups across different countries. For example, there is evidence that the ALF group in the UK has trained ALF branches throughout the world, including the USA, Canada, Germany and Japan.[127] Evidence further suggests that this trend occurs in 'both directions'. Bilouri reported that US support enabled European ALF members to carry out attacks, including in 1998 ten arsons against McDonald's restaurants in Genk, Belgium, to protest the killing of animals and the levelling of rainforests to feed the West's appetite for beef cattle.[128]

Communication and the Use of Media

From the early 1970s until the mid 1980s, Ronnie Lee was the 'leading press contact' for the ALF.[129] Arslan argues that by the 1990s, the ALF began to disseminate its own publicity, particularly in the USA. The group began to utilize the potential of the internet to get out its message and began to release all communications through a website. Robin Webb became the senior press officer of the organization in 1991, after leaving the 'national committee of the RSPCA' (he was later banished from the RSPCA 'for ALF connections').[130] According to the Anti-Defamation League, Katie Fedor (an activist) set up the group's North American press office in Osseo, Minnesota while Craig Rosebraugh served as a spokesperson between 1997 and 2000 for the group while in Portland, Oregon. In the summer of 1999, David Barbarash succeeded Fedor and moved the office to Vancouver, Canada.[131]

The ALF sometimes communicated through its press office's website including threats, incitements and claims of responsibility. However, at other times, PETA functions as a 'mouthpiece network' for the organization.[132] Furthermore, activists in the field are kept abreast of the campaign through 'Action Reports', which report activities from local cells.[133] There has been debate within the organization regarding the necessity of a press office.[134] Now the preferred approach appears to be that following direct actions activists now send an anonymous email or fax to online journals such as *Bite Back Magazine*, *No Compromise* and *Arkangel*, which now publish direct action reports, personal interviews and alerts for upcoming actions.[135] Along with communiqués and information regarding direct actions, these online forums encourage legal strategies and tactics, with information on fund-raisers, collaborative work with environmental and other animal liberation groups, and suggested literature.

Radical activists understand the value of heart-wrenching stories, for example: the exploitation of baby animals, the use of cramped cages and crates.[136] ALF activists welcome publicity for their actions in the hope that it will change public attitudes. As Mann points out though, this has not yet been the case as: 'the small minority affected are vastly outnumbered by those who either forget what they've seen, those who abnegate from taking any responsibility because "someone else" will do something about it, or those who simply don't care'.[137]

However, the ALF is not above engaging in false dissemination of information to bolster its cause. It has emerged that the ALF has been issuing false communiqués and press releases – it has been reported that an examination of claimed actions when compared with police reports demonstrated that these actions never happened.[138] It has also been argued that such false press releases are not uncommon.[139]

THE ANIMAL LIBERATION FRONT AND VIOLENCE

In the beginning, ALF activists vowed to take all precautions to ensure lives were not threatened by their actions.[140] Kim Stallwood writes that Ronnie wrote in *Peace News* in 1974 that militant action should be 'limited only by reverence for life and hatred of violence'.[141] Lyle Monroe maintains that the overall animal rights movement members are not violent and the aim is to achieve publicity for its cause and to challenge mainstream thinking about how humans treat animals.[142]

In a publication released in 1979 by the anarchist magazine *Freedom*, Gary Treadwell and Ronnie Lee wrote:

> The ALF is not violent in that much care is taken to prevent injury to people and many raids have been called off because of possible confrontation. In any case our aims are for human as well as (other) animal liberation. The ALF is destructive, but only to property used to inflict, promote or transport animal exploitation.[143]

Property Damage Equals Violence?

One of the more interesting questions played out within the ALF is whether destruction of property is to be considered an act of violence.[144] Publicly the ALF actively denounces the use of violence as a tactic. However, it is important to note that they do not believe the destruction of property can or should be labelled 'violence'. One key principle to this organization is the notion that animal exploitation laws are unjust and one can break such laws in defence of a higher moral principle of animal rights. As stated by David Barbarash, 'the basic premise is that if someone's property is used to inflict pain, suffering, and death on innocent animals' lives, then the destruction of the property is morally justified. It is not unlike freedom fighters in Nazi Germany destroying the gas chambers. The ALF believe that life is more important than things.'[145]

For example, one militant wrote in *Snarl! Handbook of the Leeds Animal Liberation Front* in 1986:

> Personally speaking, as an activist for some time, I wouldn't plant a 'bomb' ... on or near any human or animal; no matter how cruel they may be. However, I would be prepared to use a device against empty property. This may sound contradictory, but it's not. Sure, give these people the beating they deserve, but don't harm anyone else. To kill or seriously main [sic] someone seems very contradictory, to me at least.[146]

Those who support the notion that sabotage should be considered a form of 'violence' assert two points: (1) that violence is 'in the action itself'; and (2) its potential effect on human targets. To be more specific, in the first instance, objects are destroyed; and in the second case, they argue, 'activists do some kind of harm or injury to those who own the property or have a stake in it'.[147]

However, according to Best and Nocella, 'if sabotage is violence, it pales in comparison to what industries inflict on animals in the specieist Gulags, factories and killing fields/seas of industrial capitalism'.[148] Robin Webb poses the problem with such justification as such: 'In my opinion, arson does not fall under the classification of "damage to property" but rather, actions that endanger life.'[149]

Violence Against Humans

It has been argued that the aims of movements such as the animal rights movement will only be supported by 'elites in government and media' if their actions are non-violent. As a result, the majority of activists, including those involved in the animal rights movement, favour a non-violent approach.[150] However, the public perception of the animal rights movement is often one connected to violence, 'especially in the UK where the ALF has been most active'. It is important to note that even in Australia (where the leading advocate for animal liberation Peter Singer was born) 'peaceful animal activists have been unfairly labeled "terrorists" and "extremists" and their campaigns linked to those of the ALF'.[151]

According to Stallwood, the shift in rhetoric from a non-violent strategy of illegal direct action to the use of violence was detrimental in that it cost the organization sympathetic media coverage and growing public support. Other non-violent animal rights groups were forced into 'defensive positions' in justifying the actions of the entire movement.[152]

The animal liberationist ethics that allow (and promote) the labelling that the killing of non-human, sentient animals is equivalent to murder, and that vivisection equals torture, provide a logic that can justify violence as a means to prevent such perceived atrocities. Taylor believes that this explains why animal liberationists appear to be willing to use violence and even potentially commit murder against those they have branded torturers/murderers.[153] According to Mann, as perceived abusers are seen to thrive and are able to commit violence against sentient species with impunity, breaking the law presents a very attractive alternative to the unpalatable status quo.[154]

Ronnie Lee had initially believed that direct action was needed due to the frustration that activists had with traditional methods of lobbying.[155] He has stated that 100 years of campaigning utilizing legal methods such as peaceful protest and petitions had been futile and that the Gandhian approach was not a useful strategy to follow.[156] He saw non-violence as the preferred option of many animal rights movement members and this was due to their middle-class origins – he believed such individuals 'don't like to get personally involved in violence'.[157]

Furthermore, Lee is quoted as saying that they needed to show their opponents that they could be more violent than they are. Only members who were 'resolved on the lightning of violence' could truly be considered committed to the cause; the rest were merely playing games. Lee concludes: 'Animal liberation will not be achieved if we treat the struggle for it as a social club or garden party.'[158]

Lee has publicly stated that the only reason the ALF so far has not killed any of the enemy is not a principle position, but rather a matter of tactics and they do not commit murder: 'not because we love the scum who brutally exploit animals, nor because we believe the emotive [sic] unbalanced statement that violence against them would "make us as bad as they are"'.[159] Furthermore, Lee states: 'It is a war without killing, but a war nonetheless. To advocate anything less than a war when faced with the brutal tyranny of the human race against all other creatures is a form of treachery against the animals.'[160]

Lee in recent years, however, appears to have rethought and revised his views on violence and now says that the ALF's long-standing non-violence policy was a mistake, arguing: 'Most animal rights and animal liberation activity needs to be educational and therefore non-violent, but I don't see anything morally wrong in using violence against animal abusers.'[161] As he argues: 'First of all, I'd like to make it clear that I don't promote unlawful violence. I would not suggest or advocate the unlawful use of violence against animal abusers. For personal and tactical reasons, it's not something I'd be willing to do myself, so I would consider it unethical to encourage other people to do it, especially when they would be putting themselves at risk of severe judicial punishment.'[162]

There was and still is an ongoing debate within the organization regarding the 'nature of the support base for the ALF'. Richard Course argues that the use of violence as an approach is due to anarchist members and influences, stating:

> There is a hard core who have turned their back [on the parliamentary process] ... and they are anarchists. They see the animal rights issue growing and regard it as fertile, attractive ground.[163]

Henshaw does not agree with this view, arguing that the support base is very wide ranging from anarchists to fascists to Conservative-voting pensioners and teenagers.[164] Arguably, few activists have joined the animal liberation movement with the intention of breaking the law. However, many are soon convinced 'of the effectiveness of such an approach compared to the other options available'.[165] It is important to note that violence against humans did occur despite the official disapproval of the ALF. According to Henshaw:

> If a human happened to be on the premises in the middle of a raid, then the chances were they would get thumped. Farmers woke up to find themselves covered in broken glass after a 'bricking'. A huntmaster in Surrey was thrown into a ditch by hooded raiders, who then broke his arm with blows from a walking stick. And then there were the 'vigilante' actions carried out against known animal abusers, often as a result of press coverage of a particularly nasty court case. In January 1987, a gang of five ALF members went round to the home of nineteen-year-old Scott Goodman in Swindon. Goodman had been sent to jail for three weeks the year before for kicking a puppy to death. The vigilante squad turned up at his flat wearing masks and carrying knives, truncheons and rice flails. Clearly they were not out for a piece of quiet remonstrance but unfortunately Goodman happened to be out that evening, leaving two lodgers and a friend on the premise. These innocent parties were nonetheless attacked, two of them being stabbed in the back and the shoulder. The flat was wrecked.[166]

Animal rights activists maintain, however, that the movement is 'non-violent even though some have been implicated in acts of intimidation'.[167] Yet many critics argue that it is 'only a matter of time' before an ALF action leads to an injury or death or the organization decides to shift their practices to include violence.[168] It is very easy for an intimidation/harassment campaign to lead to more violent actions.[169] According to Fiala, 'a small number of animal rights activists have made the leap from civil disobedience to extremist activities, with some engaging in serious terrorist activities'.[170] According to the FBI, beginning in 2002 'there has been an escalation in violent rhetoric and tactics, particularly within the animal rights movement'.[171]

Munro argues that while it is indisputable that violent factions exist on the fringes of the mainstream movement, 'they are a minority who evidently do not accept the non-violence stance of the mainstream movement'.[172] As late as 2004, Best and Nocella stressed the ALF's continuing commitment to non-violence, quoting an ALF website: 'The ALF does not, in any way, condone violence against any animal, human or nonhuman. Any action involving violence is by definition not an ALF action, any person involved is not an ALF member.'[173]

Best and Nocella argue that any definitions of violence and terrorism must 'include the obscene suffering humans inflict on animals, yet common usage conveniently ignores this barbarity toward animals while targeting activists who protest the enormity of such evil'.[174] They argue that, 'given the enormity and magnitude of animal suffering, and the righteous anger that animal liberationists feel, one should notice that the ALF has demonstrated remarkable *restraint* in their war of liberation'.[175]

Lee has pointed out that animal activists who have defended the use of arson by arguing that they were able to clear buildings of all animals (and/or humans) are wrong. He states: 'This is clearly untrue. Since every building is home to countless very small animals, e.g. insects, who could not be evacuated to safety and who would therefore be murdered, do you support the use of fire? … I think we were naive to think that animals would not be harmed.'[176]

It is clear from an analysis of the various actions undertaken that ALF adherents are willing to condone property damage, including arson and physical threats against persons, although the majority of members would draw the line at murder.[177] Some members, though, have gone so far as to publicly suggest that the killing of certain humans involved with the agricultural/industrial complex would be justified and the implications of this stance need to be more fully teased out by reference to the actions undertaken by the ALF's 'offshoot' groups.[178]

NOTES

1. Keith Mann (2008) *From Dusk 'til Dawn: An Insider's View of the Growth of the Animal Liberation Movement* (US: Voice of the Voiceless), p. 55.
2. Donald R. Liddick (2006) *Eco-Terrorism: Radical Environmental and Animal Liberation Movements* (Westport, Connecticut: Praeger), p. 40.
3. Rachel Monaghan (1999) 'Terrorism in the name of animal rights', *Terrorism and Political Violence*, **11** (4), p. 164.
4. David Henshaw (1989) *Animal Warfare: The Story of the Animal Liberation Front* (London: Fontana), pp. 50–51.
5. Ibid., p. 51.
6. Nick Harding (2010) 'Eco-anarchists: the new breed of terrorist', *The Independent (UK)*, 18 May.
7. Monaghan, 'Terrorism in the Name of Animal Rights', p. 164.
8. Henshaw, *Animal Warfare: The Story of the Animal Liberation Front*, p. 51.
9. Ron Arnold (1997) *Ecoterror: The Violent Agenda to Save Nature, The World of the Unabomber* (Bellevue, WA: Free Enterprise Press), p. 209; Nicholas Roe (1988) 'Crusaders against cruelty: whether sabotaging hunts, fire-bombing or burgling, anti-vivisectionists are sure right is on their side', *London Independent*, 12 December, p. 21.
10. Monaghan, 'Terrorism in the name of animal rights', p. 165.
11. David Henshaw, *Animal Warfare: The Story of the Animal Liberation Front*, p. 52.
12. Hasan T. Arslan (2008) 'The social and operational intersections of environmental extremism in North America and Europe' (PhD dissertation, Sam Houston State University, Huntsville, TX), p. 7; Donald R. Liddick (2006) *Eco-Terrorism: Radical Environmental and Animal Liberation Movements, Liberation* (Westport, Connecticut: Praeger), p. 41.
13. Arslan, 'The social and operational intersections of environmental extremism in North America and Europe', p. 23.
14. Rachel Monaghan (1997) 'Animal rights and violent protest', p. 112.
15. Liddick, *Eco-Terrorism: Radical Environmental and Animal Liberation Movements, Liberation*, p. 41.
16. Keith Tester and John Walls (1996) 'The ideology and current activities of the Animal Liberation Front', *Contemporary Politics*, **2** (2), p. 82.
17. Arslan, 'The social and operational intersections of environmental extremism in North America and Europe, p. 39; D. Kuipers (1995) 'The tracks of the coyote', *Rolling Stone*, **709**, 1 June, p. 52.
18. Tester and Walls, 'The ideology and current activities of the Animal Liberation Front', p. 82.
19. Henshaw, *Animal Warfare: The Story of the Animal Liberation Front*, p. 130.
20. 'To the Death', *The Guardian*, 7 November 2001, http://www.theguardian.com/g2/story/0,,588987,00.html.
21. Liddick, *Eco-Terrorism: Radical Environmental and Animal Liberation Movements*, p. 41.
22. Tester and Walls, 'The ideology and current activities of the Animal Liberation Front', p. 82.
23. Rachel Monaghan (2006) 'Animal rights and violent protest', *Terrorism and Political Violence, Liberation* (Westport, Connecticut: Praeger), p. 112.
24. Animal Liberation Fund.com, Worldwide News & Information Resource about the ALF, 'Funding your actions from no compromise issue 9', http://www.animalliberationfront.com/ALFront/Activist%20Tips/LettersfromUnderground3.htm. For example, putting 10 per cent of individual members' salary into a fund (but not a personal fund that could be tied back to a member by the authorities) is suggested, as is having a financial backer 'adopt' a cell. Such adopters should not be hounded for money but rather ideally should be known to a cell member as a trusted supporter who shares the ALF philosophy. Such donors should never be allowed access to other cell members nor should they be told future plans or targets. Members are also encouraged to fund-raise, for example car wash,

bake sale or keep a donations jar handy. Donators are not told the money is raised for illegal activities but rather done to 'help animals'. Donations should be solicited at events like school fairs, Earth Day events, street fairs or concerts. Members are also encouraged if fund-raising under the guise of legitimate organizations to siphon money off for ALF purposes. The idea is to continue fund-raising until individual cells have enough money to carry out their plans. Tom Kelly (2008) 'Guilty: animal terror gang who raised £1million rattling tins on the high street', *The Daily Mail*, http://www.dailymail.co.uk/news/article-1100822/Guilty-Animal-terror-gang-raised-1million-rattling-tins-high-street.html, 24 December.

25. Kelly, 'Guilty: animal terror gang who raised £1million rattling tins on the high street'.
26. Tester and Walls, 'The ideology and current activities of the Animal Liberation Front', p. 82.
27. Henshaw, *Animal Warfare: The Story of the Animal Liberation Front*, p. 129.
28. http://www.hedweb.com/alffaq.ht.
29. People for the Ethical Treatment of Animals (PETA), Activist Facts, https://www.activistfacts.com/organizations/21-people-for-the-ethical-treatment-of-animals/.
30. People for the Ethical Treatment of Animals (PETA), activist facts, https://www.activistfacts.com/organizations/21-people-for-the-ethical-treatment-of-animals/.
31. Ibid.
32. Rodney Coronado, http://www.targetofopportunity.com/coronado.htm).
33. Russell Lee Young (2004) 'A time series analysis of eco-terrorist violence in the United States: 1993–2003' (PhD dissertation, Sam Houston State University, Huntsville, TX), p. 142; G.G. McClellan (2004) 'The terrorists among us', (PhD Dissertation, Sam Houston State University, Huntsville, TX) pp. 42, 34.
34. 'Animal rights, terror tactics', *BBC News*, http://news.bbc.co.uk/2/hi/uk_news/902751.stm, 30 August 2000.
35. Arnold, *Ecoterror: The Violent Agenda to Save Nature, The World of the Unabomber*, p. 209; Peter Carlson (1991) 'The great silver spring monkey debate', *The Washington Post Magazine,* 24 February, p. W17.
36. Arnold, *Ecoterror: The Violent Agenda to Save Nature, The World of the Unabombe*r, p. 209; Carlson, 'The great silver spring monkey debate', p. W17.
37. Harding, 'Eco-anarchists: the new breed of terrorist'.
38. Rachel L. Einwohler (2002) 'Bringing the outsiders in: opponents' claims and the construction of animal rights activists' identity', *Mobilization: An International Journal,* **7** (3), p. 261.
39. Ibid., p. 257.
40. Ibid.
41. Steven Best and Anthony Nocella (2004) 'Behind the Mask: Uncovering the Animal Liberation Front', in Steven Best and Anthony Nocella (eds) *Terrorists or Freedom Fighters: Reflections on the Liberation of Animals* (New York: Lantern Books), p. 23.
42. Young, 'A time series analysis of eco-terrorist violence in the United States: 1993–2003', p. 142; B. Laurent (2001) 'Eco-vandals put a match to "progress"', *Christian Science Monitor*, 5 July.
43. David Henshaw, *Animal Warfare: The Story of the Animal Liberation Front*, p. 26.
44. Ibid., p. 34.
45. Lee Hall (2006) *Capers in the Churchyard: Animal Rights Advocacy in the Age of Terror* (Darien, Connecticut: Nectar Bat Press), p. 66.
46. Ibid., p. 64.
47. Rik Scarce (2006) *Eco-Warriors: Understanding the Radical Environmental Movement (Updated Edition)* (CA: Left Coast Press), pp. 135–6.
48. Henshaw, *Animal Warfare: The Story of the Animal Liberation Front*, p. 32.
49. Alexandra Plows et al. (2004) Covert repertoires: ecotage in the UK, *Social Movement Studies*, **3** (2), p. 212.
50. Andrew N. Rowan (1984) *Of Mice, Models and Men: A Critical Evaluation of Animal Research* (New York: SUNY Press), p. 32.

51. Denise Case, 'The USA Patriot Act: adding bite to the fight against animal rights terrorism?', *Rutgers Law Journal*, **187** (Fall), p. 194; Gary Francione (2000) *Introduction to Animal Rights: Your Child or the Dog?* (Philadelphia, P.A: Temple University Press), p. 98; Helena Silverstein (1996) *Unleashing Rights: Law, Meaning, and the Animal Rights Movement* (Detroit: University of Michigan Press), p. 202.
52. Mann, *From Dusk 'til Dawn: An Insider's View of the Growth of the Animal Liberation Movement*, p. 247.
53. Paul Joosse (2007) 'Leaderless resistance and ideological inclusion: the case of the Earth Liberation Front', *Terrorism and Political Violence*, **19** (3), p. 359.
54. Arslan, 'The social and operational intersections of environmental extremism in North America and Europe', p. 39; S.E. Paris (1995) 'Firebombing "animal liberationist" given prison sentence for his terrorism', *Human Events*, **51** (33), 25 August, p. 17.
55. Arslan, 'The social and operational intersections of environmental extremism in North America and Europe', p. 14; V. Richardson (2002) 'Law catches up to eco-terror: some find threat as dangerous as al Qaeda', *The Washington Times*, 24 March, p. A1.
56. Kevin Grubs (2010) 'Saving lives or spreading fear: the terroristic nature of eco-extremism', *Animal Law*, **16**, p. 355; PETA, 'General FAQs', url: http://www.peta.org/about/faq.asp.
57. Douglas Long (2004) *Ecoterrorism: Library in a Book* (New York: Facts on File, Inc), p. 45.
58. Mann, *From Dusk 'til Dawn: An Insider's View of the Growth of the Animal Liberation Movement*, p. 56.
59. Monaghan, 'Animal Rights and Violent Protest', p. 110; Author unknown, 'Regulation of 'eco-terrorism' in the United States' (date unknown), p. 2: Animal Liberation Front 'Mission Statement', http://www.animalliberationfront.com/ALFront/mission_statement.htm.
60. Maxwell Schnurer (2004) 'At the gates of hell: the ALF and the legacy of Holocaust resistance' in Steven Best and Anthony Nocella (eds), *Terrorists or Freedom Fighters: Reflections on the Liberation of Animals* (New York: Lantern Books), p. 114.
61. Mann, *From Dusk 'til Dawn: An Insider's View of the Growth of the Animal Liberation Movement,* p. 57.
62. http://www.animalliberationfront.com/ALFront/alf_credo.htm.
63. Anthony Nocella (2007) 'Unmasking the Animal Liberation Front using critical pedagogy: seeing the ALF for who they really are', *Journal for Critical Animal Studies*, **V** (1), p. 7.
64. Monaghan, 'Animal rights and violent protest', p. 109.
65. Tester and Walls, 'The ideology and current activities of the Animal Liberation Front', p. 84.
66. Best and Nocella, 'Behind the mask: uncovering the Animal Liberation Front', p. 27.
67. Ibid., pp. 44–5.
68. Arslan, 'The social and operational intersections of environmental extremism in North America and Europe', p. 40; J.L. Lewis (2004) Deputy Assistant Director, Counter-terrorism Division Federal Bureau of Investigation, 'Congressional testimony before the Senate Judiciary Committee', Washington, DC., 18 May, http://www.fbi.gov/congress/congress04/lewis051804.htm.
69. Arslan, 'The social and operational intersections of environmental extremism in North America and Europe', p. 40; Scott E. Hendley and Steve Wegelian (1993) 'Report to Congress on the extent and effects of domestic and international terrorism on animal enterprises', Washington, DC: U.S. Department of Justice, p. 6; A.R. Morrison (1996) 'Rights, reason drive research', Forum for Applied Research and Public Policy, 11 September, pp. 21–6; Horacio R. Trujillo (2005) 'The radical environmentalist movement', *Aptitude for Destruction* 2, p. 163.
70. Arslan, 'The social and operational intersections of environmental extremism in North America and Europe', p. 40.
71. Monaghan, 'Terrorism in the Name of Animal Rights', p. 161.

72. 'Animal Liberation Front: Complete U.S. Diary of Actions, the First 30 Years', p. 1.
73. Hall, *Capers in the Churchyard: Animal Rights Advocacy in the Age of Terror*, p. 64.
74. Arslan, 'The social and operational intersections of environmental extremism in North America and Europe', p. 160.
75. Hall, *Capers in the Churchyard: Animal Rights Advocacy in the Age of Terror*, p. 64; Jenifer Johnston (2004) 'Of mice and men', *Sunday Herald – Scotland*, 19 September.
76. Scarce, *Eco-Warriors: Understanding the Radical Environmental Movement,* p. 136.
77. Monaghan, 'Animal Rights and Violent Protest', p. 110.
78. Liddick, *Eco-Terrorism: Radical Environmental and Animal Liberation Movements*, p. 37.
79. Steve Best (2010) 'War against animals: time to stop playing nice', *The Scavenger*, blog, 10 July.
80. Author unknown, 'A discussion of the animal enterprise terrorism act', p. 3.
81. Best and Nocella, 'Behind the mask: uncovering the Animal Liberation Front', p. 40.
82. Ibid.
83. Young, 'A time series analysis of eco-terrorist violence in the United States: 1993–2003', p. 30; G.G. McClellan (1993) 'The terrorists among us', *Security Management*, **6** (July) pp. 56–9.
84. Young, 'A time series analysis of eco-terrorist violence in the United States: 1993–2003', p. 30.
85. Bite Back Magazine, http://www.directaction.info; North American Animal Liberation Press Office, http://animalliberationpressoffice.org/NAALPO/; Global Terrorism Database, http://www.start.umd.edu/gtd/; 325, http://325.nostate.net.
86. 'Animal Liberation Front: complete U.S. diary of actions, the first 30 years' (United States: Voice of the Voiceless Communications), 2010, p. 1.
87. Young, 'A time series analysis of eco-terrorist violence in the United States: 1993–2003', p. 42; J.F. Jarboe (2002) 'The threat of eco-terrorism', statement of James F. Jarboe, Domestic Terrorism Section Chief, Counter-Terrorism Division, Federal Bureau of Investigation, made before the House Resources Committee, Subcommittee on Forests and Forest Health, http://www.fbi.gov/congress/congress02jarboe021202.htm.
88. Arslan, 'The social and operational intersections of environmental extremism in North America and Europe', p. 7.
89. 'Animal Liberation Front: complete U.S. diary of actions, the rirst 30 years', p. 1.
90. Mann, *From Dusk 'til Dawn: An Insider's View of the Growth of the Animal Liberation Movement*, p. 60.
91. Ibid., p. 63.
92. Arnold, *Ecoterror: The Violent Agenda to Save Nature, The World of the Unabomber*, p. 209; Henshaw, *Animal Warfare: The Story of the Animal Liberation Front*, pp. 53–4.
93. Arnold, *Ecoterror: The Violent Agenda to Save Nature, The World of the Unabomber*, p. 209.
94. Ehud Sprinzak (1998) '"The psychopolitical formation of extreme left terrorism in a democracy: the case of the Weathermen"', in Walter Reich (ed.), *Origins of Terrorism: Psychologies, Ideologies, Theologies, States of Mind* (Washington, DC: Woodrow Wilson Center Press), p. 82.
95. Carolyn Bailey, 'Transcript of Ronnie Lee's ARZone Live Guest Chat', http://arzone.ning.com/profiles/blogs/transcript-of-ronnie-lees-live.
96. Henshaw, *Animal Warfare: The Story of the Animal Liberation Front*, p. 91.
97. Hall, *Capers in the Churchyard: Animal Rights Advocacy in the Age of Terror*, p. 92.
98. Rachel Monaghan (2013) 'Not quite terrorism: animal rights extremism in the United Kingdom'. *Studies in Conflict & Terrorism*, **36** (11), p. 935.
99. Ibid., pp. 935–6.
100. Ibid., p. 936.
101. Ibid., p. 94.
102. Ibid., p. 91.
103. Ibid., p. 58.
104. Monaghan, 'Animal rights and violent protest', p. 111.

105. 'The early history of animal rights extremism, Animal Liberation Front', http://www.understandinganimalresearch.org.uk/policy/animal-rights-extremism/the-early-history-of-animal-rights-extremism/.
106. During both his prison sentences, he gave up smoking and used the education offered in the system to learn new languages so that he was able to reach out and write to non-English speaking followers. Keeping fit he believed was his way of getting back the time they had taken from him. He believed that by living longer he would beat the system. He replaced smoking with running and badminton and believes that if it was not for prison, he would have continued to be a smoker today. He still continues to run but not as much as he used to in prison. He also used this time to read up on and to increase his knowledge of the labour movement, http://www.spokeo.com/Ronnie+Lee+1.
107. Lyle Munro (2005) *Confronting Cruelty: Moral Orthodoxy and the Challenge of the Animal Rights Movement* (Boston, Leiden: Brill), p. 133.
108. Munro, *Confronting Cruelty: Moral Orthodoxy and the Challenge of the Animal Rights Movement*, p. 133; 'People and animals: also part of creation', *The Economist*, 19 August 1995, pp. 17–19.
109. Best and Nocella, 'Behind the mask: uncovering the Animal Liberation Front', p. 21.
110. Scarce, *Eco-Warriors: Understanding the Radical Environmental Movement*, p. 121; Alex Pacheco (1985) 'The silver spring monkeys' in Peter Singer (ed.) *In Defense of Animals* (New York: Basil Blackwell), pp. 135–47.
111. Sam Howe Verhovek, 'Radical animal rights groups step up protests', *New York Times*, 12 November 2001, p. 1.
112. Liddick, *Eco-Terrorism: Radical Environmental and Animal Liberation Movements*, p. 43.
113. Monaghan, 'Not quite terrorism: animal rights extremism in the United Kingdom', p. 937.
114. 'Animal rights, terror tactics', *BBC News*, 30 August 2000, http://news.bbc.co.uk/2/hi/uk_news/902751.stm.
115. Sandra Laville, 'Animal Militants Set Fire to Oxford Boathouse', *The Guardian*, 21 July 2005, https://www.theguardian.com/uk/2005/jul/21/businessofresearch.animalwelfare.
116. Jesse McKinley (2008) 'Firebombings at homes of 2 California researchers', *The New York Times*, 4 August.
117. 'ALF claims planting carbomb in CA researcher's car', *Thomas Paine's Corner*, blog, 9 March 2010.
118. Peter Young, 'Egg farm denies raid by ALF', *Voice of the Voiceless*, (blog), 7 April 2010.
119. 'Animal Liberation Front: complete U.S. diary of actions, the first 30 years', United States, p. 1.
120. Liddick, *Eco-Terrorism: Radical Environmental and Animal Liberation Movements*, p. 41.
121. Henshaw, *Animal Warfare: The Story of the Animal Liberation* Front, p. 200.
122. Author unknown, 'Activists claim French arson', *Bite Back Magazine*, 21 January 2011, http://directaction.info/news_jan21_11.htm.
123. Author unknown, 'ALF visit another fortress executive', *Bite Back Magazine*, 2 December, 2010.
124. Author unknown, 'Dove gets another chance at life', *Bite Back Magazine*, 8 February 2010.
125. Author unknown, 'Two pigs liberated, graffiti and a call to action', *Bite Back Magazine*, 24 October 2010.
126. Author unknown, 'KFC bombed', *Bite Back Magazine*, 12 May 2010.
127. Trujillo, 'The radical environmentalist movement', p. 162.
128. Ibid.
129. Tester and Walls, 'The ideology and current activities of the Animal Liberation Front', p. 81.
130. Tester and Walls, 'The ideology and current activities of the Animal Liberation Front', p. 81.
131. Arslan, 'The social and operational intersections of environmental extremism in North America and Europe', p. 41; Anti-Defamation League (2006) 'Eco-terrorism: extremism

in the animal rights and environmentalist movements', http://www.adl.org/learn/ext_us/Ecoterrorism.asp?LEARN_Cat=Extremism&LEARN_SubCat=Extremism_in_America&xpicked=4&item=eco.

132. Arslan, 'The social and operational intersections of environmental extremism in North America and Europe', p. 38.
133. Henshaw, *Animal Warfare: The Story of the Animal Liberation Front*, p. 53.
134. Tester and Walls, 'The ideology and current activities of the Animal Liberation Front', p. 81.
135. Arslan, 'The social and operational intersections of environmental extremism in North America and Europe', p. 41; Liddick, *Eco-Terrorism: Radical Environmental and Animal Liberation Movements*, p. 42.
136. Hall, *Capers in the Churchyard: Animal Rights Advocacy in the Age of Terror*, p. 100.
137. Keith Mann, *From Dusk 'til Dawn: An Insider's View of the Growth of the Animal Liberation Movement*, p. 66.
138. 'ALF issues false press releases', *FCUSA*, 7 April 2010.
139. Ibid. The following are cases where ALF 'crimes' 'are known to be fabricated': 2 April 2010 – Utah, 72 chickens stolen from egg farm: http://www.directaction.info/news_apr02_10.htm; 1 April 2010 – Utah, incendiaries at homes of researchers: http://www.directaction.info/news_apr01_10.htm; 4 March 2010 – California, incendiary in exhaust pipe of researcher's vehicle: http://www.directaction.info/news_mar05_10.htm.
140. Hall, *Capers in the Churchyard: Animal Rights Advocacy in the Age of Terror*, p. 63.
141. Bailey, 'Transcript of Ronnie Lee's ARZone live guest chat'.
142. Arslan, 'The social and operational intersections of environmental extremism in North America and Europe', p. 52; L. Munro (2005) 'Strategies, action repertoires and DIY activism in the animal rights movement', *Social Movement Studies*, **4** (1) (May), p. 76.
143. Kim Stallwood (2004) 'A personal overview of direct action in the United Kingdom and the United States' in Steven Best and Anthony Nocella (eds), *Terrorists or Freedom Fighters: Reflections on the Liberation of Animals* (New York: Lantern Books), p. 83.
144. Monaghan, 'Terrorism in the name of animal rights', p. 160.
145. Best and Nocella, 'Behind the mask: uncovering the Animal Liberation Front', pp. 25–6; 'The ALF unmasked – interview with David Barbarash', http://www.animallib.org.au/more_interviews/barbarash.
146. Tester and Walls, 'The ideology and current activities of the Animal Liberation Front', p. 85.
147. Best and Nocella, 'Behind the mask: uncovering the Animal Liberation Front', p. 32.
148. Ibid.
149. Ibid., p. 37.
150. Munro, *Confronting Cruelty: Moral Orthodoxy and the Challenge of the Animal Rights Movement*, p. 133.
151. Ibid., p. 134; Lyle Munro (1999) 'Contesting moral capital in campaigns against animal liberation', *Society & Animals*, **5** (2), pp. 43–4.
152. Kim Stallwood (2004) 'A personal overview of direct action in the United Kingdom and the United States' in Steven Best and Anthony Nocella (eds), *Terrorists or Freedom Fighters: Reflections on the Liberation of Animals* (New York: Lantern Books), p. 85.
153. Bron Taylor (2003) 'Threat assessments and radical environmentalism' , *Terrorism and Political Violence*, **15** (4), pp. 173–82, Winter, p. 180.
154. Mann, *From Dusk 'til Dawn: An Insider's View of the Growth of the Animal Liberation Movement*, p. 247.
155. Monaghan, 'Animal rights and violent protest', p. 114.
156. Wall, 'Snowballs, elves and skimmingtons?: genealogies of environmental direct action', p. 86; Ronnie Lee (1983) 'Free the 4,344,843', *Peace News* **2201**; Henshaw, *Animal Warfare: The Story of the Animal Liberation Front*, p. 94.
157. Henshaw, *Animal Warfare: The Story of the Animal Liberation Front*, p. 100.
158. Ibid.
159. Ibid., p. 56.

160. Ibid.
161. Bailey, 'Transcript of Ronnie Lee's ARZone live guest chat.
162. Ibid.
163. Davidson Smith (1985) 'Political violence in animal liberation', *Contemporary Review*, **247** (July), p. 28, cited in Monaghan, 'Animal rights and violent protest', pp. 112–13.
164. Monaghan, 'Animal rights and violent protest', p. 113.
165. Mann, *From Dusk 'til Dawn: An Insider's View of the Growth of the Animal Liberation Movement*, p. 58.
166. Henshaw, *Animal Warfare: The Story of the Animal Liberation Front*, p. 71.
167. Harding, 'Eco-anarchists: the new breed of terrorist'.
168. Hall, *Capers in the Churchyard: Animal Rights Advocacy in the Age of Terror*, p. 67.
169. Arslan, 'The social and operational intersections of environmental extremism in North America and Europe', p. 158.
170. Ibid., p. 7; J. Fiala (2004) 'String of attacks: ALF targets universities', *The Newsmagazine of Veterinary Medicine* (May), http://www.swaebr.org/cfaar/newsletters/2004/July%2020 04%20news.pdf.
171. Arslan, 'The social and operational intersections of environmental extremism in North America and Europe', p. 26; Young, 'A time series analysis of eco-terrorist violence in the United States: 1993–2003', p. 48.
172. Munro, *Confronting Cruelty: Moral Orthodoxy and the Challenge of the Animal Rights Movement*, p. 134.
173. Bailey, 'Transcript of Ronnie Lee's ARZone live guest chat.
174. Best and Nocella, 'Behind the mask: uncovering the Animal Liberation Front', p. 31.
175. Ibid., p. 36.
176. Bailey, 'Transcript of Ronnie Lee's ARZone live guest chat.
177. Tester and Walls, 'The ideology and current activities of the Animal Liberation Front', p. 85.
178. Ibid.

3. By other means: the Animal Liberation Front and its purported splinter groups

> It is never governments or well funded organizations that affect revolutionary change, but the common people, unwilling to sit back any longer and watch the animals they love be destroyed.
>
> Rod Coronado

INTRODUCTION

There is evidence to suggest that many ALF extremists came to the view that violence was necessary, and that new names were needed in order to keep the ALF's non-violent reputation intact.[1] Those ALF members who expressed a wish to be violent towards other human beings were encouraged not to utilize the ALF name (which remained the primary named animal liberation organization), rather they adopted nom de plumes such as Stop Huntingdon Animal Cruelty (SHAC), the Animal Rights Militia (ARM) and the Justice Department (JD).[2] With their emergence came questions as to whether or not entities like ARM and the Justice Department were legitimate animal rights groups or just agents, *provocateurs* acting on behalf of the ALF.[3]

This chapter examines the hiving off of more extreme members who were supposedly willing to commit physical violence against humans and questions the splinter group's relationship with the ALF. It briefly considers the domestic legal and law enforcement responses to radical animal liberation groups and the future of this phenomenon. The conclusion and analysis section will critically examine the ALF and its purported offshoot groups in the light of the radicalization theories proposed in the Introduction, to consider what insights such theories can offer regarding the evolution of radical animal liberation groups.

ANIMAL LIBERATION OFFSHOOT GROUPS

It is clear that names such as 'Animal Rights Militia', 'Stop Huntingdon' and the 'Justice Department' were flags of convenience only.[4] It appears that the ALF invented these various nom de guerres so that these 'groups' could accept responsibility for actions considered too extreme for the ALF, given its stated public position of being non-violent towards sentient beings. As Robin Webb, the ALF's press officer, stated: 'If someone wishes to act as the Animal Rights Militia or Justice Department, simply put, the ... policy of the Animal Liberation Front, to take all reasonable precautions not to endanger life, no longer applies.'[5]

These groups used the ALFSG newsletter to publish their 'communiqués' and it has been suggested that some activists participate in all three organizations. While the 'main strategy' of the ALF is purportedly 'economic sabotage and destruction', the ARM (and, especially, the JD) have utilized different approaches and have proudly proclaimed publicly that they are willing to use violence against humans to achieve their ends.[6] For example, in 1999 in the UK there were 1,200 fire bombings, acts of vandalism and physical attacks organized by the ALF and linked groups (ARM, JD and SHAC).[7] The groups also broke into laboratories, eventually sending letter bombs and placing explosives under cars.[8]

Animal Rights Militia

The Animal Rights Militia was established in England in 1982 and adopted what it considered a more proactive approach to dealing with perceived opponents of the animal rights movement and was willing to target humans explicitly. Similarly to the ALF, the ARM does not have a website or single online community dedicated to their actions and instead relied on others (especially ALF.com, ALF Press Office and *Bite Back Magazine*) to distribute their communiqués.[9]

The ARM, going further than the ALF was willing to publicly proclaim they 'are prepared to engage in direct action that might endanger human life'.[10] While the ARM supported the acts committed by the ALF, it was their publicly stated belief that the ALF was not tactically going far enough to achieve their goals. The ARM believed that a more effective path to victory would be by engaging in poisoning hoaxes and other strategies that targeted humans, particularly their enemies, for physical harm.[11] The group publicly stated:

> We do not shy away from violence against individual animal abusers for, even if a vivisector were to die, it would be just a tiny fraction of the blood and

> terror on which animal abuse industries are based ... What we plan to do is attack the real abusers, the vivisectors, huntsmen and slaughterhouse owners ... Every day our comrades and fellow animals stay behind bars their torment will be avenged, even if this means some of the filth will lose their lives.[12]

The ARM defends such actions with the aid of Singer's works, stating that all sentient beings suffer. However, the ARM 'takes that proposition much further than Singer would ever allow to justify the claim that the suffering counts strictly from one creature to another'. They claim that 'a farmer is responsible for the death of, say 5,000 chickens, and consequently, in a rather vulgar utilitarian calculation, the unhappiness and denial of preferences caused by the murder of the single farmer would be more than counterbalanced by the liberation of the chickens from their suffering'. The ARM has gone so far as to argue that such a killing could be considered an 'ethical' act.[13]

On 30 November 1982, letter bombs were sent to the leaders of the four UK main political parties. While three incendiary devices were successfully identified and disarmed, the fourth bomb exploded causing minor injuries to a civil servant. The bombs were claimed by a new organization, calling itself the Animal Rights Militia (ARM), which has proved to consist of ALF members who did not want to sully the above-ground reputation of the ALF – that they did not officially target humans for violence.[14] The offenders were never located but Henshaw argues it was a one-off act.[15]

ARM activists claimed they were not 'irresponsible lunatics or madmen', but rather they 'no longer saw any point in persuasion'. ARM members believed that the animal rights struggle was part of a broader fight. Their public communiqué (Christmas, 1982) after the bombing read:

> Animal liberation must be part of a wide spectrum of revolutionary change in the structure of society, for British democracy is based on more blood, terror and exploitation than any other country in history. It has a brutal police force whose crimes against people and animals the media will not report, and whose government blatantly supports repressive systems of governments [sic] around the world.[16]

Furthermore, the organization was responsible for firebombing cars and targeted the homes of employees of the British Industrial Biological Research Association and the Wellcome Foundation.[17] In a second communiqué released by the ARM, the organization referred to an incident in which a Dr Sebesteny found what appeared to be a bomb strapped to the underside of his car. The statement read: 'In line with our "no more warnings" policy, we planted a powerful bomb at the home of a cancer research vivisector in north London. Unfortunately, shortly before it was due to explode the vivisector saw it and it was defused by the bomb squad. Next time the scum won't be so lucky ... We could have killed all four bastards [referring to car bombs planted in January], but we didn't.'[18]

In 1985 the group claimed to have injected eggs with rat poison.[19] The ARM's biggest action to date occurred in January 1986 when explosives were planted under the cars of scientific animal experimenters in Sussex, London, Yorkshire and Staffordshire. In July 1994, the ARM claimed responsibility for planting explosives at a Boots store in Cambridge, causing £1.5 million worth of damage, and £550,000 worth of damage to an Edinburgh Woollen Mill store. Two weeks later, the organization also admitted to planting two more devices at a Boots store on the Isle of Wight, which cost £2 million. The ARM claimed it had instituted 'a campaign against High Street animal abuse in towns and cities across Britain'.[20]

In the USA the ARM has been responsible for targeting businesses in San Jose, California and burnt down a warehouse owned by San Jose Valley Veal Inc. on 1 September 1987, causing $100,000 in damage. They also torched the Ferrara Meat Company on 26 November 1987.[21] The second action was even more costly, causing $230,000 worth of damage to the corporation.[22]

Furthermore, the ARM instituted a series of public hoaxes with the aim of causing major economic damage to their opponents. For example, in January 1992 in Canada the group claimed they had injected Cold Buster Bars with oven cleaner. The required recall of the product cost the company $1 million.[23] The ARM was also blamed for an incident whereby Boots' own brand of toothpaste was allegedly contaminated with mercury.[24] In 1994 the ARM was to blame for a Christmas turkey poisoning hoax in Vancouver, British Columbia.[25]

Earlier, in 1984, activists claimed they had poisoned Mars candy bars because Mars had been performing tooth-decay experiments on animals. Financially, the hoax to the Mars Company was astronomical. For the first couple of days sales of the chocolate bar were effectively zero and it took approximately ten weeks for sales of single bars to return to the pre-hoax level and between three to four months for sales of the multipack option to recover.[26] According to 'Ben', when discussing the Mars hoax the group believed of the tactic that:

> It was incredibly successful. We managed to get approximately fifty bars into shops in ten different regions, which I think shows that people have got to

> realize that we are more co-ordinated than we're given credit for. The point of it fundamentally is to create a shock wave.[27]

While the hoax had a significant impact (unlike the letter bombs), it backfired in that many potential sympathizers were upset with this approach since it appeared to engender callousness towards innocent citizens.[28] Recently, the ARM has claimed responsibility for arson attacks against leather shops in Britain. The organization continues to be very active in Sweden, where most of their actions revolve around animal liberations.[29] The ARM also threatened to kill ten research scientists in the event of the death of imprisoned animals rights activist Barry Horne who was on a hunger strike.[30]

While the ARM have been known to use threats against individuals, arson and letter bombs, they are arguably best known for 'removing from a grave in October 2004, the body of Gladys Hammond, the mother-in-law of Christopher Hall, part-owner of Darley Oaks Farm, which bred guinea pigs for Huntingdon Life Sciences [HLS], and which had been the target of the animal rights campaign "Save the Newchurch Guinea Pigs"'.[31] In 2006, three activists were sentenced to 12 years in prison for their part in the campaign against HLS (which, in addition to grave robbing, included letter bombs and property destruction), while a fourth activist was given four years. On 30 August 2007 the group claimed to have contaminated tubes of the antiseptic Savlon in England to protest its maker Novartis's support of Huntingdon Life Sciences.[32] Their last reported actions were in Sweden in 2011 and 2012 where they targeted fur farmers and vivisectionists with threats of bombs against individuals' houses.[33]

At the time of writing, in total the ARM has been responsible for 63 incidents since 2000, with the vast majority (43 incidents) taking place in Europe. However, the use of the ARM nom de guerre peaked in 2004 with 13 incidents and has been little invoked in the past few years.[34]

Justice Department

The use of the descriptor 'Justice Department' first emerged in the UK in 1993.[35] They have claimed responsibility for hundreds of attacks primarily in the UK, Canada and the USA. The group publicly declared they were willing to use physical violence against their enemies.[36]

The Independent newspaper has described the organization's actions as 'the most sustained and sophisticated bombing campaign in mainland Britain since the IRA was at its height'.[37] The organization 'soon surpassed any of the "achievements"' of ARM in both scope of attacks and through its violent rhetoric. It should be noted that again it is believed that there is a large amount of overlap of members between the JD and the ALF. John Curtain (former Hunt Retribution Squad member, ALF activist and spokesman, 1995) claimed: 'it is accurate to put the figure of activists who are willing to engage in actions (such as burning meat lorries) at around 200'. However, police believe that there are approximately '60 hard-core activists' who were willing to utilize different group affiliations to suit their cause.[38]

Similarly structured to the ALF, the JD works in anonymous cells and has utilized letter bombs that have injured several people.[39] The group had its supporters from within the ALF but also some mainstream RSPCA supporters approved of their actions.[40] They have claimed hundreds of attacks in the UK, the USA and Canada against animal research, animal testing companies and hunters.[41] A 1993 report to the US Congress from the Departments of Justice and Agriculture on terrorism on enterprises claimed the group was responsible for 313 violent and destructive incidents between 1979 and 1993.[42]

The JD sought to: 'intimidate those involved in certain industries [what is identified by them as the specieist oppression of animals] ... in order to halt the perceived torture of animals'.[43] To that end the JD was willing to target individuals, their families and personnel of 'offending' companies to require them through fear to rethink their approach to animals.[44]

The JD was first 'noticed' in October 1993, when a letter bomb exploded at the Post Office sorting centre in Watford. The package was addressed to 'someone involved in blood sports'. The police declared that they had successfully intercepted earlier devices.[45] Almost a month later on 23 November, the ALF press office received a communiqué from a new group calling itself the 'Justice Department', claiming responsibility for the bombings. To prove their bona fides the statement included a video that showed the 'internal components of the bomb and its construction'. The statement declared:

> On the 28th October two animal abusers were injured and given the shock of their pathetic lives when they opened parcel bombs sent by us. We don't need to explain why these two ... were targeted, suffice to say they cause animals to suffer great cruelty; and they deserve it. In spite of their minor injuries they will now be very much aware that we mean business and, were they not our 'guinea pigs' for the testing of our experimental devices would have been more permanently physically injured. This will be the case next time. We've sat back for years and watched AR activists ask nicely for abuse to stop – the more daring risk their lives and liberty but still the unacceptable number of tortured animals keep rising ... the torturers become more extreme; they kill the non-violent opponents ... In light of recent parcel bombs sent by the HRS

> (Hunt Retribution Squad) ... The lack of media hysteria suggests we didn't get through but we will ... We only have to get lucky once ... We make no excuses for our violent intervention. They've had it too good for too long. NO MORE TORTURES NO MORE LIES.[46]

From October to December 1993, the JD claimed to be involved in 31 attacks including poster tubes (fitted with hypodermic needles), video-cassettes and timed incendiary devices. Their targets included fieldsport individuals, furriers and companies linked to animal experimentation. In 1994, the JD claimed responsibility for approximately 100 attacks.[47]

In February 1994 the JD adopted a new tactic and sent out metal mousetraps fitted with superglued razor blades. After these attacks, the organization claimed: 'One former member stated the campaign was a significant success in that, "the first device from the Justice Department against the (live export) trade was dispatched with six more following ... for the first time in all those years major ferry companies announced that they would no longer be carrying live animals for slaughter".'[48]

Their first known attack in the USA was in 1999, when it sent razor blade-filled packages to university researchers and furriers along with letters promising 'full retribution' and, 'Your violence will be turned back upon you.' One letter noted: 'the ALF have a clear policy of adherence to non-violence. We do not.'[49]

Justice Department member Gurj Aujila (eventually apprehended and sentenced to six years in jail) who headed the letter-bomb campaign maintained their operations were carefully planned and studied, arguing:

> This wasn't token protest, or mindless retribution, or even economic sabotage ... it was strategic action. I researched that the meat trade is massive and can't be easily beaten, but live export is one vulnerable aspect of that trade that could be defeated. Furthermore, the ferry companies are not primary animal abusers, they could exist perfectly well without live exports, so hit them and they will withdraw – and they did.[50]

The JD was not involved in any known campaigns for most of the early 2000s until in November 2008 the group claimed responsibility for vandalizing the home of a University of California, San Francisco researcher. Since then, it has claimed responsibility for mailing needles covered in rat poison to two primate researchers at Wake Forest University in North Carolina, and razor blades covered in rat poison to at least one other primate researcher at the University of California, Los Angeles (UCLA).[51]

In November 2010, David Jentsch, a UCLA psychologist and neuroscientist conducting schizophrenia, amphetamine and addiction research on rodents and vervet monkeys received a razor blade-filled package and a note threatening to slash his throat, sent by another extremist group calling itself the Justice Department.[52]

Stop Huntingdon Animal Cruelty

Another offshoot was the organization called Stop Huntingdon Animal Cruelty (SHAC). SHAC was established in the UK in 1999. Their primary objective was to persuade Huntingdon Life Sciences (HLS), a research laboratory, to stop ongoing animal experimentation.[53] The HLS is one of the world's largest animal testing laboratories and has been the target of a prolonged attack by animal liberation activists.[54]

SHAC funded their operations in a similar manner to the ALF with cash collected at Saturday stalls on shopping streets across the UK, displaying emotive pictures of animals in distress to entice donations. One cell that targeted HLS for six years funded their campaign with £1 million raised from collection tins on main street stalls.[55]

SHAC also took its campaign abroad and targeted companies in Switzerland, Holland, Sweden, France, Belgium and Germany where they broke into offices and harassed staff with late-night demonstrations outside workers' homes.[56] After direct action attacks by SHAC, which ranged from vandalism of the company's headquarters to the brutal beating of its president, the company relocated to New Jersey in 2001. While the HLS laboratory hoped to avoid future attacks with the transferring of their operations, other environmental activists continued the attacks on the company in the USA.[57]

SHAC also believed that attacks on secondary targets linked to the HLS would be a viable strategy to economically hurt the company. It was a successful campaign since over 100 companies, including Deloitte & Touche, Marsh & McLennan, and both the Royal Bank of Scotland and the Stephens Group, chose to sever ties with the HLS in the face of SHAC actions.[58] The group was willing to go after the customers of the HLS since they made the enterprise profitable; suppliers; as well as shareholders, banks and markets linked to the company. For example, in February 2000, the ALF threatened bomb attacks against HLS's major shareholders that led to Phillips and Drew, a fund manager, quitting its stake in the HLS after allegedly receiving death threats and hate mail. Private investors, suppliers and employees were also subjected to the usual tactics including arson, bombs, threats, physical assaults, threatening and abusive communications and false allegations of paedophilia.[59]

Over 40 companies were eventually targeted and Brian Cass, HLS managing director, was attacked outside his home with a pickaxe handle.

In 2007, after a pan-European police operation, 32 members were arrested and the leadership jailed, which broke the movement. Six members of the US branch of SHAC were also jailed in 2006.[60] They were prosecuted under the US Animal Enterprise Protection Act (1992), which made stealing from or causing damage or property loss to an 'animal enterprise' a criminal activity.[61]

Debbie Vincent (a SHAC leader) was jailed in 2014 for blackmail; while Gregg Avery, his wife Natasha, and his former wife, Heather Nicholson, were jailed in 2009. Avery claimed there was only ever a hard-core membership of ten people. He denied that SHAC ever was involved in violence, attributing such actions to the ALF.[62]

As seen in *Bite Back Magazine* and the North American Animal Liberation Press Office, while the attack on the HLS occurred in both the UK and the USA, the vast majority of the communiqués released regarding actions against the HLS were either uncredited or attributed to the ALF. According to John Lewis, deputy assistant director of the FBI in a Senate Committee Hearing in 2005:

> When these companies or individuals are threatened or attacked, it is not necessarily the work of SHAC itself. There may be overlap in membership in extremist movements which can make it difficult to identify the actual perpetrators. Also, in the past 18 months, a number of SHAC splinter groups have been created, which use SHAC tactics and focus on SHAC targets. This is most likely an attempt by animal rights extremists to continue the SHAC campaign while appearing to distance themselves from the SHAC organization. However, while the SHAC organization attempts to portray itself merely as an information service or media outlet, it is closely aligned with these groups, as well as with the Animal Liberation Front.[63]

In August 2014 SHAC announced – due to police operations and the 'onslaught of government repression' against the animal rights movement – that they were ceasing to operate.[64]

GOVERNMENT AND INDUSTRY RESPONSE

The main response to the threat of ecoterrorism has been the creation of joint task forces, with federal and local agency (and, at times, international) cooperation, the continued monitoring of online communities by law enforcement and changes to legislation, which have allowed activists to be labelled 'terrorists' and have promised more criminal charges and longer sentences.

The UK government has slowly responded to the shifting strategies of animal liberation groups and their use of violence. In 1984 they established a new squad attached to New Scotland Yard's C11 branch (responsible for intelligence gathering), which became known as the Animal Rights National Index (ARNI). In 1986 it became an autonomous national unit liaising with animal rights officers in every police force. The responsibility of ARNI was to create an intelligence database on illegal animal rights activity.[65]

The Animal Enterprise Protection Act (AEPA) was passed in 1992 and created 'the new crime of "animal enterprise terrorism"'. The law refers to 'anyone who "intentionally damages or causes the loss of any property" of and "animal enterprise", or who causes an *economic loss* of any kind'.[66] The AEPA defines an 'animal rights or ecological terrorist organization' as 'two or more persons organized for the purpose of supporting any politically motivated activity intended to obstruct or deter any person from participating in any activity involving animals or an activity involving natural resources'. It further criminalized any action that disrupted 'any lawful activity involving the use of natural resources with an economic value'.[67]

Under the Act, the actions of more than two people can be labelled as 'terrorist' if they leaflet a circus, or protest an experimental lab, or engage in a tree-sit or even organize an effective boycott.[68] Even though the AEPA was passed in 1992, it has rarely been utilized. The first activist was not jailed under the legislation until 1995.[69]

In September 2006, the US Senate passed a modified version of the AEPA, renamed as the 'Animal Enterprise Terrorism Act' (AETA). The bill was fast-tracked without hearings or debate in order to forestall public criticism. In November 2006, the bill was approved and it was signed into law by President George W. Bush.[70]

The updated version extends the range of potential legal prosecutions of activists, including internet protest campaigns, and enforced stiffer penalties for 'terrorist' actions. As it was passed with the intention to prevent SHAC-style campaigns from succeeding in the future, the law not only makes it a criminal offence to interfere with so-called 'animal enterprises' directly, but also with affiliated parties such as insurance companies, law firms and investment houses that do business with them.[71]

The ALF has recognized that regular police scrutiny means they 'cannot report what they would like to' so they purposefully self-censorship articles submitted to them, and have in some cases legal advice prior to publication. Raids on ALF offices have occurred multiple times, resulting in paperwork, computers and newsletters being confiscated by the authorities.[72]

The UK government also introduced Sections 145–9 of the British Serious Organised Crime and Police Act (2005), which were also amended as a result of the SHAC campaign. These sections cover 'interference with contractual relationships so as to harm animal research organisations' and the 'intimidation of persons connected with animal research organisations'.[73] In other words, it became an offence to intimidate someone into breaking their contract with an animal research laboratory. In addition, anti-social behaviour orders were placed on activists in the UK, preventing them from having any contact with the HLS and any other target company.[74]

Legal Consequences

It is important to note that there have been approximately 300 prosecutions, most of them successful against ALF members, and many activists have served time in prison (usually for property damage, which can mean a prison sentence of up to seven years). According to Scarce, while American ALFers have been nearly untouched by the law over a dozen British activists have served jail sentences.[75]

In early 1978, the ALF (UK) had five of its members imprisoned. Gary Treadwell (21), David Hough (48) and Michael Huskisson (24) were imprisoned after being convicted of damaging John Peel's grave. Activist Rodney Coronado pleaded guilty and served 57 months in jail for aiding and abetting in arson (the firebombing of a Michigan State University research laboratory on 28 February 1992).[76]

On 2 March 2006, the 'SHAC 7' were 'found guilty of multiple federal felonies' for advocating the closure of the HLS and all were sentenced to prison.[77] Following a 'defiant speech' to the court, stating that 'carrying out Animal Liberation Front actions "was the proudest and most powerful thing I have ever done"', Walter Bond was sentenced to a minimum of five years in prison.[78] Bond boldly told the court:

> I know many people think I should feel remorse for what I've done. I guess this is the customary time where I'm suppose[d] to grovel and beg for mercy. I assure you if that's how I felt I would. But, I am not sorry for anything I have done … I doubt the court is interested in the precautions that I took to not harm any person or by-stander … Do what you can, do what you must, be vegan warriors and true animal defenders and never compromise with their murderers and profiteers. The Animal Liberation Front is the answer. Seldom has there been such a personally powerful and internationally effective movement in human history. You cannot join the A.L.F. but you can become

> the A.L.F. and it was the proudest and most powerful thing I have ever done … Every time someone liberates an animal and smashes their cage, it lives on! Every time an activist refuses to bow down to laws that protect murder, it lives on! … That's all Your Honor, I am ready to go to prison.[79]

ANALYSIS AND CONCLUSION

It is clear that animal rights violence within the UK and the USA has a long history and at times the campaigns undertaken by the ALF have tipped over into terrorist acts.[80] By far, the Animal Liberation Front, compared to other radical environmental groups, appears to be the most active and far-reaching organization, with a global extent.

There is no doubt that Ronnie Lee was a hugely charismatic and influential leader of both the Band of Mercy and the ALF. It was his vision that, despite the creation of the affinity cell model, actually fuelled the early version of the groups. His being imprisoned, while valuable as a martyr for the cause, was a great loss to the group. While it continued on without him, the law enforcement crackdown, particularly in the UK, appears to have rendered a crippling blow to the ALF.

Ronnie Lee believes that, in the UK at least, the decimation of the fur trade and a big reduction in the number of animals vivisected by businesses have been the greatest accomplishments achieved by the ALF.[81] They also have made many businesses that utilize animals as part of their business model – and the people who worked for them – scared. For example, in February 2011 a *Nature* magazine poll showed that almost 25 per cent of animal research scientists undertaking the poll were affected by or knew someone affected by animal rights militants. A little more than 15 per cent had changed practices or direction as a result of such targeting or knowledge of such attacks.[82]

As noted earlier, it is almost impossible to definitively determine the average ALF member. They come from all types of backgrounds, classes and genders – from professionals, full-time and part-time workers to retirees. They come from 'normal' homes and are not particularly motivated by money. The young are drawn to the organization; it also attracts those who are not interested in conventional politics.[83]

What binds them all together as Einwohler discovered is their emotional attachment to animals or their strong emotional reactions to animal abuse.[84] Further, they perceive that their awareness of such cruel practices distinguishes them from the majority of society who are either unaware or unwilling to recognize this ongoing holocaust.[85] Such a distinction can prove fertile ground for sowing an 'us versus them' angry mentality, which can tip over into violence when the minority think the majority is ignoring their viewpoint or demand because they are already perceived as 'other'.[86]

Becoming More Radicalized

The purpose of terrorism is to instil fear, or to terrorize, and it is clear that ALF adherents under both their own name and other pseudonyms were willing to use personal violence to that end. This is evidenced not only by the reaction of their targets, but also by the response of the 'larger target audience'. For example, due to the letter-bomb campaigns carried out, there was a forced 'introduction of specially designed machines to check the contents of incoming mail'. Individuals involved in animal experimentation were required to continually check their vehicles in case they had been targeted with car bombs.[87]

When the FBI initially labelled the ALF a terrorist organization, many treated it as a joke. Until the passage of the Animal Enterprise Protection Act (1992), such actions were not prosecuted as 'terrorism'. As is pointed out by Kuipers, 'sinking empty whaling boats was not terrorism. Spiking trees was not terrorism. Even burning barns was not terrorism. Not legally.' Prior to the passage of the AEPA, terrorism had largely been defined as 'being an act of violence against a person – not property – designed to influence government or private action'.[88] However, it is clear from a look at the historical record that at times it has deserved that appellation.

Smith's research indicates that ALF attacks within the USA went from three attacks in 1991 increasing to eight in 1999, peaking in 2001 with 13. There were eight attacks in 2003 before plummeting dramatically to ones and twos in 2004–9 and four attacks in 2010.[89] In the early part of the twenty-first century, 3,119 actions were reported from 2000 to 2015, with the ALF claiming responsibility for 2,847 of them, and the majority taking place in Europe, followed by the UK and North America. The data collected for the ALF shows the number of reported activities significantly decreasing over the past several years (specifically after 2008). While there have still been 45 reported actions in 2015, it is a sharp contrast to the 556 they claimed responsibility for worldwide in 2008.[90]

Of the radical environmental groups examined here the ALF hews most closely to Sprinzak's process model of radicalization. Lee started out utilizing non-violent methods before deciding to engage in more militant forms of action with the Band of Mercy and the ALF. It can be observed that this was a relatively short process over several years.

Clearly Lee and his adherents believed that the urgent need to protect animals was not being met.

As per Sprinzak's projected radicalization trajectory, the ALF very rapidly developed a devoted following of perhaps as many as 2,500 participants, with a hard core of approximately 100 willing to commit arson and violence (although it is difficult to quantify exact numbers).[91] Building from the work done by Singer, the ALF developed their own distinctive philosophy, goals and the affinity cell structure to carry out its mission to save animals and end animal suffering.

It is clear that Lee and his followers went through a crisis of confidence stage whereby they experienced a 'profound disenchantment' with the current society, due to accumulated frustration with prevailing societal conditions that allowed animals to be used for research or as part of the food chain. They were convinced that something needed to be done to startle society out of its lethargy as regards animal rights and to educate people as to what was happening to defenceless creatures – but, more importantly, to save the creatures from human oppressors.[92] Almost from the start it was clear that the ALF was seeking to challenge the established political system with violent attacks against property.

What precipitated the entry into Sprinzak's conflict of legitimacy stage by the Band of Mercy and then the ALF was a perception that not enough animals were being protected; society was not moving fast enough in the desired direction.[93] As Rowan noted, activists were frustrated at the glacial pace of change and believed that mainstream tactics such as dialogue and conciliation were not working.[94] They believed that a system that allowed animal suffering was not legitimate and needed to be challenged, with the aim of creating a mass movement for change. They spoke of inspiring a revolution of thought and practice. In terms of the use of violence by the group the initial method utilized was liberation raids but that quickly progressed to violence against property using a variety of methods, including arson. However, there appears to be little evidence of them adopting further countercultural practices.[95]

To many ALF adherents they were involved in a war with an enemy. For Lee, anything less than fighting a war is committing treachery against other species. Many perceived themselves as freedom fighters on behalf of animals, fighting the moral equivalent of Nazi Germany.[96] The ALF rejected engagement with the mainstream political discourse, seeking rather to end the prevailing political structures.[97] The language and rhetoric utilized on their websites and on missives left behind at the scene of their actions in many cases were filled with warnings against their enemies to change their ways, while denouncing them.[98]

Certainly the ALF did engage in 'terrorist' actions against humans and thus can be considered to have crossed the threshold into Sprinzak's third phase, the crisis of legitimacy. Under the nom de guerres of the ARM, the JD and SHAC, and sometimes in their own name, the ALF considered their opponents as the enemy and they were willing to use physical violence against people in pursuance of their objectives. Lee has argued that ALF members needed to be willing to be more violent than their opponents. If they were not willing to go this far then they were not truly committed.[99] In some ways the philosophy underpinning the ALF equating animal life to human life made it easy to make the leap to harming humans because it was considered to be the defence of 'another' and thus legitimate.

The ALF cells evolved along the radicalization continuum to the point where they see the world in stark 'us and them' terms and to a point where they are willing to kill humans. From statements made there was very much a Manicheistic break where the ALF members were fighting against the forces of darkness. For many their participation was part of a cosmic fight between opposing forces representing good (them) and others (the rest of society).[100] Lee has argued that the ALF not officially allowing killing in pursuit of their goals is not a principled position, but rather merely a tactical decision.[101] Given this, it is relatively easy to adopt physical violence if it is perceived as a winning strategy.

However, the official position of the ALF was that cells were forbidden to injure life and members had to take all reasonable precautions to prevent injury.[102] Some members tried adopting other names to commit physical attacks such as the ARM, the JD and SHAC, allowing the ALF to keep a relatively benign public stance on the question of physical violence. However, there is evidence that threats to commit physical force and acts of violence were undertaken under the ALF banner.

However, Sprinzak's analysis is incorrect in a number of regards: while the cells tended to be small, they did not tend to isolate themselves from the community, with many also engaged with the broader environmental movement at the same time.[103] Further, they did not tend to impose on members a new set of behavioural and moral standards to adhere to. Rather, the evidence suggests that the activists were already committed vegetarians or believed in a world without animal suffering. However, being in such tight-knit cells no doubt reinforced previous beliefs. As Hall notes, being in such cells offered an identity and friends to the members who then face an enemy that needs to be fought to avenge animal suffering.[104]

There is a great deal of evidence in Sprinzak's derogatory language to signal that the group has evolved to a point where they have dehumanized their opponents.[105] The language used by the ALF to describe their opponents was full of vitriol, equating their opponents with evil to the point that they became depersonalized and dehumanized as 'killers of defenceless creatures'.[106] There are numerous examples of ALF members and supporters using derogatory language to describe their enemies. They have been called 'scum' and 'scumbags';[107] 'desensitized butchers' and 'oppressors';[108] 'cowards';[109] 'subhumans';[110] a 'stupid, cold-hearted bitch';[111] and a 'monster'.[112] Members tended to be dismissive of those not part of the animal liberation collective. Members saw themselves as morally superior from mainstream society and this was key to their own self-understanding as to who they were.

However, there is no evidence that ALF members engaged in other forms of criminality, or non-conventional sexual activity. Rather their focus on their special interest issue of protecting animals appears to be the focus of their criminal activity rather than a generalized rejection of all of society's mores.[113]

Why Has the ALF Lost Momentum?

The above figures indicate that the ALF as a group and potential mass movement appears to have lost momentum (particularly in Western countries), and while not a spent force is a severely depleted one. A combination of extra police powers and stricter laws appears to be working in limiting ALF activities. Those convicted of carrying out operations received near-maximum or maximum sentences. Actions reported in *Bite Back Magazine* have declined in both number and severity, with most actions carried out being merely minor criminal damage and vandalism, similar to how the organization started.[114]

In the late 1980s ALF adherents believed they had to work outside the system to achieve their goals. Nicholls wrote: 'animal liberation has to be achieved outside the legal system!' He further believed that the actions of the welfare animal groups distracted good people who 'would otherwise be doing really useful work'. He had pride in the fact that 'the ALF is now feared by animal abusers' (for example, according to Henshaw, 'people who worked in laboratories where vivisection was practised would no longer be named in public, for fear for their personal safety'). According to Nicholls, this was just 'the beginning of justified retaliation'.[115]

However, in the late 1990s in the UK animal rights bombings and arson attacks committed in the name of animal rights plunged. Robin Webb, the ALF press officer, believed this was due to the Labour Party coming to power in 1997 and pledging to ban hunting and fur farming and to establish a Royal Commission on animal experimentation. However, liberation missions were still carried out: for example, 600 guinea pigs were liberated from a guinea pig breeder (Darley Oaks Farm) in Staffordshire. The failure to set up the promised Royal Commission caused the ALF to again turn to arson in 1999 and 2000, with members carrying out firebomb attacks on trucks from a meat firm (Weddel Swift) in Devon, and an attack on Unigate Dairies and a poultry farm in Oxfordshire.[116]

According to Best and Nocella, one of the biggest challenges facing the ALF was their attempt to 'be as militant and effective as possible without losing the moral high ground, without alienating public support, and without diluting the values of freedom and compassion'.[117] However, they appear to have failed. As Liddick argues, 'if there is a lack of support in the movements themselves for radical direct action, the general public's view of illegal actions is certainly far worse. Those who burn down buildings and physically attack scientists have an insurmountable image problem with average citizens.'[118]

The Association of the British Pharmaceutical Industry, a lobby group, claimed that the increasingly militant actions of the ALF and its sister organizations led to many activists abandoning the animal rights cause and the activists did not return to the fold until after militant attacks ceased in 2009.[119] By 2011, however, in the UK animal rights moderates' revulsion at the ALF's activities has been seen as calming animal rights actions – illegal attack numbers were down while legal protests at UK animal-testing facilities were up.[120]

The ALF organization has also altered significantly over the decades, with many representative members having been bankrupted for breaches of injunctions applied to the whole organization. Members have also been sued by both companies and individuals affected by the ALF's activities. The use of the nom de guerres ALF and ARM are now merely badges for carrying out actions, not viable organizations.[121]

Further, the issue of animal rights has also gone mainstream in many Western countries. Inhumane practices such as chaining dogs is now outlawed in many US states; law schools teach animal-law courses with massive student interest; countries like Spain debate granting legal rights to primates and outlawing animal experimentation.[122]

An analysis of the *Bite Back* 'Diary of Actions' for the last few years indicates that while ALF actions tend to be global in nature (Brazil, Canada, Australia, Italy, the USA, Spain, the Netherlands, Japan, Colombia, Turkey, the UK, Sweden, Finland and Poland) they are primarily liberation actions or ecotage, with the odd arson occurring (in Australia a slaughterhouse was burnt out in December 2014[123]). In 2014 there were over 180 actions reported to the Bite Back website by ALF adherents and sympathizers and in 2015 there were over 100 reported attacks. Graffiti has been daubed, animals have been rescued and buildings destroyed or damaged.[124] While it cannot be stated with certainty it appears that ALF cells have retreated from the physical attacks and threats that characterized the ARM and SHAC and have gone back to the type of actions that occurred in the ALF's infancy. Whether this trend will continue, however, remains to be seen.

Global Reach

While the UK government has had considerable success in curtailing the ALF's activities the group has become more active in other jurisdictions, particularly in Europe. On 27 July 2009 militants stole the ashes of Mr Vasella's (the Novartis pharmaceutical company's chief executive officer, CEO) mother in the eastern Swiss city of Chur, and left the message, 'Drop HLS Now', spray-painted on the gravestone. On 4 August that same year Mr Vasella's holiday home was firebombed and a message was left on the North American Animal Liberation Press Office website claiming, 'We personally can only regret that Mr. Vasella was not present in the home when it burned.'[125]

The ALF appears to have a wider reach than its counterparts, with actions being reported in countries worldwide. Unlike the ELF, the vast majority of actions took place in Europe (particularly Sweden and Germany) and the UK. In addition to these countries, which have historically also had an environmental rights presence, the ALF has had successful actions in smaller, lesser known countries such as Malaysia,[126] Lithuania,[127] Costa Rica[128] and Israel.[129] The ALF has also given support and advice to like-minded groups that have burgeoned in countries such as Canada, Germany, Japan and the USA.[130]

The Future of the ALF

Ronnie Lee, the charismatic creator of the group (and initial leader), no longer swears by the methods utilized by the ALF and is now urging a strategy instead of exposure and shaming the individual abuser. Targeting them personally in their own homes financed by exploitation of the 'innocents' (animals) would streamline their strategy. Educational approach and peaceful campaigning aside, he does not totally rule out animal rights groups resorting to violence if required to deter animal abusers.[131]

Lee has also come to believe that taking animals out of laboratories or 'concentration camps', as he sometimes calls them, can do more harm than good.[132] Such raids he has come to accept only lead to the animals being replenished and do not necessarily lead the facilities to cease operations. Sent to rescue organizations, these animals then occupy spaces that could have saved two others. He argues that animal liberation groups should focus on the source of the problem: people's behaviour rather than the animals. Education and coercion are the two effective methods to bring about change in attitude and behaviour.[133]

Lee argues that the ALF will continue to exist but merely as a small subset of the overall continuing struggle for animal liberation – and it is hard to disagree with his assessment. He thinks that 'times have changed' and most people are not willing to engage in ALF-style operations. However, he does not believe this is necessarily a bad thing, since such operations are not critical to bringing about the achievement of animal liberation within society (but it can help).[134]

Lee believes that the highpoint of the ALF is past, because it did not metamorphize into a mass movement due to the short-sightedness of ALF adherents themselves. Lee argues that in the UK in the late 1970s/early 1980s there was a real 'feeling' amongst animal protectionists for the carrying out of direct action. The problem was that the affinity cell structure of the organization prevented new members joining pre-existing cells to learn needed methods, and many established groups would not take on new members. Those members who did not have the initial confidence to find their own group could have gone on to building a mass movement. The established cells were not thinking of the big picture but only the need to carry out their individual operations. Training new people was critical if the ALF was ever to become a mass movement but the failure to do so, in part, crippled the potential growth of the movement.[135]

However, the ALF is not totally defunct and still carries out actions and is attracting a new generation of adherents. According to a report in 2011, universities have 'more of a problem with animal rights extremists than Islamist radicals'.[136] The report stated that, 'animal rights was the most commonly experienced issue on campus, particularly protests, public campaigns and attempts to gain access to animal-testing facilities'.[137] There may well be a new generation of ALF adherents currently being born out of the university system if the political conditions are right to radicalize them.

The ALF to date has not, however, developed into a mass movement of adherents as was originally envisaged. However, its original vision may no longer be necessary given how society has adopted animal rights norms over the last four decades. More people have adopted vegetarianism; there are animal rights and law courses taught at universities; and more companies are phasing out animal testing than ever before. This is not to say that the ALF may not surge again if a charismatic leader arises or enough people believe that animal suffering is inexcusable. However, for now most activists appear willing to forgo militant and/or terrorist actions since they believe they are progressing towards creating the type of society that they (and animals) would wish to live in.

NOTES

1. Animal Rights Extremism, 'Violent extremism', http://www.animalrightsextremism.info/animal-rights-extremism/history-of-animal-rights-extremism/violent-extremism/.
2. Carolyn Bailey, 'Transcript of Ronnie Lee's ARZone live guest chat, http://arzone.ning.com/profiles/blogs/transcript-of-ronnie-lees-live.
3. Keith Tester and John Walls (1996) 'The ideology and current activities of the Animal Liberation Front', *Contemporary Politics*, **2** (2), p. 86.
4. Hasan T. Arslan (2008) 'The social and operational intersections of environmental extremism in North America and Europe' (PhD dissertation, Sam Houston State University, Huntsville, TX), p. 38. For example, the desecration of John Peel's grave was publicly claimed by a group calling themselves the 'Hunt Retribution Squad', but all perpetrators were veterans of ALF actions; David Henshaw, *Animal Warfare: The Story of the Animal Liberation Front*.
5. Rachel Monaghan (2013) 'Not quite terrorism: animal rights extremism in the United Kingdom', *Studies in Conflict and Terrorism*, **36**, 11, p. 940.
6. Tester and Walls, 'the ideology and current activities of the Animal Liberation Front', p. 85.
7. Ibid.
8. Rachel Monaghan (1997) 'Animal rights and violent protest', *Terrorism and Political Violence*, **9** (4), p. 114.
9. Animal Rights Extremism, 'Violent extremism'.
10. Animal Liberation Front, 'Animal Rights Militia', http://www.animalliberationfront.com/ALFront/ARMilitia.htm.
11. Russell Lee Young (2004) 'A time series analysis of eco-terrorist violence in the United States: 1993–2003' (PhD dissertation, Sam Houston State University, Huntsville, TX), p. 43.
12. Animal Rights Militia Communiqué (1985) *Animal Liberation Front Supporters' Group Newsletter*, **17**; Tester and Walls, 'The ideology and current activities of the Animal Liberation Front', p. 86.
13. Ibid.
14. Henshaw, *Animal Warfare: The Story of the Animal Liberation Front*, p. 115.
15. Ibid., p. 116.
16. Ibid., p. 118.
17. Donald R. Liddick (2006) *Eco-Terrorism: Radical Environmental and Animal Liberation Movements* (Westport, Connecticut: Praeger), p. 44.
18. Ibid., p. 120.
19. Ibid.
20. Tester and Walls, 'The ideology and current activities of the Animal Liberation Front', p. 87.
21. Liddick, *Eco-Terrorism: Radical Environmental and Animal Liberation Movements*, p. 44.

22. Young, 'A time series analysis of eco-terrorist violence in the United States: 1993–2003', p. 43.
23. Liddick, *Eco-Terrorism: Radical Environmental and Animal Liberation Movements*, p. 44.
24. Rachel Monaghan (2006) 'Animal rights and violent protest', *Terrorism and Political Violence, Liberation* (Westport, Connecticut: Praeger), pp. 111–12; see also http://envirolink.org/ALF/ezines/ugl_lhtml.
25. Liddick, *Eco-Terrorism: Radical Environmental and Animal Liberation Movements*, p. 44.
26. Henshaw, *Animal Warfare: The Story of the Animal Liberation Front*, p. 65.
27. Ibid., p. 64.
28. Ibid.
29. Ibid., p. 44.
30. Liddick, *Eco-Terrorism: Radical Environmental and Animal Liberation Movements*, p. 44; Animal Liberation Front, 'Animal Rights Militia Fact Sheet', http://www.animaliberationfront.com/ALFront/Actions-UK/alfarm.htm.
31. Animal Liberation Front, 'Animal Rights Militia'.
32. Anonymous Communiqué, 'Will Novartis products ever be safe?', *Bite Back*, 8 October 2007, http://www.animalliberationfront.com/ALFront/Premise_History/Biteback2007.htm.
33. Bite Back, 'Diary of Actions 2011–12', http://directaction.info/news.htm.
34. Animal Rights Extremism, 'Violent extremism'.
35. Liddick, *Eco-Terrorism: Radical Environmental and Animal Liberation Movements*, p. 44.
36. Justice Department – Animal Rights, Terrorism Research & Analysis Consortium, http://www.trackingterrorism.org/group/justice-department-animal-rights.
37. Liddick, *Eco-Terrorism: Radical Environmental and Animal Liberation Movements*, p. 44.
38. Tester and Walls, 'The ideology and current activities of the Animal Liberation Front', p. 87.
39. Liddick, *Eco-Terrorism: Radical Environmental and Animal Liberation Movements*, p. 44.
40. Tester and Walls, 'The ideology and current activities of the Animal Liberation Front', pp. 88–9.
41. Justice Department – Animal Rights, Terrorism Research & Analysis Consortium.
42. Arslan, 'The social and operational intersections of environmental extremism in North America and Europe', pp. 38–9.
43. Tester and Walls, 'The ideology and current activities of the Animal Liberation Front', p. 88.
44. Ibid.
45. Ibid., p. 87.
46. 'The Justice Department … The Story So Far', *Liberator* (1994, winter), cited in Tester and Walls, 'The ideology and current activities of the Animal Liberation Front', p. 88.
47. Monaghan (1997) 'Animal rights and violent protest', p. 112; Tester and Walls, 'The ideology and current activities of the Animal Liberation Front', p. 88.
48. Tester and Walls, 'The ideology and current activities of the Animal Liberation Front', p. 88.
49. 'Extremism in America – updates, "Justice Department" claims responsibility for threats against UCLA animal researcher', http://archive.adl.org/learn/extremism_in_america_updates/movements/ecoterrorism/justice_department_ucla.html#.VmI_gGSGRHw, 3 Dec 2010.
50. Monaghan, 'Not quite terrorism: animal rights extremism in the United Kingdom', pp. 936–7.
51. 'Extremism in America – updates, "Justice Department" claims responsibility for threats against UCLA animal researcher.'
52. Sue Russell (2012) 'When extreme animal rights activists attack', *Pacific Standards, Politics & Law*, 17 March, http://www.psmag.com/politics-and-law/when-extreme-animal-rights-activists-attack-40430.
53. Horacio R. Trujillo (2005), 'The radical environmentalist movement', *Aptitude for Destruction*, **2**, pp. 141–78.

54. Animal Liberation Front, 'SHAC', http://www.animalliberationfront.com/ALFront/SHAC.htm.
55. Tom Kelly (2008) 'Guilty: animal terror gang who raised £1million rattling tins on the high street', *The Daily Mail*, http://www.dailymail.co.uk/news/article-1100822/Guilty-Animal-terror-gang-raised-1million-rattling-tins-high-street.html, 24 December.
56. Ibid.
57. Trujillo, 'The radical environmentalist movement', p. 156.
58. Ibid., p. 157.
59. Monaghan, 'Not quite terrorism: animal rights extremism in the United Kingdom', p. 938.
60. 'Animal rights group ends 15-year campaign against experiments at Huntingdon: activists have changed their tactics due to an "onslaught of government repression"', http://www.independent.co.uk/news/uk/crime/animal-rights-group-ends-15-year-campaign-against-experiments-at-huntingdon-9687843.html.
61. Russell, 'When extreme animal rights activists attack'.
62. 'Animal rights group ends 15-year campaign against experiments at Huntingdon: activists have changed their tactics due to an "onslaught of government repression"'.
63. John Lewis, Deputy Assistant Director, FBI, Eco-Terrorism, Senate Committee on Environment and Public Works (2005), http://www.epw.senate.gov/hearing_statements.cfm?id=247787.
64. 'Animal rights group ends 15-year campaign against experiments at Huntingdon: activists have changed their tactics due to an "onslaught of government repression"'.
65. Rachel Monaghan (1999) 'Terrorism in the name of animal rights', *Terrorism and Political Violence*, **11** (4), p. 165.
66. Steven Best (2007) 'The Animal Enterprise Terrorism Act: New, Improved and ACLU Approved', *Journal for Critical Animal Studies*, **5** (1), p. 5.
67. Ibid.
68. Ibid.
69. Denise Case (2002) 'The USA Patriot Act: adding bite to the fight against animal rights terrorism?', *Rutgers Law Journal*, **187** (Fall), p. 196; *PR Newswire* (1995) 'For first time in U.S. history – animal rights extremist to go to jail for A.L.F. related terror activity', 4 March.
70. Best, 'The Animal Enterprise Terrorism Act: New, Improved and ACLU Approved', p. 7.
71. Ibid.
72. Monaghan, 'Terrorism in the name of animal rights', p. 165.
73. Serious Organized Crime and Police Act 2005, http://www.legislation.gov.uk/ukpga/2005/15/contents.
74. 'If you don't fight, you've already lost', *Corporate Watch*, 17 April 2014, https://corporatewatch.org/news/2014/apr/17/if-you-dont-fight-youve-already-lost.
75. Rik Scarce (2006) *Eco-Warriors: Understanding the Radical Environmental Movement* (California: Left Coast Press), p. 141.
76. Case, 'The USA Patriot Act: adding bite to the fight against animal rights terrorism?', p. 197; 'For first time in U.S. History – animal rights extremist to go to jail for A.L.F. related terror activity'.
77. Anthony Nocella (2007) 'Unmasking the Animal Liberation Front using critical pedagogy: seeing the ALF for who they really are', *Journal for Critical Animal Studies*, **V** (1), p. 2.
78. Peter Young (2011) 'Walter Bond receives minimum sentence in A.L.F. arson', *Voice of the Voiceless*, 13 February.
79. Ibid.
80. Monaghan, 'Not quite terrorism: animal rights extremism in the United Kingdom', p. 945.
81. Bailey, 'Transcript of Ronnie Lee's ARZone live guest chat'.
82. Russell, 'When extreme animal rights activists attack'.
83. Ibid., p. 34.

84. Rachel L. Einwohler (2002) 'Bringing the outsiders in: opponents' claims and the construction of animal rights activists' identity', *Mobilization: An International Journal*, **7** (3), p. 261.
85. Ibid., p. 257.
86. Henshaw, *Animal Warfare: The Story of the Animal Liberation Front*, p. 26.
87. Monaghan, 'Terrorism in the Name of Animal Rights', p. 167.
88. Dean Kuipers (2009) *Operation Bite Back: Rod Coronado's War to Save the American Wilderness* (New York: Bloomsbury), p. 4.
89. Phillip Andrew Smith (2014) 'The axe without the handle: an exploratory analysis of eco-terrorism and its relationships to U.S. public policy towards terrorism: 1990–2010', p. 109.
90. Bite Back Magazine, http://www.directaction.info; Global Terrorism Database, http://www.start.umd.edu/gtd/; North American Animal Liberation Press Office, http://animalliberationpressoffice.org/NAALPO/; 325, http://325.nostate.net.
91. Monaghan, 'Animal rights and violent protest', p. 112.
92. Ehud Sprinzak (1991) 'The process of delegitimation: towards a linkage theory of political terrorism', *Terrorism & Political Violence*, **3** (1), p. 54.
93. Sean Parson, 'Understanding the ideology of the Earth Liberation Front', https://libcom.org/forums/theory/understanding-ideology-earth-liberation-front-21012009, p. 51.
94. Andrew N. Rowan (1984), *Of Mice, Models and Men: A Critical Evaluation of Animal Research* (New York: SUNY Press), p. 32.
95. Sprinzak, 'The process of delegitimation: towards a linkage theory of political terrorism', p. 54.
96. Steven Best and Anthony Nocella (2004) 'Behind the mask: uncovering the Animal Liberation Front', in Steven Best and Anthony Nocella (eds) *Terrorists or Freedom Fighters: Reflections on the Liberation of Animals* (New York: Lantern Books), p. 23.
97. Manuel Castells (2000) 'Toward a sociology of the Network Society', *Contemporary Sociology*, **29** (5), p. 693.
98. Ehud Sprinzak (1998) 'The psychopolitical formation of extreme left terrorism in a democracy: the case of the Weathermen', in Walter Reich (ed.), *Origins of Terrorism: Psychologies, Ideologies, Theologies, States of Mind* (Washington, DC: Woodrow Wilson Center Press), pp. 81–2.
99. Ibid.
100. Lee Hall (2006) *Capers in the Churchyard: Animal Rights Advocacy in the Age of Terror* (Darien, Connecticut: Nectar Bat Press), p. 66.
101. Sprinzak, 'The process of delegitimation: towards a linkage theory of political terrorism', p. 56.
102. Craig Rosebraugh (2004) *Burning Rage of a Dying Planet: Speaking for the Earth Liberation Front* (New York: Lantern Books), pp. 263–4.
103. Gerry Nagtzaam and Pete Lentini (2008) 'Vigilantes on the high seas?: the Sea Shepherds and political violence', *Terrorism and Political Violence*, **1**, p. 118.
104. Sprinzak, 'The process of delegitimation: towards a linkage theory of political terrorism', p. 64.
105. Sprinzak, 'The psychopolitical formation of extreme left terrorism in a democracy: the case of the Weathermen', p. 82.
106. Ibid.
107. 22 April 2003, England; 5 May 2003, Sacramento California, http://www.animalliberationfront.com/ALFront/Premise_History/2003_Chronicle_of_Direct_Actions.htm.
108. 'Dutch ALF Communiqué', http://www.animalliberationfront.com/ALFront/Actions-Netherlands/DutchALF.htm.
109. Mandy in Camden, 'SHAC – letter from Heather Nicholson VM 4859 serving 11 years for animal rescue', 22 February 2009, http://www.animalliberationfront.com/ALFront/Activist%20Tips/FromPOW-Heather.htm.
110. http://www.animalliberationfront.com/Saints/Authors/Quotes/ARQuotesLyrics.htm.
111. Ibid.

112. http://scienceblogs.com/insolence/2010/02/24/animal-rights-thugs-researchers-children/.
113. Sprinzak, 'The psychopolitical formation of extreme left terrorism in a democracy: the case of the Weathermen', p. 83.
114. Ibid.
115. Henshaw, *Animal Warfare: The Story of the Animal Liberation Front*, p. 92.
116. Monaghan, 'Not quite terrorism: animal rights extremism in the United Kingdom', pp. 936–7.
117. Best and Nocella, 'Behind the mask: uncovering the Animal Liberation Front', p. 57.
118. Liddick, *Eco-Terrorism: Radical Environmental and Animal Liberation Movements*, p. 112.
119. The Economist (2011) 'A beastly business – peacerful protests against animal testing is on the rise', 22 October, http://www.economist.com/node/21533451.
120. Russell, 'When extreme animal rights activists attack'.
121. Monaghan, 'Not quite terrorism: animal rights extremism in the United Kingdom', p. 944.
122. Adam Cohen (2010) 'Case study: can animal rights go too far?', *Time Magazine*, 14 July.
123. Anonymous (2015) 'News from the frontline', *Bite Back*, 27 December, http://directaction.info/news_dec27_14.htm.
124. Bite Back, 'Diary of Actions 2011–12' http://directaction.info/news.htm.
125. Speaking of Research (2009) Grave robbing by animal rights extremists, 5 August, http://speakingofresearch.com/2009/08/05/graverobbing-by-animal-rights-extremists/.
126. Bite Back Magazine, http://www.directaction.info/news_jan03_08.htm.
127. Bite Back Magazine, http://www.directaction.info/news_jan27_14.htm.
128. Bite Back Magazine, http://www.directaction.info/news_nov10_14.htm.
129. Bite Back Magazine, http://www.directaction.info/news_jan02_15.htm.
130. 'Animal rights, terror tactics', *BBC News*, 30 August 2000, http://news.bbc.co.uk/2/hi/uk_news/902751.stm.
131. Claudette Vaughan, 'Animal Soldiers-A Rare Exclusive Interview with Ronnie Lee'.
132. Ronnie Lee, 'Animal Liberation But Not Too Much?', http://www.animalliberationfront.com/ALFront/Arkangel/Arkangel2.htm#nottoomuch, *Arkangel*, spring 1990.
133. Claudette Vaughan (2010) 'Animal soldiers – a rare exclusive interview with Ronnie Lee', https://carmen4thepets.wordpress.com/2010/03/22/animal-soldiers-a-rare-and-exclusive-interview-with-ronnie-lee/.
134. Bailey, 'Transcript of Ronnie Lee's ARZone live guest chat'. As for Ronnie Lee today, he thinks he is no longer an inspiration and wants to keep a low profile. He now works for animal protection organizations that try to educate the public about the need for animal rights and protection. He claims his administrative workload even prevents him from appearing at animal rights events.
135. Bailey, 'Transcript of Ronnie Lee's ARZone live guest chat'.
136. Duncan Gardham (2011) 'University extremism: AR a bigger problem than Islamists', *The Telegraph (UK),* 18 February.
137. Ibid.

PART II

4. Direct action in defence of living systems: Earth First!

Growth for the sake of growth is the ideology of the cancer cell.

Edward Abbey

INTRODUCTION

Environmental activists in the USA, upset at what they saw as the deficiencies of the capitalist system they were operating under, were determined to find a way to put the environment front and centre in society's calculations. Building on lessons absorbed from Edward Abbey's popular 'ecoterrorist' novel, *The Monkey Wrench Gang* (1975), and a desire to build a new ecological society, a group of environmental activists led by David Foreman, Bart Koehler and Howie Wolke – who had always worked in the system – created a new entity: Earth First!. The new group was dedicated to protecting the biosphere through the use of direct actions to highlight their cause. Eschewing one underlying philosophy Earth First! was influenced by a 'grab bag' of different philosophies and approaches including deep ecology, spirituality and anti-capitalism. Seeing itself more as a movement rather than a group, Earth First! proudly thought of itself as a 'disorganization' dedicated to protecting the environment.

This chapter details the history, philosophical strategy, tactics and key people involved in creating Earth First!. It examines the role played by Edward Abbey and the impact of his 1975 novel on radical biosphere environmentalism. The chapter also seeks to explain the demise of Earth First! as a functioning group.

EARTH FIRST!: EDWARD ABBEY AND *THE MONKEY WRENCH GANG*

The Earth First! environmental group was inspired in part by Edward Abbey's 1975 novel *The Monkey Wrench Gang*.[1] Others argue, however, that the novel is actually based on the activities of American Southwest radical environmentalists who were operational in the 1960s and 1970s.[2] Regardless of the truth, in many ways the book acted as a 'battle plan, manifesto and spiritual guide' to Earth First!.[3] Many activists were moved by Abbey's work and saw a potential home for their subversive actions within the loose structure of Earth First!.[4]

The novel provided lessons that Earth First!ers took to heart. For example, in the book one of the saboteurs decided that any group ideology should be 'made up' as they go. This concept of permitting 'practice [to] inform … doctrine, thus assuring precise theoretical coherence' was mirrored in Foreman's later statement that Earth First! activists should 'let our actions set the finer points of our philosophy'.[5] In a second example of how the novel transcended to reality, the book's activists imagined a disorganized movement made up of small, discrete groups, with no one group being in contact with another, committing sabotage across the USA. This decentralized vision was later adopted by Earth First!, the ELF and the ALF to carry out their visions.[6]

However, in an excerpt from a piece, 'Earth First! and *The Monkey Wrench Gang*', Edward Abbey writes:

> As for the book, please note that *The Monkey Wrench Gang* is a novel, a work of fiction, and – I like to think – a work of art. It would be naïve to read it as a tract, a program for action, or a manifesto … The book does not condone terrorism in any form. Let's have some precision in language here: terrorism means deadly violence – for a political and/or economic purpose – carried out against people and other living things, and is usually conducted by governments against their own citizens.[7]

However, despite Edward Abbey's rejection of his novel as a manifesto for ecoterrorism, Dave Foreman in 1981 acknowledged that one of the original aims of Earth First! was 'to inspire others to carry out activities straight from the pages of *The Monkey Wrench Gang* even though Earth First! [we agreed] would itself be ostensibly law-abiding'.[8] More than just a wellspring of ideas and approaches, Edward Abbey later spoke at rallies on behalf of Earth First! and wrote the foreword to Earth First!'s 'controversial' book, *Eco-Defense: A Field Guide to Monkeywrenching*. It is important that while Abbey is not an official member of the group, he has supported the organization in a variety of ways.[9]

PRIOR ACTS OF ECOTAGE

While Earth First! garners a lot of the press around the issue of environmental direct action and ecosabotage, it is important to realize that in the USA there has been a long history dating back to at least the end of the Second World War – isolated and discrete groups cut down billboards and survey stakes as well as disabling bulldozers.[10] In the early 1970s militant groups like the Black Mesa Defense disrupted international environmental conferences. In Chicago the 'Fox' plugged industrial drains and smokestacks and dumped effluent at corporate offices.[11] At the same time groups such as the 'Bolt Weevils' (Minnesota),[12] the 'Tucson Ecoraiders' (Arizona),[13] the 'Billboard Bandits' (Michigan) and the 'Eco-Commandos' (Florida)[14] were all involved in acts of sabotage on behalf of the environment.[15]

FAILURE OF RARE II

Despite the long history of environmental actions the issue (and publicity of the phenomenon) of ecoterrorism was fairly obscure throughout the 1970s. A catalyst, however, occurred in 1979, when the US Forest Service had completed an evaluation (the Roadless Area Review Evaluation or RARE II) of the 80 million acres of wilderness under its control and chose to allow 65 million to be open to timber, mining and tourism interests.[16] Arguably, the goal of RARE II was to critique the national forest system and categorize it as either wilderness or study areas, and determine areas for resource exploitation. This evaluation was meant to be the culmination of the agency's inventory of all domestic forest lands eligible for being designated as wilderness areas.[17]

The decision to designate such a low number of acres as off-limits initiated a large amount of opposition from a variety of sources.[18] However, to the dismay of many environmental activists the mainstream movement, in the face of a corporate backlash campaign, 'gave up' the fight – going so far as to pressure the grass roots not to bring a lawsuit against the government. To many activists these actions highlighted the cravenness and limited influence and effectiveness of the mainstream environmental movement in domestic politics.[19]

Dave Foreman, who co-founded Earth First!, began as a volunteer in the movement and was ultimately named the chief lobbyist for the Wilderness Society but at this stage was the number three man in the organization.[20] Like many, Foreman found himself increasingly unhappy with the US mainstream environmental movement.[21] Foreman argued that: 'in their attempts to be "reasonable and credible and politically pragmatic", the environmental movement would come out of those meetings having made all the concessions'.[22] Considering President Carter a 'traitor' and angered by the RARE II decision, Foreman resigned his position in Washington and resumed his old job as the society's Southwest representative.[23]

The review and internal conflict within the Wilderness Society left Foreman feeling 'disillusioned and … discarded'.[24] The decision of the Carter administration, who were meant to be pro-environment, convinced Foreman that this was the inevitable result of the professional lobbyists compromising by working within 'the system' and that the government is the problem, not the solution to protecting the wilderness. Foreman claimed that their opponents had 'gained control' of the battle, stating: 'the anti-environmental side had been extreme, radical, emotional … their arguments had been easily shot full of holes. We had been factual, rational. They looked like fools. We looked like statesmen. Who won? They did.'[25]

Thus 1979 saw three 'disillusioned participants of the mainstream environmental movement' resign from their posts. These activists included Foreman and Bart Koehler (Wilderness Society) and Howie Wolke (Friends of the Earth). All three headed west after 'losing faith' in the system and hoping to create a new and different way to protect the earth.[26] *The Monkey Wrench Gang* novel soon became Foreman's inspiration and his 'model for action'.[27]

Given the problems with the mainstream movement, many environmentalists had come to believe that 'direct action' was the only way to 'counter the softening of the mainstream environmental movement'. Foreman visualized using more aggressive confrontation tactics as 'a means of persuasion':

> It was time for a new joker on the deck. Something more than commenting on dreary environmental-impact statements and writing letters to participants of Congress. Politics in the streets. Civil disobedience. Media stunts. Holding the villains up to ridicule. Using music to charge the cause … all that would be required to join us, we decided, was a belief in Earth first.[28]

ORIGINS OF EARTH FIRST!

Foreman, Koehler and Wolke's loss of faith in the US system and the mainstream environmental movement led to the point where they felt it was necessary to create a new group to protect the biosphere. This maps neatly within Sprinzak's crisis of confidence stage.

The group they created, Earth First!, was established in 1980, possibly after being inspired by Sea Shepherd activists. Foreman stated that he began the group because there was: 'a need for a radical wing that would make the Sierra Club look moderate. Someone needs to say what needs to be said, and do what needs to be done, and take the strong actions to dramatize it.'[29] The creation of Earth First! as an organization has become part of the movement's mythology and many variations of the origin story abound.[30] The creation of Earth First! remains highly contested but some basic facts are known. In April 1980, Foreman and four activist friends – Ron Kezar (Sierra Club), Bart Koehler, Mike Roselle (left-wing groups) and Howie Wolke – went hiking in Mexico's Pinacate Desert. One reporter colourfully described a version of their trip to Mexico:

> They hit the Mexican border running on beer and tequila and an agenda: preserve natural diversity by any means, legal or not, and reclaim lost ground – close logging roads, tear down dams, reintroduce grizzlies and wolves and elk. They united as a 'disorganization' with no official participants and no directors, and called themselves 'Earth First!.[31]

While travelling in Foreman's VW Bus from the Pinacate Desert back to Albuquerque in New Mexico, Foreman is credited on the trip with yelling out 'Earth First', which inspired Roselle to draw a clenched fist logo on the van while Kezar contributed the slogan of 'No Compromise in Defense of Mother Earth'. Together these ideas inspired them to found an environmental group.[32] Part of the mythos of this creation, according to Lee, is that the creation of the new movement happened while the group was drunk in an attempt to emulate *The Monkey Wrench Gang*'s wild-eyed leader Abbey.[33] According to some accounts, Earth First! was created while the group was in the desert or a whorehouse.[34]

At the time, all but Roselle had dedicated their lives to protecting the environment and had worked to that end with mainstream environmental groups.[35] As Martha Lee has pointed out, all the founding participants of Earth First! were remarkably similar in age, education and background. They also all believed that the ongoing destruction of the natural world could only end in an apocalyptic crisis.[36] The men were inspired to action by Rachel Carson's book *Silent Spring*, Aldo Leopold's land-ethic philosophy and Edward Abbey's *The Monkey Wrench Gang*.[37]

During the week away on the Mexico trip from 'the evils of technology and the mores of American society', the four men became even more convinced that Earth was in 'imminent danger' and that the traditional political system was not the solution capable of effectively remedying the crisis.[38] The men also discussed issues such as the environmental movement's current lack of vision; the futility of moderation as an approach; the schism between the movement's professional leadership and the grass-roots activists, and corporate and governmental hostility towards the notion of environmental protection.[39]

Dave Foreman explained: 'the people who started Earth First! decided there was a need for a radical wing that would make the Sierra Club look moderate. Someone needs to say what needs to be said, and do what needs to be done, and take the strong actions to dramatize it.'[40] It was thought, by the four men, that an organization similar to the group in Edward Abbey's *The Monkey Wrench Gang* was required. Such an entity would adopt a neo-Luddite approach that privileged a direct action approach above what they perceived as failing mainstream approaches to protecting the environment.[41] The establishment of the new group was partly a 'rational and strategic act' since the domestic government had failed the environment and a new way forward to protect wilderness was needed. There are thus clear differences between Earth First! and other environmental groups. From its inception the group wanted to operate outside of traditional politics and was concerned with the freedom and simplicity of the wilderness. They wished to provide a 'standard of good' for wilderness that existed prior to political society.[42]

The group determined to ignore the traditional 'anthropocentric' view ('human is first, central and dominant') in support of a 'biocentric' belief system ('humans are only one species in the much grander scheme of things'). They also supported Aldo Leopold's land ethic: 'a thing is right when it tends to preserve the integrity, stability, and beauty of the biotic community, and it is wrong when it tends otherwise'.[43]

The goal of the group was primarily to 'avoid the pitfalls of co-option and moderation'.[44] Further, the time for talk was past and action was needed – but a new kind. They wanted to bring joy back to the environmental movement; keep mainstream groups honest; to provide an outlet to many hardliner conservationists who, disillusioned, had left the movement; they wanted to inspire using *The Monkey Wrench Gang* as a template even though Earth First! would be ostensibly law abiding; and to question the system and develop a new world view, that of biocentrism.[45]

So, according to Dave Foreman, in discussing the establishment of the group the new group needed to make cause, whenever possible, with other progressive elements of society such as feminists, anti-nuclear groups and Native American rights groups, and that they needed to avoid the tending of radicals for 'righteous seriousness' and be willing to laugh at themselves, since it 'preserve[s] individual and group sanity, it retards hubris, a major cause of environmental rape, and it is also an effective weapon'.[46] Earth First! publicized themselves as a 'radical' organization. Foreman declared, 'it was ridiculous that off-roaders were macho men and backpackers were considered wimps'. Roselle further claimed, 'not all environmentalists are granola-crunching hippies. Some of us are rednecks and cowboys'.[47]

Post the Road Trip

Following the trip to Mexico, on 4 April 1980 Foreman and his friends set about establishing an 'Earth First!' that they believed would 'take an uncompromising, militant stand in defense of the environment and engage in direct action ranging from civil disobedience to terrorist attacks'.[48]

However, they were unsure how to translate their high-minded goals into concrete steps. First they created a mailing list of 75 influential contacts they knew, sent them the biodiversity listing, and considered what was the next step.[49] In autumn 1981, Foreman, Kezar and Koehler began a cross-country trip they called the 'inaugural Earth First! "Road Show"' to publicize their new organization, celebrate wilderness values and the need to fight to protect nature.[50] They spoke at colleges and held meetings (a mixture of populism, protests, humour and ecological agitation), believing people were ready to hear their message.[51]

Earth First! began slowly with only 13 participants, and has increasingly grown into a large organization; 75 people attended a rally in 1981, but at the second in 1982 more than 400 attended.[52] Earth First! is well known for accepting diversity in its participants and being tolerant to various points of view and beliefs, providing that participants accept the need for direct action:

> [W]hile there is a broad diversity within Earth First! from animal rights vegans to wilderness hunting guides, from monkeywrenchers[53] to careful followers of Gandhi, from whiskey-drinking backwoods riffraff to thoughtful philosophers, from misanthropes to humanists there is agreement on one thing, the need for action![54]

Within a year of its creation, participants in Earth First! increased to more than 1,500 (as measured by the group's newsletter subscriptions), arguably 'making Earth First! … the fastest-growing environmental group in history'.[55] According to *Japenga*, by 1985 over 6,500 readers were on the mailing list for Earth First!'s newsletter.[56] The group continued to grow, numbering about 10,000 participants by 1989. Furthermore, as pointed out by Manes, Earth First! sympathizers in the mainstream environmental movement was estimated to be many times that figure.[57] According to

Roselle, the most important thing to him was to engage, and that meant confrontation with their opponents. Such vigorous confrontation was how Earth First! defined itself, and its initial victories validated that tactical approach.[58] Earth First! introduced a new culture, tactics, discourse, a rejuvenated optimism and explored different forms of non-violent direct actions including civil disobedience, guerilla theatre, non-violent demonstrations and, ultimately, 'monkeywrenching'.[59]

EARTH FIRST! PHILOSOPHY

Members of Earth First! believed a biocentric approach to nature is correct in that 'nature has an inherent right to exist and should not be exploited'.[60] Many of the leaders of the organization were familiar with the biocentric philosophy of Aldo Leopold, Arne Naess, Bill Devall and George Sessions.[61] A recurring theme in the organization is its belief in the philosophy of deep ecology.[62] Lee argues that the views and beliefs of deep ecology became a fundamental part of the movement's ideology in 1984.[63] During a speech in Sacramento, California, Foreman discussed deep ecology as a reason he joined the environmental movement:

> Why preserve a wilderness area? Because it's a nice place to go and relax? Because you can make pretty books of pictures of it? To protect a watershed? No. You protect a river because its [sic] a river. For its own sake. Because it has a right to exist by itself. The grizzly bear in Yellowstone Park has as much right to her life as any one of us has to our life. Each of you is an animal and should be proud of it.[64]

The group believes that humans are not divinely granted dominion over other species and are merely one life form amongst many. The concept promoted by some groups of a notion of 'benevolent stewardship' towards the earth is rejected as that implies dominance of the planet.[65] Rather the group promoted that large areas needed to be quarantined from industrial human civilization.[66] Earth First!ers further believed that they would have a leading role in creating new biocentric communities.[67]

The group was also inspired by Aldo Leopold's philosophy and the need to protect wilderness. Dave Foreman argued:

> That in *any* decision, consideration for the health of the Earth must come first, or as Aldo Leopold said, 'A thing is right when it tends to preserve the integrity, stability, and beauty of the biotic community. It is wrong when it tends otherwise ... It is not enough to protect our few remaining bits of wilderness. The only hope for Earth (and humanity for that matter) is to

withdraw huge areas as inviolate natural sanctuaries from the depredations of modern industry and technology.[68]

It is important to understand that Earth First!'s radical stance involved the biocentric belief that 'the natural world should be preserved *for its own sake*, not for the sake of any real or imagined benefits to humanity'.[69] Earth First! saw itself as not so much a reform group calling, for example, for stronger air-quality standards but engaged in ethical and cultural defiance with the aim of reframing the environmental issue.[70] Thus it has been argued that Earth First!, inspired by the deep ecology philosophy, introduced the extremist agenda to the broader environmental movement with its ideas of civil disobedience as the central idea of direct actions:[71]

Lee argues that the immediate political imperative of Earth First! was to preserve as much remaining wilderness as achievable to enable continued life and evolution on the planet.[72]

No Real Underlying Philosophy

While undoubtedly influenced by biocentric writings it is clear, however, that Earth First! as a group adhere to no real underpinning philosophy. Writing about Edward Abbey's statement that there is no 'underlying philosophy in *The Monkey Wrench Gang* and therefore none in Earth First!', Foreman has written, 'let our actions set the finer points of our philosophy … To act, to trust your instincts, to go with the flow of natural forces, *is* an underlying philosophy. Talk is cheap. Action is dear.'[73] George Draffan (Earth Front! activist) once told a reporter, 'most people in Earth First! are not dependent on books to explain their own view of things. I don't think it has much effect. We have a pretty simple philosophy and very simple feelings about things.'[74]

This is reflected in the group's early publications of the group's newsletter that are striking in their paucity of philosophical discussion. Rather, contributors focused on ending the current political system.[75] Liddick argues that while most Earth Front! activists abhorred philosophy they had no issue in identifying their 'enemy'.[76] Most Earth Front!ers were uncomfortable with 'identifying a philosophical source for their beliefs', maintaining that their beliefs are bolstered by scientific documents and evidence observed from the world around them that there is an environmental crisis.[77]

Thus their approach to their beliefs was almost an intuitive one.[78] Many Earth First!ers preferred this intuitive approach, arguing that it was not necessary to read philosophy in order to 'have their lives explained to them'.[79] The founding participants attempted to convey their ideas in 'myth, ritual and song'. According to Arnold, the written word was problematic for Earth First!ers as it could lead to dogma, and the downgrading of their beliefs to just another interpretation.[80]

However, it is important to note that, despite a general aversion to philosophy and the written word by participants, it is clear that their 'intuitive feelings' approach was clearly influenced by deep ecology.[81] Bron Taylor argues that as the group developed there was a decreasing emphasis on the tenets of deep ecology and a corresponding increase in the influence of green anarchist thought, leading to a privileging of primitivism as an approach.[82] According to Martha Lee, Earth First!'s ecological-centred philosophy and tactics also embodied aspects of both millenarian and apocalyptic movements. Lee views biocentric philosophy and the use of direct action as identical to the approach used by apocalyptics, who were willing to go to any lengths to prepare for the end of the world.[83] Earth First! activists also believed that they were destined to have 'a special role in this imminent end of history'.[84]

Earth First! and the Concept of Wilderness

Earth First!'s major issue of concern, at least initially, was the loss of wilderness. In early Earth First! documents, Wolke and Foreman define wilderness as 'areas that are large enough to support a complete ecosystem and that are free from human influence'.[85] Dave Foreman, in keeping with biocentric thought, insisted that wilderness and the diversity of life it contained had an inherent right to exist that should not be justified by reference to its use to humans.[86] According to Foreman, Earth First! had a more ambitious goal – that of restoring the natural world to its homeostatic wild state. Foreman stated:

> Wilderness is the essence of everything we're after. We aren't an environmental group. Environmental groups worry about environmental health hazards to human beings, they worry about clean air and water for the benefit of people and ask us why we're so wrapped up in something as irrelevant and tangential and elitist as wilderness.[87]

Early publications of the group's newsletter focused on the need to save what remained of the North American wilderness, and reclaim greater wilderness.[88] The organization's initial platform demanded the creation of 41 wilderness areas covering 137 million acres.[89] Earth First! advocated for a national wilderness proposal whereby ecological reserves would be set up and 'the developments of man will be obliterated'. Such reserves would have no permanent human habitation (with the exception of indigenous peoples with traditional lifestyles) and no technology allowed within the regions.[90] Furthermore, this proposal called for 'restoration ecology' to occur, which would include the removal of exotic species, reintroducing extirpated species (such as timber wolves), and the dismantling of industrial features, for example, dams and roads. However, it is important to note, it did not propose for the removal of civilization.[91] In June 1983, 'Earth First! revealed its 'Wilderness Preserve System'. It called for 50 reserves comprising 716 million acres to be established that would be off-limits to human civilization.[92] For about a decade, according to Zakin, proposals put forth by Earth First! for biological reserves were largely ignored. By the 1990s, those ideas had come to mainstream environmental groups and were even debated in the pages of the *New York Times* and *The Atlantic*.[93]

Earth First! and Spirituality

Taylor argues that, for the most part, many Earth First! participants were motivated by their own 'spiritual experiences' as regards nature, which had convinced them of the 'interrelatedness and sanctity of all life'.[94] Foreman, though, insisted: '[Earth First!ers] are not devotees of some Teilhardian New Age eco-la-la that says we must transcend our base animal nature and take charge of our evolution in order to become higher moral beings'.[95] According to Arnold, Foreman was not impressed with the 'Dungeons and Dragons' direction the organization was taking, being concerned that the new organization was too 'New Age' in its emphasis on vegetarianism and non-aggression.[96]

However, this did not mean that Foreman did not possess religious feelings for the earth. He once told an interviewer that the environment is: 'religious in a non-supernatural sense … we have an ethical, reciprocal relationship with the land. We are, for lack of a better term, talking about our souls.'[97]

While Earth First! has no ties to Christianity, Arnold argues that is has emerged as a 'civil religion', with 'the characteristics of more traditional millenarian religious movements: the participants were the chosen people; all subsequent history would be understood as a battle between good and evil, where good was defined as progress toward their goals and evil as reaction; the innocence and purity of the first creation will reappear in a future time; their politics constituted the good'.[98]

Foreman proudly announced his own paganism, stating: 'I hold my personal religious views towards Mother Earth just as strongly and sincerely as any Christian.' He went on to portray himself as a 'howling-at-the-moon-pantheist'.[99] Foreman, however, became increasingly uncomfortable with the overt, organized role of paganism within Earth First!. As a result, in 1983 he wrote an article (under the pseudonym 'Chim Blea') 'criticizing the preoccupation with spiritual enlightenment as detrimental to effective environmental action'.[100]

Industrial Civilization

Earth First! believed that the industrial complex, in collusion with the US government, was destroying the 'planet's vital ecosystems'.[101] They were concerned that the prevailing industrialization was facilitating a 'biological meltdown' whereby one-third to one-half of the world's biodiversity would become extinct, creating a cataclysmic event that would threaten the world.[102] Foreman argued that the decimation of human civilization was required so that the planet could recover from 'humanpox'. He perceived that humans were a 'disease plaguing the earth', a view that had been supported by many radical greens.[103] As such, Earth First!ers hoped and worked towards ending 'industrial civilization to protect wilderness areas and thus were drawn to a primitivist ethos'.[104] Activists within the Earth First! organization considered it their responsibility to save as much of the wilderness as feasible, so that after the impending apocalypse, biodiversity and evolution would continue.[105]

According to the group, the prevention of the end of human civilization required fundamental changes to government, a halt to industry and cultural changes such as banning cars and range cattle. However, such calls for sweeping change, by their nature, rendered such alterations highly unpalatable and nigh on impossible to achieve.[106]

Earth First! and Overpopulation

Many Earth First!ers perceived human overpopulation as a fundamental cause of the environmental crisis. As such, to live those beliefs many participants volunteered to be sterilized. One Earth First!er explains, 'My strongest belief is that the human population needs to allow people who want to die to have the right to die, and we need to really cut down on having kids … I personally have had my tubes tied. I practice what I preach.'[107] However, not all Earth Firster!s held this view. While denouncing others for reproducing, many Earth First!ers believed that they had a duty to reproduce, because 'all people are *not* equal in comprehending or defending the earth'.[108]

Given the belief that human overpopulation was a critical issue for many Earth First!ers, that concern on a number of occasions spilt over into issuing racist proclamations, in particular calling for restrictions on

Hispanic immigration into the USA.[109] Foreman voiced his support of Edward Abbey's view that the USA needed to impose an immigration moratorium in order to 'put an end to social and environmental ills from "mass unemployment" and "an overload welfare system" to "rotting cities and a poisoned environment"'.[110]

Some participants also went so far as to invite a misanthropic reading of their statements.[111] Infamously, Foreman once made the following comment regarding famine in Ethiopia: 'the best thing would be to let nature seek its own balance and let the people there starve'.[112] As Chase argues, Foreman's comments with regards to immigration and famine suggest an indifference to human suffering similar to the power elites Foreman has criticized – 'the thugs who run modern society'.[113]

John Davis (the original editor of the *Earth First! Journal*) once advocated that eradicating smallpox would be wrong since it plays a role in balancing ecosystems. Critics pointed to an *Earth First! Journal* article of 1 May 1987, which argued that the Acquired Immunodeficiency Syndrome (AIDS) disease was a welcome development since it undermined industrial civilization and would lead to preserving wilderness areas.[114] That article written by Christopher Manes (under the penname 'Miss Ann Thropy') suggested to its readers that AIDS: 'was nature's way of protecting the planet from excess population … I take it as axiomatic that the only real hope for the continuation of diverse ecosystems on this planet is an enormous decline in population. If the AIDS epidemic didn't exist, radical environmentalists would have to invent one.'[115] While some sympathizers argued that the more misanthropic statements were mere hyperbole, designed to attract public attention to their cause, other participants believed that such articles were a 'public relations nightmare'.[116]

For 'Miss Ann Thropy' and those activists who agreed with her views, altering the beliefs and norms of the populace was futile. The release of Miss Ann Thropy's article and the ensuing controversy, however, demonstrated that many participants rejected this approach, instead arguing that education could bring about meaningful change.[117] Thus we can observe a distinct division occurring in Earth First! at this point, with conflict and debate raging around the movement's ideology and vision. Those participants who supported Foreman were misanthropic, leading them to conclude that human nature was immutable and the goal was merely to save as much wilderness as they could until the environmental meltdown eventuated. Mike Roselle led the 'social justice faction', which linked human issues with environmental needs and adopted the millenarian ideal that the end goal was establishing a post-apocalyptic ideal (socially and environmentally) society.[118] They argued that since humans would live through the collapse of industrial civilization and biological meltdown that thought needed to be given as to how such a human society would look.[119]

According to Liddick, the organization's belief system is a millenarian one where participants are on a mission of historic importance to save future generations after the pending environmental catastrophe.[120] However, Tayor argues that Lee characterizes one strand of Earth First!ers as 'apocalyptic biocentrists' who are more willing to undertake terrorist violence.[121]

PRINCIPLES OF EARTH FIRST!

It is also important to note that within the group there is a 'set of core tenets' to which all activists are meant to adhere.[122] Foreman later set out a list of principles by which the new organization was to live. The final point was 'Earth is Goddess and the proper object of human worship'. While this one was quickly dropped from the list, both the religious (and feminist) themes are apparent.[123] Foreman claimed the Earth Goddess clause was a result of his fleeting interest in a feminist theologian named Starhawk.[124]

The group's 'Statement of Principles' was developed by Dave Foreman and Howie Wolke and distributed to participants who had expressed a commitment to the cause Wyoming Rendezvous.[125] The Statement of Principles read:

- Wilderness has a right to exist for its own sake.
- All life forms, from virus to the great whales, have an inherent and equal right to existence.
- Humankind is no greater than any other form of life and has no legitimate claim to dominate Earth.
- Humankind, through overpopulation, anthropocentrism, industrialization, excessive energy consumption/resource extraction, state capitalism, father-figure hierarchies, imperialism, pollution and natural area destruction, threatens the basic life processes of EARTH.
- All human decisions should consider Earth first, humankind second.
- The only true test of morality is whether an action, individual, social or political, benefits Earth.
- Humankind will be happier, healthier, more secure and more comfortable in a society that recognizes humankind's true biological nature and which is in dynamic harmony with the total biosphere.

- Political compromise has no place in the defence of Earth.
- Earth is Goddess and the proper object of human worship.[126]

These principles embodied a biocentric perspective. The idea of promoting wilderness is considered an absolute good, against which all subsequent actions should be judged with all species considered equal and of intrinsic value.[127] In response to negative reactions of public and government officials following the release of his book, Foreman was forced to further outline the guiding principles of the movement in a May (1985) article published in the Earth First! journal. Foreman clarified that Earth First!ers believed in biocentrism and the need to place Earth first. He also noted that the group was non-hierarchical and welcomed diverse participants, from 'animal rights vegetarians to wilderness hunting guides, from monkeywrenchers to followers of Gandhi … from bitter misanthropes to true humanitarians'.[128]

Foreman cautioned, however, that Earth First! was a militant organization and would not change to suit those who did not like it. If participants were unhappy with militancy they should leave to form their own entity.[129] An editorial published by Foreman argued that Earth First!ers were not terrorists but rather radicals – compared to the mainstream environmental movement they were radicals. He told the readers that the symbol of Earth First! was a clenched fist, with all that it entailed.[130]

ROUND RIVER RENDEZVOUS: ANNUAL MEETING

Earth First!'s first annual meeting, also known as the Round River Rendezvous, occurred during the fourth of July weekend, 1980 at the T-Cross Ranch in DuBois, Wyoming. The name of the meeting was inspired by Aldo Leopold's work, *The Round River – A Parable*.[131] Over 60 activists attended the first Round River Rendezvous. According to Lee, the majority of the attendees were from the western states or Washington DC.[132] At the meeting organizational details were elucidated, as were proposed ideological parameters.[133]

It developed into an annual event with seminars on 'civil disobedience training' on chaining themselves to equipment and how best to blockade various site entrances.[134] All were welcome to the event no matter what their political beliefs or lifestyle choices. What brought them all together was a wish to save the environment.[135]

The first meeting also created a central authority divided into two governing structures: the Circle of Darkness and *La Manta Mojada* ('The Wet Blanket'). A breakdown of the two structures was as follows:

1. The Circle of Darkness had 12 participants, including the five Buckaroos and Susan Morgan, who was put in charge of the bank account, participant dues, the participant list and the newsletter.
2. *La Manta Mojada* was made up of eight advisors to the Circle, whose names were kept secret because they all came from moderate conservative groups.[136]

Movement, Not an Organization

Earth First! claimed it was an anti-hierarchical disorganization with no official leaders, no national headquarters, no participant lists, no dues paid by participants, no board of directors and, unlike mainstream environmental groups, no tax-exempt status as it refused to seek being designated a non-profit organization.[137] Dave Foreman, in *More on Earth First! and the Monkey Wrench Gang*, points out that Earth First! is a movement as opposed to a formally organized group. He further argues that, for example, there are many opinions within the movement regarding the use of direct action and monkeywrenching but, as at the time the editor of *Earth First! Journal*,[138] he maintains, 'I do not advocate it nor do I *not* advocate it. It is a personal decision.'[139]

The lack of apparent structure within the Earth First! organization was 'reinforced by the movement's 1982 declaration that individuals were not *participants* of Earth First!', that they were not compelled to the movement by being participants but rather by their espoused ideals.[140] The putative disorganized manner of the organization was done purposefully. According to co-founder Dave Foreman, 'we felt that if we took on an organization of the industrial state, we would soon accept their anthropocentric paradigm, much as Audubon and the Sierra Club already had'.[141] Foreman reportedly posed the following question to the activists: 'So what is the one kind of human organization that's really worked?' The answer was the hunter-gatherer tribe, which the organization attempted to model itself after.[142] According to Arnold, it is important to note, contrary to many proclamations that 'Earth First has always been a "movement" and not an "organization", and that its participants are "Earth Firsters" and not "participants", it was well-organized at the beginning and participants were called participants'.[143]

However, as noted earlier, there was a leadership group at the core of the 'movement'. According to Lee, the Circle of Darkness was to be the organization's 'national coordinating committee', a group of individuals whose role was to determine policy, approve participants and state and local groups, select new participants of the Circle, and generally 'run the outfit'.[144] Furthermore, Circle participants had to be willing to be publicly identified with the movement but were barred from being employees or officers of mainstream environmental groups. Curiously, Foreman was unsure if the new group needed officers but he wanted a treasurer appointed immediately.[145]

The organization's second 'original governing structure' was *La Manta Mojada*, 'an official and secret group of advisors to the Circle'.[146] This group of advisors was made up of participants already part of moderate environmental groups.[147] As *La Manta Mojada* was never again mentioned within the group's newsletters, Lee notes, it is impossible to make an analysis of its evolution. However, it is important to note that, in later interviews, Foreman suggested that, 'its existence was short-lived and implied that is was also ineffectual; Earth First!'s doctrine and actions were independent in both spirit and practice.'[148] However, according to Arnold, the notion of 'rejecting hierarchy and authority' was beyond the entity's grasp and the group quickly turned to a structure of hierarchy and authority.[149]

Despite these controlling entities, ostensible public leadership of the movement was frowned upon: 'any figure who even begins to consider her or himself an authoritative leader is usually quickly and effectively blocked or deposed of by other activists within this radically egalitarian group'.[150] Despite the principal role played by Dave Foreman, Earth First! appears to have had no charismatic leader to enforce their will on the group. Without the assistance of a public leader there is, arguably, an increased amount of (and continual) debate within the organization. One forum that allows for such debate is *Earth First! Journal*, which: 'insist[s] that every one be allowed to speak in favour of unpopular articles apparently promoting violence'. Such a forum can create a 'moderating effect' within the debate.[151]

EARTH FIRST! DIRECT ACTION MANUAL

Earth First! put out a do-it-yourself guide to sabotage actions. According to the disclaimer within the manual, 'the attached document, the "Earth First! Direct Action Manual", hereby referred to as "The Manual", has been written for entertainment purpose only'.[152] According to the manual, before any action, the activist must:

- Know the people in your Affinity Group (AG) by name and face.
- Know any pertinent medical information for each person.
- Know who the support coordinators are (if applicable).
- Know where people who are arrested are likely to be taken.
- Know contact phone numbers to update the organizers.
- Be sure your name, phone number where you can be reached, and how long you will be available for support work are written on your AG data list.[153]

The manual further outlines what the group considers to be good security measures, including: 'sharing action information on a need to know basis and only within your affinity group, reserving sensitive issue discussions to be held person to person and never over the phone, adopting aliases, selectively using code language when needed'.[154] According to the manual, one effective strategy for preventing or intervening with such actions is through hunt sabotage, meaning 'direct intervention and are meant to disrupt or stop a hunt. Actions can take the form of blockades, harassment, propaganda, etc.'[155]

These small 'affinity' groups are responsible for the majority of acts of sabotage. Often, such acts are not publicized, even to other participants of the larger organization, due in part to a lack of trust.[156] Many activists who engaged in direct action did so in tiny, insular cells that had little interaction with other cells. As such, the movement can be best understood as a 'leaderless resistance' model, albeit with some qualification, as some participants were suspected of playing more central roles within Earth First![157] However, some activists had concerns regarding the 'closed nature' of some groups, worrying that the movement could eventually 'drop out of sight' and there was no way to build a mass movement with such an approach – a concern shared eventually by Ronnie Lee, the creator of the ALF.[158]

The make-up of the organization (for example, leadership structure and the use of 'decentralized cells') and its fundamental values were all modelled after the ALF. It was agreed that the new environmental organization would attempt to:

1. Cause as much economic damage as possible to a given entity that is profiting off the destruction of the natural environment and life for selfish greed and profit.
2. To educate the public on the atrocities committed against the environment and life.
3. To take all precautions against harming life.[159]

GLOBAL REACH OF EARTH FIRST! CELLS

A complete and accurate tally of Earth First! chapters is impossible, as the groups tend to be ad hoc and issue specific. An examination of the Earth First! website includes a list of cells that have operated globally, including: EF! Cascadia, EF! Britain, EF! Melbourne, EF! Netherlands, EF! Prague, EF! Sierra Nevada, and also in Poland, Nigeria, Mexico and the Philippines.[160] While Earth First! has not been as active in Europe, research suggests that, when they are involved in a campaign, it is usually modelled from previous activities by radical environmentalists in the USA.[161] According to Liddick, the 'big tent' approach favoured by the social justice faction of the organization enlarged the Earth First! group to include anti-Iraq war petitions, 'Impeach Bush Now' and 'Stop the Seal Pup Slaughter'.[162]

EARTH FIRST! PARTICIPANTS

As a 'disorganization' the number of activists in the group can only be estimated. It is believed that the organization has at different times included approximately 12,000–15,000 non-participants. The group prides itself on having no paid staff, no centralizing hierarchy and no by-laws to constrain participants' activities.[163] Participants of Earth First! are thus individually responsible for their actions during protests.[164] As of 19 January 2006, of those named for committing Earth First! actions, of 11 indictments five were men and six were women.[165]

Viewing Themselves as Radicals?

In their demands to preserve and recreate wilderness, Earth First!ers did not view themselves as radicals. Instead, they claimed it was those destroying the earth, what they termed the 'corporate/industrial monolith', who were the aggressors.[166] In Foreman's book, *Ecodefense: A Field Guide to Monkeywrenching*, he claims that direct action undertaken by Earth First! 'does not aim to overthrow any social, political or economic system'.[167] However, his does not necessarily accord with other pronouncements where members have stated their preference for a different political and economic system. Perhaps the discrepancy can be explained that members were not calling for the violent overthrow of the system, but rather 'prodding' or cajoling the system to evolve.

THE FIRST ACTION: GLEN CANYON

Following the trip to Mexico, Dave Foreman quietly began a programme of guerilla theatre tactics that would soon become the calling card of Earth First! actions. One of the first such acts involved Foreman and several other activists trekking to Cooney (New Mexico, Gila Wilderness), where they put up a plaque honouring the Apache tribe for raiding a mining camp in 1880 and for being willing to protect mountains from the depredations of the white race.[168]

The fundamental goal of the 'Monkey Wrench Gang' (in Edward Abbey's novel), that of destroying the Glen Canyon Dam, was one shared by many environmentalists. Activists saw the dam as a key symbol of the mainstream environmental movement's compromise with the government.[169] Foreman and his fellow activists organized their first public action on 21 March 1981 (spring equinox) when 75 activists rallied at the dam holding signs with slogans including 'Free the Colorado' and 'Let It Flow'.[170]

Earth First! activists knew the importance of their action at Glen Canyon Dam even then. According to Roselle, the activists knew they were making history and this was the birth of a needed radical environmental movement if the planet was to endure.[171] The activists brought with them an 'awkward black bundle'; four men and one woman on the dam attached ropes to the dam, and while shouting 'Earth First!' released 300 ft of black plastic to activist cheers, creating the impression of a growing crack in the dam wall. The dam breaking was a particular fear of the downwater local community and the carrying out of this act in the eyes of some made this a terrorist act, but for others it was merely a prank.[172]

The activists knew that such actions could capture the attention of the media and the US public. According to Foreman:

> The Glen Canyon Dam caper brought EARTH FIRST! an unexpected degree of media attention. Participantship in our group has spiraled to more than a thousand participants from Maine to Hawaii. Even the Government is interested – according to reliable reports, the FBI dusted the entire Glen Canyon Dam crack for fingerprints![173]

ACTIONS IN THE 1980s

Following the Glen Canyon protest in November 1982, Earth First! organized its first civil disobedience action, a protest near to New Mexico's Salt Creek Wilderness Area, where Yates Petroleum had mineral rights to an exploration site with a lease set to run out on 1 November. The proposed site intersected a national wildlife refuge, next to their site. The company had begun drilling, after the US Fish and Wildlife Service challenged the exploration without success.[174] On 25 April 1983, Earth First!'s first blockade of the Bald Mountain Road commenced, when four Earth First!ers blockaded a caterpillar tractor involved in a construction project.[175]

By May 1982, there were over 2,000 activists in the organization and the organization had 'cell groups scattered across the United States'. In the beginning, Foreman supported such diversity believing that anyone who was willing to adopt the creed that 'the earth must come first' was welcome. However, by this time Foreman could no longer assume that all joining activists believed in his vision of biocentrism. The majority of early adopters had shared his political experience and beliefs, but these new participants did not necessarily do so.[176]

For example, the first major campaign for the organization was the 'No G-O Road' in California and Oregon. However, many of the people flocking to help were younger people with differing political histories and political goals to the founders, with many being 'career activists' involved in multiple political causes, for example, pro-choice reproductive rights and anti-nuclear protesting. For these activists environmental issues were 'only one of the world's many problems' that needed to be addressed and biocentrism was not necessarily the solution.[177]

By December 1982, over 50 local Earth First! groups had sprung up and it had begun a global presence with a group forming in New South Wales, Australia.[178] A second 'global campaign' commenced in Australia in 1984. While few Earth First! activists actually travelled to Australia to participate in the Australian Rainforest Campaign, the movement tendered its support in other ways. According to Lee, these offshoot Earth First! organizations grew both in size and visibility and functioned as informal umbrella organizations for the many local affinity cell groups that existed in different locales, such as Florida and Montana.[179]

Earth First! quickly set up a second civil disobedience protest, this time in New Mexico at the Bisti Badlands in 1983, which had been initially proposed for a new wilderness designation but instead had been again designated a mining site. Approximately 50 Earth First! activists trespassed on the site, burned in effigy Interior Secretary James Watt and Sunbelt mining executive Jerry Geist, and sang 'America the Beautiful', with the goal of being arrested in the glare of the media. The stunt failed when the police did not arrive and private security had been advised not to engage with the protesters. In the end the activists declared their action a success, since the site was included on the next round of wilderness studies.[180]

In terms of actions undertaken, Earth First! was most active during the mid-1980s.[181] Following a series of small actions in 1986, public awareness was raised but problematically few tangible results were achieved. Few wilderness areas, their key demand, were actually protected. The Reagan administration proved particularly intractable on this point, given their overall attitude to environmental protection.[182]

By 1988, the Earth First! group had an annual budget of approximately $50,000.[183] That year, the organization was making a profit of over $200,000,[184] and its 'Ned Ludd Books' and 'Trinkets and Snake Oil' were selling well. From its initial creation, it is important to note, Foreman had wanted the group to be a 'small, ideologically united tribe' but given the growth in numbers and financial success, Lee argues the movement went from being millenarian in nature to apocalyptic.[185]

Offshoot radical environmental groups not officially affiliated with Earth First! were willing to go much further than Earth First!'s publicly stated position on violence. These participants were convinced that Earth First!'s civil disobedience approach was not radical enough and wanted to adopt a more militant method (Sprinzak's conflict of legitimacy category) – that of ecotage.

One such group facetiously calling itself the Evan Mecham Eco Terrorism International Conspiracy (EMETIC), named after the then Republican Governor of Arizona, operated out of Prescott, Arizona. In 1986 the group first damaged ski lifts at the Fairfield Snow Bowl near Flagstaff causing US $50,000 worth of damage. They also sent a letter to the CEO containing the unlikely threat to: 'chain the Fairfield CEO to a tree at the 10,000-foot level and feed him shrubs and roots until he understands the suicidal folly of treating the planet primarily as a tool for making money'.[186]

On 5 October 1987, EMETIC participants, angered by a resort's planned expansion on to sacred Native American land, struck again utilizing a propane-cutting torch to damage the main cable chairlift at the Fairfield ski resort in Arizona. Earth First! participants Mark Davis (an anti-nuclear activist), Marc Baker (a biologist) and Peg Millet (a self-described 'redneck woman' who worked at planned parenthood) were involved in the action. On 25 September 1988 EMETIC participants, once again including Davis, Millet and now Ilse Asplund, collapsed power-line poles leading to a uranium mine near the Grand Canyon in Arizona. A month later, they were involved in an action that severed the 'chairlift's main support pylon' at Fairfield.[187]

During this time, an FBI agent (Mike Fain) had infiltrated the group under the assumed name of Mike Tait as part of Operation THERMCON.[188] According to the *New York Times*, the FBI spent two years investigating Earth First!, believing the group to be part of a 'domestic terrorism network'. According to Long, in-fighting within Earth First! had seen Foreman distance himself from his own organization, but Fain and the FBI made every effort to involve him with the goal of implicating him in the activities of EMETIC. Furthermore, according to Long, the FBI plan was to convince Earth First! activists to use thermite to topple a power line so that Foreman could be accused of being a terrorist willing to utilize explosives.[189]

On 30 May 1989, several participants of EMETIC (including Mike Fain) planned to topple a transmission tower near Wenden, Arizona. Just as the cutting was about to occur, 50 FBI agents revealed themselves and arrested Davis and Baker but Millet evaded capture. Both she and Foreman, however, were arrested the next day.[190] The FBI argued that bringing down the power lines in Wenden was a 'dry run' before attempting to do the same to electrical transmission lines that led to the Rocky Flats, Colorado nuclear weapons base.[191]

At least 15 people with links to Earth First!'s international organization were subpoenaed by a federal grand jury in Phoenix, Arizona.[192] Although not on the actual raid Foreman was charged on the basis that he had supplied \$580 and two copies of his book *Ecodefense* to the other activists.[193] As part of the case, the FBI maintained that the group's activities were 'dry runs for a larger conspiracy to damage power lines leading to nuclear facilities in Arizona, California and Colorado'. The legal trial ran through the summer of 1991. In the end, all the defendants accepted plea bargains, with Asplund and Baker sentenced to one year in federal prison as well as fines and community service. Millet served three years in federal prison and Davis six, and both had to pay restitution to Fairfield in the amount of US \$19,821.[194]

Foreman was the main target because the US government maintained that he was the ringleader. Assistant US Attorney Roger Dokken told the court: 'Mr. Foreman is the worst of the group, he sneaks around in the background ... I don't like to use the analogy of a Mafia boss, but they never do anything either. They just sent their munchkins out to do it.'[195]

Foreman was successfully distanced from the rest of the defendants, with his attorney arguing that he had not been directly involved with any of the actions. Furthermore, Foreman's lawyer (Gerry Spence) argued that the entire scheme had been an egregious example of law enforcement entrapment. This was inadvertently echoed by the undercover FBI agent who was caught on his body tape stating: '[Foreman] isn't really the guy we need to pop … in terms of the actual perpetrator … This is the guy we need to pop to send a message, and that's all we're really doing … If we don't nail this guy, we're not sending a message.'[196]

Foreman effectively used the tape as proof that the FBI's goal was to 'intimidate the entire environmental and social-justice movement in this country'.[197] Despite this, Foreman eventually pleaded guilty to conspiracy to commit property destruction and was sentenced to five years' jail, postponed for five years when he could either change his plea or plead guilty to a misdemeanour.[198] Foreman eventually paid a fine of US $250 in 1996.[199]

Even prior to the arrest and trial of the 'Arizona 5' as they became known, Earth First! had been riven between the deep ecologist factions who were focused on wilderness and environmental issues (including Foreman), and social ecologists who stressed the need for social justice and change as the *raison d'être* of the organization.[200] By 1987, its participants reflected this divide. Whereas early activists (prior to campaigns in California and Oregon) were older than 30, had been conservationist activists, primarily lived in the American Southwest and believed in biocentrism and monkeywrenching, newer participants were younger, West Coast career activists involved in multiple political causes.[201]

The social ecologist faction was led primarily by Judi Bari and Mike Roselle.[202] Bari's aim was to expand Earth First! into a broad environmental movement and she believed the use of direct and violent action would alienate other like-minded activists, which Foreman opposed.[203] For Bari's faction, 'opposing social injustice ha[d] an importance equal to that of working for wilderness protection'.[204] They were determined to take Earth First! in a more explicit 'leftist' direction heavily influenced by anarchist and, to some extent, feminist political thought.[205] The newer activists' beliefs made them hesitant to participate in any action that might prevent their activities or lead others to question the legitimacy of their broader causes. As such, the new recruits were more interested in civil disobedience than direct action.[206]

Many of this bloc believed that environmental initiatives would be unable to bring about radical change without a larger-scale social change (tackling large-scale problems such as racism and poverty). The new activists believed that, to achieve biocentric equality, it would mean that changes to human nature were required to bring about biocentrism and social justice outcomes:

> [W]e have to deal with humans in order to save as much wilderness as we can, we have to change as much human behaviour as we can … therefore we

> are engaged in the activity of changing human consciousness and changing human behaviour.[207] (Interview, Darryl Cherney, 10 April 1991, Ballard, WA)

Foreman disagreed, however, claiming Earth First! was 'big enough to contain street poets and cowboy bar bouncers, agnostics and pagans, vegetarian and raw steak eaters, pacifists and those who think that turning the other cheek is a good way to get a sore face'.[208]

By 1987, Foreman and other activists who believed in biocentrism were worried about the size of the movement and this preference for civil disobedience acts over monkeywrenching. Foreman argued that the focus on public education was in opposition to the doctrine, as it 'suggested that human welfare was more important than wilderness'.[209] That same year the 'Miss Ann Thropy' AIDS article further split the organization. The biocentrists supported the sentiments expressed while the social justice faction was horrified. This opposition was further intensified when Edward Abbey wrote a letter to the *Bloomsbury Review* in 1987 to suggest that 'to prevent further population pressure on its borders, the United States should close its borders to all immigrants'.[210]

The ideological cleavages the organization was experiencing were demonstrated by the quest to control the journal. In the beginning, with a small number of activists, only Earth First!'s 'governing body', 'The Circle of Darkness' produced work to be disseminated in the journal, allowing for a sense of 'purity' with regards to ideological beliefs. However, with the schism between the two factions, the journal became a 'forum for ideological debates'. These debates were also fought out at the national conferences (when representatives from many chapters met) where the atmosphere was characterized as 'hostile' and 'unproductive'.[211] For Foreman, such ideological disagreements were antithetical to what he thought the group should stand for and he came to believe such internal wrangling threatened to 'compromise the basic tenets of Earth First!, or make [it] impotent'.[212]

The transfer of *Earth First! Journal* to the social justice faction marked the movement's formal separation.[213] From 1987 onwards Earth First! became primarily a direct action organization aimed at preventing logging and development that threatened wildlife habitats or unspoiled land.[214] The focus on direct action proved attractive to many activists, particularly those of an anarchist or counterculture bent. For the original or founding participants such as Dave Foreman, Howie Wolke, Bart Koehler, Christopher Manes, George Wuerthner and *Earth First! Journal* editor John Davis, such a direction was intolerable.[215] Foreman and many of the early activists (who supported his biocentric view) were becoming irritated with lack of success in achieving their stated goals, as well as the social ecological direction of Bari's faction. As such, they developed an 'increasingly apocalyptic view of the movement and its role in the world'.[216]

Bari suggested that the movement would be better off by dividing strategically. She proposed that such a division should be based on activists' attitudes toward the use of violence, stating, 'I think we need a split, like the Weather Underground and SDS [Students for a Democratic Society] so those who want to do such tactics can do so without any official connection to Earth First!.'[217]

By 1989 Foreman's faction argued that 'neither they nor any human beings should have an important role in the millennium' and still hoped for the pending end of human industrial civilization. Lee believed that due to concerns over human population growth their belief system was evolved from a millenarian viewpoint into an apocalyptic doctrine.[218] The social justice faction, however, remained millenarian in outlook with its calls to remake human society before the impending biological meltdown and to adopt a long-term view to bringing about change.[219]

Foreman argued at the 1989 Rendezvous meeting that 'old commonly held checks' are no longer being used, after some anarchist participants burnt the American flag (a move supported by Bari).[220] It is important to note that by 1989 the social justice wing had by sheer numbers come to dominate many of the movement's committees, including the Round River Rendezvous organizing committee.[221] Seemingly disillusioned, Foreman wondered not only if Earth First! was going to survive but whether it should, given the direction in which it was travelling.[222]

Foreman Leaves Earth First!

Following his trial, Foreman completely separated himself from Earth First! He acknowledged that the organization had riven in two with increasing numbers of leftist participants desiring more to end capitalism than protect the wilderness.[223] His sentence of parole was effectively the end of his active participation in Earth First!.[224] On 12 August 1990 Foreman publicly denounced the direction of Earth First!. He stated that 'West Coast yippies and hippies ha[d] taken over' and that they were 'more interested in pursuing the wildness within than the wildness out in the forests'.[225] He further stated, 'I found myself in recent years more comfortable at Sierra Club meetings than I have at Earth First! meetings.'[226] As such, he announced, he was demanding, 'a no fault divorce' from the movement.[227] Foreman went on to use his arrest record as a warning to potential and current activists, warning that activists could go to jail or die.[228] It would also appear as though participant numbers within the Earth First! organization began to decrease following Foreman's trial. However, it is important to note that its 'radical' actions did not.[229]

By 22 September 1990 the Earth First! movement, as Dave Foreman had envisaged it, was no more. According to Lee, in just ten years it had gone from a tiny millenarian movement into a big, diverse movement containing both apocalyptic and millenarian wings.[230] Foreman argued that he left because social issues had become dominant over natural ones and that the group should not ally with other social causes.[231] However, he stated in a farewell statement that he would still support the actions of Earth First! but he personally renounced ecosabotage.[232] He established *Wild Earth*, a journal that reflected his ideological orientation.[233] John Davis followed Foreman out of the organization and helped to set up the new journal and planned the Wildlands Projects (TWP), which aimed to 're-wild' 50 per cent of America.[234]

After the departure of Foreman and his supporters, the social humanist faction asserted control and the concept of biocentric equality was further downgraded. In 1990 Judi Bari, speaking on behalf of Earth First! community, issued a public denunciation of the tactic of tree spiking.[235] According to Rowell, by renouncing tree spiking and announcing their commitment to non-violent tactics, Earth First!ers were making it more difficult for others to brand them 'mindless eco-terrorists'.[236] Long argues that Bari's renouncement of tree spiking signalled a general, but not total, move away from monkeywrenching as the preferred tactic and towards civil disobedience.[237]

Further, in July 1990, several major changes were announced by Bari and Daryl Cherney:

1. There would be an expansion of the recruitment of minority participants to 'better reflect the organization's majority'.
2. That some radical slogans (for example 'AIDS is a cure to the population problem' and 'Let Ethiopians Starve') did not properly reflect the 'opinions on how to deal with the world population problems'.[238]

The split placed Earth First! as a more moderate and 'mainstream' group.[239] From the early 1990s onwards Earth First! became a global ecological mass movement with a broad social justice focus. It financed campaigns and projects that are administered through the affiliated regional chapters and continued to publish *Earth First! Journal*. While it still maintains a commitment to direct action, it primarily advocates (and occasionally litigates) and organizes civil disobedience actions such as tree sittings and road blockages.[240] Bari goes as far to argue that Earth First! advocates should leave ecosabotage to ELF participants (a decision that could be considered strategic – Earth First! operating in the daylight while the ELF participants (elves) carry out militant actions at night).[241]

POST FOREMAN: THE BOMBING OF BARI AND CHERNEY

Earth First! continued on without Foreman and Davis. The lack of structure and authority in the organization allowed Bari to forgo ecosabotage and embrace non-violence based on the civil rights movement. The Redwood Summer protests against logging would focus on actions such as marches, tree sits, blockades and rallies. Despite this newfound rhetoric, however, several encounters between activists and loggers ended in violence.[242]

On 24 May 1990, Judi Bari and Darryl Cherney were on their way to the Redwood Summer protests when 'a motion activated pipe bomb' exploded in the car.[243] Bari was very badly injured, her pelvis and coccyx shattered in the blast and her spine dislocated, leaving her physically maimed for life.[244] The FBI and Oakland Police Department immediately arrested them both on suspicion of possessing explosives. Their fellow activists, however, claimed that anti-environmentalists or law enforcement officers had planted the bomb.[245]

On 17 July the district attorney announced that no charges would be laid in relation to the bombing, as there was no evidence on which to proceed.[246] Bari and Cherney sued the FBI for civil rights infractions, and were vindicated at a 2002 trial when a jury awarded them US $4.4 million in damages (posthumously for Bari, as she succumbed to cancer in 1997).[247]

The car bombing did not deter the organization and they continued to promote their political agenda. Without a hierarchical, central structure, the group was able to continue its operations, even when key participants were threatened with charges or jail.[248]

EARTH FIRST! AND THE MAINSTREAM ENGO MOVEMENT

It is important to note that some mainstream environmental groups and leaders are quite content with the existence of Earth First!. As Robert Hattoy (former Southern California Representative of the Sierra Club) explains, 'Frankly, it makes us look moderate. When Earth First! is out there demanding a hundred million acres of wilderness and we know we can only get ten, I can turn to a congressman and say, Look, we're the voice of reason.'[249] Howie Wolke also worried that Earth First! would make other mainstream environmental groups look more moderate by comparison.[250] He also pointed out: 'if you look at any social reform movement, there has always been a radical arm of that movement. We want to push the traditional environmentalists back into the roots, away from the political establishment that governs it and further toward the extreme.'[251]

Radical and mainstream environmental organizations have been able to maintain a symbiotic relationship. Many radicals have accepted this arrangement, with Foreman noting there has to be room for other environmental groups less radical than Earth First!.[252] He believes, as opposed to Wolke, that a major accomplishment of the group has been to allow groups such as the Sierra Club to be perceived as moderates.[253]

EARTH FIRST! AND VIOLENCE

For Earth First!ers, violence against sentient beings was not officially permissible in pursuit of their goals. All participants had to agree that: 'At no time should anyone physically or verbally assault anyone or contribute to escalating violence from the police, workers, management or general public at an Earth First! action.'[254] Rather its preferred methods included non-violent direct actions, civil disobedience and ecotage acts, perceiving these methods as legitimate in defence of the Earth.[255]

Edward Abbey, whose views and 1975 novel aided in encouraging the formation of Earth First!, believed there was a clear distinction between terrorism and sabotage, 'the first being a form of deadly violence directed against people and other living things, the second being the use of force against inanimate objects'.[256] Such sabotage, Abbey noted, has never meant or implied the utilization of violence against sentient beings.[257]

Abbey further clarified that terrorism should only be categorized as 'deadly violence – for a political and/or economic purpose – carried out against people and other living things, [that] is usually conducted by governments against their own citizens … or by corporate entities … against the land and all creatures that depend upon the land for life and livelihood'.[258]

Earth First! used many traditional methods of direct action and non-violent civil disobedience protests, including: tree sittings, road blockades, chaining themselves to equipment, computer 'hacktivism' and office occupations (sometimes refilling or removing paperwork to disrupt corporate activities).[259] However, what made Earth First! distinct from other mainstream environmental groups was its willingness to commit 'ecotage' or 'ecosabotage' in furtherance of its goals. Dave Foreman's book *Ecodefense* was an 'ecotage manual' and 'was widely distributed to members detailing how to carry out acts of ecosabotage'.[260] Generally, ecotage was seen as one of many tactics of 'public action', not as a 'strategy for the movement as a whole'. It was the preferred method of 'affinity groups', as it was considered an opportunistic, low-risk tactic.[261] However, Foreman argued that 'ecotage is only a last resort [for participants], one tool among many' and goes on to argue that the act of 'monkeywrenching' defines us. It is a litmus test.[262]

Many activists pointed to the efficacy of this approach because:

> Economic sabotage is far more effective [a tool] against corporate enterprises to cost them money, and the most effective way to do that is to physically damage their property … yeah. It's the only thing that they recognize and take notice of … that's my strategy.[263] ('Andrew' (2001) – interview, name has been changed)

Earth First! activists were also aware that such bold acts of ecotage had the capacity to elicit increased media attention for their cause.[264] As with other direct action repertoires, emotional responses are interwoven with other rationales with many participants arguing they were 'angry' and needed to do something. For some participants such actions also come 'with an element of macho posturing', a certain 'swagger'. There has also been acknowledgement that acts are sometimes done simply to 'show off' to friends.[265]

Tree Spiking

One prominent form of ecotage was 'tree spiking'. In 1984, participants of Earth First! began using more 'violent methods' to protect the Earth, prompting a heated debate about the legitimacy and consequences of such actions.[266] Tree spiking can be defined as the act of 'driving metal or hardened ceramic nails in trees to damage blades at the sawmill as a means of deterring logging'.[267] Tree spiking can cause logging saws to shatter into dangerous shrapnel upon contact and are potentially deadly.[268] Such actions are aimed to deter many loggers from entering forests known to be spiked.[269] According to activists, the aim of tree spiking is to thread the needle in aiming to deter logging but not cause harm to sentient beings.[270]

Some activists thrived on 'demonizing' their opponents, which left open the door for physical violence.[271] There has also been continued controversy over using arson as a legitimate tactic, with Craig Rosebraugh arguing that arson attacks are 'to be seen as an act of love for the environment', a position vehemently opposed by many other participants.[272] For some Earth First! activists, the only 'moral response' was 'active resistance' such as tree spiking.[273] Abbey himself is quoted as telling the organization: 'oppose, resist and if necessary subvert. Of course, I never advocate illegal action at any time. Except at night …'[274]

The use of sabotage continues to be a point of controversy within the organization, although there is no 'official position' regarding it.[275] While it is a subject of debate, most Earth First! activists defend such methods as: 'it is nonviolent; it is aimed at the guilty parties; it is an effective threat; it is in defense of the earth; it does not hurt living things.'[276] It is important to note that even Judi Bari (a long-time opponent of a 'violence promoting rhetoric' and who has condemned tree spiking as 'ineffective' and 'dangerous') has not completely ruled out the use of violence (however, as noted previously, most radical members were more attracted by the actions done by the elves).[277]

Likelihood of Violence Increasing?

It must be first noted that there is no 'continuity' that leads such a group from ecotage to intentionally harming humans.[278] It is common for radical environmentalists and their opponents to engage in face-to-face confrontations. This 'plays an important role in humanizing the "enemy"', which reinforces that although the parties are rivals they are human. As Sprinzak notes, humanizing an enemy goes a long way to preventing terrorist actions against an enemy.[279]

David Rapoport argues that non-violent action has often been a first step in the road to full-on terrorism, but there is little evidence of elves progressing to become terrorists.[280] It can occur if participants and their opponents continue to fight, with both attempting to justify their stances and actions. For example, problems can occur if a participant decides that God or Gaia is calling on them personally to wage a 'holy war' against the earth's despoilers. Most likely, if there is continuing confrontation then 'relatively minor injuries' will occur. However, if monkeywrenching activities continue it is only a matter of time before someone is injured.[281]

As such, Earth First! participants appear less likely to give in to the type of 'unbridled extremism' that sees participants pursuing violence against sentient beings. The organization does not require or encourage activists to cut ties with their families and loved ones, as do many terrorist groups. While some may have chosen to sever such ties, there is no evidence to suggest there is an inclination or pattern to do so.[282] It is also important to note that the FBI has classified Earth First! as a 'soft core' terrorist group to distinguish it from 'hard-core' terrorists willing to take life to promote their cause.[283]

Monkeywrenching

The preferred method of ecotage has often been described as monkeywrenching. Foreman defined strategic 'monkeywrenching' as 'a non-violent response to the excesses of industrial and urban growth ... It's directed toward inanimate objects, and never toward people or any other life-forms.'[284] He writes that among other features, 'monkeywrenching should be nonviolent, not organized, the act of individuals, targeted, timely, simple, dispersed among all regions, and fun'.[285] The act should be distinguished from performance of vandalism since monkeywrenching is undertaken with purpose and respect, and adhering to the highest moral standards whilst vandalism is pointless and insensitive.[286]

Earth First! activists argued monkeywrenching did not constitute violence because it was not aimed at the 'natural' world but rather inanimate machinery that was destroying life.[287] However, the nature of many such acts is such that there was a risk of death or injury to sentient beings. Earth First!ers of the biocentric persuasion accepted this prospect since the rights of the Earth should be prized even above human welfare if required.[288] Mike Roselle once 'scoffed' at Foreman's assertion that 'monkeywrenching is not a revolutionary act, declaring that sabotage was radical in nature and, to him: 'There are no innocent bystanders, because in these desperate hours, bystanders are not innocent.'[289]

Given its nature and similarity, at least on the surface, to vandalism it is important to note that it is impossible to 'map' the actions and levels of ecotage, as often, the only people who are knowledgeable about the action are the people responsible and the target. While cases of ecotage are sometimes reported, most information regarding an action is detailed in communiqués, which are written by the activists themselves and forwarded on to the media.[290]

There was constant debate regarding the usefulness of tactics such as 'monkeywrenching', particularly there was concern that any injury or death would cause public opinion to turn against wilderness preservation or that it would provide a moral justification for practitioners of mere vandalism.[291] The debate regarding the use of monkeywrenching tactics versus simple civil disobedience occurring within the Earth First! organization continued throughout the 1990s. Following Foreman's arrest and trial, several activists who remained wedded to monkeywrenching went underground and became participants of the ELF.[292] However, even Foreman could see in some cases that it went too far. On one occasion Foreman publicly reprimanded activists who sabotaged logging equipment belonging to a small, family-owned timber company and draped an Earth First! banner nearby. This act of destruction was merely petty vandalism as opposed to monkeywrenching, which targeted corporate logging activities.[293]

EARTH FIRST! (UK)

In 1987 UK Earth First! was created by Chris Laughton (a physics graduate).[294] Laughton had worked with Greenpeace and was in communication with Earth First! (USA) and subscribed to *Earth First! Journal* upon his return to the UK. He found the group inspirational and thought Greenpeace was a mainstream organization but Earth First! was a partly subversive organization.[295] In his attempt to begin a UK-based Earth First! organization, Laughton imported 50 copies of *Ecodefense* (written by Foreman and Haywood), which he sold to radical bookshops. Within each copy, he added his name and address as an Earth First! contact. Furthermore, he contacted green journals including *Green Line* and *Green Anarchist* in an attempt to publicize his manifesto but was unable to elicit much interest.[296]

A longer-lasting network was created by two students (Burbridge and Torrance) in Hastings in 1991. According to Torrance, they had previously been involved with several other organizations, including Friends of the Earth, the Green Party and Greenpeace but were looking for a new approach.[297] Earth First! UK quickly became the fastest-growing organization in Britain.[298] The UK faction, once established, consisted of a few thousand activists and focused on the use of direct action as a tactic. While their campaigns concentrated on anti-road-protest camps, their targets grew to include other development projects they disapproved of.[299] The anti-road movement was created to fill a void caused by the apparent inability of mainstream environmental groups to act on the ever-growing problem of increased road building.[300]

The first of many direct actions undertaken by Earth First! in Twyford Down occurred in December 1992.[301] Wall argues that during the 1990s, particularly 1992–6, the anti-road movement was the most visible form of environmental direct action.[302] After 1995–6, the protests targeted airport construction, quarrying, open-cast mining and, in particular, genetically modified (GM) foods. They also began to focus on global capitalism as the enemy.[303]

According to Wall, there were several characteristics shared by Earth First! activists that are important for the creation of a green agency/identity, including: 'a sense of urgency', a 'largely undogmatic approach', an emphasis on 'personal empowerment' and the 'ability to link "militant particularist" struggles to global concerns'.[304]

ANALYSIS AND CONCLUSION

The Earth First! organization today barely resembles the organization that Foreman and the others created in 1980. Liddick further argues that it may be more accurate to describe Earth First! at present as a 'collection of social movements loosely tied together under a familiar banner'.[305] However, in its prime, estimates regarding the destruction attributed to Earth First! actions are quite high, ranging from approximately US $20–25 million a year, but now it is a shadow of the group set up by Foreman and his friends.[306]

Earth First!ers wanted and anticipated that their brand of radical ecological resistance would promulgate and influence the technological/capitalist system.[307] According to Taylor, we can see the 'emergence of Earth First!-style actions in Czechoslovakia in opposition to the Gabcikovo dam project, in England where activists claim significant victories in resisting road building and in Switzerland where there have been violent anti-automobile demonstrations'.[308] Moreover, reportedly, optimism is arising from the 'Celtic renewal and ecological resistance movements of Scotland, Wales, and Ireland'.[309]

Earth First! also still believes that, 'we are in the midst of an unprecedented, anthropogenic extinction crisis, and consequently, many ecosystems are presently collapsing'. This belief strongly aids in the justification for the use of militancy to achieve their goals but to date this has not occurred.[310]

Finally, Earth First! continues to argue that 'democracy in the United States is a sham, thoroughly thwarted by corporate economic power, or, even if not a complete sham, the democratic political system is so distorted by corporate power and regressive human attitudes that it cannot respond quickly enough to avert the escalating extinction catastrophe'.[311] Furthermore, with regard to their political claims, many participants of Earth First! argue that 'in light of nature's intrinsic value, governing processes that disregard the interests of nonhumans are illegitimate' and can be discounted.[312]

Taylor argues that such political claims simply allow participants to validate illegal or militant acts. He states that by 'asserting either that democratic procedures never existed, or that they have broken down, or that they camouflage domination, these activists argue that illegal tactics are morally justifiable'.[313]

Earth First! participants have 'celebrated ecological resistance movements wherever they could be found'. According to Taylor, 'popular environmental movements are interpreted as kindred movements in different cultural garb, particularly when they appear to be motivated by nature-based spirituality'. As a result Earth First! activists attempt to act in solidarity with such groups.[314] Earth First! participants have also formed alliances with groups including the US-based Rainforest Action Network (RAN) and the Australian-based Rainforest Information Center (RIC).[315]

According to Sarkar, 'there is little doubt that Earth First! extended the realm of the environmental debate in the United States'.[316] However, despite their actions between 1980 and 1987, Earth First! was considered a 'bit player' in the broader environmental political debates. Attention was focused on the group's activities, versus their environmental agenda. However, in 1988, this stance changed, when the organization 'found itself under concerted attacks from not only industrial interests but also law enforcement agencies, the federal government and even other environmental groups'.[317]

Certainly there is some evidence that Dave Foreman in particular was a charismatic leader of the early Earth First! incarnation. He was greatly admired by the rank and file and his pronouncements on the group – and then his fears the group was heading in the wrong direction – were closely heeded by both original participants and those who wished to use monkeywrenching as a tactic. His decision to leave Earth First! robbed the organization of its most articulate voice, just at the time when the decision to embrace political violence against property rendered it vulnerable to a law-enforcement crackdown.

The types of people who joined Earth First! were an eclectic group from cowboys and middle-class professionals to former mainstream environmental members. The group made a point of being inclusive and inviting a wide range of people from hippies to rednecks, vegetarians to hunters, college dropouts to professors and those of all political philosophies, who were only bound together by their desire to protect the biosphere.[318] Early Earth First! followers tended to be older than 30, but as the group evolved younger people became more dominant.[319] Women were particularly involved with Earth First! – from the influence of Judi Bari to the fact that of those indicted for committing Earth First! actions the majority were women.[320]

Since the creation of the ELF, Earth First! arguably appears to have taken a back seat in terms of actions and growth as compared to its spin-off organization. Very few direct actions have been recorded and claimed by Earth First! since 2000 and, while there are several branches still active, they appear to have refocused their efforts on above-ground, legal protests. For example, the Hudson Valley Earth First! website outlines their active campaigns as including anti-fracking in the Marcellus Shale, the Minisink Compression Station, Wawayanda Power Plant and the Indian Point Nuclear Plant.[321] These campaigns are all local campaigns and Earth First!'s recognized and encouraged actions against each include: attending public hearings and rallies, organizing protests, bullhorn announcements in the streets and handing out fliers to drum up local support.[322] Further, the Earth First! UK website outlines recent actions taken again coal conveyor belts and mines through peaceful protest and blockades.[323]

All Earth First! websites outline actions undertaken by other environmental groups worldwide, so long as the organizations and incidents adhere to the general principles outlined by Earth First! – 'direct action, eco-justice, respect for all life, and a "no compromise" stance'.'[324] Further to each individual website, *Earth First! Journal* still provides online community support for Earth First! cells across the world, information on how to form your own Earth First! group, prisoner support and action resources (including manuals and information on monkeywrenching and direct action).[325]

NOTES

1. Russell Lee Young (2004) 'A time series analysis of eco-terrorist violence in the United States: 1993–2003' (PhD dissertation, Sam Houston State University, Huntsville, TX) p. 26; Edward Abbey (1975) *The Monkey Wrench Gang* (New York: Avon) Dedication Page. The book tells the tale of four environmentally motivated individuals who came together to use 'monkeywrenching' or sabotage tactics to damage those individuals or organizations they considered environmentally destructive, with the aim of preserving America's wilderness. Abbey has claimed, 'this book, though fictional in form, is based strictly on historical fact. Everything in it is real and actually happened.' Young, 'A time series analysis of eco-terrorist violence in the United States: 1993–2003', p. 26.
2. Ibid., p. 119.
3. Brant Short (1991) 'Earth First! and the rhetoric of moral confrontation', *Communication Studies*, **42** (2), p. 177; Bill McKibben (1989) *The End of Nature* (New York: Random House), pp. 177–82; Roderick Nash (1989) *The Rights of Nature: A History of Environmental Ethics* (Madison: University of Wisconsin Press), pp. 191–4.
4. Jay Hasbrouck (2005) 'Primitive dissidents: Earth Liberation Front and the making of a radical movement' (PhD dissertation, University of Southern California, Los Angeles, CA, 2005), p. 9.

5. Douglas Long (2004) *Ecoterrorism: Library in a Book* (New York: Facts on File, Inc.), p. 29; Dave Foreman (1991) *Confessions of an Eco-Warrior* (New York: Crown), p. 20.
6. Long, *Ecoterrorism: Library in a Book*, p. 29.
7. Peter C. List (1993) *Radical Environmentalism: Philosophy and Tactics* (Belmont, CA: Wadsworth, Inc.), p 252.
8. Long, *Ecoterrorism: Library in a Book*, p. 29; Dave Foreman, quoted in List's *Radical Environmentalism: Philosophy and Tactics*, p. 254.
9. Short, 'Earth First! and the rhetoric of moral confrontation', p. 177. For example, at one rally at the Glen Canyon Dam, Abbey declared, 'oppose! Oppose the destruction of our homeland… And if opposition is not enough, we much subvert.' Short, 'Earth First! and the rhetoric of moral confrontation', p. 177.
10. Young, 'A time series analysis of eco-terrorist violence in the United States: 1993–2003', p. 31. For example, in 1958 Edward Abbey and co-workers on a Taos newspaper sawed down a dozen billboards owned by the Melody Sign Company as a protest. In 1959 in Flagstaff, Arizona Marc Gaede and others cut down billboards on Route 180 between Flagstaff and the Grand Canyon. In 1970 at Black Mesa Arizona, a lone protester known as the 'Arizona Phantom' vandalized heavy equipment owned by the Peabody Coal Company and tore up railway tracks for two years. He was never identified. See Long, *Ecoterrorism: Library in a Book*, p. 19; Susan Zakin (1993) *Coyotes and Town Dogs: Earth First! and the Environmental Movement* (New York, Viking), p. 41.
11. Young, 'A time series analysis of eco-terrorist violence in the United States: 1993–2003', p. 31; S. Hays et al., 'Radical environmentalism and crime' in T. Edwards et al. (1996) *Environmental Crime and Criminality: Theoretical and Practical Issues* (New York: Garland Publishing), pp. 163–81. The Fox is considered by many to be the first unequivocally criminal acts clearly guided by an ideological goal to save nature that gained public attention. See Ron Arnold (1997) *Ecoterror: The Violent Agenda to Save Nature, The World of the Unabomber* (Washington: Free Enterprise Press), pp. 123–4. Mike Royko (a reporter for the *Chicago Daily News*) managed to get the Fox to agree to an interview. Royko described the activist as the 'antipollution Zorro' and as, 'an ordinary soft-spoken citizen who is approaching middle age, has a respectable job, a family, and has never before gone outside the law'. See Long, *Ecoterrorism: Library in a Book*, p. 18. When asked why he began his campaign, the Fox responded, 'I've always lived in Kane County and I remember how beautiful it was.' Mike Royko and the Fox, quoted in Sam Love and David Obst's (1972) *Ecotage!* (New York: Pocket Books), pp. 144–5. The Fox's campaign was broadcast by the national media and provoked feelings of sympathy from many Americans. See Long, *Ecoterrorism: Library in a Book*, p. 18; Love and Obst, *Ecotage!*, p. 151.
12. A group of Minnesota farmers (calling themselves the Bolt Weevils) were upset over the potential health implications of the installation of high-voltage power lines across their land. The group used wrenches to bring down at least 15 towers over two years from 1976. Thousands of farmers protested and 140 were arrested and charged with sabotage and civil disobedience. See Long, *Ecoterrorism: Library in a Book*, p. 18.
13. In the summer of 1971, a group of activists using the pseudonym the 'Tucson Eco-Raiders'; they cut down billboards, sabotaged locks and bulldozers. One activist later told a reporter that they, 'bore a grudge against developers who go in and flatten out everything. In general, if we see a nice area of the desert being destroyed, we'll do something about it.' See Long, *Ecoterrorism: Library in a Book*, p. 19.
14. A group that called itself the Eco-Commando Force was active briefly in Miami, Florida. Claiming to be a five-member 'clandestine guerilla organization', the group focused on water issues being affected by sewerage and used yellow dye to highlight the issue in Miami's waterways. See Long, *Ecoterrorism: Library in a Book*, p. 18.
15. Young, 'A time series analysis of eco-terrorist violence in the United States: 1993–2003', p. 31.
16. Sean P. Eagan (1996) 'From spikes to bombs: the rise of ecoterrorism', *Studies in Conflict and Terrorism*, **19**, p. 5.

17. Anthony Vincent Silvaggio (2005) 'The Forest Defense Movement, 1980–2005: resistance at the point of extraction, consumption, and production' (PhD dissertation, University of Oregon, Eugene, OR), p. 58.
18. Eagan, 'From spikes to bombs: the rise of ecoterrorism', p. 5.
19. Silvaggio, 'The Forest Defense Movement, 1980–2005: resistance at the point of extraction, consumption, and production', pp. 58–9.
20. Anonymous (1985) 'The plowboy interview: Dave Forman: no compromise in the defense of Mother Earth', *The Mother Earth News*, **91**, pp. 17–18.
21. Martha F. Lee (1995) 'Violence and the environment: the case of 'Earth First!', *Terrorism and Political Violence*, **7** (3), p. 112.
22. Short, Earth First! and the rhetoric of moral confrontation', p. 176.
23. Eagan, 'From spikes to bombs: the rise of ecoterrorism', p. 5.
24. Arnold, *Ecoterror: The Violent Agenda to Save Nature, The World of the Unabomber*, p. 214.
25. Short, 'Earth First! and the rhetoric of moral confrontation, p. 176.
26. Ibid.
27. Lee, 'Violence and the environment: the case of 'Earth First!'; Foreman, *Confessions of an Eco-Warrior*, p. 12.
28. Short, 'Earth First! and the rhetoric of moral confrontation', p. 176.
29. Eagan, 'From spikes to bombs: the rise of eco-terrorism', p. 6
30. Arnold, *Ecoterror: The Violent Agenda to Save Nature, The World of the Unabomber*, p. 211.
31. Jonathan Lange (1990) 'Refusal to compromise: the case of Earth First!', *Western Journal of Speech Communication*, **54** (Fall), p. 479.
32. Lange, 'Refusal to compromise: the case of Earth First!', pp. 478–9.; Martha F. Lee (1995) *Earth First! Environmental Apocalypse* (Syracuse, N.Y.: Syracuse University Press), pp. 31–2, Rik Scarce (2006) *Eco-Warriors Updated Edition: Understanding the Radical Environmental Movement* (Walnut Creek, California: Left Coast Press), pp. 58–62.
33. Lee, 'Violence and the environment: the case of 'Earth First!', p. 112.
34. Scarce, *Eco-Warriors: Understanding the Radical Environmental Movement* (updated edn, 2006), p. 61.
35. Christopher Manes (1990) *Green Rage: Radical Environmentalism and the Unmaking of Civilization* (Boston: Little Brown), pp. 65–9; Rik Scarce (1990) *Eco-Warriors: Understanding the Radical Environmental Movement* (Chicago, IL: Noble Press), pp. 58–61.
36. Arnold, *Ecoterror: The Violent Agenda to Save Nature, The World of the Unabomber*, p. 219.
37. Lee, 'Violence and the environment: the case of 'Earth First!', p. 111.; Scarce, *Eco-Warriors: Understanding the Radical Environmental Movement* (updated edn, 2006), p. 58.
38. Lee, 'Violence and the environment: the case of 'Earth First!', p. 112.
39. Eagan, 'From spikes to bombs: the rise of ecoterrorism', pp. 5–6.
40. Ibid., p. 6.
41. Ibid.; Manes, *Green Rage: Radical Environmentalism and the Unmaking of Civilization*, pp. 66–9.
42. Lee, 'Violence and the environment: the case of 'Earth First!', pp. 112–13.
43. Lange, 'Refusal to compromise: the case of Earth First!', p. 479; Aldo Leopold (1949) *A Sand County Almanac, and Sketches Here and There* (New York: Oxford University Press).
44. Lange, 'Refusal to compromise: the case of Earth First!', p. 480.
45. List, *Radical Environmentalism: Philosophy and Tactics*, pp. 187–8.
46. Ibid., p. 189.
47. Short, 'Earth First! and the rhetoric of moral confrontation', p. 177.
48. Eagan, 'From spikes to bombs: the rise of ecoterrorism', p. 6; Manes, *Green Rage: Radical Environmentalism and the Unmaking of Civilization*, p. 69.

49. Scarce, *Eco-Warriors: Understanding the Radical Environmental Movement* (updated edn, 2006), p. 62.
50. Ibid., p. 63.
51. Manes, *Green Rage: Radical Environmentalism and the Unmaking of Civilization*, p. 76.
52. Short, 'Earth First! and the Rhetoric of Moral Confrontation', p. 175.
53. Monkeywrenching can be defined as industrial or commercial sabotage against inanimate objects but that does not target sentient beings. Ibid., p. 178.
54. Paul Joosse (2007) Leaderless resistance and ideological inclusion: the case of the Earth Liberation Front', *Terrorism and Political Violence*, **19**, (3), p. 356; url: http://www.earthfirst.org/about.htm.
55. Manes, *Green Rage: Radical Environmentalism and the Unmaking of Civilization*, p. 76; Earth First! (1982) *Earth First! Newsletter*, 20 March, p. 10.
56. Short, 'Earth First! and the rhetoric of moral confrontation', p. 175.
57. Manes, *Green Rage: Radical Environmentalism and the Unmaking of Civilization*, p. 76; Mike Roselle (1989) 'Co-founder of Earth First! on Direct Action', *Ecology Center Newsletter* (Berkeley, California) (July), p. 3.
58. Mickey Z. (2010) 'From Earth First! to Climate Ground Zero, Mike Roselle is a radical lifer', *Truth Out*, blog, 9 October, http://truth-out.org/archive/component/k2/item/92225:from-earth-first-to-climate-ground-zero-mike-roselle-is-a-radical-lifer.
59. Silvaggio, 'The Forest Defense Movement, 1980–2005: resistance at the point of extraction, consumption, and production', p. 66.
60. Short, 'Earth First! and the rhetoric of moral confrontation', p. 178.
61. Arnold, *Ecoterror: The Violent Agenda to Save Nature, The World of the Unabomber*, p. 218.
62. Short, 'Earth First! and the rhetoric of moral confrontation', p. 178.
63. Lee, *Earth First! Environmental Apocalypse*, p. 37.
64. Short, 'Earth First! and the rhetoric of moral confrontation', p. 178.
65. Lee, *Earth First! Environmental Apocalypse*, p. 71; Dave Foreman et al. (1983) 'The Earth First! Wilderness Preserve System', *Earth First!*, **3** (5), 21 June, p. 9.
66. Lee, *Earth First! Environmental Apocalypse*, p. 71; Foreman et al., 'The Earth First! Wilderness Preserve System', p. 9.
67. Reed Noss (1984) 'Deep ecology, elitism and reproduction', *Earth First,* **4** (5), 1 May, p. 16.
68. List, *Radical Environmentalism: Philosophy and Tactics,* p. 188.
69. Manes, *Green Rage: Radical Environmentalism and the Unmaking of Civilization*, p. 71.
70. Ibid., pp. 71–2.
71. Hasan T. Arslan (2008) 'The social and operational intersections of environmental extremism in North America and Europe' (PhD dissertation, Sam Houston State University, Huntsville, TX), p. 45.
72. Lee, *Earth First! Environmental Apocalypse*, p. 37.
73. List, *Radical Environmentalism: Philosophy and Tactics*, p. 253.
74. Arnold, *Ecoterror: The Violent Agenda to Save Nature, The World of the Unabomber*, p. 218; Lee, *Earth First! Environmental Apocalypse*, p. 37.
75. Ibid., p. 40.
76. Donald R. Liddick (2006) *Eco-Terrorism: Radical Environmental and Animal Liberation Movements* (Westport, Connecticut: Praeger), p. 57.
77. Lee, *Earth First! Environmental Apocalypse*, p. 37.
78. Liddick, *Eco-Terrorism: Radical Environmental and Animal Liberation Movements*, p. 57.
79. Lee, *Earth First! Environmental Apocalypse*, p. 37.
80. Arnold, *Ecoterror: The Violent Agenda to Save Nature, The World of the Unabomber*, p. 218.
81. Lee, *Earth First! Environmental Apocalypse*, p. 37.
82. Sean Parson (2008) 'Understanding the ideology of the Earth Liberation Front', *Green Theory & Praxis: The Journal of Ecopedagogy*, **4** (2), p. 56.

83. Silvaggio, 'The Forest Defense Movement, 1980–2005: resistance at the point of extraction, consumption, and production', p. 29; Lee, *Earth First! Environmental Apocalypse*, p. 19.
84. Lee, 'Violence and the environment: the case of 'Earth First!', p. 115.
85. Lee, *Earth First! Environmental Apocalypse,* p. 38; Howie Wolke and Dave Foreman (September 1980) *Memorandum Regarding Earth First*, p. 1.
86. Arslan, 'The social and operational intersections of environmental extremism in North America and Europe', p. 46.
87. Manes, *Green Rage: Radical Environmentalism and the Unmaking of Civilization*, p. 72; Dave Foreman (speech), Grand Canyon, Arizona (7 July 1987).
88. Lee, *Earth First! Environmental Apocalypse,* p. 42; 'Editorial' (1980) *Earth First! Newsletter*, **1** (1), 1 November, p. 1.
89. Lee, *Earth First! Environmental Apocalypse*, p. 42; 'Earth First Platform', *Earth First! Newsletter*, **1** (1), 1 November 1980, pp. 2–4. The document also demanded the entire island of Hawaii be considered off limits for development, the end to all development in Alaska, RARE II's 'Alternative J' wilderness zones be implemented, and that all Bureau of Land Management Roadless areas be considered wilderness. See Lee, *Earth First! Environmental Apocalypse*, p. 42; 'Earth First Platform', *Earth First! Newsletter*, pp. 2–4.
90. Long, *Ecoterrorism: Library in a Book*, p. 32.
91. Ibid.; Dave Foreman, quoted in List, *Radical Environmentalism: Philosophy and Tactics,* p. 188.
92. Scarce, *Eco-Warriors: Understanding the Radical Environmental Movement* (updated edn, 2006), p. 66.
93. Susan Zakin, *Coyotes and Town Dogs: Earth First and the Environmental Movement,* p. 7.
94. Bron Taylor (1995) 'Earth First! and global narratives of popular ecological resistance' in Bron Taylor (ed.) *Ecological Resistance Movements: The Global Emergence of Radical and Popular Environmentalism* (Albany, NY: State University of New York Press), p. 16.
95. Arnold, *Ecoterror: The Violent Agenda to Save Nature, The World of the Unabomber,* p. 245.
96. Ibid., p. 245; John Hayes (1983) 'Environmental radicalism backed – local response favourable', *Portland Oregonian*, 23 January, p. C2.
97. Arnold, *Ecoterror: The Violent Agenda to Save Nature, The World of the Unabomber*, p. 245; Lee, *Earth First! Environmental Apocalypse*, p. 56; Jim Robbins (1998) 'The environmental guerillas', *Boston Globe Magazine*, 27 March.
98. Arnold, *Ecoterror: The Violent Agenda to Save Nature, The World of the Unabomber*, p. 232.
99. Bron Taylor (2001) 'Earth and nature-based spirituality (part 1): from deep ecology to radical environmentalism', *Religion*, **31** (2), p. 185.
100. Ibid., p. 186.
101. Lee, 'Violence and the environment: the case of 'Earth First!', p. 113.
102. Ibid., p. 114.
103. Taylor, 'Earth and nature-based spirituality (part 1): from deep ecology to radical environmentalism', p. 186.
104. Lee, 'Violence and the environment: the case of 'Earth First!', p. 113.
105. Ibid., p. 114.
106. Lee, *Earth First! Environmental Apocalypse,* p. 40.
107. Ibid., p. 62; Interview with Helen Wilson, Tucson, Arizona (26 January 1992).
108. Lee, *Earth First! Environmental Apocalypse,* p. 64; Noss, 'Deep ecology, elitism and reproduction', p. 16.
109. Derek Wall (1999) *Earth First! and The Anti-Roads Movement: Radical Environmentalism and Comparative Social Movements* (London and New York: Routledge), p. 44; Lee, *Earth First! Environmental Apocalypse*, pp. 106–11.

110. Scarce, *Eco-Warriors: Understanding the Radical Environmental Movement* (updated edn, 2006), p. 92; Edward Abbey (1988) 'Immigration and liberal taboos', in *One Life at a Time, Please* (New York: Henry Holt), p. 42.
111. Wall, *Earth First! and The Anti-Roads Movement: Radical Environmentalism and Comparative Social Movements*, p. 44; Foreman, *Confessions of an Eco-Warrior*, pp. 55–8; Lee, *Earth First! Environmental Apocalypse*, p. 61.
112. Long, *Ecoterrorism: Library in a Book*, p. 33; Dave Foreman quoted in Mark Dowie (1995) *Losing Ground: American Environmentalism at the Close of the Twentieth Century* (Cambridge, Mass: MIT Press), p. 210; Scarce, *Eco-Warriors: Understanding the Radical Environmental Movement* (updated edn, 2006), p. 92.
113. Steve Chase (1991) 'Whither the radical ecology movement' in Murray Bookchin and Dave Foreman (eds) *Defending the Earth: A Debate Between Murray Bookchin and Dave Foreman* (New York, Quebec: Black Rose Books), p. 21; Dave Foreman, interviewed by Bill Devall (1986) *Social Living*, **2** (12).
114. Horacio R. Trujillo (2005) 'The radical environmentalist movement', *Aptitude for Destruction 2*, pp. 141–78, 167.
115. Long, *Ecoterrorism: Library in a Book*, pp. 32–3; Christopher Manes quoted in Dowie, *Losing Ground: American Environmentalism at the Close of the Twentieth Century*, p. 10.
116. Scarce, *Eco-Warriors: Understanding the Radical Environmental Movement* (updated edn, 2006), p. 92.
117. Lee, *Earth First! Environmental Apocalypse*, p. 93.
118. Liddick, *Eco-Terrorism: Radical Environmental and Animal Liberation Movements*, p. 59.
119. Lee, *Earth First! Environmental Apocalypse*, p. 63.
120. Liddick, *Eco-Terrorism: Radical Environmental and Animal Liberation Movements*, p. 57.
121. Bron Taylor, 'Religion, violence and radical environmentalism: from Earth First! to the Unabomber to the Earth Liberation Front', *Terrorism and Political Violence*, **10** (4), p. 22.
122. Lee, *Earth First! Environmental Apocalypse*, p. 33.
123. Liddick, *Eco-Terrorism: Radical Environmental and Animal Liberation Movements*, p. 56.
124. Lee, *Earth First! Environmental Apocalypse*, p. 39.
125. Lee, 'Violence and the environment: the case of 'Earth First!', p. 115.
126. Lee, *Earth First! Environmental Apocalypse*, p. 39; Wolke and Foreman, 'Memorandum regarding Earth First', p. 2.
127. Lee, *Earth First! Environmental Apocalypse*, p. 9.
128. Ibid., p. 86; Dave Foreman,'Welcome to Earth First!', *Earth First*, No. 5, Beltane, 1 May 1985, p. 16.
129. Lee, *Earth First! Environmental Apocalypse,* p. 86; Foreman, 'Welcome to Earth First!', p. 16.
130. Lee, *Earth First! Environmental Apocalypse*, p. 66.
131. Ibid., p. 34.
132. Lee, *Earth First! Environmental Apocalypse*, p. 34; 'Earth First!: The First Three Years', *Earth First! Newsletter*, **4** (1), 1 November 1983, p. 11.
133. Lee, *Earth First! Environmental Apocalypse,* p. 34.
134. Lange, 'Refusal to compromise: the case of Earth First!', p. 483.
135. Ibid., p. 481.
136. Arnold, *Ecoterror: The Violent Agenda to Save Nature, The World of the Unabomber*, p. 217.
137. Kevin Michael Deluca (1999) 'Unruly arguments: the body rhetoric of Earth First!, Act Up, and Queer Nation', *Argumentation and Advocacy*, **36** (summer), p. 9; Short, 'Earth First! and the rhetoric of moral confrontation', p. 175.
138. Foreman released the first newsletter, originally called 'Nature More' following the general meeting. The name was from a famous line in Lord Byron's poem, *Childe Harold's Pilgrimage*, '*I love not man the less, but nature more*'. Others objected that the title was too literary and it was quickly amended to 'Earth First! Newsletter', and later, simply called *Earth First! Journal*. See Arnold, *Ecoterror: The Violent Agenda to Save Nature, The World of the Unabomber*, p. 217. According to Douglas Long, a more

detailed agenda was proffered in the journal's pages and it soon had 1,500 subscribers, growing to more than 5,000 by the end of the 1980s. With no formal structure, these subscriptions were the closest the organization had to a participantship list. The journal 'published photographs, editorials, accounts of protest actions, poetry, and how-to advice for monkeywrenchers'. See Long, *Ecoterrorism: Library in a Book*, p. 32. The journal was initially published eight times a year and, with every publication, included a disclaimer that, 'the contents do not necessarily represent the viewpoint of the journal, the Earth First! movement, local Earth First! groups, or individual Earth First!ers'. See Lange, 'Refusal to compromise: the case of Earth First!', p. 482.

139. List, *Radical Environmentalism: Philosophy and Tactics*, p. 253.
140. Lee, 'Violence and the environment: the case of 'Earth First!', p. 120.
141. Deluca, 'Unruly arguments: the body rhetoric of Earth First!, Act Up, and Queer Nation', p. 9.
142. Arnold, *Ecoterror: The Violent Agenda to Save Nature, The World of the Unabomber*, p. 217; Dave Foreman, quoted in Lee's, *Earth First! Environmental Apocalypse*, p. 35.
143. Arnold, *Ecoterror: The Violent Agenda to Save Nature, The World of the Unabomber*, p. 216.
144. Lee, *Earth First! Environmental Apocalypse*, p. 35.
145. Ibid., p. 35; Dave Foreman, *Nature More*, 0 (July 1980), p. 2.
146. Lee, *Earth First! Environmental* Apocalypse, p. 36; Foreman, *Nature More*, p. 1.
147. Lee, *Earth First! Environmental Apocalypse,* p. 36; Foreman, *Nature More*, p. 1.
148. Lee, *Earth First! Environmental Apocalypse,* p. 36; Interview with Dave Foreman, cited in Scarce, *Eco-Warriors: Understanding the Radical Environmental Movement*, p. 61.
149. Arnold, *Ecoterror: The Violent Agenda to Save Nature, The World of the Unabomber*, p. 217.
150. Taylor, 'Religion, violence and radical environmentalism: From Earth First! to the Unabomber to the Earth Liberation Front', p. 14.
151. Ibid.
152. *Earth First! Direct Action Manual: Uncompromising Resistance in Defense of Mother Earth* (Eugene, OR: DAM Collective, 1997) p. ii.
153. Ibid., p. 8.
154. Ibid., p. 21.
155. Ibid., p. 131.
156. Trujillo, 'The radical environmentalist movement', p. 153.
157. Ibid.
158. Alexandra Plows et al. (2004) 'Covert repertoires: ecotage in the UK', *Social Movement Studies*, **3** (2), p. 209.
159. Parson, 'Understanding the ideology of the Earth Liberation Front', p. 52.
160. Liddick, *Eco-Terrorism: Radical Environmental and Animal Liberation Movements*, p. 61.
161. Trujillo, 'The radical environmentalist movement', p. 162.
162. Liddick, *Eco-Terrorism: Radical Environmental and Animal Liberation Movements*, p. 61.
163. Lange, 'Refusal to compromise: the case of Earth First!', p. 481.
164. Taylor Horne (2006) 'The Radical Environmental Movement: Incorporating Empire and the Politics of Nature', *Green Theory & Praxis Journal*, 2 (1), pp. 31–51.
165. Ibid., p. 34.
166. Lee, *Earth First! Environmental Apocalypse*, p. 43.
167. Steve Chase (1991) 'Whither the radical ecology movement' in Murray Bookchin and Dave Foreman (eds) *Defending the Earth: A Debate Between Murray Bookchin and Dave Foreman* (New York, Quebec: Black Rose Books), p. 21; Dave Foreman (1989) *Ecodefense: A Field Guide to Monkeywrenching* (Tucson: Ned Ludd Books), p. 16.
168. Long, *Ecoterrorism: Library in a Book*, p. 31; Dave Foreman, quoted in Manes, *Green Rage: Radical Environmentalism and the Unmaking of Civilization*, p. 73.
169. Lee, 'Violence and the environment: the case of 'Earth First!', p. 111.
170. Long, *Ecoterrorism: Library in a Book*, p. 31.
171. Manes, *Green Rage: Radical Environmentalism and the Unmaking of Civilization*, p. 7.

172. List, *Radical Environmentalism: Philosophy and Tactics*, p. 190.
173. Ibid., p. 191.
174. Arnold, *Ecoterror: The Violent Agenda to Save Nature, The World of the Unabomber*, p. 234.
175. Lee, *Earth First! Environmental Apocalypse*, p. 72; 'Wilderness War in Oregon, Blockaders Assaulted by Bulldozer', *Earth First!*, **3** (5), 21 June 1983, p. 1.
176. Lee, 'Violence and the environment: the case of 'Earth First!', p. 120.
177. Ibid.
178. Lee, *Earth First! Environmental Apocalypse*, p. 70.
179. Ibid., pp. 80–1; Peggy Bond (1984) 'Montana Earth First! takes senator's office', *Earth First!*, **4** (8),1 August, p. 1.
180. Arnold, *Ecoterror: The Violent Agenda to Save Nature, The World of the Unabomber*, p. 35.
181. Frederick Meekins (2010) 'The radical nature of "deep ecology"', *Canada Free Press*, 2 June.
182. Liddick, *Eco-Terrorism: Radical Environmental and Animal Liberation Movements*, p. 59.
183. Lee, *Earth First! Environmental Apocalypse* p. 116; 'Earth First! Foundation Fiscal Report – December 31, 1987', *Earth First!*, **8** (4), 20 March 1988, p. 17.
184. Lee, *Earth First! Environmental* Apocalypse, p. 116; Mike Roselle, quoted in Susan Zakin, *Coyotes and Town Dogs: Earth First! and the Radical Environmental Movement*, p. 384.
185. Lee, *Earth First! Environmental Apocalypse*, p. 117.
186. Jeffrey St Clair and Joshua Frank (2015) 'Dave Foreman and the First Green Scare Case', *Counter Punch*, 20 November 20, http://www.counterpunch.org/2015/11/20/dave-foreman-and-the-first-green-scare-case/.
187. Long, *Ecoterrorism: Library in a Book*, p. 36.
188. Ibid.
189. Ibid.
190. Taylor, 'Religion, violence and radical environmentalism: from Earth First! to the Unabomber to the Earth Liberation Front', p. 6.
191. St Clair and Frank, 'Dave Foreman and the First Green Scare Case'.
192. Eagan, 'From spikes to bombs: the rise of ecoterrorism', p. 7; Rae Tyson (1991) 'For Activist, earth still first: defendant to tone down his tactics', *USA Today*, 15 August, p. 3A.
193. Douglas Long, *Ecoterrorism: Library in a Book*, p. 36.
194. Ibid., p. 37.
195. St Clair and Frank, 'Dave Foreman and the First Green Scare Case'.
196. Long, *Ecoterrorism: Library in a Book*, p. 37; Gerry Spence (1991) quoted in Mark Shaffer, 'Eco-terrorism trial underway', *Arizona Republic*, 20 June, p. B1; Mike Fain, quoted in Lee, *Earth First! Environmental* Apocalypse, p. 132.
197. Long, *Ecoterrorism: Library in a Book*, p. 37; Dave Foreman, quoted in Sam Negri (1990) 'Earth First! setup alleged', *Arizona Republic*, 25 April, p. B2.
198. Donna E Correll (1992–3) 'No peace for the greens: the criminal prosecution of environmental activists and the threat of organizational liability', *Rutgers Law Journal*, **24** (3), pp. 773–806, p. 792, fn, 90.
199. St Clair and Frank, 'Dave Foreman and the First Green Scare Case'.
200. Long, *Ecoterrorism: Library in a Book*, p. 37.
201. Trujillo, 'The radical environmentalist movement', p. 150.
202. Jay Hasbrouck (2005) 'Primitive dissidents: Earth Liberation Front and the making of a radical movement' (PhD dissertation, University of Southern California, Los Angeles, CA), p. 11; Judi Bari (1990) 'Expand Earth First!', *Earth First!: The Radical Environmental Journal*, **10** (8), p. 5; Judi Bari (1994) *Timber Wars* (Monroe, ME: Common Courage); Lee,, *Earth First!: Environmental Apocalypse*; Zakin, *Coyotes and Town Dogs: Earth First! and the Environmental Movement.*

203. Hasbrouck, 'Primitive dissidents: Earth Liberation Front and the making of a radical movement', pp. 11–12; Dave Foreman (1982) 'Foreman replies', *Earth First!: The Radical Environmental Journal*, **2** (5), p. 2.
204. Wall, *Earth First! and The Anti-Roads Movement: Radical Environmentalism and Comparative Social Movements*, p. 45; Judi Bari (1993) 'Earth First! in Northern California: interview with Judi Bari', *Capitalism, Nature, Socialism*, **4** (4); Bari, *Timber Wars*).
205. Scarce, *Eco-Warriors: Understanding the Radical Environmental Movement* (updated edn, 2006), pp. 87–90.
206. Trujillo, 'The radical environmentalist movement', p. 150.
207. Lee, 'Violence and the environment: the case of 'Earth First!', pp. 120–1.
208. Long, *Ecoterrorism: Library in a* Book, p. 32; Dave Foreman, quoted in List, *Radical Environmentalism: Philosophy and Tactics*, p. 189.
209. Lee, 'Violence and the environment: the case of 'Earth First!', p. 121.
210. Ibid., pp. 121–2.
211. Paul Joosse, 'Leaderless resistance and ideological inclusion: the case of the Earth Liberation Front', p. 357.
212. Ibid., p. 358.
213. Lee, *Earth First! Environmental Apocalypse*, p. 143.
214. Liddick, *Eco-Terrorism: Radical Environmental and Animal Liberation Movements*, p. 59.
215. Wall, *Earth First! and the Anti-Roads Movement: Radical Environmentalism and Comparative Social Movements*, p. 45.
216. Trujillo, 'The radical environmentalist movement', p. 150.
217. Ibid., p. 151; Taylor, 'Religion, violence and radical environmentalism: from Earth First! to the Unabomber to the Earth Liberation Front', p. 11.
218. Lee, 'Violence and the environment: the case of 'Earth First!', p. 121.
219. Lee, *Earth First! Environmental Apocalypse*, p. 145; Karen Wood (1994) 'Getting back to (our) grass roots', *Earth First!*, **14** (6), 21 June, p. 2.
220. Scarce, *Eco-Warriors: Understanding the Radical Environmental Movement* (updated edn, 2006) p. 89.
221. Lee, *Earth First! Environmental Apocalypse*, pp. 128, 134.
222. Scarce, *Eco-Warriors: Understanding the Radical Environmental Movement* (updated edn, 2006), p. 94; Dave Foreman interviewed by Rik Scarce, Visalia, California (2 October 1989).
223. Long, *Ecoterrorism: Library in a Book*, p. 37.
224. Trujillo, 'The radical environmentalist movement', pp. 141–78, p. 150.
225. Lee, *Earth First! Environmental Apocalypse*, p. 139; Mike Geniella (1990) 'Leadership dispute splits Earth First!', *Press Democrat*, 12 August, p. A1.
226. Eagan, 'From spikes to bombs: the rise of ecoterrorism', p. 7.
227. Lee, *Earth First! Environmental Apocalypse*, p. 140; Geniella, 'Leadership dispute splits Earth First!', p. A14.
228. Short, 'Earth First! and the rhetoric of moral confrontation', p. 182.
229. Eagan, 'From spikes to bombs: the rise of ecoterrorism', p. 7.
230. Lee, *Earth First! Environmental Apocalypse*, p. 140.
231. Wall, *Earth First! and the Anti-Roads Movement: Radical Environmentalism and Comparative Social Movements*, p. 45; Lee, *Earth First! Environmental Apocalypse*, p. 57.
232. Long, *Ecoterrorism: Library in a Book*, p. 37; Foreman, *Confessions of an Eco-Warrior*, pp. 217–20.
233. Joosse, 'Leaderless resistance and ideological inclusion: the case of the Earth Liberation Front', p. 358.
234. Long, *Ecoterrorism: Library in a Book*, p. 38; John Davis (1991) *The Earth First! Reader: Ten Years of Radical Environmentalism* (Salt Lake City, Utah: Peregrine Smith), p. 14.
235. Trujillo, 'The radical environmentalist movement', p. 151.

236. Andrew Rowell (1996) *Green Backlash: Global Subversion of the Environment Movement* (London, New York: Routledge), p. 157.
237. Long, *Ecoterrorism: Library in a Book*, p. 39.
238. Lee, 'Violence and the environment: the case of 'Earth First!', p. 122.
239. Joosse, 'Leaderless resistance and ideological inclusion: the case of the Earth Liberation Front', p. 359.
240. Lee, 'Violence and the environment: the case of 'Earth First!', p. 123; Liddick, *Eco-Terrorism: Radical Environmental and Animal Liberation Movements*, pp. 61–3.; Long, *Ecoterrorism: Library in a Book*, p. 39.
241. Joosse, 'Leaderless resistance and ideological inclusion: the case of the Earth Liberation Front', p. 355.
242. Long, *Ecoterrorism: Library in a Book*, p. 38.
243. Ibid.
244. Rowell, *Green Backlash: Global Subversion of the Environment Movement*, p. 159; J.S. Zer and Judi Bari (1991) *High Times* (June), p. 14.
245. Long, *Ecoterrorism: Library in a* Book, p. 38.
246. Scarce, *Eco-Warriors: Understanding the Radical Environmental Movement* (updated edn, 2006), p. 84.
247. Liddick, *Eco-Terrorism: Radical Environmental and Animal Liberation Movements*, p. 61.
248. Short, 'Earth First! and the rhetoric of moral confrontation', p. 182.
249. Ibid., p. 18; Interview with Robert Hattoy, Los Angeles (9 September 1987).
250. Manes, *Green Rage: Radical Environmentalism and the Unmaking of Civilization*, p. 18; Howie Wolke (1983) 'The Grizzly Den', *Earth First!*, 1 May, p. 2.
251. Short, 'Earth First! and the rhetoric of moral confrontation', p. 172.
252. Manes, *Green Rage: Radical Environmentalism and the Unmaking of Civilization*, p. 19; Dave Foreman, speech at the Seventh Annual Round River Rendezvous, Grand Canyon, Arizona (10 July 1987).
253. Teale Phelps Bondaroff (2008) 'Throwing a wrench into things: the strategy of radical environmentalism', *Journal of Military and Strategic Studies*, **10** (4), p. 17.
254. http://www.earthfirstjournal.org/subsection.php?id=1 accessed 10/03/10.
255. Parson, 'Understanding the ideology of the Earth Liberation Front', p. 51.
256. Long, *Ecoterrorism: Library in a Book*, p. 7.
257. List, *Radical Environmentalism: Philosophy and Tactics*, p. 252.
258. Long, *Ecoterrorism: Library in a Book*, p. 7; Edward Abbey, quoted in List, *Radical Environmentalism: Philosophy and Tactics*, p. 252.
259. Deluca, 'Unruly arguments: the body rhetoric of Earth First!, Act Up, and Queer Nation', pp. 12, 16; Alexandra Plows et al. (2001), 'From the Earth Liberation Front to universal dark matter: the challenge of covert repertoires to social movement research', Paper for the Workshop on Democracy and Extremism European Consortium for Political Research Joint Sessions Grenoble, 6–11 April, p. 4.
260. Plows et al., 'From the Earth Liberation Front to universal dark matter: the challenge of covert repertoires to social movement research', p. 5.
261. Plows et al., 'Covert repertoires: ecotage in the UK', p. 209.
262. Lange, 'Refusal to compromise: the case of Earth First!', p. 484.
263. Plows et al., 'Covert repertoires: ecotage in the UK', p. 208.
264. Trujillo, 'The radical environmentalist movement', p. 149.
265. Plows et al., 'Covert repertoires: ecotage in the UK', p. 208.
266. Eagan, 'From spikes to bombs: the rise of ecoterrorism', p. 6.
267. Taylor, 'Religion, violence and radical environmentalism: from Earth First! to the Unabomber to the Earth Liberation Front', p. 6.
268. Trujillo, 'The radical environmentalist movement', p. 149.
269. Young, 'A time series analysis of eco-terrorist violence in the United States: 1993–2003', p. 36; 'The Green Threat', *Economist*, **361**, 1 December 2001, pp. 31–2.
270. Trujillo, 'The radical environmentalist movement', p. 149.

271. Taylor, 'Religion, violence and radical environmentalism: from Earth First! to the Unabomber to the Earth Liberation Front', p. 10. For example, 'stuffed "Smokey the Bear" dolls symbolizing Forest Service employees (who are often called 'freddies' – a derogatory term meaning 'forest rape', eagerly done and done in endless succession) are occasionally hung in effigy from trees in movement campsites. See Taylor, 'Religion, violence and radical environmentalism: from Earth First! to the Unabomber to the Earth Liberation Front', p. 10.
272. Michael Stratmoen (2008) 'Arson on Vail Mountain: a case study of the Earth Liberation Front', James Madison University, May, p. 21.
273. Short, 'Earth First! and the rhetoric of moral confrontation', p. 178.
274. List, *Radical Environmentalism: Philosophy and Tactics*, p. 250; Edward Abbey (1983) 'Earth First! and the Monkey Wrench Gang', *Environmental Ethics*, **5** (Spring), pp. 94–5.
275. Taylor, 'Religion, violence and radical environmentalism: from Earth First! to the Unabomber to the Earth Liberation Front', p. 15.
276. Lange, 'Refusal to compromise: the case of Earth First!', p. 484.
277. Taylor, 'Religion, violence and radical environmentalism: from Earth First! to the Unabomber to the Earth Liberation Front', p. 11.
278. Plows et al., 'Covert repertoires: ecotage in the UK', p. 209.
279. Ehud Sprinzak (1995) 'Right-wing terrorism in a comparative prospective: the case of split delegitimization', in Tore Bjørgo (ed.), *Terror From the Extreme Right* (London: Frank Cass & Co. Ltd), p. 20; Taylor, 'Religion, violence and radical environmentalism: from Earth First! to the Unabomber to the Earth Liberation Front', p. 13.
280. David Rapoport (1984) 'Fear and trembling: terrorism in three religious traditions, *American Political Science Review*, **78**, p. 671; Taylor, 'Religion, violence and radical environmentalism: from Earth First! to the Unabomber to the Earth Liberation Front', p. 9.
281. Taylor, 'Religion, violence and radical environmentalism: from Earth First! to the Unabomber to the Earth Liberation Front', p. 11.
282. Ibid., p. 12.
283. Long, *Ecoterrorism: Library in a Book*, p. 35.
284. Short, 'Earth First! and the rhetoric of moral confrontation', p. 178.
285. Ibid.
286. Ibid.
287. Lee, 'Violence and the environment: the case of 'Earth First!', p. 117.
288. Ibid., p. 118.
289. Taylor, 'Religion, violence and radical environmentalism: from Earth First! to the Unabomber to the Earth Liberation Front', pp. 17–18.
290. Plows et al., 'Covert repertoires: ecotage in the UK', p. 203.
291. Lee, 'Violence and the environment: the case of 'Earth First!', p. 117.
292. Long, *Ecoterrorism: Library in a Book*, p. 40.
293. Ibid., p. 49.
294. Wall, *Earth First! and the Anti-Roads Movement: Radical Environmentalism and Comparative Social Movements*, p. 45.
295. Ibid.
296. Ibid., pp. 45–6.
297. Ibid., p. 46.
298. Noel Molland (2006) 'A spark that ignited a flame: the evolution of the Earth Liberation Front', in Steven Best and Anthony Nocella (eds), *Igniting a Revolution: Voices in Defense of the Earth* (Oakland, CA: AK Press) p. 48.
299. Plows et al., 'Covert repertoires: ecotage in the UK', p. 201.
300. Rowell, *Green Backlash: Global Subversion of the Environment Movement*, p. 331.
301. Ibid., p. 334; J. Torrance, Interviewed by Andrew Rowell (16 October 1994).
302. Derek Wall (2000) 'Snowballs, elves and skimmingtons?: Genealogies of environmental direct action' in B. Seel et al. (eds) *Direct Action in British Environmentalism* (London and New York: Routledge), p. 81.

303. Brian Doherty et al. (2000) 'Direct action in British environmentalism' in B. Seel et al. (eds) *Direct Action in British Environmentalism* (London and New York: Routledge), p. 9.
304. Wall, *Earth First! and the Anti-Roads Movement: Radical Environmentalism and Comparative Social Movements*, pp. 190–91.
305. Liddick, *Eco-Terrorism: Radical Environmental and Animal Liberation Movements*, p. 63.
306. Manes, *Green Rage: Radical Environmentalism and the Unmaking of Civilization*, p. 9. For example, according to Manes, in the late 1980s, Australian activists caused more than US $1 million in damage to timber equipment. Furthermore, in Thailand, activists were responsible for the firebombing (in 1986) of a chemical plant, which produced tantalum with an estimated cost of US $45 million. See Manes, *Green Rage: Radical Environmentalism and the Unmaking of Civilization*, p. 9.
307. Bron Taylor (1995) 'Earth First! and global narratives of popular ecological resistance' in Bron Taylor (ed.) *Ecological Resistance Movements: The Global Emergence of Radical and Popular Environmentalism* (Albany, NY: State University of New York Press), p. 23; Scarce, *Eco-Warriors: Understanding the Radical Environmental Movement*, p. 140.
308. Taylor, 'Earth First! and global narratives of popular ecological resistance', p. 23; see also Tomas Kolenka (1993) 'Resistance in Slovakia: Earth First! defends Danube', *Earth First!*, **8** (5).
309. Ibid., p. 24; see also Oxford Earth First! (1993) 'Twyford down but not out', *Earth First!*, **13** (6); Jake Burbridge and Jason Torrance (1993) 'Road war victory', *Earth First!*, **13** (7); Alistair McIntosh et al. (1994) 'Reclaiming the Scottish Highlands: clearance, conflict and crofting', *The Ecologist*, **24** (2).
310. Taylor, 'Earth First! and global narratives of popular ecological resistance' p. 16.
311. Ibid., p. 17.
312. Ibid.
313. Ibid.
314. Ibid.
315. Ibid.
316. Arslan, 'The social and operational intersections of environmental extremism in North America and Europe', p. 46; S. Sarkar (1996) 'Review of the book *Between Millenarianism and the Apocalypse: Earth First!: Environmental Apocalypse', Bioscience*, **46** (8) (September), pp. 628–30.
317. Short, 'Earth First! and the rhetoric of moral confrontation', p. 180.
318. Ibid., p. 481.
319. Trujillo, 'The radical environmentalist movement', p. 150.
320. Ibid., p. 361.
321. Hudson Valley Earth First!, 'Campaigns', https://hudsonvalleyearthfirst.wordpress.com/gas-infrastructure/.
322. Ibid.
323. Earth First!, 'Rest of Europe', https://earthfirst.org.uk/actionreports/resteurope.
324. Hudson Valley Earth First!, 'Who we are', https://hudsonvalleyearthfirst.wordpress.com/about/.
325. *Earth First! Journal*, media from the frontlines of ecological resistance, http://earthfirstjournal.org/submissions/. As evidence of how close Earth First and the ELF still are, Earth First! News publishes many of the ELF operations. See earthfirstjournal.org.

5. Elves running through the forest: the Earth Liberation Front

I love not man the less, but nature more.

Childe Harold's Pilgrimage, Lord Byron

INTRODUCTION

Radical movements have a tendency to adapt over time into unexpected permutations where external circumstances and internal dynamics can either break up a group or it becomes more extremist and willing to use greater violence in the furtherance of its goals. In the case of Earth First! that occurred when it metastasized into the Earth Liberation Front (ELF) when some group members believed that Earth First! was not radical enough in its methods.[1] The ELF is now the most highly visible 'ecoterrorist' group currently operating.[2] The group based itself on the ALF with the ELF acronym based on the ALF initials.[3] The ELF describes itself as 'the dying rage of the burning planet',[4] and can best be understood as 'an international underground organization that uses direct action in the form of economic sabotage to stop the exploitation and destruction of the natural environment'.[5]

ELF participants proclaimed themselves 'elves',[6] and were more than willing to commit crimes against property but would not target humans.[7] The ELF, however, rejects the label 'ecoterrorist', its participants considering themselves to be 'ecosaboteurs', a militant action rather than terrorist.[8] However, according to many state agencies, ELF activists are without a doubt 'ecoterrorists'.[9] Prior to the 9/11 attacks in 2001 the FBI considered the ELF to be a significant domestic terrorist threat, given the amount of destruction (in monetary amounts) they committed as well as the potential for (accidental) physical injury given its modus operandi.[10] Rosebraugh points out that, in February 2001, then FBI director Louis Freeh publicly stated that the ELF was the number one domestic terrorist threat currently operating.[11] According to Wade, the FBI believed that ELF acts should not be classified as isolated vandalism but were rather a global 'thoughtful, coordinated campaign'.[12]

According to Young, post-9/11 the ramping up of ELF's activities surprised and concerned terrorism scholars who were worried the group would become a classic revolutionary organization.[13] Pickering claims, however, that the organization is working to build a revolutionary movement that is less concerned with theories and strategies and more focused on action, but to date this has not happened, nor have they developed into a mass movement.[14] The ELF publicly argues that it is more concerned with raising awareness of environmental issues than the support of the public, since many activists believe that the public is part of the problem. While the controversy continues to rage regarding the use of violence against persons rather than property by the group, there was, for a time, a clear indication of 'an erosion of the ELF's existing restraints on causing harm to human beings'.[15]

Section 1 of this chapter charts the split of the ELF from Earth First!. It examines how its philosophy, strategies and tactics differed from Earth First! and charts its development. It evaluates how the ELF started in the UK in 1992 and how it spread globally. It examines this cell structure with, in the case of the ELF, their emphasis on 'affinity groups', which are usually autonomous and self-funded, and further evaluates their strengths and weaknesses.

Section 2 of this chapter provides a history of the various militant acts carried out by the ELF. Lastly, using the proposed radicalization approach outlined in the Introduction, this chapter considers whether the organization is still an effective radical environmental group and analyses the extent of the process of radicalization that both Earth First! and the ELF have undergone.

SECTION 1

EARTH LIBERATION FRONT SPLITTING FROM EARTH FIRST!

When UK Earth First! participants were involved in the Fison's peat-digging operation in south Yorkshire in April 1992 they wanted to forward a communiqué to the media proclaiming responsibility for their sabotaging activities. Once the publication was released, however, internal debate began regarding the legal difficulty for the organization should they be seen to be publicly endorsing such activities.[16] Many activists associated with Earth First! believed it would be legally difficult for the organization to publicly support the use of 'ecotage'. As such, it was decided that they would create a sub-division of the organization with ELF activists carrying out raids where there was the potential for criminal damage, whilst Earth First! would publicly promote non-violent direct action.[17]

Activists who joined the ELF argued that the tactics and campaigns undertaken by Earth First! could only 'go so far against earth abusers'. Early participants insisted that 'mass protest and civil disobedience is limited in its scope and sooner or later the legal system inevitably works in favor of the earth rapist and environment destroyer'.[18] As such, the Elves concluded that their actions were necessary and hoped that their illegal action would help the earth liberation movement as similar radical actions, they believed, had helped the animal liberation movement. As such, according to Molland, the Elves wished to become an eco-ALF that, inspired by the ALF's willingness to undertake more radical action, were willing to do whatever is necessary to save the world.[19] Reportedly, the founders of the new ELF wanted the environmentalists to 'work on the same basis and have a similar name, hoping that people would instantly understand how the ELF operated and what its goals were'.[20]

Thus the Earth Liberation Front (ELF) was officially founded in 1992 in Brighton, England. The sub-group was more attractive for the more radical participants of Earth First! who believed sabotage would further the environmentalist cause better than legal protests. The division between the ELF and Earth First! has allowed both entities to focus on their preferred methods of actions, strategies and differing constituencies.[21] While the two groups were to operate separately the participants agreed there should not be competition between the two groups but rather tolerance.[22] According to Sulek:

> Frustrated that Earth First! was going too mainstream, more radical activists proposed an underground wing to keep up the sabotage ... Sadly, this never really happened, as some sections of the movement were trying to link up with the mainstream and saw the elves (ELF) as an embarrassment ... Undeterred, the more radical group broke off to form Earth Liberation Front as a separate entity.[23]

Hasbrouck notes that the group was immediately successful in England and within a year 20 clandestine cells had been established in England, using arson and other means to attack corporations.[24]

In February 1994, inspired by the actions of Earth First! UK, Judi Bari published an article in *Earth First! Journal*, recommending that Earth First! US also separate into an above-ground group and an underground one with the goal of seeking legitimacy for their movement. She argued that carrying out activities such as monkeywrenching had helped to isolate and discredit their movement, and drive away some of the best activists. In an article, she wrote, 'For the survival of both, it's time to leave the night work to the elves in the woods.'[25]

PRINCIPLES AND AIMS OF THE ELF

The ELF website lists the goals and guidelines of the organization, which are:

1. To inflict economic damage on those profiting from the destruction and exploitation of the natural environment.
2. To reveal and educate the public on the atrocities committed against the earth and all species that populate it.
3. To take all necessary precautions against harming any animal, human and non-human.[26]

All ELF participants are expected to adhere to these principles regardless of their individual cell's wishes.[27] When asked about the group's aims, an ELF spokesperson responded with:

> Our Westernized way of life comes at the expense of … the natural environment. By seeking a safer, longer, happier life – by seeking more than a bare, primitive subsistence – mankind is guilty of crimes against nature. We wish to inflict economic damage on those profiting from the destruction and exploitation of the natural environment – hoping eventually to speed up the collapse of the industry.[28]

Influenced by these goals, many actions attempt to inflate the cost of insurance, thereby increasing the 'costs of harming the environment' by the putative despoiler.[29] In a 1997 communiqué from the ELF, the group's intentions spelled out that its long-term goals are 'to speed up the collapse of industry, to scare the rich, and to undermine the foundations of the state'.[30]

IDEOLOGY OF THE ELF

Up to this point, as Parson notes, researchers have neglected to adequately investigate the ELF's ideology, focusing instead on three other organizations (Greenpeace, Earth First! and the Sea Shepherds), all of whom 'embrace variants of biocentrism and/or deep ecology', unlike the ELF.[31] The ELF describes itself as being concerned with bringing about positive social and political change, but rather than basing their actions on a deep ecology critique of society like Earth First! they are more interested in 'attacking the ideology of "capitalism and the mindset that allows it to exist", which is thought to be the root cause of injustice and the destruction of nature'.[32]

In 2002, Craig Rosebraugh (the unofficial spokesman of the ELF) testified that the ELF perceives itself as containing both anarchist and anti-capitalist elements and antecedents.[33] The ELF fully believes that the capitalist society in which we live is to blame for 'destroying all life on this planet' and to stop such destruction requires members to 'take the profit motive out of killing'.[34] Pickering points out that for the ELF, 'it is not enough to work solely on individual environmental issues; the capitalist state and its symbols of propaganda must also be targeted'.[35] For ELF participants, therefore, their actions are a form of self-defence they commit as extensions of nature on behalf of the planet.[36]

According to Long, ELF activists, unlike Earth First! with its focus on protecting wilderness, have shifted to be concerned with the broader environmental issue. In doing so they have made common cause with the ALF and are more likely to be vegans rather than the 'proud meat-eating, redneck behavior of Foreman and company' entertained within Earth First!.[37] According to Hasbrouck, the ELF while drawing on the Earth First! roots of 'noble savagery' and bringing about an 'anarcho-primitivist ecotopia', are more seized by the urgency of the situation demanding immediate action. But their vision of a more perfect (ecological) world cannot be realized until civilization, as it is currently constructed, collapses and for ELF participants it is their self-appointed obligation to achieve this goal.[38] According to Castells, to this end the ELF is not 'seeking a place at any political table' since it would prefer to end current political structures totally to be replaced with their 'version' of society.[39]

Similarly, the ELF has adopted radical action because it believes the conventional strategies adopted by mainstream environmental organizations such as protests and lobbying have failed. According to an ELF communiqué (released 1 January 2003 in response to an action in Erie, Pennsylvania):

> Despite decades of popular environmental activism, the mainstream environmental movement, which began arguably in the early 1960s, has failed in its attempts to bring about the protection needed to stop the destruction of life on this planet. In many ways, it has served only to accelerate the destruction. It's [sic] occasional 'victories', reforms or small concessions, have fostered hope in a means of social change that has proven unable to produce tangible protection of life, time after time.[40]

ELF AND ECOTAGE

Like Earth First! the primary tactics of the ELF include 'direct action' and 'ecotage'.[41] The organization has claimed responsibility for acts of property damage multiple times, including attacks against loggers, genetic engineering facilities, multinational corporations and research laboratories.[42] According to an ELF communiqué (distributed 24 October 2003, in response to the destruction at a construction site of a Wal-Mart store):

> For us, sabotage may not be a means to change any world but our own, as an expression of our feelings toward this society. We strike for ourselves, out of our own frustrations, and rage and despair ... as a means of therapy and adventure. Because to not act, or to resign oneself to such an impoverished life of working and consuming is not good enough for us. We are not content and we intend [sic] to express this.[43]

Despite having a large array of targets to choose from, no action is meant to be targeted at humans.[44] For elves, ecotage has become a 'bonafide stand alone strategy'. The ELF now believes that if enough damage can be done to a project, the entire project will be halted and rethought. In this way, ecotage is no longer used as a tactic to stall while legitimate means are pursued but is a means in and of itself.[45]

THE STRUCTURE OF THE ELF

Building on both the Earth First! and the ALF approach of leaderless resistance, the organization, according to their website, is an 'international underground movement consisting of autonomous groups of people who carry out direct action according to the E.L.F. guidelines'.[46] They have no discernable organizational structure and instead rely on individual cells understanding and accepting the organization's mission and choosing to initiate action (including determining targets) without a centralized command structure. This structure has made it difficult for police and intelligence services to identify members of these tight-knit cells.[47] This allows individuals, as the ELF website notes, to commit illegal acts such as arson as their consciences dictate, but such choices 'are not endorsed, encouraged, or approved of by the management and participants of this web site'.[48]

The separate ELF cells do not generally communicate with each other.[49] Thus it can be argued that the ELF is best conceived of as an amorphous movement rather than an organization.[50] It is important to note that while decentralization can inhibit the ELF's ability to learn and adapt at a strategic level, the evidence indicates it has enabled elves to respond quickly and effectively at least in terms of being able to disseminate and interpret information.[51] According to Rosebraugh, the ELF has no hierarchy and does not hold national meetings. This does complicate its ability to respond because there is no mechanism to amend their ideology or guidelines, nor to rein in extremist members of individual cells.[52]

However, according to articles in *Jane's Intelligence Review*, the ELF does have a tiny 'cohesive leadership core', which can nominate targets to local cells but also travels globally increasing support, which not only suggests targets to local cells but whose participants also travel between countries to garner support.[53] Further, it is believed there have been formal efforts to promote self-training materials via journals and websites as well as the training of activists.[54] Certainly there must be/or was either a leadership group or communication occurring between cells, since the ELF has shown that it is capable of coordinating attacks. For example, on 21 May 2001, the ELF launched simultaneous arson attacks against Jefferson Poplar Farms in Clatskanie, Oregon and the University of Washington's horticulture centre located in Seattle.[55]

Funding for the ELF predominantly comes from 'sympathetic organizations' (some from the animal rights movement) and 'wealthy benefactors' who support the ELF's goals.[56]

'MEMBERSHIP' OF THE ELF

It is important to understand that the ELF does not have any official membership and does not consider itself to be an 'organization' but rather providing a 'philosophy' of action. Anyone willing to carry out radical acts and publicize it, in accordance with the overarching philosophy and guidelines, is a 'member' of the ELF.[57]

Thus the ELF does not recruit from pre-existing organizations but encourages people to start their own cells of people they trust.[58] Foreman points out that the more people involved, the greater the chance of police infiltration and it is vital to avoid publicizing who individual members are.[59]

When asked how many participants make up the ELF, Pickering writes:

> It is next to impossible to estimate the number of ELF participants internationally or even country by country. Since 1997, in the United States, the ELF actions have steadily increased and have appeared in a growing number

of differing geographical areas. Therefore, it is safe to assume the group continues to grow in size.[60]

Why Participants Join the ELF

It is difficult to determine the individual make-up of the ELF affinity cells since individuals do not *join* the ELF per se and are not formal members.[61] Further, as Ackerman has pointed out, the only known ELF participants are the ones who have been identified and prosecuted, which is highly unlikely to be all of the elves.[62]

However, research indicates that the sort of person drawn to join the ELF tends to be of two types. The first and most prominent type are either teenagers or young adults, educated, drawn predominately from the middle/upper class or well-established and highly educated people in their thirties, mostly with families and an active part of their local communities, and with a background in environmental activism.[63] Gary Perlstein and Kelly Stoner argue that the first cohort 'are young white males, educated and bright, angry, politically far to the left and/or anarchist, vehemently anti-corporate America, anti-war, and often aligned with other social justice movements'.[64] Similarly, according to Ray Lauer (an FBI spokesman), officials have concluded that ELF participants are usually men aged between 18 and 26.[65] Gary Perlstein further concluded that cells are likely drawn from the nearest university population.[66]

The second, less numerous type of ELF participants are older activists who appear to become members over concerns about the long-term impact of global environmental damage on intergenerational equity. The idea of operating anonymously whilst allowing them to be 'respectable' members of their community is also appealing.[67] Many activists have joined the ELF after previously attempting to 'operate within the laws', but growing tired of the failure of the 'legitimate system' to protect the environment. Other activists felt too little was being done to protect the environment from perceived environmental catastrophes such as climate change or nuclear mishaps. Due to these types of events, many activists chose to join the ELF, preferring to use their tactics of economic sabotage to bring about governmental and corporate change.[68]

However, it is possible to make some generalizations about the typical ELF participant. If we were to build a profile they would be a Caucasian US male aged between 18 and 26, with a middle-class background and a university education, exposed to anti-authoritarian leftist thought, most likely anarchist and disenfranchised from the mainstream environmental movement. An examination of the arrests of those charged with being a member of the ELF shows that while women are involved as elves the vast majority fit the above profile.[69]

Paul Joosse argues that the ELF was particularly attractive to young men because it downplayed ideology, particularly on its website and publications. The message was particularly strong for those who saw it as a chance to be a 'hero'.[70]

COMMUNICATING THE MESSAGE

Although the group does not have a leader, Craig Rosebraugh (and later joined by Leslie James Pickering) has functioned in the past as its 'unofficial spokesman'. The ELF has been known to contact him through communiqués (usually taking responsibility for an action) and Rosebraugh would, in turn, arrange a press release to the media. He also was available for speeches and interviews on behalf of the group.[71] Participants were also able to download videos from the group's website that provide 'tutorials in arson and sabotage'.[72]

The ELF created the North American Earth Liberation Front Press Office (NAELFPRO), in Portland, Oregon, to function as a clearing house to publish organizational literature, post recruitment videos and provide a public outlet for ELF actions and communiqués.[73] Between 1997 and 2002, 46 communiqués were written and circulated by ELF cells explaining action events such as vandalism, animal liberation and arson.[74]

Following the resignations of Leslie James Pickering and Craig Rosebraugh after FBI harassment,[75] the role was filled anonymously but still many activists believed it was contrary to ELF ideology for a green, anarchist, direct action network to have a central communications hub that could be perceived as 'approving' and claiming actions and, in effect, 'approved' and 'claimed' actions on behalf of the ELF.[76] The internet (and other modern technologies) now have increased the reach of the movement, providing the ELF with the ability to contact sympathizers, distribute training and logistics information but also to function 'more as a networked entity than as a concrete group'.[77]

SECTION 2

ELF ACTIONS

At first, the ELF's actions were on a small scale and considered to be merely 'token' actions.[78] Due to the lack of 'large-scale' protests and attacks, however, the new environmental group failed to gain the same popularity that the ALF had accomplished.[79] Despite being known primarily for small-scale attacks, the English ELF was responsible for one large-scale demonstration. The campaign was against the company Fison, which was accused of causing US $100,000 worth of damage to the 'English countryside' by 'draining peat bogs'. This campaign has been the only one in which the organization (UK) has communicated with the public, through the media in the from of a statement in the *Green Anarchist*.[80]

By 1994 the organization had established itself on the European continent.[81] Early European actions included targeting Amsterdam Airport, destroying hunting platforms and attacking oil exploration equipment.[82]

By 1996, the ELF movement had become firmly entrenched in North America. The first action in Canada occurred in British Columbia (June 1995) and included vandalism against 'trophy hunting stores' and an act of arson against a 'guide outfitter'. In October, a second act of arson occurred in Alberta, against a lumber company. The movement also quickly spread to the USA, with reports of vandalism in Oregon. However, the acts quickly intensified (including arson) and spread to other states (including Michigan, Washington, California and Indiana). Reportedly, the ELF announced its US existence in October 1996 by torching a United States Forest Service truck in Oregon's Willamette National Forest.[83] Also in 1996 ELF participants orchestrated further actions within the US. In Oregon, activists wrote 'ELF' on the walls of a public relations office and vandalized a McDonalds. The next day a further two McDonalds were attacked and had their locks glued shut. Later that year a group calling itself the Great Lakes ELF participants raided a fur farm in Michigan and set free 150 minks.[84]

The movement was widespread by the time the first official 'communiqué' was issued by the group in March 1997 that stated they took inspiration from the 'Luddites, Levellers, Diggers, the Autonome squatter movement, ALF, the Zapatistas, and the little people – those mischievous elves of lore and that many elves were amassing in the Pacific Northwest and elves will leave surprises as they go'.[85] While a complete accounting of their actions is not possible, below is a number of the most significant actions carried out as well as a range of different ecotage tactics adopted by the elves.

On 28 October 1996 in Detroit, Oregon a US Forest Service vehicle was torched in the Detroit Ranger District headquarters. The building was spray painted with 'Earth Liberation Front' and anti-logging slogans. An incendiary device was located on the roof that had failed to explode.[86]

The next year on 15 March 1997 a joint ALF and ELF tree-spiking operation occurred in Mackenzie River watershed, Oregon.[87]

On 11 March 1997 in Sandy, Utah a joint ALF/ELF operation utilized pipe bombs and one firebomb to destroy four trucks and the offices of the Agricultural Fur Breeders Co-Op, causing approximately US $1 million in damage.[88] That same year on 29 November, in Burns, Oregon, the Bureau of Land Management Wild Horse Corral was burnt to the ground while the 488 wild horses and 51 burros were released. The fire caused over US $450,000 in structural damage.[89]

Again on 21 June 1998 a joint ALF/ELF cell destroyed two US Department of Agriculture Animal Damage Control Buildings in Olympia, Washington leading to US $1.5 million in research being lost and $400,000 in structural damages.[90] On 26 December 1998 in Medford, Oregon the US Forest Industries suffered damages estimated at $700,000 when a fire destroyed their logging mill offices.[91]

Since their inception they have been implicated in numerous criminal activities ranging from arson to vandalism, including destroying ski lifts and burning down condominiums in 2003. Since 1997 their actions in the USA are estimated to have caused over $100 million in damages.[92] However, despite some comments about the need for violence against people, they still appear to be very careful to target property rather than sentient beings in their action to date.

Vail Lodge Attack

On 18 October 1998 the largest ecotage attack committed (in terms of cost) to date was carried out by the ELF, which claimed responsibility for an act of arson that destroyed 'five buildings and four ski lifts' in Vail, Colorado, causing an estimated $21 million in damages. It was maintained that the action was to defend the Lynx habitat against the resort's expansion plans and the communiqué sent to the media advised skiers, for their own safety, to go elsewhere.[93]

Craig Rosebraugh announced to local and national media that he did not know the identity of those who sent him the missive, but he claimed that the ELF was responsible for the act.[94] As Garfinkel points out, regarding the arson attack in Vail, Colorado even if the ELF was not responsible for the arson, claiming it was a potent propaganda device, a photo of the burning building was shown on the front page of the ELF's website.[95]

Rick Scarce believes that the attack in Vail indicated that 'a whole different scale of sabotage had become acceptable … The environmental movement has been radicalized permanently. I don't rule out the next step … that people will be killed.'[96] However, the attack on the Vail, Colorado ski resort was counterproductive for the ELF in preventing the lodge being built. Hoping to gain sympathy for the environment from the community, the response by other environmental groups and the Vail community had the 'opposite effect'. The Vail community rallied behind the ski resort, denouncing the ELF and their tactics. According to townsman Ken Huge, 'even people who are opposed to Vail's expansion are infuriated by the devastation'.[97] Ultimately, the ELF was unsuccessful in stopping the planned expansion in Vail.[98] It can be argued that this is how acts of ecotage often conclude, as the general public does not see such strikes as the work of 'environmental heroes' but rather terrorists.[99]

'The Family' and Operation Backfire

The Vail attack led to the FBI taking over ecoterrorist attacks on the West Coast. In 2004 the FBI merged seven independent investigations from its Portland, Oregon field office under the code name *Operation Backfire*. An ELF cell that called itself 'The Family' was alleged to be behind the Vail arson attack (and up to 20 other arson and ecotage attacks over a six-year period).[100] The 20-strong cell was active from 1995 to 2001, in Oregon, Washington, California, Colorado and Wyoming. The FBI deemed them 'ecoterrorists'. They caused more than $48 million in damages and they became the prime target of the FBI operation.[101]

The group's membership was eclectic comprising college students, a firefighter and a woman employed in a group home for the developmentally disabled. Some of the members were politically aware but others were involved because of their partners (while some never told their partners of their nocturnal activities) or just wanted to 'blow things up'.[102]

'The Family' utilized 'book club' meetings as cover for sub-cells where training was provided, previous operations were analysed for errors and strategy was planned. The cells were vigilant about not being apprehended; willing to 'conceal or destroy evidence'; used code names, words and numbers; and used false identification documents to conceal their true identities. However, the group developed irreconcilable differences amongst the members leading to in-fighting about the success of their actions, which caused them to abandon their campaign.[103]

In 2003, the police learned of a suspected former member Jacob Ferguson's drug habit and used that information against him to compel him to become an informant against his former cell.[104] He helped identify family members (as a cell it was no longer active as of 2003) and the incidents they had been involved in.[105] Based on information given to them by the turned informant the taskforce successfully arrested and prosecuted members of 'The Family'.[106]

In December 2005 and January 2006, the FBI indicted six women and seven men on a total of 65 charges. Several activists initially refused to testify, but under the threat of potentially going to jail for 60 years they accepted a plea deal.[107] The alleged leader of the cell, William C. Rodgers, committed suicide in an Arizona jail cell after being indicted in 2006. Another member, Rebecca Jeanette Rubin, after avoiding police capture for a decade by having fled to Canada turned herself in to authorities at the border in Blaine, Washington.[108]

By the end of the investigation the FBI had arrested 11 people on charges ranging from arson to conspiracy. Over 40 criminal acts ranging from vandalism to arson were solved and 17 individuals were indicted; 15 of them pleaded guilty and were sentenced in 2007 to jail time ranging from 37 months to 188 months.[109] Two members of 'The Family' remain uncaptured: Josephine Sunshine Overaker is believed to have fled to Spain and Joseph Dibee is currently thought to be in Syria.[110]

According to Andrew Smith, the significance of the operation was a new-found determination by the government to prosecute ecotage as terrorist acts, whereby defendants receive stiffer penalties under the newly enhanced Patriot Act title VII. Radical environmentalists everywhere were afraid that the government would be targeting them next.[111]

The Vail attacks, however, did raise the public consciousness of radical environmental philosophy and activities within the USA like no previous action had. Further, despite the threat of prosecution and hefty jail sentences after Operation Backfire, participants were still willing to risk their freedom to commit ecotage.

On 7 August 1999 at Escanaba, Michigan two fishing boats were burnt in the driveway of a veterinarian who was once a mink rancher. A garage door was tagged with graffiti reading, 'FUR IS MURDER. E.L.F.'[112] On Christmas Day that year, fire destroyed the main office of the Boise Cascade logging company in Monmouth, Oregon costing over US $1 million in damage, with the ELF claiming responsibility for the action in a communiqué.[113] On 31 December offices at the Michigan State University were drenched with gasoline and set alight causing US $900,000 in damage. The ELF claimed responsibility and stated that the fires were set because of the work being done to force developing nations in Asia, Latin America and Africa to switch to genetically engineered crops.[114]

According to Rosebraugh, 2000 was an 'extremely busy' year for the ELF. He states that the group grew in numbers and built on having a greater global presence.[115] In Bloomington, Indiana on 23 January 2000 a fire destroyed a building site at the Sterling Woods development causing US $200,000 in damage. The site was targeted because it was part of a sprawling development in the Lake Monroe watershed under threat from building developments.[116] On 9 September 2000 the Monroe County Republican Party Committee headquarters was targeted in an arson attack. An ELF communiqué stated that it would not 'sit quietly as politicians pushed for plans to extend an ecologically destructive highway'.[117]

On 27 November 2000 there was an attack at Niwot, Colorado. The group burnt down a luxury home going up in a new sub-division. The ELF sent a note to the *Boulder Weekly* newspaper stating 'Viva la revolution! The Boulder ELF burned the Legend Ridge mansion on Nov. 27th.'[118] On 9 December 2000 on Long Island, New York a fire burned down a condominium under construction. The ELF in a missive declared 'an unbounded war on urban sprawl' but claimed it checked for occupants, both human and animal, before the fire was set.[119]

On 1 January 2001 in Glendale, Oregon the ELF claimed responsibility for an arson attack on the Superior Lumber Company offices causing $400,000 in damage. Their communiqué stated that 'This year we hope to see an escalation in tactics against capitalism and industry.'[120] That same year on 21 May the ELF set off a firebomb at the University of Washington's Center for Urban Horticulture causing US $7 million in damage. Two of the cell members responsible, Lacey Phillabaum and Jennifer Kolar, pleaded guilty to the attack in 2006. Another member, Bill Rodgers, a top ELF organizer, was caught and killed himself in an Arizona jail cell. Member Briana Waters was convicted in 2008 and sentenced to six years in prison.[121] On 2 November 2001 at Boulder, Colorado the ELF burnt down a US $2.5 million mansion owned by corporate developers.[122]

On 24 March 2002, in Erie, Pennsylvania hundreds of trees were spiked in Wintergreen Gorge and forestry equipment destroyed.[123] In September 2002 in Irvine, Pennsylvania the ELF claimed responsibility for arson at the US Forest Service Northeast Research Station. The facility was destroyed causing over US $700,000 in damage and destroying 70 years' worth of accumulated research.[124] The next year on 4 June 2003 in Chico, California and Washington, Michigan separate arson attacks by the ELF were undertaken against luxury homes under development as part of a protest against urban sprawl.[125] One of the most destructive acts attributed to the ELF occurred on 1 August 2003 when participants burned down a condominium complex in San Diego and destroyed a 100 ft crane, causing approximately US $50 million in damage. A 12 ft banner bearing the ELF acronym was put up nearby stating, 'If you build it, we will burn it'.[126]

As can be observed to date, there have been multiple arson attacks against targets that elves believe are harming the earth, as this has often been the preferred form of ecotage.[127] John Lewis, deputy assistant director in the Counterterrorism Division, further testified that 'from January 1990 to June 2004, animal and environmental rights extremists have claimed credit for more than 1,200 criminal incidents'. However, the FBI has only been able to link the ELF to 14 incidents.[128] James Jarboe (the FBI's top domestic terrorism officer) claimed they have been able to link the organization to '600 criminal acts committed between 1996 and 2002, totalling $43 million in damages'. Of these acts, according to the FBI, the most devastating was the arson attack on the Vail, Colorado ski resort.[129]

On 27 December 2004 at Lincoln, California incendiary devices were placed in three houses under construction. The letters 'ELF' were spray-painted nearby.[130] Four months later on 13 April 2005 at Sammamish, Washington the ELF partially burned down one of two buildings in a golf course development. An unexploded incendiary device was found at the second property. Nearby a sheet was found hanging stating, 'Where are all the trees? Burn, rapist, burn. E.L.F.'[131]

On 19 November 2005 the elves set four fires at Hagerstown, Maryland in newly constructed unoccupied homes. One building was completely destroyed. Credit was claimed by the ELF using the email address, tree_beard1234@yahoo.com. The name Treebeard is a character (an Ent) in J.R.R. Tolkien's *The Two Towers*. The message left read:

> Last night we, the Earth Liberation Front, put the torch to a development of Ryan Homes in Hagerstown, Maryland (off of Route 40, behind the Wal-Mart). We did so to strike at the bottom line of this country's most notorious serial land rapist … We warn all developers that the people of the Earth are prepared to defend what remains of the wild and the green … We encourage all who watch with sadness while developers sell out the future of us and our children to join us in resisting them in any and every possible way … The Ents are going to war.[132]

In late 2005 at least four separate incidents occurred, three in the USA and one in Greece. Approximate damage (inclusive of all four attacks) was US $567,600.[133] In 2006 Steven James Murphy (an ELF participant) was sentenced to five years' imprisonment for the attempted arson of Pasadena condominiums.[134] On 17 January 2006, at Camano Island, Washington the ELF burnt down a close-to-completion 890 m^2 US $3 million, trophy house.[135] In March 2008, at Street of Dreams, Washington the ELF is suspected of setting fire to four multimillion-dollar homes costing US $7 million in damage. Their initials were spray-painted in red letters along with a message, '*Built Green? Nope black! McMansions in RCDs r not green. ELF.*'[136]

ELF actions also continue to be carried out on a global scale. An anonymous report from Russia in 2011 outlines an ELF action where bulldozers were destroyed with Molotov cocktails,[137] at Jesse's Marine (North Plymouth), where a warning left at the scene read: 'Commercial fishing first class rape' and 'sea life kidnapped, murdered, maliciously'.[138] Below the messages were the letters ELF.[139] Two communiqués were also released in Orebro, Sweden where a McDonald's was vandalized by 'The ALF & ELF Family!'[140] According to a communiqué in 2010 (jointly made by the ALF and the ELF, Mexico State) machines critical to an infrastructure highway project were destroyed.[141] In Sweden in the same year an action on behalf of the ELF saw windows and doors smashed.[142]

In a sign that at least some ELF participants believe that Earth First! is not hard core enough the *Earth First! Journal* office in Lake Worth, Florida was burnt down on 1 April 2013 by elves. The local news station KTIV received an anonymous communiqué, signed by the ELF stating that:

> The Earth Liberation Front takes credit for torching the Earth First! Journal office in Lake Worth, Fla. The Journal continues to print articles that exhibit capital letters at the beginning of each sentence. In light of global opposition to capitalism, and the murder of our planet at the hands of capitalists, the Journal's use of capitalization needs to be stopped … We are the burning rage of a dying planet. Welcome to the struggle of all species to be free![143]

In January 2013, a UK cell destroyed a Bathampton radio and TV relay station in an arson attack. The attack caused hundreds of thousands of pounds worth of damage, and shut down TV channels and national analogue and digital radio stations.[144] On New Year's Eve 2013–14 Russian elves destroyed two vehicles in southern Moscow using petrol. They cite that no harm to humans occurred but damage was done to the 'developers purse'.[145] In December 2014, elves in Istanbul damaged a road roller in solidarity with the Greek anarchist prisoner Nikos Romanos.[146] A Greek cell of the ELF on 12 April 2015 used incendiary devices to destroy a poultry company and its vehicles in Peristeri.[147]

While there are still ELF actions occurring, the volume of events appears to be well down from their heyday even if the geographic reach of the ELF has expanded. As shown above, there has been a rise in actions in other states such as Mexico, Russia, Western Europe and South

America. Further, an examination of the *Earth First News Wire*, *Earth First! News* and *Back Bite* reveals that actions, particularly in the USA and the UK – once the most active sites – appear to have tailed off dramatically between 2005 and 2015. The scale of operations appears to have also been downsized, with most actions being relatively small-scale property damage as opposed to the preferred tactic in the 1990s and early 2000s of committing arson.

ELF AND VIOLENCE

Similar to Earth First!, the ELF claims that 'its actions are guided by a nonviolent, nonterrorist ideology whose aim is to "protect all life on planet earth".'[148] As noted above, while the ELF has taken responsibility for acts of ecotage and property damage that have resulted in millions of dollars of damage, the group has to date never intentionally (or even unintentionally) brought harm to a human.[149] The ELF's website (www.earthliberationfront.com) claims that activists should engage only in 'non-violent activism' while committing ecotage. The website also instructs that activists should 'make absolutely sure that no animals, human or otherwise, will be inadvertently injured or killed'.[150] For ELF participants ecotage is not considered a form of 'violence'. An activist who was interviewed in 1999 stated:

> I don't count violence to property as violence, I don't count the destruction of property… the destruction of machinery I think is perfectly valid, something that I enjoy immensely [laughs] and is something that is important to do.[151] ('Anonymous' interview, 1999)

Certainly, however, there is some evidence that the commitment to non-violence against humans is not watertight. There have been a number of statements by ELF representatives that threaten violence against individuals.[152] The attempt to mainstream Earth First! left some participants disenchanted, leading to a number breaking away to form the ELF to continue direct, criminal actions in support of the environment.[153] Even ELF spokesman Craig Rosebraugh admits to an internal debate within the ELF regarding the use of violence, with the group publicly promoting non-violence while privately questioning their commitment to it.[154] Rosebraugh declared in an interview: 'terrorism can be OK, can be justified and … bombing and assassination can under certain circumstances be legitimate forms of self-defense against political oppression'.[155]

However, in 2000, the tactics used by the organization changed dramatically when 'unknown' activists placed three canisters containing low levels of cyanide in various places around Minneapolis. The action was a protest against a 'conference on genetic engineering'. This event brought to light the possibility of more radical activists within the organization, ones who were willing to ignore one of the fundamental principles, to go further than petty property damage and risk the lives of themselves and others.[156]

Further, elves have not been adverse in issuing personal threats. When the ELF sent out a communiqué detailing an action against the United States Forest Service Northeast Research Center in Irvine, Pennsylvania (2002), it stated: 'While innocent life will never be harmed in any action we undertake, where it is necessary, we will no longer hesitate to pick up the gun to implement justice, and provide the needed protection for our planet that decades of legal battles, pleading, protest, and economic sabotage have failed so drastically to achieve'.[157]

In June 2009 a letter that claimed to be from an ELF participant in Australia was posted to the website of the ELF press office in the USA. The letter had been delivered to the home address of Graeme York, the CEO of a company International Power Australia, and stated that he was 'responsible for the dirtiest power station in Australia and the most polluting in the industrialised world ... We hold you personally accountable for this assault against our Earth. We do not take lightly to the perpetual destruction of our land-base for the selfish and short-term objective of fattening your bank account.'[158] However, despite the threatening tone, no further action took place.

Before the Senate Judiciary Committee (18 May 2004), John Lewis testified that activists had discussed physical harming of food producers, biomedical researchers and even law enforcement officers. Improvised explosive devices against consumer product-testing companies have been employed along with threats of bigger bombing campaigns, and even potential assassinations of researchers and employees have been voiced.[159]

Leader and Probst noted that a self-proclaimed Seattle ELF sympathizer testified before a grand jury in Portland, Oregon that if the federal government developed a nuclear power industry it would be targeted. If the sites were too difficult to penetrate he stated that the cells would target plant executives and/or their homes.[160]

Up until the early 2000s, the ELF had consistently followed their three guiding principles for the actions of the organization, including taking precautions against anyone being injured.[161] When asked what would happen if someone were to be injured during an ELF action (followed by the question of whether or not this has ever occurred), Pickering stated:

> The guidelines for the ELF specifically require participants to take all necessary precautions to ensure no one is physically injured. In the history of the ELF internationally, no one has ever been injured from the group's actions and that is not a coincidence … [Furthermore] if an action similar to one performed by ELF occurred and resulted in an individual being harmed, this would not be considered an ELF action.[162]

However, the release of these varied statements and the actions in Minneapolis, coupled with the threatening letter in Australia, appeared to signify that some ELF cells had moved past the non-violence guidelines, and were willing to commit political violence, if and when necessary, against humans.[163] However, to date there appears no other evidence of actual physical violence being occasioned on ELF opponents.

ANALYSIS AND CONCLUSION

In comparison to Earth First!, the ELF has continued its use of direct actions in recent years. Most campaigns appear to be against 'urban sprawl' across the USA, targeting luxury apartment complexes and car dealerships. While no individual has ever been reported injured following an ELF action, their choice of arson, incendiary devices and fire bombs as weapons have caused concern,[164] and ultimately, resulted in the FBI categorizing them as 'ecoterrorists' and the 'top domestic terror' threat within the USA in late 2001.[165]

Elves were also a varied bunch but the people going out on actions tended, although not exclusively, to fit Sageman's stereotypical 'bunch of guys'. They also tended to be Caucasian, relatively young (between 18 and 26 years of age), university educated, recruited locally from known associates, had a leaning towards left-wing politics and a dissatisfaction with mainstream environmental group efforts, believing they were neither sufficient nor timely. As Ackerman points out, of the members arrested for actions or suspected of engaging in ecotage throughout the 1980s and 1990s, all but one were young men (juveniles to age 28).[166] However, 'The Family' cell certainly had women members and no doubt women were committed elves.

The reasons why people joined Earth First! or the ELF tended to be varied and in some cases no doubt overlapping. For some Earth First!ers and elves Neumann and Rogers's analysis was correct in that for some it provided a mission in life and a sense of superiority over others.

Similarly, Joosse notes that many joined the ELF for the chance to be a hero in both their own eyes and in the eyes of fellow participants.[167] As the research indicates, there were also participants who did act 'for ourselves, out of our own frustrations, and rage and despair ... as a means of therapy and adventure'.[168]

However, as the closer examination of 'The Family' cell demonstrated, people joined for a variety of reasons that could also include having a partner involved or just wanting to blow things up. Similarly some members, as per Einwohler's research, did join out of a shared connection with the biosphere but others participated because they had a shared connection with the group members or no real connection.

ELF actions have been primarily focused within the USA. Between 2000 and 2015, of the approximate 201 actions attempted and successfully achieved and accredited to ELF, 118 occurred on US soil.[169] The actions of the ELF seem to have dropped off in the last few years and, while they peaked several years after the ALF (in 2011), there are several potential reasons for the decrease in activity. First, as the ELF does not seem to have a dedicated website or single online community (the ELF press office used to act as a legal and above-ground entity to publicize ELF actions but has since been disbanded, with the website stating that the 'account has been suspended'),[170] the ELF now relies on magazines, other organizations and online communities to distribute their communiqués and actions.

Second, successful prosecution of ELF activists may have worked as a deterrent for others. In particular, with regards to 'the 15 convictions in 2007 [of ELF activists] ... not only did several ELF members get long prison sentences – Stanislas Meyerhoff got 13 years – but also many activists testified against each other to get lighter punishments'.[171] Members who turned informants may have affected the organization, with activists questioning one another's loyalty and trustworthiness.

Finally, according to some, the political environment that has helped shape the USA over the past two presidential terms may have contributed to the decreased activity. FBI intelligence analyst Erin Weller argues, '[ELF and ALF] activists may view a Democratic administration as more sympathetic to their goals and be less inclined to take radical steps. Obviously, if you think there is going to be support for your position, you're going to use legal means rather than illegal means.'[172] It should be noted that this also potentially aids in explaining the apparent shift of Earth First! activists to more legal, above-ground actions, as outlined above.

When the ELF was first established, it attempted to 'somehow give the mainstream environmental organizations more leverage in negotiating environmental protectionism with the government'. As time went on, however, they have abandoned such aims, instead acting 'as though the mainstream no longer exists and they, the eco-activists, are the only ones left to carry on the struggle'.[173]

A similar story occurred in the UK in the 1990s. In that decade, covert ecotage became a standard part of many participants' repertoire. Problematically, though, the organization devolved into an 'uncoordinated, widespread and crucially mostly unclaimed "pixie-ing"'.[174]

Becoming More Radical?

Sprinzak's delegitimation model, at least for the first two stages, maps on to the Earth First!/ELF evolution as a group. As this analysis contends, Earth First! activists Foreman and his compatriots began with non-violent activities before progressing to utilizing militant forms of ecotage, and further contends that political activists do not just suddenly decide to engage in terrorism. Rather, a relatively lengthy process was undertaken over a decade before militant actions were formally adopted by the ELF.

It can clearly be seen that Earth First! followed Sprinzak's projected radicalization trajectory initially – that the group rapidly recruited followers, quickly developed their own distinctive philosophy, aims, operational structure and set themselves up in opposition with law enforcement. It is clear that the founders of Earth First! suffered a crisis of confidence and experienced a 'profound disenchantment' due to accumulated frustration with prevailing societal conditions and a passionate belief that the state and mainstream environmental groups were not protecting the environment.[175]

It also appears that at their formative stage they were seeking to challenge the established political system, not so much with violence but to rethink society's relationship with the environment. As Daryl Cherney noted, Earth First! needed to change human behaviour and human consciousness.[176] Also as Sprinzak's model predicts, many of their behaviours at round-ups and other meetings were countercultural in nature, a rejection of dominant cultural mores.[177]

In terms of the use of violence Earth First! began by using stunts such as their first action at Glen Canyon to publicize their cause.[178] Their initial campaigns were civil disobedience protests such as the Bisti Badlands in 1983, which gibes with Sprinzak's radicalization process predictions. For Earth First!ers violence against sentient beings was not permitted in the pursuance of their goals. All participants had to agree that they do not physically or verbally assault anyone.[179]

That definition of violence that Earth First!ers embraced did not, however, in their estimation include monkeywrenching or ecotage applied to property, which precipitated the group entering into Sprinzak's conflict of legitimacy stage.[180] By the mid-1980s cells were engaging in not only demonstrations but ecotage against selected targets, for example the Earth First! offshoot EMETIC.[181] However, there is no evidence of small-scale physical violence occurring as Sprinzak's model predicts.

It can also be observed that Earth First! participants underwent a schism over the use of ecotage. By 1987, Foreman and his biocentric supporters were championing the committing of monkeywrenching over civil disobedience acts as the way forward. Bari suggested that the disorganization should split, like the Weather Underground and Students for a Democratic Society did, with the more militant wing engaging in ecotage in the form of the ELF leaving no official connection to Earth First!, which would pursue a social justice mandate using civil disobedience strategies and tactics only.[182]

The Earth First! bloc, which became the elves, had become frustrated at the direct action stunts mostly favoured by Earth First! participants and their failure to bring about a more environmentally harmonious society quickly enough. The breakaway Earth First! forces that left to join the ELF clearly viewed non-violent political action as being limited. They were willing to allow Earth First! to function above ground but wanted the option of pursuing more militant actions.[183]

Many of this bloc believed that environmental initiatives would be unable to bring about radical change without a larger-scale social change (for example systems tackling large-scale problems such as racism and poverty). The new activists believed that, to achieve biocentric equality, it would mean that changes to human nature were required to bring about biocentrism and social justice outcomes.

They codified as part of the new entity ELF, first in the UK in 1992 and then in the USA, a more militant strategy involving campaigns of ecotage against individuals or corporations that they considered to be enemies of the planet. The elves certainly had come to see themselves as involved in a 'just war' against environmental oppressors that would inspire a mass movement, but that did not occur. Sprinzak's characterization of a 'great disappointment' prefacing this change in tactics does appear to have occurred, primarily occasioned by the pace of change desired being too slow.[184]

For example, Jeff Luers who was sentenced to 22.5 years in jail for setting fire to three SUVs in a Eugene, Oregon Chevrolet dealership in June 2000, stated in an interview that he moved towards this type of activity after going through all the legal channels that were available, and that he felt that this act of violence was the only means left that he could use to have a political impact.[185] Such statements suggest that broader forms of environmental political violence may also conform to Sprinzak's model.

The ELF noted that few wilderness areas were actually being protected. The Reagan administration proved particularly intractable on this point given their overall attitude to environmental protection.[186] The elves argued that this failure could be laid at the feet of mainstream environmental organizations and their use of civil disobedience tactics.[187] Thus, similar to Earth First! the elves rejected engagement with the mainstream political discourse seeking to rather end the prevailing political structures.[188] The language and rhetoric utilized on their websites and on missives left behind at the scene of their actions in many cases were filled with warnings against their enemies to change their ways, while denouncing them.[189]

Sprinzak's conflict of legitimacy stage presupposes the creation of an alternative ideological and cultural approach that delegitimates the current regime and its social norms, rather seeking to implement, at least in the eyes of the radicals, superior ones.[190] While the ELF has claimed to have no underlying philosophy, just intuition or action, it is clear that biocentric writings, deep ecology, anti-capitalist and anarchist philosophies came together to create a coherent approach, at least in the eyes of the elves, which could feasibly be adopted by the wider society.

Elves carried out political ecotage as opposed to vandalism (although to opponents they can be considered the same) throughout the 1990s before peaking in the early 2000s. As can be observed from examining 'The Family' cell, intense radicalization occurred with members becoming insular and closed off, in some cases even from their own partners. These small 'affinity' groups were responsible for the majority of acts of sabotage. Often, such acts were not publicized, even to other participants of the larger organization due, in part, to a lack of trust.[191] The ELF manual informed cell members not to share information with outsiders and to adopt security protocols that reinforced that outsiders were not to be trusted.[192]

Certainly Earth First! did not engage in 'terrorist' actions against humans and thus cannot be considered to have crossed the threshold into Sprinzak's third phase, the crisis of legitimacy. Even the FBI only ever considered Earth First! to be a 'soft core' terrorist group, not willing to deliberately kill.[193] In terms of whether the ELF should be considered to be engaging in 'terrorist' activities the situation becomes more murky and complex. While most of their actions in carrying out ecotage fit more comfortably at the militant end of the spectrum, there are signs of

Sprinzak's derogatory language signal that the group evolved to a point where they have demonized and dehumanized their opponents.[194]

There is a great deal of evidence of misanthropy amongst ELF participants, which has the potential to escalate to a point where members may be willing to carry out targeted attacks against humans.[195] The language they use to describe corporations or governments accuses them of being evil, greedy and corrupt exploiters with little or no redeeming qualities ascribed to them. An example of such dehumanizing language is the September 1989 issue of *Earth First! Journal*, where 'Gula' acknowledges that life is sacred and therefore should not be a target but states that many participants doubt that those who harm the environment should be considered life forms (the author uses the term 'robotoids').[196]

There is no evidence, however, that cells like 'The Family' embraced other forms of criminality (beyond arson and property damage) let alone engaged in non-conventional sexual activity. While cells did consider their opponents the enemy they were not willing to use physical violence against people in pursuance of their objectives.

While the cells tended to be small, they do not tend to isolate themselves from the community, with many also engaged with the broader environmental movement at the same time.[197] However, they did impose on members a new set of behavioural and moral standards such as not 'snitching' on fellow participants and engaging in ostensibly illegal activity such as ecotage. However, most participants came to Earth First! or the ELF already trying to live a life that incorporated biodiversity protection within it.[198] These cells do not seem to have evolved along the radicalization continuum to the point where they see the world in stark 'us and them' terms and to a point where they are willing to kill humans.

ELF guidelines state that cells are expected to adhere to forbid injuring life, and go so far as to insist that all reasonable precautions be undertaken to prevent injury.[199] However, despite the guidelines ELF participants have threatened people with violence on a number of occasions, including the 2002 threats issued against the United States Forest Service Northeast Research Center in Irvine, Pennsylvania; and in June 2009 Graeme York, the CEO of International Power Australia, received a threatening letter delivered to his home address.[200]

Craig Rosebraugh has publicly stated that assassination might well be a legitimate tactic in the right circumstances.[201] But this appears to be part of an internal debate with the ELF as to the use of violence against humans, which has to date not been adopted as 'official' policy. There has been one incident linked to the ELF where physical violence was offered. In 2000 perpetrators placed canisters of low-level cyanide in and around a genetic engineering conference.[202] While such an attack has an extremely low probability of hurting someone the attack was a salient reminder that the elves are just a 'rogue cell' or change-of-heart away from moving into Sprinzak's third stage. Further, it is arguable that carrying out a sufficiently large property damage attack, or sustained use of arson as a tactic, as adopted by the Family, may see the ELF accurately characterized as entering Sprinzak's third stage.

Ackerman argues that if anarchists become dominant within the ELF then the group may be subsumed into a broader anarchist revolution that may promote violence unencumbered by the ELF's philosophy of physical non-violence. The model of affinity cells means there is no leadership to rein in more extreme cells. Lastly, given that most ELF members are young and male, a group of criminologists have determined that in terms of creating most societal physical violence, there is a chance that a group comprised solely of young men is more likely to commit violence to further its goals.[203]

Further, given that the ELF's belief structure tends towards an apocalyptic view that the environment is at risk from corporate greed and a corrupt system, then self-defence of the Earth is possible. *Igniting the Revolution*, a self-produced video by the ELF, argued that such a tactic was permissible. Such a doctrine can easily allow for an escalating series of violent acts.

It is evident that some environmental activists believe that they are 'under attack' by a government they consider both hostile and corrupt. For example, Craig Rosebraugh argues that the US government is both oppressive and comprised of 'vicious thugs who serve the state' and who aim to silence him.[204] Such beliefs can prove fertile ground for radicalization methods. As Leslie James Pickering points out, it is likely to be government repression that is likely to foment ongoing radicalization of environmental activists.[205]

The elves currently appear to be a spent force. While their geographical reach has expanded, the number of incidents occurring is well down between 2000 and 2015. This may be partly due to the cessation of 'The Family' cell, which had been so instrumental in many of the attacks on the US West Coast in 2003 and the eventual apprehension and imprisonment of many of its members. Second, elves have been most prevalent in the USA and concerted law enforcement action led by the FBI has seen many operatives imprisoned. But it may also be that, as demonstrated, many activists were not willing to engage in militant or terrorist acts if other options are available for them to engage in the political process, which under President Obama's administration has been a more viable option.

Certainly at this stage they seem extremely unlikely to develop into the mass movement that Foreman and his friends hoped for when they first dreamed Earth First! into existence. Any group that 'believes a higher law mandates violent acts in order to bring about what it considers to be salvation' – in this case to save the planet – has tended to struggle to build a mass movement. The failure to do so can mean that the smaller group of disaffected participants becomes more fanatical and violent over time, but there is no sign of this occurring at the present time.[206]

Again, like with the ALF, the limitations of the affinity cell, which tended only to recruit close friends or those known to other cell members because of fear of law enforcement infiltration, hindered development. Similarly, the insistence on being a 'disorganization' meant that Earth First! participants and the elves were unable to grow as a mass political force. This is not to say that the elves may not rise again, but it would most likely take a significant environmental incident, or perhaps the rise of a charismatic leader, to inspire terrorist action – but for now, the elves are quiescent.

NOTES

1. Gary Ackerman (2003) 'Beyond arson? A threat assessment of the Earth Liberation Front', *Terrorism and Political Violence*, **15** (4), p. 163.
2. Russell Lee Young (2004) 'A time series analysis of eco-terrorist violence in the United States: 1993–2003' (PhD dissertation, Sam Houston State University, Huntsville, TX), p. 38; B. Laurent (2001) 'Eco-vandals put a match to "progress"', *Christian Science Monitor*, (5 July), p. 11.
3. Hasan T. Arslan (2008) 'The social and operational intersections of environmental extremism in North America and Europe' (PhD dissertation, Sam Houston State University, Huntsville, TX), p. 34.
4. Ibid., p. 34; K.L. Ziner (2001) 'Burning down the houses', *E Magazine: The Environmental Magazine*, **12** (3) (May/June), p. 17.
5. Jay Hasbrouck (2005) 'Primitive dissidents: Earth Liberation Front and the making of a radical movement' (PhD dissertation, University of Southern California, Los Angeles, CA, 2005), p. 1; 'Anonymous (2001) frequently asked questions about the Earth Liberation Front (ELF)' (Portland, OR: North American ELF Press Office).
6. According to Wall, the terms 'elf' and 'elving' (also 'pixieing') to describe ELF participants evolved from the acronym ELF. Derek Wall (2000) 'Snowballs, elves and skimmingtons?: Genealogies of environmental direct action', in B. Seel et al. (eds), *Direct Action in British Environmentalism* (London and New York: Routledge), p. 86.
7. Steve Vanderheiden (2005) 'Eco-terrorism or justified resistance? Radical environmentalism and the "war on terror"', *Politics and Society*, **33** (3), p. 427.
8. Ibid., p. 426.
9. Hasbrouck, 'Primitive dissidents: Earth Liberation Front and the making of a radical movement', p. xii; Office of US Representative Phil English (2003) 'English introduces bill condemning eco-terror', http://www.house.gov/apps/list/press/pa03_english/ecoterror.html. According to Phil English (US Representative), announcing the 2003 Congressional Resolution titled *Expressing the Sense of the Congress Regarding the Earth Liberation Front and Ecological Terrorism*, ELF members are 'self-righteous hooligans' who are

home-grown ecoterrorists. See Hasbrouck, 'Primitive dissidents: Earth Liberation Front and the making of a radical movement', p. xii; Office of US Representative Phil English, 'English Introduces Bill Condemning Eco-Terror'.

10. Ackerman, 'Beyond arson? A threat assessment of the Earth Liberation Front', p. 144.
11. C. Rosebraugh (2004) Burning rage of a dying planet: speaking for the Earth Liberation Front (New York: Lantern Books), p. 213.
12. John Wade (2006) 'Radical environmentalism: is there any other kind', in Steven Best and Anthony Nocella (eds), *Igniting a Revolution: Voices in Defence of the Earth* (Oakland: AK Press), p. 281.
13. Young, 'A time series analysis of eco-terrorist violence in the United States: 1993–2003', p. 38.
14. Leslie James Pickering (2006) 'People ain't feeling this bullshit', in Steven Best and Anthony Nocella (eds), *Igniting a Revolution: Voices in Defense of the Earth* (Oakland, CA: AK Press), p. 305.
15. Ackerman, 'Beyond arson? A threat assessment of the Earth Liberation Front', p. 154.
16. Plows et al. (2001) 'From the Earth Liberation Front to universal dark matter: the challenge of covert repertoires to social movement research', Paper for the Workshop on Democracy and Extremism European Consortium for Political Research Joint Sessions Grenoble, 6–11 April, p. 5.
17. Wall, 'Snowballs, elves and skimmingtons?: Genealogies of environmental direct action' p. 85.
18. Noel Molland (2006) 'A spark that ignited a flame: the evolution of the Earth Liberation Front', in Steven Best and Anthony Nocella, *Igniting a Revolution: Voices in Defense of the Earth* (Oakland, CA: AK Press), p. 50.
19. Ibid.
20. Ibid., p. 49.
21. Stefan Leader and Peter Probst (2003) 'The Earth Liberation Front and environmental terrorism', *Terrorism and Political Violence*, **15** (4), p. 38.
22. Alexandra Plows et al. (2004) 'Covert repertoires: ecotage in the UK', *Social Movement Studies*, **3** (2), p. 202.
23. Hasbrouck, 'Primitive dissidents: Earth Liberation Front and the making of a radical movement', p. 12; Julia Prodis Sulek (1998) 'Evolution of a movement: environmental terrorism contrasts with maturing radicals', *San Jose Mercury News*, 1 November.
24. Hasbrouck, 'Primitive dissidents: Earth Liberation Front and the making of a radical movement', p. 12; Bron Taylor (2005) 'Earth First! and the Earth Liberation Front', *Continuum International*, http://www.religionandnature.com/bron/ern/Taylor,Bron–EF+ELF.pdf.
25. Ron Arnold (1997) *Ecoterror: The Violent Agenda to Save Nature, The World of the Unabomber* (Bellevue, WA: Free Enterprise Press), p. 271; Judi Bari (1994) 'Monkey-wrenching', *Earth First* (February), p. 8.
26. Leader and Probst, 'The Earth Liberation Front and environmental terrorism', p. 40.
27. Taylor Horne (2006) 'The Radical Environmental Movement: Incorporating Empire and the Politics of Nature', *Green Theory & Praxis Journal*, 2 (1), pp. 31–5.
28. Young, 'A time series analysis of eco-terrorist violence in the United States: 1993–2003', pp. 39–40; E. Journo (2002) 'Homegrown terrorism', 16 April, http://www.aynrand.org/medialink/greenterror.shtml.
29. Rosebraugh, *Burning Rage of a Dying Planet: Speaking for the Earth Liberation Front*, p. 154.
30. Taylor Horne, 'The radical environmental movement: incorporating empire and the politics of nature', p. 6.
31. Sean Parson (2009) 'Understanding the ideology of the Earth Liberation Front', https://libcom.org/forums/theory/understanding-ideology-earth-liberation-front-21012009, p. 50.
32. Douglas Long (2004) *Ecoterrorism: Library in a Book* (New York: Facts on File Inc.), p. 48.
33. Leader and Probst, 'The Earth Liberation Front and environmental terrorism', p. 40.

34. Leslie James Pickering (2007)*The Earth Liberation Front: 1997–2002* (Portland, OR: Arissa Media Group,), p. 47.
35. Ibid., p. 44.
36. Michael Becker (2006) 'Ontological anarchism: the philosophical roots of revolutionary environmentalism', in Steven Best and Anthony Nocella, *Igniting a Revolution: Voices in Defense of the Earth* (Oakland, CA: AK Press), p. 77.
37. Long, *Ecoterrorism: Library in a Book*, p. 48.
38. Hasbrouck, 'Primitive dissidents: Earth Liberation Front and the making of a radical movement', p. 140.
39. Ibid., p. 68; Manuel Castells (2000) 'Toward a sociology of the Network Society', *Contemporary Sociology*, **29** (5), p. 693.
40. Hasbrouck, 'Primitive dissidents: Earth Liberation Front and the making of a radical movement', p. 2.
41. Michael Stratmoen (2007) 'Arson on Vail Mountain: a case study of the Earth Liberation Front', p. 9.
42. Ibid.
43. Hasbrouck, 'Primitive dissidents: Earth Liberation Front and the making of a radical movement', p. 122.
44. Stratmoen, 'Arson on Vail Mountain: a case study of the Earth Liberation Front', p. 9.
45. Parson, Understanding the ideology of the Earth Liberation Front, p. 53.
46. Leader and Probst, 'The Earth Liberation Front and environmental terrorism', p. 38.
47. Stratmoen, 'Arson on Vail Mountain: a case study of the Earth Liberation Front', p. 6; Leader and Probst, 'The Earth Liberation Front and environmental terrorism', p. 39.
48. Paul Joosse, 'Leaderless resistance and ideological inclusion: the case of the Earth Liberation Front', p. 354, www.earthliberationfront.com.
49. Joosse, 'Leaderless resistance and ideological inclusion: the case of the Earth Liberation Front', p. 354.
50. Leader and Probst, 'The Earth Liberation Front and environmental terrorism', p. 39.
51. Trujillo, 'The radical environmentalist movement', p. 153.
52. Rosebraugh, *Burning rage of a dying planet: speaking for the Earth Liberation Front*, p. 264.
53. Trujillo, 'The radical environmentalist movement', p. 162.
54. Ibid., p. 161.
55. Ackerman, 'Beyond arson? A threat assessment of the Earth Liberation Front', pp. 151–2.
56. Leader and Probst, 'The Earth Liberation Front and environmental terrorism', pp. 43–4. For example, in January 1995, PETA reportedly provided a $45,200 payment to the 'Rodney Coronado support committee'. Coronado had been convicted of arson against a Michigan State University research facility. See Leader and Probst, 'The Earth Liberation Front and environmental terrorism', pp. 43–4.
57. Hasbrouck, 'Primitive dissidents: Earth Liberation Front and the making of a radical movement', p. 84; Anonymous (2001) *Frequently Asked Questions About the Earth Liberation Front (ELF)* (Portland, OR: North American ELF Press Office).
58. Joosse, 'Leaderless resistance and ideological inclusion: the case of the Earth Liberation Front', p. 354.
59. Hasbrouck, 'Primitive dissidents: Earth Liberation Front and the making of a radical movement', p. 126; Dave Foreman and Bill Haywood (1993 [1985]) *Ecodefense: A Field Guide to Monkeywrenching* (Chico, CA: Abbszug Press).
60. Leslie James Pickering (2007) *The Earth Liberation Front: 1997–2002* (Oakland, CA: PM Press), p. 44.
61. Helios Global Inc. (2008) 'Ecoterrorism: environmental and animal-rights militants in the United States', *Washington DC, Helios Global Inc./US Department of Homeland Security* 7, p. 9.
62. Ackerman, 'Beyond arson? A threat assessment of the Earth Liberation Front', p. 151.
63. Donald R. Liddick (2006) *Eco-Terrorism: Radical Environmental and Animal Liberation Movements* (Westport, Connecticut: Praeger), p. 83; Kelly Stoner and Gary Perlstein

(2005) 'Implementing "justice" through terror and destruction: ecoterror's violent agenda to save nature', in Lynne L. Snowden and Bradley C. Whitsel (eds), *Terrorism: Research, Readings and Realities* (Upper Saddle River, NJ: Prentice Hall), p. 93; Trujillo, 'The radical environmentalist movement', p. 154.

64. Liddick, *Eco-Terrorism: Radical Environmental and Animal Liberation Movements*, p. 83; Stoner and Perlstein, 'Implementing "justice" through terror and destruction: ecoterror's violent agenda to save nature', p. 93; Trujillo, 'The radical environmentalist movement', p. 154.
65. Hasbrouck, 'Primitive dissidents: Earth Liberation Front and the making of a radical movement', p. 86; Ray Lauer, quoted in Diana Hefley (2004) 'ELF activists claim fires: group takes responsibility in statement', *HeraldNet*, http://www.heraldnet.com/stories/04/4/24/18523003.cfm.
66. Hasbrouck, 'Primitive dissidents: Earth Liberation Front and the making of a radical movement', p. 86; Perlstein, quoted in Diana Hefley, 'ELF activists claim fires: group takes responsibility in statement'.
67. Trujillo, 'The radical environmentalist movement', p. 154.
68. Stratmoen, 'Arson on Vail Mountain: a case study of the Earth Liberation Front', p. 8.
69. Helios Global Inc., 'Ecoterrorism: environmental and animal-rights militants in the United States', p. 3; Joosse, 'Leaderless resistance and ideological inclusion: the case of the Earth Liberation Front', p. 356.
70. Joosse, 'Leaderless resistance and ideological inclusion: the case of the Earth Liberation Front', p. 360.
71. Ibid., p. 7.
72. Leader and Probst, 'The Earth Liberation Front and environmental terrorism', p. 43; Joosse, 'Leaderless resistance and ideological inclusion: the case of the Earth Liberation Front', p. 354.
73. Liddick, *Eco-Terrorism: Radical Environmental and Animal Liberation Movements*, p. 64.
74. Trujillo, 'The radical environmentalist movement', p. 153.
75. Following their departures from the ELF, Rosebraugh and Pickering established 'Arissa', an 'anarchist social-revolution group that espouses greater violence to foment social change'. Rosebraugh and Leslie James Pickering maintain they wanted to establish a broader revolutionary movement, similar to the American revolution with the goal, 'to create a political and social revolution in the United States', which opens up the door to potentially violent tactics to achieve their goals, although there is no evidence of this occurring to date. See Ackerman, 'Beyond arson? A threat assessment of the Earth Liberation Front', p. 149; Liddick, *Eco-Terrorism: Radical Environmental and Animal Liberation Movements*, p. 67.
76. Hasbrouck, 'Primitive dissidents: Earth Liberation Front and the making of a radical movement', p. 84.
77. Trujillo, 'The radical environmentalist movement', pp. 153–4.
78. Molland, 'A spark that ignited a flame: the evolution of the Earth Liberation Front', p. 51. For example, during British Earth Front!'s 'Mahogany Means Murder' campaign of the early 1990s, elves would mingle in with the EF! activists carrying out direct actions like unfurling their banners, the elves would glue the locks of targeted buildings. They also engaged in 'Earth Nights' where ecotage was carried out on a chosen night. See Molland, 'A spark that ignited a flame: the evolution of the Earth Liberation Front', p. 51.
79. Parson, 'Understanding the ideology of the Earth Liberation Front', p. 52.
80. Ibid.
81. Teale Phelps Bondaroff (2008) 'Throwing a wrench into things: the strategy of radical environmentalism', *Journal of Military and Strategic Studies*, **10** (4), pp. 13, 16.; Liddick, *Eco-Terrorism: Radical Environmental and Animal Liberation Movements*, pp. 65–6.
82. Molland, 'A spark that ignited a flame: the evolution of the Earth Liberation Front', p. 52.
83. Arslan, 'The social and operational intersections of environmental extremism in North America and Europe', p. 35; A. Baker (2001) 'Police say an anti-sprawl group burned new Long Island homes', *The New York Times*, 3 January, p. B1.

84. Liddick, *Eco-Terrorism: Radical Environmental and Animal Liberation Movements*, p. 65.; Parson, 'Understanding the ideology of the Earth Liberation Front', p. 53.
85. Parson, 'Understanding the ideology of the Earth Liberation Front', p. 53; Arslan, 'The social and operational intersections of environmental extremism in North America and Europe', p. 35.
86. 'Fanning the flames: the Earth Liberation Front in North America, *Do or Die*, **10**, pp. 137–9, http://www.eco-action.org/dod/no10/flames.htm.
87. Ibid.
88. 'Intelligence report', *Southern Poverty Law Centre*, https://www.splcenter.org/intelligence-report.
89. 'Fanning the flames: the Earth Liberation Front in North America, pp. 137–9.
90. Ibid.
91. Ibid.
92. Bondaroff, 'Throwing a wrench into things: the strategy of radical environmentalism', pp. 13, 16.; Liddick, *Eco-Terrorism: Radical Environmental and Animal Liberation Movements*, pp. 65–6.
93. Bron Taylor (1998) 'Religion, violence and radical environmentalism: from Earth First! to the Unabomber to the Earth Liberation Front', *Terrorism and Political Violence*, **10** (4), pp. 27–8.
94. Bryan Denson and James Long (1999) 'Eco-terrorism sweeps the American West', *The Oregonian*, 26 September.
95. Joosse, 'Leaderless resistance and ideological inclusion: the case of the Earth Liberation Front', p. 361.
96. Trujillo, 'The radical environmentalist movement', p. 158.
97. Stratmoen, 'Arson on Vail Mountain: a case study of the Earth Liberation Front', p. 23.
98. Ibid., p. 21.
99. Ibid., p. 24.
100. Carlton Purvis (2012) 'Operation backfire, eleven down, two to go', *NAALPRO*, 3 December, https://animalliberationpressoffice.org/NAALPO/2012/12/03/operation-backfire-eleven-down-two-to-go/ accessed 28 December 2015.; Global Terrorism Database, ID: 200110150005; http://www.start.umd.edu/gtd/search/IncidentSummary.aspx?gtdid=200110150005.
101. Young (2015) 'The Family: America's most prolific domestic terrorism cell', *news.com.au*, 13 December, http://www.news.com.au/technology/environment/the-family-americas-most-prolific-domestic-terrorism-cell/news-story/62da5ed8a0f54112834e207846783946.
102. Ibid.
103. Ibid.
104. Ibid.
105. 'Countering ecoterrorism in the United States: the case of "Operation Backfire"', *Final Report to the Science & Technology Directorate, U.S. Department of Homeland Security*, September 2012, http://www.start.umd.edu/sites/default/files/files/publications/Countermeasures_OperationBackfire.pdf.
106. Global Terrorism Database, ID: 200110150005, http://www.start.umd.edu/gtd/search/IncidentSummary.aspx?gtdid=200110150005.
107. Andrew Smith, 'An axe without the handle: an exploratory analysis of eco-terrorism and its relationships to public policy towards terrorism: 1990–2010', doctoral dissertation, Nova Southeastern University, http://nsuworks.nova.edu/cgi/viewcontent.cgi?article=1004&context=shss_dcar_etd.
108. Purvis, 'Operation backfire, eleven down, two to go'.
109. 'Operation Backfire: help find four ecoterrorists', 19 November 2008, https://www.fbi.gov/news/stories/2008/november/backfire_11908.
110. Young, 'The Family: America's most prolific domestic terrorism cell'.
111. Smith, 'An axe without the handle: an exploratory analysis of eco-terrorism and its relationships to public policy towards terrorism: 1990-2010'.

112. 'Intelligence report', *Southern Poverty Law Centre*, https://www.splcenter.org/intelligence-report.
113. 'Fanning the flames: the Earth Liberation Front in North America', pp. 137–9.
114. 'Fanning the flames: the Earth Liberation Front in North America', pp. 137–9.
115. Rosebraugh, *Burning Rage of a Dying Planet: Speaking for the Earth Liberation Front*, p. 153.
116. 'Fanning the flames: the Earth Liberation Front in North America', pp. 137–9.
117. Ibid.
118. 'Intelligence report', *Southern Poverty Law Centre*, https://www.splcenter.org/intelligence-report.
119. 'Fanning the flames: the Earth Liberation Front in North America', pp. 137–9.
120. Ibid.
121. Hal Bernton and Christine Clarridge (2006) 'Earth Liberation Front members plead guilty in 2001 firebombing', *The Seattle Times*, 5 October, http://community.seattletimes.nwsource.com/archive/?date=20061005&slug=uwfire05m; 'US woman convicted of being lookout during arson gets prison, restitution', *AP*, 19 June.
122. 'Fanning the flames: the Earth Liberation Front in North America', pp. 137–9.
123. 'Intelligence report', *Southern Poverty Law Centre*, https://www.splcenter.org/intelligence-report.
124. ''Fanning the flames: the Earth Liberation Front in North America', pp. 137–9.
125. 'Fanning the flames: the Earth Liberation Front in North America', pp. 137–9.
126. Liddick, *Eco-Terrorism: Radical Environmental and Animal Liberation Movements*, p. 66.
127. Ackerman, 'Beyond arson? A threat assessment of the Earth Liberation Front, p. 143.
128. Stratmoen, 'Arson on Vail Mountain: a case study of the Earth Liberation Front', p. 10.
129. Joosse, 'Leaderless resistance and ideological inclusion: the case of the Earth Liberation Front', p. 352.
130. 'Intelligence report', *Southern Poverty Law Centre*, https://www.splcenter.org/intelligence-report.
131. Ibid.
132. http://www.bombsandshields.com/2005/11/hagerstown-maryland-underground-earth.html.
133. Ibid.
134. Ruby Gonzales (2010) 'Environmental extremist gets 5 years for attempted arson of Pasadena condos', *Pasadena Star-News*, 5 April.
135. 'Intelligence report', *Southern Poverty Law Centre*, https://www.splcenter.org/intelligence-report.
136. Debera Harrell, Paul Shukovsky and Aubrey Cohen (2008) *Street of Dreams homes burned, eco-terrorists suspected*, Seattlepi.com.
137. ELF Russia (2011) 'ELF claims arson in RU', *Bite Back Magazine*, 28 January.
138. Herald Staff (2011) 'Struggling fishermen targeted by vandals', *Boston Herald*, 12 January.
139. Ibid.
140. Author Unknown (2011) 'Hot dog stand gets new look', *Bite Back Magazine*, 2 January.
141. 'Culmine' (2010) 'ALF & ELF attack ecosystem-devastating machines in Mexico', *This is our Job*, blog, 9 December.
142. Author Unknown (2010) 'Broken windows at HLS financial supporter', *Bite Back Magazine*, 28 November.
143. 'Earth Liberation Front burns down Earth First1 journal office', *Earth First! News Wire*, 1 April 2013, http://earthfirstjournal.org/newswire/2013/04/01/earth-liberation-front-burns-down-earth-first-journal-office/.
144. 'FAI / ELF new horizons of burning rage take responsibility for media sabotage (UK)' *Guerilla News*, https://guerrillanews.wordpress.com/tag/earth-liberation-front/.
145. 'Moscow, Russia: RLF torch excavator and dozer during New Year festivities', *Earth First! Newswire*, http://earthfirstjournal.org/newswire/2014/01/14/moscow-russia-elf-torch-excavator-and-dozer-during-new-year-festivities/.

146. 'Istanbul: ELF sabotages road Roller', *Earth First! News*, Number XVIII, Spring 2015, http://earthfirstjournal.org/merch/wp-content/uploads/sites/2/2015/04/EFNBeltane2015.pdf.
147. http://325.nostate.net/?tag=earth-liberation-front.
148. Long, *Ecoterrorism: Library in a Book*, p. 7; Pickering, *The Earth Liberation Front: 1997–2002*, p. 77.
149. Ackerman, 'Beyond arson? A threat assessment of the Earth Liberation Front', p. 162.
150. Trujillo, 'The radical environmentalist movement', p. 145.
151. Plows et al., 'From the Earth Liberation Front to universal dark matter: the challenge of covert repertoires to social movement research', p. 7.
152. Ackerman, 'Beyond arson? A threat assessment of the Earth Liberation Front ', p. 146.
153. Plows et al., 'Covert repertoires: ecotage in the UK', p. 202.
154. Ackerman, 'Beyond arson? A threat assessment of the Earth Liberation Front', p. 149.
155. Ibid.
156. Leader and Probst, 'The Earth Liberation Front and environmental terrorism', p. 42.
157. Rosebraugh, *Burning Rage of a Dying Planet: Speaking for the Earth Liberation Front*, p. 263.
158. 'Earth Liberation Front leaves message for Hazelwood CEO Graeme York in Australia', Earth Liberation Front Communique, 3 June 2009.
159. Stratmoen, 'Arson on Vail Mountain: a case study of the Earth Liberation Front', p. 11.
160. Ackerman, 'Beyond arson? A threat assessment of the Earth Liberation Front', p. 158; Stratmoen, 'Arson on Vail Mountain: a case study of the Earth Liberation Front', pp. 11–12.
161. Rosebraugh, *Burning Rage of a Dying Planet: Speaking for the Earth Liberation Front*, pp. 263–4.
162. Pickering, *The Earth Liberation Front: 1997–2002*, p. 61.
163. Rosebraugh, *Burning Rage of a Dying Planet: Speaking for the Earth Liberation Front*, p. 264.
164. Global Terrorism Database, Earth Liberation Front, Attack Type, http://www.start.umd.edu/gtd/search/Results.aspx?charttype=bar&chart=attack&search=earth%20liberation%20front.
165. James Jarboe (2002) Domestic Terrorism Section Chief, Counterterrorism Division, FBI, Before the House Resources Committee, Subcommittee on Forests and Forest Health, Washington: DC, https://www.fbi.gov/news/testimony/the-threat-of-eco-terrorism.
166. Ackerman, Beyond arson? A threat assessment of the Earth Liberation Front, p. 148.
167. Joosse, 'Leaderless resistance and ideological inclusion: the case of the Earth Liberation Front', p. 360.
168. Hasbrouck, 'Primitive dissidents: Earth Liberation Front and the making of a radical movement', p. 122.
169. Bite Back Magazine, http://www.directaction.info; Global Terrorism Database, http://www.start.umd.edu/gtd/; North American Animal Liberation Press Office, http://animalliberationpressoffice.org/NAALPO/; 325, http://325.nostate.net.
170. ELF Press Office, http://www.elfpressoffice.org/cgi-sys/suspendedpage.cgi.
171. Juliet Eilperin (2012) 'As eco-terrorism wanes, governments still target activist groups seen as threat', *The Washington Post*, 10 March, https://www.washingtonpost.com/national/health-science/as-eco-terrorism-wanes-governments-still-target-activist-groups-seen-as-threat/2012/02/28/gIQAA4Ay3R_story.html.
172. Ibid.
173. Paul J. Karasick (2009) 'Curb your ecoterrorism: identifying the nexus between state criminalization of ecoterror and environmental protection policy', *Environmental Law and Policy Review*, **33** (2) (Winter), p. 586; Xavier Beltran (2002) 'Applying RICO to eco-terrorism: fanning the radical flames of eco-terror', *29 BC ENVTL. AFF. L. REV*, pp. 302, 304.
174. Plows et al., 'From the Earth Liberation Front to universal dark matter: the challenge of covert repertoires to social movement research', p. 7.

175. Ehud Sprinzak (1991) 'The process of delegitimation: towards a linkage theory of political terrorism', *Terrorism & Political Violence*, **3** (1), p. 54.
176. Martha F. Lee (1995) 'Violence and the environment: the case of 'Earth First!', *Terrorism and Political Violence*, 7 (3), pp. 120–1.
177. Sprinzak, 'The process of delegitimation: towards a linkage theory of political terrorism,' p. 54.
178. Gerry Nagtzaam and Pete Lentini (2008) 'Vigilantes on the high seas?: The Sea Shepherds and political violence', *Terrorism and Political Violence*, **1**, p. 118; Ehud Sprinzak (1998) 'The psychopolitical formation of extreme left terrorism in a democracy: the case of the Weathermen', in Walter Reich (ed.), *Origins of Terrorism: Psychologies, Ideologies, Theologies, States of Mind* (Washington, DC: Woodrow Wilson Center Press), pp. 80–1.
179. http://www.earthfirstjournal.org/subsection.php?id=1.
180. Parson, 'Understanding the ideology of the Earth Liberation Front', p. 51.
181. Long, *Ecoterrorism: Library in a Book*, p. 36.
182. Taylor, 'Religion, violence and radical environmentalism: from Earth First! to the Unabomber to the Earth Liberation Front', p. 11.
183. Nagtzaam and Lentini, 'Vigilantes on the high seas?: The Sea Shepherds and political violence', p. 118.
184. Sprinzak, 'The process of delegitimation: towards a linkage theory of political terrorism', pp. 56–7.
185. Olivia Rousset (reporter, producer), 'ELF – "Green With a Vengeance"', *Dateline* (Sydney: SBS Television), broadcast 10 October 2001.
186. Liddick, *Eco-Terrorism: Radical Environmental and Animal Liberation Movements*, p. 59.
187. Hasbrouck, 'Primitive dissidents: Earth Liberation Front and the making of a radical movement', p. 2.
188. Ibid., p. 68; Manuel Castells (2000) 'Toward a sociology of the Network Society', *Contemporary Sociology*, **29** (5), p. 693.
189. Sprinzak, 'The psychopolitical formation of extreme left terrorism in a democracy: the case of the Weathermen', pp. 81–2.
190. Sprinzak, 'The process of delegitimation: towards a linkage theory of political terrorism,' p. 55.
191. Trujillo, 'The radical environmentalist movement', p. 153.
192. Ibid., p. 21.
193. Long, *Ecoterrorism: Library in a Book*, p. 35.
194. Sprinzak, 'The psychopolitical formation of extreme left terrorism in a democracy: the case of the Weathermen', p. 82.
195. S. Kamieniecki et al. (1995) 'The effectiveness of radical environmentalists', in Bron Taylor (ed.), *Ecological Resistance Movements: The Global Emergence of Radical and Popular Environmentalism* (New York: University of New York Press), p. 326.
196. Gula (1989) 'Eco-kamikazes wanted', *Earth Journal First!*, 22 September, p. 21.
197. Nagtzaam and Lentini, 'Vigilantes on the high seas?: The Sea Shepherds and political violence', p. 118.
198. Sprinzak, 'The psychopolitical formation of extreme left terrorism in a democracy: the case of the Weathermen', p. 83.
199. Rosebraugh, *Burning Rage of a Dying Planet: Speaking for the Earth Liberation Front*, pp. 263–4.
200. Ackerman, 'Beyond arson? A threat assessment of the Earth Liberation Front ', p. 146.
201. Ibid.
202. Leader and Probst, 'The Earth Liberation Front and environmental terrorism', p. 42.
203. Ackerman (2003) Beyond arson? A threat assessment of the Earth Liberation Front, p. 147.
204. Ibid., p. 154; 'Interview with Craig Rosebraugh', *No Compromise*, **16**, http://www.nocompromise.org/issues/16craig.html.

205. Stratmoen, 'Arson on Vail Mountain: a case study of the Earth Liberation Front', pp. 154–5.
206. Trujillo, 'The radical environmentalist movement', p. 167.

PART III

6. Gaia's Navy: the Sea Shepherd Conservation Society

> Paul Watson is the greatest Eco-Warrior of all. Operating largely on their own dedication, Paul and his crews enforce international treaties and agreements on the high seas to protect marine mammals and ocean birds from criminal destruction by industrial fishing ... Because of this, Watson and his ships have become the international policeman of the sea.
>
> Dave Foreman[1]

INTRODUCTION

Since 1977 the Sea Shepherd Conservation Society (SSCS) has gone about its self-appointed task to protect the oceans and their inhabitants from human depredation.[2] The Sea Shepherd organization has expanded from one ship and a small crew seeking to protest Canadian sealing to a worldwide organization with multiple ships and the ability to carry out its mission globally. Its leader, Paul Watson, is greeted as an 'ecological rock-star' in many Western democracies, with his own television series *Whale Wars* on the Discovery Channel and celebrity supporters willing to donate to his cause. He is perceived by many of his followers as willing to do what other ecological groups are not prepared to do and commit militant direct acts that disrupt ongoing whaling and the exploitation of marine life.

However, in states where whaling or overfishing continues Watson and the group he leads are reviled as ecoterrorists, pirates or vigilantes and constantly threatened with legal action under both domestic and international law.[3] In response to such allegations Paul Watson and his members proudly wear such appellations, arguing that they have to enforce international wildlife law since no other global agency will act. The SSCS has argued for years that the current slaughter of whales by Japanese whalers under the rubric of 'scientific research' is illegal under international laws such as the International Convention for the Regulation of Whaling and the World Charter for Nature.[4] In the absence of a world community unwilling or unable to end the killing, they believe it is incumbent upon them to act as vigilantes by shining a media spotlight on their foes' actions, and by carrying out direct actions that make the cost of marine exploitation uneconomic.

The strategies and tactics employed by Sea Shepherd against the annual Japanese whaling fleet are sensational, sometimes violent, and intended to inflict property damage with the stated goal of ending global whaling in all forms and the exploitation of the ocean's resources. Every year the ever-expanding Sea Shepherd flotilla sets sail from Australian waters to do battle with the Japanese whaling fleet. Over the decades the SSCS has been implicated in ramming whaling ships; sinking whaling vessels; utilizing lasers to blind Japanese whalers; flinging butyric acid (rancid butter) at ships to disrupt on-ship whale-meat processing; fouling the propellers of ships; playing 'chicken' with and/or harassing ships; and boarding ships at sea.[5] Further, Watson and his organization have proudly proclaimed responsibility for sinking ten 'illegal' whaling ships.[6]

Yet at the height of its powers the SSCS and its leader Paul Watson finds itself challenged like never before. In the past, despite a myriad of militant direct actions undertaken by the group in the service of their goals, states have being mostly unwilling to challenge them in domestic courts, fearing a global media backlash. Further, the SSCS has demonstrated a sophisticated knowledge of the limitations of international oceanic law as applied to their actions, exploiting a lacuna at the centre of international maritime law that has allowed the group to operate virtually unhindered to date. However, a number of domestic court actions being brought by the group's opponents targeting Paul Watson and the SSCS threaten their ability to continue to carry out direct actions with impunity.

This chapter details the background of the group's totemic leader Paul Watson, and his childhood influences that led him to want to work to save oceanic creatures. It describes his oft-times fiery relationship with the environmental non-governmental organization (ENGO) Greenpeace and Watson's rancorous exit from that organization. The chapter then critically examines the formation of Earthforce, the stillborn antecedent group to the SSCS and the creation in 1977 of the SSCS. It goes on to critically analyse the group's ethos; its organizational structure; its strategy and tactics: its use of diplomacy, the global media and militant direct action to achieve its goals. Lastly this chapter examines the SSCS's attitude to violence carried out in the service of its mission and its distinction between violence against humans and property damage, which the group argues should not be considered a violent act.

BACKGROUND OF PAUL WATSON

Paul Watson claims that his attraction to the ocean began when he was six, when his family relocated to St Andrews, a colonial resort town situated on Canada's east coast.[7] According to Watson he was 'an eco-warrior before puberty' and has related a number of incidents that have profoundly affected him and his relationship to the biosphere.[8] Watson has often told a story that he befriended a beaver (in some accounts it is an otter) near his domicile when he was a child.[9] In 1960, Watson became a member of the Kindness Club, founded by Aida Flemming in New Brunswick. After trappers killed and skinned one of his beaver friends, Watson set out (at the age of nine in some accounts) with his brothers and sisters to confiscate and destroy leg-hold traps. He was also known to disrupt deer and duck hunters, and to prevent other boys from shooting at birds.[10] Watson maintains that his passion for saving animal life developed early. In his book *Seal Wars* (2003) Watson recounts his revulsion at an uncle who took him to a seal hunt and states:

> Ever since I was a boy of nine, I have abhorred the killing of seals. That was in 1960, when I first saw evidence of the seal hunt with my own eyes. To this day, forty-two years later, I can still recall the vivid, scarlet-on-white images that so disturbed me as a child. In my nightmares, newborn seal pups were bludgeoned by men whose cold, savage eyes held a ruthlessness I had never before encountered or imagined. In some dreams, I was the seal pup, shivering in the shadow of a huge hairy creature who brutally wielded a spiked club dripping with blood. I remember feeling frustrated, angry, and extremely helpless.[11]

Watson spent much of his youth at a marine biology station, including a volunteer position he held when he was 11, which: 'helped set the course that led to my activist protests against nuclear testing in 1971 and, by extension, most of my other expeditions'.[12] According to Watson his personal view of how humans treat the planet was shaken to the core when:

> [d]uring the winter of 1965, I stumbled across a book that shook me to the very core of my being ... Published by the New York Zoological Society in 1913, the study by William T. Hornady was entitled *Our Vanishing Wild Life – Its Extermination and Preservation.* The book documents human atrocities against the natural world and calls for the formation of an army of defence for non-humans. I still have that copy of Hornaday's book and view it as my personal bible.[13]

By 1970, Watson was working part-time for the Canadian Coast Guard, whilst writing for an underground newspaper, the *Georgia Straight*, and studying at Simon Fraser University.[14] Although he studied archaeology, linguistics and communications at Simon Fraser University, Watson never graduated.[15] Yet his studies in media seem to have had a profound effect on him and he has become a master manipulator of the medium. According to Watson, 'survival in a media culture meant developing the skills to understand and manipulate media to achieve strategic objectives'. As such, Watson concluded that whaling as an activity for most people is 'purely academic unless high drama is introduced to make it newsworthy' and his reporting of his own actions indicates he lives by this credo.[16]

Needing money, Watson joined the Canadian Coast Guard in 1968 at the age of 18 and then worked as a merchant marine, and according to his biography has no educational qualifications past high school.[17] Over the next few years, he would occasionally accept positions as a 'merchant marine', gaining experience as a sailor on Norwegian and Swedish merchant vessels, and Mediterranean yachts.[18]

On the Sea Shepherd website Watson's epiphany that whales need to be protected sprang from an incident when, as a member of a Greenpeace expedition to disrupt whaling in 1975, he came face-to-face with a dying sperm whale and thought he saw a flicker of comprehension in the dying whale's eyes. This encounter changed him and he vowed to become the defender of marine life.[19] Recalling an event when he came 'eye to eye' with a whale, Watson remembers:

> His eye fell upon Fred and me, two tiny men in a little rubber raft, and he looked at us. It was a gaze, a gentle, knowing, forgiving gaze. Slowly, slowly, as if he did not want to disturb the water unduly, as if taking care that his great tail did not scrape us from our little perch, he settled into the quietly lapping waves. I had one more glimpse of that gazing eye, and then he was gone from our world.[20]

He goes on to say of the incident that it changed the course of his life because he believed that the whale understood what Watson was attempting to do.[21] Watson recalls: 'I no longer try to understand what happened between that dying Sperm whale and me. I know only that I felt a commitment.'[22]

However, Scarce in his book on eco-activism tells a different story, as Watson has also claimed that his bond with whales derives from a vision he had in an Oglala Sioux sweat lodge during an initiation ceremony subsequent to the Wounded Knee uprising in 1973, where Watson served the Native American cause as a medical aide. He maintains that a bison appeared to him and advised him to focus on preserving sea mammals and, in particular, whales.[23] Manne similarly records that the inspiration behind Watson's ongoing 'ecological mission' is rooted in Watson's experience at Wounded Knee.[24]

Watson has also been involved in Canadian politics and he has run for elected office as a Member of Parliament for Vancouver Centre at the Federal elections, has been a candidate for the Green Party twice, and ran for the position of Mayor of Vancouver in 1995.[25] Watson has also been involved in many committees and organizations over the course of his career. However, he resigned from the Sierra Club's national board over a policy disagreement and has been expelled from attending International Whaling Commission (IWC) meetings after he successfully sunk two of Iceland's vessels in 1986.[26]

Leaving Greenpeace

A defining moment in Watson's career was his relationship with the ENGO Greenpeace. Watson claims that he was an original member of the Greenpeace organization but Greenpeace refers to him now merely as an 'influential early member'.[27] In 1969 Watson, then a part-time university student, joined other Canadian activists to protest US nuclear testing in Alaska. What is not in dispute is when those members combined three years later with other activists to form Greenpeace Watson was 'a driving force'.[28]

The group's first confrontation was with a Soviet whaling fleet off the coast of California on 27 June 1975.[29] In that first action Greenpeace activists discovered Soviet whalers harvesting sperm whales. However, it was Watson who stepped on to the carcass of a whale calf, determined to make his point.[30] The original plan was to use inflatable crafts to position themselves between the whalers and the animals. During the campaign (and while in a 'Zodiac'), an injured sperm whale approached the small dinghy and, without attacking, swam by. Both men in the dinghy (including Watson) were wrought with emotion. Speaking of the encounter, Watson said: 'in an instant, my life was transformed and a purpose for my life was reverently established'.[31]

In 1976, Paul Watson and Robert Hunter (then President of Greenpeace) prevented a sealer from the hunt by physically standing in its path. As a result, they were nearly run over.[32] In his experience in Labrador and with the seal hunters Watson explains that he refused to compromise, wanting to save as many seal pups as possible and that he was willing to take any legal consequences that might befall.[33] Determined to do more, Watson says: 'I threw myself between a sealer and his prey, and, when he shrugged and walked off, I followed him and did it again. I blocked another sealer nearby. I could see other orange-clad figures doing the same, and, to my surprise, I could hear myself swearing in Norwegian.'[34]

With the public's support and the Canadian government discussing the creation and release of a film that defended the hunt, Watson and his crew went back to Newfoundland in 1977 to again disrupt the seal hunt.[35] This time Watson increased the stakes by being willing to commit assault, recalling approaching a sealer busy with his kill, saying:

> As the sealer bent to his task, assiduously ignoring me and quickly carving the pelt from the warm little body, I walked slowly behind him. I picked up his club decorously, almost ceremoniously, I threw it into an open lead. Unfortunately, it floated. But the sealer would have to retrieve it.[36]

Camera footage of Watson's actions increased publicity and, subsequently, monetary donations for Greenpeace. After some debate, the group also became involved in protesting the annual seal hunt in Canada.[37]

The actual reasons why Watson left Greenpeace are contested. Scarce maintains that Watson's actions on the Greenpeace seal hunt campaign in 1977 in Newfoundland, where he threatened sealers with their own clubs and threw clubs and seal pelts into the water, saw him expelled from the ENGO. His actions were a crime under Canadian law, and threatened Greenpeace with losing its tax-exempt status in the USA.[38] Greenpeace charged that the action carried out by Watson was 'too radical' and some within the organization argued that it went against the group's pacifist ethos. In the end, the ENGO determined that Watson's actions had breached Greenpeace policy and had potentially endangered the group's capability of raising funds, and Watson was expelled from the organization.[39]

Watson himself claims on his website rather that he resigned from Greenpeace because he felt that the organization's original vision had been compromised and that there was a need for an organization willing to use direct action methods to enforce maritime law with the aim of preserving marine species.[40] Watson further writes of the incident:

> It was an emotional parting. All of us had given too much of ourselves over too many years for there to be dispassionate goodbyes. Those in control at Greenpeace were going one way, others of us were going another.[41]

Paul Watson still does not agree with Greenpeace's methods or effectiveness in stopping ongoing marine-life exploitation. Watson has argued: 'as far as I can see they have no intention of stopping illegal Japanese whaling … I don't think they will make any difference this year.'[42] For

Watson, Greenpeace, the group he helped found, was not radical enough for him and his agenda of saving marine mammals. He refers to his former friends as merely: 'money-grubbing, publicity-grabbing hypocrites self-victimized by size and inertia … and regards Greenpeace scornfully as the Avon ladies of the environmental movement.'[43]

Greenpeace on the other hand has denounced Watson's methods and use of violence as 'morally wrong' and 'counterproductive'.[44] The acrimony between the two groups continues to this day. Watson has accused Greenpeace of telling British authorities that 'his organisation was an eco-terrorist group'. Greenpeace, however, has firmly denied this accusation, releasing a statement that declared: 'no Greenpeace employee has intervened at any level with any authorities in relation to the registration of the Sea Shepherd vessels'.[45]

CREATING THE SSCS

Watson's disgust with Greenpeace at what he considered to be their weakness – and that led him to decide to create his own environmental group to more directly tackle marine despoilers – fits neatly within Sprinzak's crisis of confidence stage. In June 1977, Watson and several others, including Al 'Jet' Johnson, a disillusioned Greenpeace activist, established a short-lived organization called 'Earthforce' in Vancouver, Canada, in the hope of creating a model ecological activist organization.[46] Earthforce held to the tenet that a chorus of voices could gain global attention to their cause and achieve quantifiable results, an approach that Watson and the SSCS continue to this day with their focus on influencing the global media to highlight their cause. Watson envisaged that the group 'could investigate crucial environmental problems, advise authorities in responsible positions, encourage some actions and oppose others, and in that way affect decisions about the basic environmental issues'.[47] However, it ceased operations before it could carry out its strategy to stop the global ivory trade.[48]

After the failure to successfully launch Earthforce, Watson focused on creating an organization as an alternative to Greenpeace: the Sea Shepherd Conservation Society. Many activists and volunteers within the organization were former members of Greenpeace. They too became disappointed with the more 'bureaucratic' path that Greenpeace had chosen and the SSCS was founded with the express purpose of being 'devoted to aggressive but non-violent methods' of protection.[49] Watson founded the still ongoing SSCS in 1977 with the aim of protecting global marine life.[50]

Watson needed financial assistance in order to establish the Sea Shepherds. Grants from the Fund for Animals (New York) and the Royal Society for the Prevention of Cruelty to Animals (RSPCA, based in Britain) provided the initial funding for the SSCS.[51]

In 1977, Watson reportedly pleaded with Greenpeace to give him the *Ohana Kai*, which they were planning to 'sell for scrap'. He and another activist, Ross Thornwood, offered the organization a dollar for the vessel and planned to use it to ram whaling ships, either the *Dalyni Vostok* or the *Sierra*. According to Watson, they: 'called our plan Operation Asshole and the objective was to run the ex-U.S. Navy submarine chaser straight up the stern slipway of a whaler, jamming her in so tightly that she would incapacitate the target vessel'.[52]

After discussion, Greenpeace concluded that the plan was too violent and refused to give Watson the ship. In response, Watson mailed out letters to other environmental organizations, hearing back only from Cleveland Amory (founder of the Fund for Animals in New York City). Watson and Amory met in 1978, with Watson telling him his plan to bring the battle to the whalers on the high seas. They found a 200 ft (60 m) British-registered Yorkshire side trawler, the *Westella*.[53] On 5 December 1978, with the renaming of the *Westella* (now known as the *Sea Shepherd*), Watson's vessel became the 'first ship in history dedicated exclusively to the enforcement of international marine wildlife conservation law'.[54]

Watson claims, 'the name was my idea and I insisted on it as the most appropriate one we could think of'.[55] Elsewhere, though, Paul Watson has expanded on how the group was named, claiming that it stems from an incident in 1977, where he stopped a large sealing vessel by blocking its passage by standing on ice. A newspaper article run in the *Georgia Strait* newspaper had the headline, 'Shepherds of the Labrador Front', which inspired the naming of the vessel and the organization.[56]

PHILOSOPHY OF THE SSCS

In Paul Watson's own words: 'I intend to change the world. I believe, with Margaret Mead, that any single person can make a difference if he allows his passion to be expressed through action. My passion is the living Earth, especially her oceans. I am a conservationist, a protector of species and ecological systems, and a defender of the rights of nature.'[57] Watson compares the killing of whales to the murder of a human and justifies his statements by claiming whales are smarter than mankind and that their ongoing killing is a tragedy comparable to the Holocaust.[58]

Watson points out that, for the most part, the modern environmental movement has been too passive and reactionary.[59] According to Watson: 'activities by environmentalists are for the most part a series of small, inexpensive skirmishes against a powerful, better equipped opposition. A direct face-to-face encounter will almost always result in failure because of the superior financial resources of the opposition. A prolonged face-to-face campaign on open ground will certainly result in failure. The way of the Earth Warrior is to rely on the covert attack, the surprise attack, and planned defense security.'[60] He argues that it is better for environmental activists to be proactive and carry out campaigns of direct action such as tree spiking.[61] How Watson sees his and his group's *raison d'être* is encapsulated in Watson's declaration that: 'right now we're in the early stages of World War III ... we are the navy to Earth First!'s army'. Watson declares his commitment to the cause by saying: 'at the risk of sounding dramatic, my crew and I are prepared to die for these whales if need be'.[62]

ORGANIZATIONAL STRUCTURE AND PERSONNEL

The SSCS is predominantly run by volunteers and through donations. The SSCS support structure comprises both paid professionals and volunteer positions for their campaigns. The SSCS seeks volunteers for their crews who are willing to do it for no pay and work long hours in a variety of skilled and unskilled positions. Applicants are warned that 'no whiners, malcontents, mattress lovers, or wimps need apply'.[63] They also have volunteer positions for on-shore personnel to help in outreach activities and fund-raising activities, distribute information about the SSCS or conduct relevant research.[64] Some personnel on board ships are also permanent paid members of staff such as Peter Hammarstedt, the current captain of the ship *Sweden* and director of ship operations, who has been with the SSCS for over ten years.[65]

The members of the SSCS tend to be of varying ages, gender and background, ranging from youthful to older people. They also range in terms of class and gender, with staff and volunteers coming from many different countries including the USA, the UK, Canada, Australia, Sweden and the Netherlands.[66] As opposed to the ELF, which had a preponderance of men involved, there is no evidence of such gender disparity in the SSCS.

The organization has an annual budget of approximately US $2 million and has a paid staff of 14 people. Watson is rather strict on how the group receives its funding and does so mainly by delivering paid lectures, asking for donations on the internet and soliciting large donors.[67] As of 2010 Watson himself is paid US $120,000 to head up the Sea Shepherds, with the overall organization, according to its tax filings, making US $9.8 million in the 2010 fiscal year.[68] As of 2013 the SSCS had declared assets of US $3 million.[69] It has sought charitable status in a number of jurisdictions it operates within and has been granted US charitable status but has been refused in some states such as Australia, despite the country traditionally being a supporter of its actions.[70]

The Sea Shepherd organization's leader Paul Watson is the president of a tax-exempt charity headquartered in Washington State. The Japanese government tried to get the US government to revoke that status in 2009, but without success. Annual charity documents supplied to the Washington state government indicate that the organization made most of its money (US $11.4 million) through received 'solicitations' and had assets of $6.2 million in 2010. It also holds fund-raisers to help it fund its campaign in Australia; receives AUD $635,000 from the Dutch national lottery and US $750,000 from the makers of the *Whale Wars* documentary series, which features the Sea Shepherd direct action campaigns; 84 per cent of its income comes from individual donors and it has 30 people on its global payroll. Its ongoing charity status has seen it become the beneficiary of large donations from people such as Bob Barker (US $5 million) and Ady Gil (US $1 million).[71]

While the Sea Shepherd organization does not spend money on fund-raising, it often 'receives donations through media attention and word of mouth'.[72] Despite its radical tactics, the SSCS has attracted a large following of supporters, including some celebrities. For example, when Watson was arrested in 1983 for 'interfering with Canada's seal hunt, his ten-thousand dollar bail was posted by actor Mike Farrell of the television series MASH, who not coincidentally is a spokesman for the animal rights group People for the Ethical Treatment of Animals'.[73] Maxwell Gail (from the *Barney Miller* series) 'did a commercial for the Sea Shepherds that aired on local stations in California'.[74] Steve Wynn (a Las Vegas casino owner) 'once helped Watson buy a submarine'.[75] Several celebrities have also provided donations, including Pierce Brosnan, Martin Sheen, Christian Bale, John Paul DeJoria (CEO of Paul Mitchell hair-products company) and Yvon Chouinard (founder of Patagonia).[76]

Large donations have enabled the Sea Shepherds to purchase the vessels they use to disrupt their opponents. Ady Gil, a co-owner of Hi Definition Inc., donated US $1 million to the group. The money was used to buy a 'sleek, speedy and stealthy carbon-fiber trimaran', which was subsequently named after Gil.[77] After the disputed collision with a

Japanese whaling ship that sank, a second activist ship, the *Bob Barker*, rescued crew members of the *Ady Gil*. This vessel was purchased following a $5 million donation from television game-show host Bob Barker.[78]

The SSCS also has a Board of Directors headed by a president, currently Ethan Wolf, and a secretary/president, Ana Prezyna, who is also the organization's General Legal Counsel.[79] A Board of Advisors has also been created to give expert advice in their area to the organization. They range across legal, financial management, media and scientific and technical advice from a range of people volunteering their services to the organization.[80]

While many similar organizations use 'democratic consensus' as a method in the decision-making process, Watson does not believe this is a good approach. He states: 'this is not wise, but if this is the way accepted by the group, then it should always be consensus less one. There is a psychology of some individuals who will block a decision simply for the sense of power that it gives them. In fact, some of these individuals often seek out such groups for this purpose. Their priorities lie in dealing with their own psychological problems and not with the issues at hand.'[81]

Watson's autocratic behaviour and chosen actions have led many people to disassociate themselves with him. According to a former member, his method of control is 'anarchy run by God' and 'he doesn't like people who disagree with him'.[82] It is essential in Watson's view that leaders never give up their control to a bureaucracy. Furthermore, in Watson's opinion: 'confrontations must be in the control of a defined leadership. When confrontation begins, the time for democratic discussion of strategy and tactics had ended. All decisions must then be entrusted to a recognized command.'[83] Watson is a believer in the Captain James T. Kirk leadership approach, who when speaking to a crew member aboard the *Starship Enterprise*, maintained that: 'When this ship becomes a democracy, you'll be the first to know' – and Watson also runs the organization and his ship as a dictatorship with him firmly ensconced at the apex.[84]

STRATEGY AND TACTICS

Watson is a firm believer that his opponent's numbers, financial resources and technology can be defeated with superior strategy and tactics.[85] To achieve its goals the SSCS has a multi-prong strategy that ranges from diplomacy, economic and direct actions to a brilliant media strategy designed to quickly highlight the 'nefarious' operations of their opponents. The Sea Shepherds have been known to use diplomatic means to achieve their goals but have tended to prefer an economic damage approach to their opponents, coupled with a global media campaign.[86] According to Paul Watson, the objective of the Sea Shepherds is to simply damage whaling vessels enough that they will be forced back to dock for repair, though the SSCS has often committed far more damage than that, including the sinking of whaling ships.[87] As recently as January 2007 Watson argued that the group's activities would be confined to inflicting damage to any whaling vessel of sufficient magnitude to force it to comply with safety regulations and return to dock to be repaired rather than commit violence.[88] Watson maintained in late 2006 that through his (then) two ships (the *Farley Mowat* and the *Leviathan*; the *Robert Hunter* accompanied the *Farley Mowat* to the Antarctic in 2007) his organization could both keep up with Japanese whaling ships and possess the means and wherewithal to damage them.[89] The *Farley Mowat* was fitted with 'a solid steel hydraulic ram with a bulldozer-strength blade'.[90]

It has been noted that the organization thrives on publicity (both positive and negative). Such claims were evidenced by the significant increase in the Sea Shepherd's profile since the filming of the documentary series *Whale Wars* began.[91] Watson has learnt to use the media to achieve his stated goals. He declares cynically that the 'nature of mass media today is such that truth is irrelevant', and goes on to explain that, to the general public, the truth is simply what is written by the mass media.[92] When discussing the use of the media as a tactic, Watson explains, 'in the realm of eco-warfare, the camera is much more powerful than the sword'.[93]

Acting Outside the Law

According to Watson, there are times when it is essential to break the law in order to challenge its validity, and the SSCS has certainly put that precept into practice on numerous occasions. One method Watson prefers is what he refers to as the 'Brer Rabbit' ploy whereby, if you think you have the political or moral advantage, be willing to let the authorities put you on trial to further your cause. He has successfully used this strategy several times, asking to be arrested and charged on many occasions.[94] Watson claims that many states are reluctant to charge him for his and the group's activities for fear it would bring to light their own unlawful activities and draw unnecessary global media attention.[95] Watson recalls:

> In January 1988, I flew to Iceland to demand that the Icelandic authorities charge me for the sinking of half of Iceland's whaling fleet which we had sunk in 1986. I told the authorities that they should charge me and that I was at their mercy to decide what should be done with me. This action resulted in a debate in the Icelandic parliament where an Icelandic Member of Parliament stated that they would not play into my hands by doing what I wanted to do. As a result, I was deported without charge and Iceland was publicly and internationally embarrassed.[96]

SEA SHEPHERD AND ATTITUDES TO VIOLENCE

Initially Watson believed in the Greenpeace ethos of non-violence and non-militant direct action.[97] Watson argues that very few changes have occurred historically through non-violent tactics. He further argues: 'to remain nonviolent totally is to allow the perpetuation of violence against people, animals, and the environment'.[98] Watson argues that little change has occurred by embracing a non-violent ethos.[99] Thus, over time and since leaving Greenpeace his views have evolved regarding violence, particularly against property.

According to Watson, he continues to search for an agreeable compromise between violent and non-violent tactics. He claims: 'I have progressed in my thinking since 1975 to this: sometimes, to dramatize a point so that effective steps may follow, it is necessary to perform a violent act. But such violence must never be directed against a living thing. Against property, yes. But never against a life.'[100] Watson emphasizes that all of SSCS's actions have been undertaken without harm to any individual.[101] Further, the use of militant direct action methods by the SSCS against commercial whaling in the 1970s and 1980s also proved to bring 'international attention to this new form of confrontational environmental protest' and its potential as an agent of change.[102]

In practice, however, the Sea Shepherds appear to have an almost schizophrenic attitude to violence committed by the organization. On the one hand the self-imposed, supposedly inflexible rules under which they operate maintain:

1. Crew members cannot carry weapons.
2. We cannot use explosives.
3. Actions cannot be undertaken that will risk injury or death of our opposition.
4. We accept complete responsibility for our actions.
5. We accept legal and moral consequences for our actions.
6. We never compromise on the lives of those we defend.[103]

Further, Watson has outlined the guidelines to successfully completing a covert action. According to him, his rules include – besides not getting caught – that members should 'not kill or injure any living thing'.[104] Watson argues that what he does is rather a form of 'aggressive non-violence' whereby if property is used to 'break' the law it can be destroyed by his group.[105]

Lethal force against humans is not permitted by the SSCS and its members. Their policy is that action against opposition will be undertaken without firearms/explosives and without violence being directed 'against life'. However, the policy dictates that self-defence is permitted. The policy on property damage is also clear – any property being used unlawfully to take 'sentient life' will be destroyed.[106]

The Sea Shepherds have a rigid policy on the use of weapons. When the opposition is a government agency, weapons are not permitted on board at all. Rather, the SSCS believes that when fighting with a government, a camera can be a better weapon. However, if the opposition is a non-government organization, the Sea Shepherds will carry weapons. Captain Paul Watson admits to having a 'Confederate Navy Black powder revolver'.[107] Further, within the ship's armoury, the following weapons can be found: body armour, Kevlar helmets, flak jackets and gas masks. A shotgun and rifle are also carried on board. These weapons are all kept locked up and the only set of keys belongs to the captain.[108] Some argue that having the weapons on board results in a temptation to use them, to which Paul Watson argues that there has been no temptation and no incidents in which they have been used in over a decade.[109]

Watson takes great satisfaction in the claim that no one has ever been injured or killed during a campaign (on either side).[110] They claim that this is proof that the SSCS is 'operated safely and efficiently'.[111] However, they do not consider themselves a pacifist or anti-violent group and do not condemn the use of violence as a method of action.[112]

However, there have been incidents of violence against humans reported by Sea Shepherd members. In 1986, Sea Shepherd activists, using a line rifle, shot at Faroese police. A report by the police following the incident states that the attack 'is considered to have endangered the lives of the police crew members seriously'. It should also be noted that '"toads" ("rotating iron spikes, pointed and sharp at both ends") were used against rubber dinghies and petrol was poured on the dinghies (after which signal flares were also thrown)'. While the Sea Shepherds claim they only retaliated once the police had fired upon them, 'the report stresses that tear gas and gas cartridges from shotguns were the only weapons used by police'.[113]

Further, in 2010 it was alleged that a Maltese diver reportedly had his 'arm ripped by a fishing hook during a clash with conservationists who were trying to free caged tuna being towed by two fishing vessels'. The conflict occurred approximately 35 nautical miles north of Tripoli when activists with the Sea Shepherd 'accosted the two vessels – a tug boat and a supply vessel – towing the cage with hundreds of tuna belonging to Maltese company Fish and Fish'.[114] A second diver, who was also airlifted, was bruised as a result of the attack.[115]

However, there have been several conflicting versions of the event. The captain of the Sea Shepherd's *Steve Irwin* 'denied the accusations, insisting it was the ship's crew that repelled a "violent assault" by the fishermen'.[116] Paul Watson reportedly told *The Times* that they 'had no evidence of anyone being injured' and that the Sea Shepherd organization had: 'every reason to suspect that the tuna was caught illegally in the last couple of days when the fishing season is closed. We asked to inspect the cage but the fishermen were defensive and did not cooperate when we asked for information.'[117] The Sea Shepherds, though, have been more sanguine about causing property damage to achieve their goals and have not been shy about promoting their actions to a global audience.[118]

The SSCS has been growing in the last three decades from a small organization to a multimillion-dollar organization with a flotilla of ships, dozens of staff, hundreds of volunteers and thousands of supporters worldwide – all inspired by their autocratic leader and his vision of taking on who he perceives to be the enemies of Gaia. His willingness to directly confront Japanese whalers and illegal fishermen has seen him win global accolades from environmental activists, even from amongst members of his former ENGO Greenpeace. Paul Watson has also proven himself to be a master media manipulator, ever willing to subvert the truth to achieve his goals. The SSCS's attitude towards violence remains problematic, however. The willingness to use violence, even if limited to attacking property or in self-defence, runs the risk that every operation could see a loss of life on both sides – a price Paul Watson says he would personally gladly pay to defend his beloved oceans.

NOTES

1. Quoted in Paul Watson (1993) *Earthforce!: An Earth Warrior's Guide to Strategy* (Los Angeles, CA: Chaco Press) p. v.
2. http://www.seashepherd.org/.
3. Amanda M. Caprari (2010) 'Lovable pirates? The legal implications of the battle between environmentalists and whalers in the Southern Ocean', *Connecticut Law Review*, 42 (5), July, p. 1507.

4. Article VIII of the International Convention of the Regulation of Whaling (ICRW) 1946 allows member states a scientific research exception to the global whaling moratorium put into effect since 1986. Joseph Elliott Roeschke (2009) 'Ecoterrorism and piracy on the high seas: Japanese whaling and the rights of private groups to enforce international conservation law in neutral waters', *Villanova Environmental Law*, **20** (XX), p. 111.
5. Teale Phelps Bondaroff (2011) 'Sailing with the Sea Shepherds', *Journal of Military and Strategic Studies*, **13** (3) (Spring), pp. 1–55, pp. 42–3 fn 72; Caprari, 'Lovable pirates? The legal implications of the battle between environmentalists and whalers in the Southern Ocean', p. 1508; Anthony L.I. Moffa (2012) 'Two competing models of activism, one goal: a case study of anti-whaling campaigns in the Southern Ocean', *Yale Journal of International Law*, **37** (201), p. 209.
6. Joseph Elliott Roeschke (2009) 'Ecoterrorism and piracy on the high seas: Japanese whaling and the rights of private groups to enforce international conservation law in neutral waters', *Villanova Environmental Law,*, **20**, p. 99.
7. Paul Watson (2003) *Seal Wars: Twenty-Five Years on the Front Lines with the Harp Seals* (Buffalo, NY: Firefly Books), p. 43.
8. Raffi Khatchadourian (2007) 'Neptune's Navy: Paul Watson's wild crusade to save the oceans', *The New Yorker*, 5 November, p. 63.
9. Daniel Rosenthal (2012) 'High seas hijinks for Paul Watson', *Macleans.ca*, 22 May,, http://www2.macleans.ca/2012/05/22/high-seas-hijinks/.
10. 'Captain Paul Watson', http://www.seashepherd.org/who-we-are/captain-watsons-biography.html; Rosenthal, 'High seas hijinks for Paul Watson'.
11. Watson, *Seal Wars: Twenty-Five Years on the Front Lines with the Harp Seals*, p. 11.
12. Paul Watson (1982) *Sea Shepherd: My Fight for Whales and Seals* (New York and London: W.W. Norton and Company), p. 47.
13. Watson, *Seal Wars: Twenty-Five Years on the Front Lines with the Harp Seals*, p. 49.
14. Ibid., p. 50.
15. Khatchadourian, 'Neptune's Navy: Paul Watson's wild crusade to save the oceans', p. 64; Watson, *Earthforce!: An Earth Warrior's Guide to Strategy*, pp. 8–9.
16. Paul Watson (1994) *Ocean Warrior: My Battle to End the Illegal Slaughter on the High Seas* (Toronto: Key Porter Books Ltd), pp. 23–4.
17. http://www.seashepherd.org/crew-watson.html.
18. Khatchadourian, 'Neptune's Navy: Paul Watson's wild crusade to save the oceans', p. 64; Watson, *Earthforce!: An Earth Warrior's Guide to Strategy*, pp. 8–9.
19. http://www.seashepherd.org/crew-watson.html.
20. Watson, *Sea Shepherd: My Fight for Whales and Seals*, p. 41.
21. 'Paul Watson tells Alex McClintock why he won't give up fighting for the whales', *Sydney Morning Herald*, 14 March 2010.
22. Watson, *Sea Shepherd: My Fight for Whales and Seals*, p. 41.
23. Rik Scarce (1989) *Eco-Warriors: Understanding the Radical Environment Movement* (updated edn) (California: Left Coast Press), p. 97; Robert Hunter (2011) *Warriors of the Rainbow: A Chronicle of the Greenpeace Movement from 1971 to 1979* (Amsterdam: Greenpeace Press), p. 165.
24. Christopher Manes (1990) *Green Rage: Radical Environmentalism and the Unmaking of Civilization* (Boston, Toronto: Little Brown and Company), p. 109. According to Watson that same experience gave him his Lakota name: 'Grey Wolf Clear Water'. See Watson, *Earthforce!: An Earth Warrior's Guide to Strategy*, p. 8. Watson later described his experience to a reporter: 'I suddenly saw myself in a grassy, rolling field, gazing into the eyes of a wolf. The wolf looked at me, then into a pond, and walked away. When I told the Sioux what had happened, they gave me my Indian name: Grey Wolf Clear Water. Then I went back into the vision, and saw a buffalo standing on a ridge. It began to speak to me. And as it told me that I must protect the buffalo of the sea, an arrow came and struck it in the back. Attached to the arrow was a cord, symbolic of a harpoon.' See Watson, *Sea Shepherd: My Fight for Whales and Seals*, p. 70.

25. Paul Watson, Alternative Radio, recorded in Alma, MI (8 October 2001), http://www.alternativeradio.org/programs/WATP001.shtml.
26. Khatchadourian, 'Neptune's Navy: Paul Watson's wild crusade to save the oceans', p. 59.
27. ABC Newcastle, NSW, 'Paul Watson: the man behind Sea Shepherd', 23 May 2012, http://www.abc.net.au/news/2012-05-15/paul-watson-sea-shepherd-profile/4011498/?site=newcastle; James Marshall Black (2012) 'Paul Watson: shining activist hero or psychopathic terrorist', blog, 22 May. Robert Hunter in his book *Warriors of the Rainbow* recounts how Watson was left out of the first crew to protest the USA exploding a series of nuclear bombs on the island of Anchitka in the Aleutians. Hunter recounts that the rest of the Don't Make Waves Committee members (Bohlen, Stowe and Cote) considered Watson to be too radical and anti-establishment. However, he was a member of the subsequent mission to the Aleutians on board the ship *Greenpeace Too*. See Robert Hunter (2011) *Warriors of the Rainbow: A Chronicle of the Greenpeace Movement from 1971 to 1979* (Amsterdam: Greenpeace Press), pp. 27, 108.
28. Rosenthal, 'High seas hijinks for Paul Watson'.
29. Khatchadourian, 'Neptune's Navy: Paul Watson's wild crusade to save the oceans', p. 64.
30. Andrew Darby (2006) 'Hunters and protectors,' *The Age*, 15 November, p. 15.
31. Khatchadourian, 'Neptune's Navy: Paul Watson's wild crusade to save the oceans', p. 64.
32. 'Sea Shepherd History', *Sea Shepherd Log* (1983, Winter), p 4.
33. Watson, *Sea Shepherd: My Fight for Whales and Seals*, p. 87.
34. Ibid., p. 93.
35. Ibid., p 121.
36. Ibid., pp. 143–4.
37. Khatchadourian, 'Neptune's Navy: Paul Watson's wild crusade to save the oceans', p. 64.
38. Scarce, *Eco-Warriors: Understanding the Radical Environment Movement*, p. 101.
39. 'Sea Shepherd History', *Sea Shepherd Log* (1983, Winter), p. 4; Khatchadourian, 'Neptune's Navy: Paul Watson's wild crusade to save the oceans', p. 65.
40. http://www.seashepherd.org/crew-watson.html.
41. Peter C. List (1993) *Radical Environmentalism: Philosophy and Tactics* (Belmont, CA: Wadsworth, Inc.), p. 170.
42. Darby, 'Hunters and protectors', p. 15 (Focus).
43. Scarce, *Eco-Warriors: Understanding the Radical Environment Movement*, p. 102.
44. Dan Murphy (2010) 'Whale wars: the aggressive tactics of Sea Shepherd Paul Watson', *The Christian Science Monitor*, 6 January, http://www.csmonitor.com/World/Global-News/2010/0106/Whale-Wars-The-aggressive-tactics-of-Sea-Shepherd-Paul-Watson.
45. Andrew Darby (2006) 'Attack plan on Japan's whale ships', *The Age*, 27 December, p. 7.
46. Watson, *Sea Shepherd: My Fight for Whales and Seals*, p. 156.
47. Ibid., p. 156. Earthforce's aim was to be a global organization with a worldwide presence. Part of their purpose was to 'bring about international commitments to preserve the habitats of wild animals and to foster deeper public understanding of the delicate interrelationship that binds all life together'. Watson, along with many members of Earthforce, believed that they were: 'at a critical point in the survival expectations of a number of species, notably harp seals and many kinds of whales'. Further, they believed that ecological stability could be achieved and: 'Nature could overcome the damage already done, if ways to restrain the ravages of man could be found and enforced.' Through Earthforce, Watson and others reached out to other organizations, suggesting that 'in exchange for financing, I [Watson] would lead an expedition against the sealers in March and a later one against whalers as a representative to the contributing groups.' The only response Watson and Earthforce received was from Cleveland Amory (Fund for Animals in New York City). Amory's organization had been 'leading the fight to get the African elephant listed as endangered and protected from demands of the United States market'. Watson and several others organized a trip to Nairobi in order to 'gather photographic and other evidence of the size and scope of the trade in animal products such as skins and ivory' within animal curio shops. While Kenya's President Jomo

Kenyatta had commanded these shops be closed, this order was later withdrawn. See Watson, *Sea Shepherd: My Fight for Whales and Seals*, pp. 156–8, 170–71.
48. Manes, *Green Rage: Radical Environmentalism and the Unmaking of Civilization*, p. 108.
49. 'Sea Shepherd History', *Sea Shepherd Log* (1983, Winter), p. 4.
50. http://www.seashepherd.org/crew-watson.html.
51. Marine Wildlife Conservation (Circa 1984), No Citation Available, on file with the author.
52. Watson, *Ocean Warrior: My Battle to End the Illegal Slaughter on the High Seas*, p. 11.
53. Ibid.
54. Ibid., p. 12.
55. Watson, *Sea Shepherd: My Fight for Whales and Seals*, p. 175.
56. Paul Watson, Alternative Radio, url: http://www.alternativeradio.org/programs/WATP001.shtml.
57. Watson, *Ocean Warrior: My Battle to End the Illegal Slaughter on the High Seas*, p. xiii.
58. Khatchadourian, 'Neptune's Navy: Paul Watson's wild crusade to save the oceans', p. 58.
59. Watson, *Earthforce!: An Earth Warrior's Guide to Strategy*, p. 53.
60. Ibid.
61. Ibid.
62. Andrew Darby (2007) 'Anti-whaling 'pirates' get more muscle for Antarctic skirmish', *The Age*, 10 January, p. 7.
63. 'A call for planetary duty! Become a shepherd of the sea', http://www.seashepherd.org/get-involved/crewing-at-sea.htm.
64. 'Becoming a Sea Shepherd onshore volunteer', http://www.seashepherd.org/get-involved/volunteer-onshore.html.
65. 'Peter Hammarstedt biography' http://seashepherd.org.au/relentless/bob-barker-crew/peter-hammarstedt.html.
66. 'Whales Wars' DVD, *Animal Planet*, seasons 1–4, 2009–13.
67. Khatchadourian, 'Neptune's Navy: Paul Watson's wild crusade to save the oceans', p. 59.
68. Daniel Proussalidis (2012) 'Germans search for eco-fugitive Paul Watson', *Toronto Sun*, 2 August, http://www.torontosun.com/2012/08/02/germans-search-for-eco-fugitive-paul-watson.
69. Caty Enders (2015) 'Can Sea Shepherds survive their own success?', *The Guardian*, 5 June, http://www.theguardian.com/environment/2015/jun/05/sea-shepherd-whale-wars-animal-planet.
70. Jane Hammond (2012) 'Absurd outcome for Sea Shepherd tax', *The West Australian*, 10 August, http://au.news.yahoo.com/thewest/a/-/breaking/14520935/absurd-outcome-for-sea-shepherd-tax/. The Australian Administrative Appeals Tribunal denied the Sea Shepherds application for charitable status on the grounds that cetaceans and other marine wildlife could not be considered 'animals without owners'. See Hammond, 'Absurd outcome for Sea Shepherd tax'.
71. Andrew Darby (2012) How Sea Shepherd stays afloat, http://www.theage.com.au/national/how-sea-shepherd-stays-afloat-20120110-1ptu6.html#ixzz1lGmK69CU.
72. Peter Heller (2007) *The Whale Warriors: On Board a Pirate Ship in the Battle to Save the World's Largest Mammals* (New York: Free Press), p. 7.
73. Manes, *Green Rage: Radical Environmentalism and the Unmaking of Civilization*, p. 116.
74. Ibid.
75. Khatchadourian, 'Neptune's Navy: Paul Watson's wild crusade to save the oceans', p. 59.
76. Heller, *The Whale Warriors: On Board a Pirate Ship in the Battle to Save the World's Largest Mammals*, p. 7.
77. Louis Sahagun (2010) 'Whaling fight highlights two key donors', *Los Angeles Times*, 7 January, p. A4.
78. Ibid.
79. 'Board of Directors', http://www.seashepherd.org/who-we-are/board-of-directors.html.
80. 'Board of Advisors', http://www.seashepherd.org/who-we-are/board-of-advisors.html.

81. Watson, *Earthforce!: An Earth Warrior's Guide to Strategy* , p. 55.
82. Khatchadourian, 'Neptune's Navy: Paul Watson's wild crusade to save the oceans', p. 67.
83. Watson, *Earthforce!: An Earth Warrior's Guide to Strategy*, p. 54.
84. Ibid., p. 55.
85. Ibid., p. 24.
86. 'Campaigns from 1984–1986', *Sea Shepherd* (1984, Summer), p. 3. For example, in the two years before the moratorium on commercial whaling (put in force by the International Whaling Commission and set to begin in 1986), the Sea Shepherds planned to use 'diplomatic and educational' methods to convince Japan, the Soviet Union and Norway (and all other nations) to discontinue the practice. 'Campaigns from 1984–1986', *Sea Shepherd* (1984, Summer), p. 3.
87. Andrew Darby (2006) 'Attack plan on Japan's whale ships: Sea Shepherd brings faster vessel', *The Age*, 27 December, p. 7.
88. Darby, 'Attack plan on Japan's whale ships: Sea Shepherd brings faster vessel', p. 7.
89. Ibid.
90. Darby, 'Anti-whaling pirates get more muscle for Antarctica skirmish,' p. 7.
91. Dan Murphy (2010) 'Whale wars: the aggressive tactics of Sea Shepherd Paul Watson', *The Christian Science Monitor*, 6 January, http://www.csmonitor.com/World/Global-News/2010/0106/Whale-Wars-The-aggressive-tactics-of-Sea-Shepherd-Paul-Watson.
92. Ibid.
93. Watson, *Earthforce!: An Earth Warrior's Guide to Strategy*, p. 61. Watson quickly learned that using the media was a helpful strategy, one that aided him in preventing the deaths of baby harp seals in Newfoundland (1984). Watson had 'staged several confrontations with sealers that drew media attention. And then he had brought Brigitte Bardot onto the ice for her famous picture with the baby seal'. According to Rowell, 'the starlet on the cold snow holding the defenseless fuzzy white pup, and the pup's huge trusting, liquid black eyes had iced it. An outcry ensued and sealing was shut down for ten years.' See Heller, *The Whale Warriors: On Board a Pirate Ship in the Battle to Save the World's Largest Mammals*, pp. 23–4.
94. Paul Watson (1993) 'Captain's Log', *Sea Shepherd Log*, third quarter, p. 2. For example, Paul Watson has been previously charged with three counts of criminal mischief by Canadian officials, two of those charges carried the potential of a life term in prison. He pleaded not guilty and opted for a trial by jury. He has said that by choosing to be tried by jury, he was hoping that more publicity would be brought to his trial and, ultimately, his cause. See Paul Watson, 'Captain's Log' third quarter, p. 2. Similarly in 1983 Watson took a ship into Canadian territorial waters seeking to test the Canadian Seal Protection Act (1966), believing it was an unjust law designed to protect the sealing industry. They were arrested, put on trial and initially convicted. They appealed and won but the Canadian government appealed and the Supreme Court of Canada ruled that the Act was unconstitutional. See Watson, *Earthforce!: An Earth Warrior's Guide to Strategy*, pp. 85–6.
95. Khatchadourian, 'Neptune's Navy: Paul Watson's wild crusade to save the oceans', p. 66.
96. Watson, *Earthforce!: An Earth Warrior's Guide to Strategy*, p. 91.
97. Watson, *Sea Shepherd: My Fight for Whales and Seals*, p. 18. For example, Watson wrote on his way to confront Soviet whalers: 'What mattered to us, and mattered desperately, was that our voyage for peace and the ecology by our Greenpeace Foundation, was bound to win. As we had promised our members and other supporters … we were on our way to put our bodies between the Soviet harpoonists and the sperm whales they were systematically and illegally slaughtering. And we would have proof, not only through our eyewitness accounts of what we saw and heard, but especially through the incontrovertible evidence for all the world of our still photographs and movie films. This was our mission, and we were fulfilling it.' Watson, *Sea Shepherd: My Fight for Whales and Seals*, p. 18.
98. Ibid., p. 26.

99. Douglas Long (2004) *Ecoterrorism: Library in a Book* (New York: Facts on File, Inc.), p. 7; Paul Watson, quoted in Peter C. List (1993) *Radical Environmentalism: Philosophy and Tactics* (Belmont, CA: Wadsworth, Inc.), p. 131.
100. Watson, *Sea Shepherd: My Fight for Whales and Seals*, pp. 26–7.
101. Watson, *Earthforce!: An Earth Warrior's Guide to Strategy*, p. 9.
102. Anthony Vincent Silvaggio (2005) 'The Forest Defense Movement, 1980–2005: resistance at the point of extraction, consumption, and production' (PhD dissertation, University of Oregon, Eugene, OR), p. 57.
103. Marine Wildlife Conservation document (Circa 1984), no citation: available on file with the author.
104. Watson, *Earthforce!: An Earth Warrior's Guide to Strategy*, p. 88.
105. Don Melvin (2011) 'Activists searching for tuna boats', *Tacoma News Tribune*, http://www.thenewstribune.com/2011/06/12/17029641/activists-searching-for-tuna-boats.html#ixzz1PMaVonDu.
106. Paul Watson (1991) 'Sea Shepherd defense policy', *Earth Island Journal*, **6** (4), p. 42.
107. Ibid. The issue of having guns aboard at one point threatened to fracture the organization asunder. Once they became involved with drift-netters, Watson's fear for the crew's safety increased. According to Watson, at a board meeting in spring 1991, he 'moved that the *Sea Shepherd II* take on two semi-automatic rifles and a shotgun so that we wouldn't be entirely defenceless in the event that we came under attack by firearms'. Taiwanese fishermen had already reportedly threatened to shoot the crew. Watson wrote that not all members agreed on the motion regarding placing firearms on the vessel. He recalls that: 'Scott [Trimingham] and Ben White were infuriated by this idea. They voted against the motion. Peter Wallerstein was not at the meeting in Virginia, which meant that Peter Brown's vote in favour tied the vote.' Brown further pointed out that the two votes in favour of the motion were made by the 'two directors who sailed on every voyage'. According to Brown, 'it was easy for Ben and Scott to be opposed to carrying firearms. They were never in a position to be shot at. Scott insisted that our rules forbade firearms.' Following the meeting, Peter Brown asked Watson what he planned to do, to which Watson responded, 'it's a tie vote. They don't want guns. WE do. I suggest we maintain the status quo – and that means we carry guns.' Watson, in response to Scott Trimmingham's opinions that arming SSCS sailors was against the Sea Shepherd rules, stated, 'rules can be changed. If our opposition is government, then I agree. These drift-netters are pirates and they carry guns, and if they start shooting at us hundreds of miles out at sea then it won't do us much good to call the police.' See Watson, *Ocean Warrior: My Battle to End the Illegal Slaughter on the High Seas*, pp. 210–11.
108. Ibid.
109. Ibid.
110. Darby, 'Hunters and Protectors', p. 15.
111. 'Sea Shepherd History', *Sea Shepherd Log* (1983, Winter), p. 5.
112. Watson, 'Sea Shepherd defense policy', p. 41.
113. 'Sea Shepherds Record of Violence', *The High North News Extra*, 7, 10 April 1994, http://www.highnorth.no/library/movements/Sea_Shepherd/se-sh-re.htm.
114. Kurt Sansone (2010) 'Sea Shepherd attacks Maltese fishermen, two sent to hospital', *Times of Malta*, 18 June.
115. Ibid.
116. Ibid.
117. Ibid.
118. Actions of the Sea Shepherd include: ramming and sinking ships, obstructing harbours, the use of intimidation and threats, the destruction of a whale processing plant and offering rewards for the conviction of offenders who kill marine animals. See Watson, 'Sea Shepherd defense policy', p. 41. They have attempted to disable Japanese whaling ship propellers through a variety of means. See Darby, 'Hunters and protectors', p. 15. The Sea Shepherds also successfully cut the drift nets off two Japanese whaling vessels. The damage of these nets was documented in 1987; and in 1990 and in 1991 Sea

Shepherd vessels successfully disabled several drift net trawlers. 'Sea Shepherd confiscates Japanese drift net', *Sea Shepherd Log* (1992, third quarter), p. 1. A fuller account of the SSCS direct action campaigns will be undertaken in Chapter 7.

7. Ramming speed: Sea Shepherd Conservation Society actions

> I do what I do because it is the right thing to do. I am a warrior, and it is the way of the warrior to fight superior odds.
>
> Paul Watson

INTRODUCTION

The SSCS and Paul Watson have made it clear that they are more than willing to use political violence against property but it is an open question as to how far they are willing to go to achieve their goals. To help determine the answer this chapter provides a history of the various militant acts done by the SSCS since its inception. It focuses in particular on the ongoing annual confrontation between the SSCS and Japanese whalers in Antarctic waters. It further asks how effective the SSCS has been in its stated goals to end Japanese whaling and whether the methods are counterproductive to its stated goals. The chapter critically examines the recent domestic state attempts to charge Watson and the SSCS for their actions, focusing on an ongoing action brought by the Institute of Cetacean Research and the action brought by Costa Rica, which has forced Paul Watson to void bail and become a fugitive limited to living on the high seas for fear of being arrested. The chapter concludes by examining the implications of the arrest of the group's totemic leader on future campaigns.

This chapter also puts into a historical context the various major militant direct actions that the SSCS has carried out since its inception, with a particular focus on the Antarctic campaigns against the Japanese whalers. It examines the evolving strategy and tactics developed by the group as it set about its quest to end oceanic creature exploitation and questions if the campaigns are becoming more violent. Major actions undertaken by the SSCS fall into several broad categories: spoiling the whaling or sealing by-product via various means; ramming ships at sea; sinking ships in harbour; harassing ships at sea via a variety of tactics and boarding of vessels while at sea.

COMMENCING OPERATIONS: THE CANADIAN SEAL HUNT

In March 1979 the *Sea Shepherd* made its first appearance targeting the ongoing Canadian seal hunt, with a crew of 32. From the start Watson understood the value of having media attention trained on his activities (and those of his opponents) and his crew had a complement of media personnel from the US, British, Australian and Canadian press.[1] The activists' participation in the first seal hunt included throwing red dye on seal pups. This dye is not harmful to the animals, but devastates their 'commercial value'. Eight crewmen, including Watson, were subsequently arrested by the Canadian Coast Guard and questioned by the Royal Canadian Mounted Police (RCMP). Watson, reportedly, was beaten and threatened by the RCMP officers. He was eventually: 'released after two hours of exposure on the main deck after being doused with water in 10 degree temperature and told … they [RCMP] would kill him if he returned to the seal hunt'.[2]

All eight crewmen were found guilty under the Canadian Seal Protection Act (1966) and were fined CAD $2,000 and sentenced to five days in jail (except for Watson, who was sentenced to a fine of CAD $8,300 and ten days in jail). They were given a further three years of probation and prohibited from protesting the seal hunt until 1983.[3] During their time in prison, it was alleged by the SSCS that the activists were unable to eat, as seal meat was mixed with their food.[4]

RAMMING THE PIRATE WHALING SHIP THE SIERRA

For the Sea Shepherds, and in particular Paul Watson, the defining moment in their turn from what would be considered to be largely civic activism to the militant activities of what Sprinzak would argue would fall under his conflict of legitimacy category, appears to be their decision to tackle the pirate whaling ships directly and violently, in particular the decision to go after the *Sierra* pirate whaling ship.[5]

Watson convinced Cleveland Amory, the president of the Fund for Animals in 1978, to provide the money (US $120,000) to buy the ship that eventually was named the *Sea Shepherd*.[6] In July 1979 Watson put to sea in the 206 ft *Sea Shepherd* – a converted trawler with a reinforced concrete bow – determined to deal with the *Sierra* and morally avenge, as he saw it, the deaths brought about by the ship and its crew.[7] But there was also a calculating aspect to the targeting of that particular ship. As

Watson stated afterwards: 'I knew, we would get maximum world attention when I rammed the *Sierra* with the *Sea Shepherd*.'[8]

In July 1979, Watson tracked down the *Sierra* off the coast of Portugal.[9] The *Sea Shepherd*, under the guidance of Peter Woof, first positioned the ship across the *Sierra*'s bow, striking the ship a glancing blow to warn its sailors it was about to be rammed.[10] Scarce argues that Watson's 'strict code of non-violence prevented him from smashing into his antagonist then, and there … risking the lives of the *Sierra*'s crew and his own',[11] since in calm waters a competent skipper can control any ramming.[12] However, Watson is quoted by Darby as warning the *Sierra* prior to ramming the ship, stating: '*Sierra*, *Sierra*, Goddamn you, you whale-killing son of a bitch, your career is going to end today.'[13]

According to Watson (once they had pursued and rediscovered the *Sierra*):

> We made straight for the *Sierra*. My intention was to try to crash our bow into her bow in such a way that the harpoon gun would be cut away. I did not want to hit too hard … I did not want to hurt anyone – not so much because I had tender feelings toward the forty-two men aboard the *Sierra*, but because I oppose causing injury to any living thing and because their injuries might provide an excuse for a backlash that could undermine whatever good will our dramatic and dangerous aggression might produce.[14]

However, Watson has told another version of the same event that paints a darker picture of how far he was willing to go. He has stated that after ramming the vessel twice, the *Sea Shepherd* came around to hit the *Sierra* again. According to Watson: 'we had jabbed, we had hooked, and now would come the knockout blow. If possible, I would cut her in half this time.'[15] They did not succeed in that goal but did tear a 6 ft hole in the ship and stove in 45 ft of the hull, crippling the ship.[16] Despite being heavily damaged, however, the *Sierra* successfully escaped.[17] The *Sea Shepherd* attempted to make for Spanish territorial waters to avoid Portuguese retribution but was overhauled and apprehended by a Portuguese destroyer.[18]

As a result of the collision, the *Sierra* was badly damaged and would require approximately US $75,000 for repairs. All three SSCS crewmen were arrested and the Portuguese authorities, pending the outcome of the case, confiscated the Sea Shepherd vessel.[19] After being captured the vessel the *Sea Shepherd* was docked at Leixões, since the authorities were uncertain how to proceed. A Liberian company, Ultra-Marine Shipping, filed a suit against Paul Watson and the Portuguese police impounded the ship and seized its crew's passports.[20]

Following the ramming of the *Sierra*, according to Watson:

> The authorities really didn't know what to do about us. It was obvious that a crime had been committed, but technically the *Sierra* did not exist, because trading whale meat to the Japanese was illegal and therefore the whale meat that had regularly been offloaded at Portuguese docks and reloaded onto Japanese reefer ships did not officially exist either. This meant, of course, that the *Sea Shepherd* could not have actually rammed a vessel that did not exist.[21]

The three activists eventually escaped Portugal: 'with Jerry Doran swimming the river to Spain, Peter Woof cycling out over the back mountain roads and Paul Watson flying out with fake papers'. A court hearing in Portugal never occurred. According to the SSCS the Sierra Whaling Company allegedly: 'passed $60,000 in bribes to the judges and without due process … the *Sea Shepherd* was given to the whalers'.[22] Watson and the SSCS were eventually served with a demand to pay $750,000 in fines and damages for the return of his ship.[23] Fearful that the ship would be converted into a whaling vessel, Watson suggested burning it. A crew member responded with, 'no, much too messy. We should scuttle her.' Thus, on 31 December, three members of the SSCS, including Watson, made their way on board to the engine room, disconnected the bolts on the sea valve and sank their own ship.[24]

After the *Sierra* incident, 'Lloyd's of London' declined to pay out insurance for the *Sierra*, as it was registered illegally and the company 'cancelled policies with other whalers'.[25] The *Sierra* was then subsequently destroyed in suspicious circumstances. As Watson tells the story, he received an anonymous phone call and met up with an individual (whose identity he promised to keep confidential) who offered to 'finish off' what Watson and his team had started when they rammed the *Sierra*. According to this individual, he: 'represented a small group of concerned professionals who had the means and the skills to help the whales'. He further claimed that he and his team 'have the funding and the technical skills to finish off what you started'.[26]

On 6 February 1980 a bomb destroyed the newly refitted *Sierra* in Lisbon's port, with an anonymous call to the press offices of United Press International stating 'the *Sierra* will kill no more whales! We did it for the *Sea Shepherd*.'[27] Within the next few weeks two of Spain's five whaling ships were also destroyed (allegedly by the same three bombers who sunk the *Sierra*). There were no injuries sustained by the personnel in the attacks and the bombers were never apprehended.[28] Watson had the perfect alibi regarding the bombings, since he was sitting in a courtroom in Quebec when he received the news that the *Sierra* had been destroyed in Lisbon's harbour.[29]

The damaging of the *Sierra* and its eventual sinking by unknown perpetrators was certainly an escalation of previous actions by Watson and his newly formed group, seeking to create Sprinzak's 'defining moment', which changes the political landscape forever, in this case, the idea that pirate whaling can be carried out with impunity. However, such actions do not seem to be the result of a great schism or setback, unless you consider Watson's leaving of Greenpeace to be such a fulcrum.

Sprinzak's analysis of the group resorting to small acts of violence seems accurate when considering the fate of the *Sierra*. However, no one has ever been able to link conclusively the bombings of that ship and the others to the Sea Shepherds. It is indeed plausible that those in sympathy with the Sea Shepherds' goals, rather than its members, may have conducted the attacks. Indeed, it has been established that this occurs frequently within the context of political violence.

Certainly, the epithets hurled at the *Sierra* and other whalers became increasingly venomous, but the critical question is whether the sinking of the *Sierra* represents an act so revolutionary that it could be considered designed to bring about an alternative, superior ideological system. On the face of it the answer is no, with Watson seeking merely to enforce the IWC edicts. However, it could be considered revolutionary in two ways. First, it seeks to replace the current ideological system, which privileges human wants and needs over those of marine creatures such as whales and, further, declares that whales intrinsically have the right to life. Recognition of such rights by the global community would fundamentally alter the present political and ethical landscape.

Second, the actions of Watson's group represent a fundamental assault on the sovereignty of states. Up until the sinking of the *Sierra*, it was assumed that the issue of pirate whaling was an issue of state jurisdiction. The actions – whether the Sea Shepherds or their supporters perpetrated them – constitute a legal grey area, and suggest that private citizens willing to take action could perform the duties entrusted to states to enforce international law.

According to Rowell, following Watson's encounter with the *Sierra* he: 'got a taste for the immediate, undeniable results of direct "enforcement"'.[30] Following the ramming of the *Sierra*, Watson was asked to do various media interviews in the USA. Regarding such interviews, Watson declared: 'there isn't much point in ramming a whaler if you can't tell the world that you did so. In a media culture, a thing just doesn't happen unless the media covers it. We need to send a message loud and clear that whaling isn't going to be tolerated any longer.'[31] Up until this point it was assumed that the issue of pirate whaling was an issue of state jurisdiction only. The actions of the SSCS in sinking the *Sierra* represented a fundamental assault on state prerogatives to deal with ongoing piracy. Further, it demonstrated that the SSCS, operating in a legal grey area, could take militant direct action.[32]

ACTIONS FOLLOWING THE SINKING OF THE *SIERRA*

Following the *Sierra* incident the Sea Shepherds were involved in a range of further actions. In 1981 Watson secretly entered Siberia and successfully obtained documented evidence that a 'food processing facility was converting illegally harvested whale meat into feed for animals at a fur farm'.[33] In 1982 the organization dropped 'paint filled light bulbs' on to a Soviet vessel from a low-flying plane.[34] Following the light bulb incident in 1982, Watson was arrested and charged with violating several sections of the Canadian Aeronautics Act. As the opposing crew could not be subpoenaed for court, Watson was the only witness to the incident and was released.[35]

However, the group's focus remained the preventing of whaling ships carrying out their operations. In 1981, Sea Shepherd agents allegedly sank the *Isba I* and *Isba II*, both ships used for whaling, in the Spanish harbour of Viga.[36] Watson later called a press conference to announce that the group had been involved in the sinkings, virtually daring the Spanish authorities to act on the information. At the same conference, Watson further announced a US $25,000 reward for the sinking of any Taiwanese whaling vessel.[37] Following the announcement of the monetary reward and just before the IWC meeting took place, the Taiwanese government issued a statement declaring they were mothballing the five illegal whaling ships still active under their auspices.[38] According to Watson in his article *Tora! Tora! Tora!*:

> The last of the Atlantic pirate whalers, the *Astrid* was shut down after I sent an agent to the Spanish Canary Islands with a reward offer of US $25,000 to any person who would sink her. The owners saw the writing on the wall and voluntarily retired the whaler.[39]

ICELAND ACTION

One of the most famous actions mounted by the Sea Shepherds was a daring raid at the heart of one of the remaining whaling powers: Iceland.[40] In 1986 the Sea Shepherds claimed responsibility for the sinking of two whaling ships and the destruction of a whaling station in

Reykjavik, Iceland.[41] Paul Watson justified these actions in a letter written about the raid on Reykjavik by arguing that the killing of whales is both a crime and a violation of international law.[42]

The militant direct action on 9 November 1986 was undertaken by two SSCS members (Rod Coronado and David Howitt), with the help of unidentified locals against the Icelandic whalers. The whaling station (Reykjavik) was disabled and two vessels out of a fleet of four were sunk (*Hvalur 6* and *Hvalur 7*). The other two could not safely be wrecked without the potential to cause personal injury, as one had a crewman aboard it and the other was in dry dock so were not targeted.[43] Actions were thoroughly planned out to ensure the safety of everyone involved, including non-activists, and the same method of disabling the ships was employed as with the *Sea Shepherd*: removing the bolts from the seacocks. A more forceful method was employed with the whaling station, where the activists used sledgehammers.[44] The damage to the ships was later estimated to be US $2.8 million, to add to the US $1.8 million of damage caused to the plant.[45]

Although the vessels were eventually successfully recovered they were effectively scrap metal. It was determined it would be more cost-effective to purchase new ships for the fleet than attempt to fix the two vessels sunk by the Sea Shepherds.[46] Very few previous campaigns had been so successful in drawing the international attention of the global media to ongoing whaling.[47] Following this incident, some Icelandic government officials referred to the Sea Shepherds as terrorists for their actions.[48]

In 1988, Paul Watson attempted to put even more pressure on the Icelandic government over the issue when he tried to surrender to Icelandic officials, claiming responsibility for the sabotage. However, once he realized he was facing several years in prison over the criminal matter he retracted his statement. Since there was no further incriminating evidence against Watson he was ordered to leave Iceland and declared *persona non grata* within the jurisdiction.[49] Manes, however, argues that although Iceland threatened to extradite Watson over the sabotage, once he was in the country, focusing global attention on continued Icelandic whaling, they wanted nothing to do with the matter.[50] The support of the locals in carrying out this action caused many Icelanders to reflect on the nation's continued whaling activities, and many concluded that whaling was morally wrong and Iceland should discontinue such activities.[51]

In 1992 the SSCS was implicated in an attempt to sink the *Nybraena* in the Loften Islands, Norway but were ultimately unsuccessful, with the ship functional but water damaged.[52] Watson was arrested and convicted for attempting to sink a Norwegian ship and spent 80 days in jail.[53] In

1993, a similar attempt was made to sink the *Senet (Gressvik)* but again was unsuccessful with that ship again only suffering water damage.[54]

2002 COSTA RICA CAMPAIGN AGAINST SHARK-FINNING

In 2002 an SSCS vessel came across an illegal shark-finning operation, run by the Costa Rican ship the *Varadero*.[55] As a Costa Rican vessel, it had no permit to fish outside Costa Rica or within Guatemala.[56] The Sea Shepherds reportedly contacted Guatemalan authorities, which asked them to escort the vessel to port for arrest.[57] The *Sharkwater* DVD, filmed by a documentary crew aboard the SSCS vessel, shows Sea Shepherd personnel asking the crew of the *Varadero* to release the lines but they were ignored.[58] The Sea Shepherd vessel then positioned itself to sink their line and stop the *Varadero* from continuing to haul in sharks (resulting in a T-collision).[59] The *Varadero* refused to stop and attempted to escape.[60] The Sea Shepherds chased the *Varadero* with water cannons with the aim of flooding or stalling the ship's engines.[61] The *Varadero* was then rammed by the Sea Shepherd ship and finally agreed to follow them back to port.[62]

In a telephone interview about the incident, Captain Hammarstedt of the SSCS said the group took control of the boat, the *Varadero*, at the urging of the Guatemalan authorities but that 'the tables turned', with the Guatemalans dispatching a gunboat to arrest Captain Watson. Why the Guatemalan authorities took this action is still unclear. The Sea Shepherd vessel took flight, sailing to the Costa Rican port of Punto Arenas. The Sea Shepherds state that the Costa Rican authorities charged Captain Watson with violating navigational regulations. The Sea Shepherds say that the charges were eventually dropped but later reinstated by another prosecutor, with an arrest warrant issued in October 2011.

However, other reports, including the *Sharkwater* documentary,[63] maintain that subsequent to these events the *Varadero* crew accused Watson of ramming their vessel and Watson was charged with attempted murder for his actions. The charges were initially dismissed when a video of the incident, which was captured by the documentary crew, was shown to the prosecutor.[64] However, in Costa Rica a defendant can be jailed for up to a year pending an official investigation, so Freeman recounts that even when the Sea Shepherds were granted permission to leave they were pursued, leading to the bizarre event of them putting a copy of the documents authorizing their ship's release in a bottle, passed to a Costa Rican patrol boat.[65]

In the *Sharkwater* video another version of events is told. Back on their vessel, Watson and Stewart are contacted by their lawyer who informs them that the Coast Guard is on the way to indefinitely detain them. As a result, the Sea Shepherds pull anchor and run for international waters. Soon after, the Coast Guard is shown chasing them with machine guns, threatening to shoot if they refuse to stop. The Sea Shepherds decide to string barbed wire around the edges of the ship to prevent being boarded. In the end, they outrun the Coast Guard to the safety of international waters.[66] While perceived as a relatively minor incident in a long-running campaign, this action was to have far-reaching consequences for Paul Watson and the SSCS in 2012 when the Costa Rican authorities reopened the matter.[67]

THE SEA SHEPHERDS VERSUS JAPANESE SCIENTIFIC WHALING

For the last two decades the main aim of the Sea Shepherd organization has been ending Japanese whaling that continues under the rubric of 'scientific research' in Antarctic waters. The SSCS appears to believe that ending Japanese whaling would sound the death knell for the global whaling industry, given the Japanese industry's long involvement in whaling. The group continues to claim that the Japanese government is using 'scientific research' as a front to allow illegal whale hunting.[68] Paul Watson and the Sea Shepherds have become the lone activist group campaigning against Antarctic whaling since Greenpeace discontinued their participation in protesting the Antarctic hunts.[69]

The conflict between the Japanese whalers and the SSCS has been getting more aggressive in recent years.[70] The Japanese government claims that the Sea Shepherd group have continually threatened the lives of whalers with their methods of protest.[71] Watson claims that the Japanese government is desperate to stop the Sea Shepherds because of the strain the activist campaign has had on their domestic whaling industry.[72] This section details some of the more serious incidents that have occurred between the two combatants, including boarding of vessels by SSCS activists and ramming of vessels by SSCS and Japanese vessels, putting lives at risk and, in one case, a SSCS ship sinking.

The Tactic of Boarding Japanese Whaling Vessels

In the 2008–9 whaling season two men, Australian Benjamin Potts and British citizen Giles Lane, boarded the *Yishin Maru No. 2* whaling vessel and ended up tied to the radar mast.[73] The men were urged on by Watson whilst knowing they could potentially be shot for boarding the ship, or arrested and jailed. Watson worked hard, as shown in the *Whale Wars* documentary, to convince crew members to do so, to the disgust of several of the crew members.[74] The aim appeared to be to create a media controversy over Japan's treatment of the boarders. The men were eventually released into the custody of the Australian customs vessel *Oceanic Viking*.[75]

The *Ady Gil* Sinking

In the 2009–10 whaling season the Japanese whaling vessel *Shonan Maru 2* cut the high-tech US $2 million *Ady Gil* in two, paralysing her. The *Shonan Maru* was at the time providing security for the whaling vessels. According to Paul Watson, the *Ady Gil* was near Commonwealth Bay (south of Hobart) when without warning it was rammed by the security vessel.[76] The captain of the *Ady Gil*, Pete Bethune, claims that the Japanese whaler (approximately 1,000 tonnes) approached the *Ady Gil* (approximately 18 tonnes) from about 75 m away and whilst most of its crew were on deck.[77] Bethune was adamant that his vessel was idling, communicating with activists aboard the *Bob Barker*, when the impact occurred. Bethune thought the Japanese vessel was simply going to use a water cannon as a deterrent, but instead the *Ady Gil* was rammed.[78] A crewman aboard the *Ady Gil* received minor injuries (two broken ribs) as a result of the collision.[79]

Pete Bethune accused the crew of the *Shonan Maru 2* of 'attempted murder', claiming that the Japanese vessel intentionally collided with the activist vessel.[80] Paul Watson alleged that the act was deliberate and 'sheared the bow right off'.[81] As a result of the collision between the Sea Shepherds' vessel (*Ady Gil*) and a Japanese whaling ship (*Shonan Maru 2*), the *Ady Gil* sunk as it was being towed – the force of the initial collision destroyed the bow of the activist vessel. Paul Watson claims that despite being responsible for the collision and subsequent sinking, the Japanese whaling vessels ignored distress calls and did not act to aid the *Ady Gil* or its crew as it was sinking. Watson was outspoken when asked if he thought the whaling vessels should have offered assistance and stated that his society's commitment to the whales would not decrease, declaring 'we now have a real whale war on our hands'.[82]

Not surprisingly the Japanese Fisheries Agency told a different story, blaming the collision on the Sea Shepherds, arguing that the ship's crew had tried to ward off the *Ady Gil* with a water cannon initially but the ship employed reducing-speed manoeuvres, going from idling to full steam ahead tactics, which brought about the collision.[83] A Japanese video of the collision between the *Ady Gil* and the *Shonan Maru 2* shows a 'frothy wake' coming from the activist vessel, though evidence from the video is inconclusive regarding whether or not it was moving at the time of the crash.[84] The video evidence shows the *Ady Gil* 'stalking' the vessel and dragging ropes from the rear of the ship. The Institute of Cetacean Research went on to accuse the *Ady Gil* of coming within 'collision distance' of the Japanese vessel and using the ropes to 'entangle ... the rudder and propeller'.[85] Further, the video reportedly shows the *Ady Gil* increasing speed and deliberately entering the path of the *Shonan Maru 2*.[86]

Boarding of the *Shonan Maru 2* and Captain Bethune's Citizen's Arrest

The situation escalated further when Pete Bethune, the New Zealand captain of the sunken *Ady Gil*, boarded a Japanese security ship on 15 February 2010 in order to effect a citizen's arrest on the captain for attempted murder of himself and his crew.[87] It has been reported that Bethune was able to climb aboard without the crew becoming aware of his presence.[88] At 8 a.m. Pete Bethune approached the crew of the Japanese vessel *Shonan Maru 2*. The Sea Shepherds filmed the exchange via helicopter. Paul Watson called this boarding a 'mission impossible' and gave Bethune only a 50/50 chance of being successful. Watson points out that Bethune had to 'dodge nets and spikes on the outside of the vessel'. Bethune reportedly planned to stay aboard the *Shonan Maru 2* until the captain agreed to his list of demands.[89] Once aboard, Bethune reportedly knocked on the door of the wheelhouse and 'handed over a letter in Japanese saying "I am here to arrest you"'.[90] Not surprisingly, he was detained and then arrested by the Japanese Coast Guard for trespassing when the boat docked in Japan.[91]

The Institute of Cetacean Research (ICR) confirmed that Pete Bethune had boarded the *Shonan Maru 2* and that the Institute had, in the past, threatened to arrest and charge protesters who board Japanese vessels.[92] The Japanese Fisheries Minister Hirotaka Akamatsu declared, 'As it is outrageously illegal behaviour, we want to deal with it strictly.'[93] The ICR said that Bethune used a knife to cut away defensive nets in order to successfully board the Japanese vessel and that the crew treated him for a slight injury (a cut) once he was aboard.[94] Pete Bethune was taken into custody and taken back to Japan to face charges.[95] He was then handed to Tokyo's prosecutors, to decide whether to charge him for illegally boarding the *Shonan Maru 2*. The Sea Shepherds, in order to highlight the case, compared Bethune's imprisonment to that of a 'prisoner of war', stating he is the 'first New Zealander POW taken by Japan since World War II'.[96]

Bethune initially faced up to three years of imprisonment or a fine of 100,000 yen if convicted in a Japanese court of law.[97] Bethune was convicted of the following charges: 'trespassing, vandalism and possession of a knife'. He pleaded guilty to all but the assault charge. Although he was sentenced to two years' imprisonment, the sentence was suspended for five years.[98] During his closing statement on 10 June, Bethune tearfully: 'apologized for the trouble and said he never intended to hurt anyone' by his actions.[99] He was also ordered to leave the country and returned to New Zealand.[100]

In another ratcheting-up of the pressure, Japanese officials announced that the founder and leader of the Sea Shepherd Paul Watson had been placed on an Interpol wanted list in late June 2010 for 'allegedly ordering Bethune's actions as part of the group's disruption of Japanese whaling in the Atlantic'.[101]

Third Boarding

As Paul Watson tells the story: while in Fremantle, Australia he was approached by three people from Forest Rescue Australia – Geoffrey Tuxworth, Simon Peterffy and Glen Pendlebury – who offered to board the *Shonan Maru 2* (the same ship Pete Bethune had boarded previously), which had tailed the *Steve Irwin* to Fremantle Port. Watson states he advised them that the Australian government might not support them and they ran the risk of being taken prisoner, but the men wanted to do something since the Australian government was failing to act.[102]

The three men were brought out by boat to the Sea Shepherd ship approximately 16 miles off the coast near Bunbury, Western Australia. Watson points out that he knew this was inside Australia's contiguous zone (where Australia exercises nautical dominion, including who enters and leaves Australia's territorial waters). Watson reasoned that within the zone, Japan had no authority to remove Australian citizens without the express permission of the Australian government.[103]

The activists disembarked from the *Steve Irwin* via rubber dinghies and circled 12 miles back and around the *Shonan Maru 2*, guided in by the *Steve Irwin* crew with satellite navigation phones. To confound the Japanese ship, the *Steve Irwin* had posted on the Sea Shepherd website (aware that the Japanese monitored the site) that the ship had engine trouble necessitating repairs. When the *Steve Irwin* stopped, so did the *Shonan Maru 2*. The three men, in attempting to board, would have to defeat large spikes, razor wire and armed Japanese Coast Guard officers. However, they had studied photos of the defences and believed they could do so. Initially there was a problem in that one boarding-vessel engine failed, but Watson ordered the mission to be completed using the Delta boat. The three men successfully boarded the Japanese ship after the Delta used its bow to create a space between two spikes and the three men climbed through the hole in the razor wire.[104]

However, the Sea Shepherd strategy initially backfired when the Australian Attorney-General Nicola Roxon publicly noted that the three men had been detained by the Japanese whalers whilst in international waters.[105] The Japanese whalers alleged that when the boarding took place, their vessel was 44 km offshore (outside the 24-mile contiguous zone). The Sea Shepherds rejected that claim, arguing that their GPS device showed the incident took place 16.2 miles off the beach at 32° 57' 48' South and 115° 20' 24' East.[106] The Australian government then stated that it would sheet home the cost of bringing back the three boarders to the Sea Shepherd organization, which Paul Watson refused to countenance.[107]

The Sea Shepherds argued that the three men were being abducted from Australian territorial waters as the *Shonan Maru 2* headed towards Antarctica.[108] On 10 January it was announced that the three boarders would be released, with the Australian government sending a ship to rendezvous with the Japanese whaling vessel to take custody of the men. Paul Watson maintained that the operation had been a great success since it focused global media attention on Japanese whaling and got the global community and its leaders talking about the issue of whaling.[109] On 13 January it was announced that the three men were transferred to the Australian vessel *ACV Ocean Protector* and brought back to Australia three days later.[110]

PETE BETHUNE VERSUS PAUL WATSON

An ugly internal spat threatened to tear the SSCS wide open and it revolved around the issue of weapons on board SSCS vessels. While on trial in Japan Pete Bethune was formally expelled from the SSCS for violating its policy on weapons. As Bethune had admitted to having the weapons on board (in a filmed documentary), the Sea Shepherds felt they had no choice but to eject him from the organization.[111] Bethune admitted he was carrying a bow and arrows but claimed to have permission to have it on board.[112] The Sea Shepherd organization has stated that it expelled Bethune because 'he violated its policies against carrying weapons'. The organization conceded that he was in possession of a bow and arrows while aboard the *Ady Gil*, although they were never used.[113]

Pete Bethune then resigned from his position in the Sea Shepherds, accusing the organization of being 'morally bankrupt' and purposefully sinking the *Ady Gil*, one of the Sea Shepherd's activist vessels, following a high-profile collision with a Japanese whaling vessel.[114] Bethune claims that Watson ordered the sinking, which was motivated by a need to 'garner sympathy with the public and create better TV'. Bethune claims that even after the initial collision the *Ady Gil* could have been repaired.[115] Pete Bethune then took his public feud with the Sea Shepherds to his Facebook page, claiming that Paul Watson had ordered him to deliberately sink the *Ady Gil*.[116] Bethune argues he had no choice but to follow the direct orders, out of 'loyalty' to Watson and the SSCS.[117]

It is Bethune's opinion that any organization that uses public funding has a responsibility to be honest and that this is not occurring with the Sea Shepherds. He has since cut all ties from the society.[118] Ady Gil, a US businessman who donated the money (US $1 million) to the SSCS for the vessel, backs Bethune's claims. He maintains that Watson has used 'publicity stunts' in order to raise money for the society.[119]

Paul Watson, however, has denied all accusations that have been levelled by Bethune, claiming he is simply upset and seeking revenge for being fired. He goes on to say that any and all action that occurred on the *Ady Gil* was under the orders of Bethune, the captain of the vessel.[120] Watson claims that Bethune did not simply leave the group, but that he was expelled for cooperating with Japanese authorities in exchange for a lighter sentence. Watson says that the Japanese authorities were given incorrect information: that Watson ordered Bethune on to the *Shonan Maru 2*. Watson states that this betrayal is the reason that Bethune is no longer welcome in the organization.[121]

Further, the SSCS leader claims that his 'main sticking point' is that he believes Bethune gave false and accusatory information to the Japanese authorities in exchange for a lighter sentence.[122] This information resulted in Watson being placed on Interpol's 'Blue Watch' list. Interpol has: 'issued a so-called blue notice, asking national police forces to pass on information about Mr. Watson's whereabouts and activities'. However, it is important to note that at that time Interpol had yet to issue a notice 'requesting his arrest'.[123] Watson reportedly said:

> [I]t's a blue notice which means it's not an arrest warrant, it's just so they can keep tabs on me. But they needn't have wasted their time, they could have just followed our website.[124]

On 2 March 2012, Interpol declared it would not publish a Red Notice sought by Costa Rica to arrest Paul Watson over the 2002 incident since it was not satisfied that the request to do so was in compliance with its constitution and rules.[125]

In September 2015 an arbitrator, Jean Kalicki, ruled that the scuttling of the *Ady Gil* by the SSCS was a 'wrongful' act since it was not in danger of fully sinking. The arbiter was critical of the SSCS, arguing that the sinking was done for the television ratings and to boost public favour of the group and enhance fund-raising efforts. She found Watson's evidence 'highly evasive, internally contradictory, or at odds with his own prior written statements, and in certain areas simply lacking the basic indicia of genuineness that instinctively inspires confidence and trust'. Ady Gil was awarded compensatory damages of $500,000 plus interest from the date of the incident.[126]

PAUL WATSON ARRESTED

In an incident that might well have vast ramifications for the SSCS Paul Watson was arrested in Frankfurt, Germany on 13 May 2012 on an outstanding warrant from Costa Rica while on a speaking tour. The arrest warrant was over the confrontation in 2002 in Costa Rica when Sea Shepherd activists confronted Costa Rican fishermen over the practice of shark-finning.[127] Costa Rican authorities alleged that the Sea Shepherd vessel *Farley Mowat* committed attempted murder by ramming a fishing boat, the *Varadero 1*. The SSCS maintains that the incident merely involved an alleged violation of ship's traffic laws.[128]

The statute of limitations on the case against Paul Watson was due to expire in June 2013. Costa Rican prosecutors first filed charges in 2002 against Paul Watson for allegedly endangering the lives of eight fishermen and for attempting to cause a shipwreck. Watson did not attend a trip there on 26 June 2006, and he was declared a fugitive by the Costa Rican courts.[129] Sea Shepherd spokesman Mr Hammarstedt said that an arrest warrant against Paul Watson had lapsed before it was reactivated in October 2011.[130]

However, the global media was reporting that the Costa Rican government wished to charge Paul Watson with attempted murder over the alleged incident.[131] A higher regional court in Frankfurt directed that the alleged incident would have been a crime under German law and that the statute of limitations for this alleged crime had not yet passed and therefore ordered Watson into custody until the extradition process was determined.[132] The prosecutor in the matter alleged that the charge in the matter before the court was one of 'putting a ship's crew in danger' not attempted murder.[133] On 18 May 2012 Paul Watson was granted bail of €250,000 while the Costa Rican extradition request was considered by the courts. Further, the court decided he was not to leave Germany and must adhere to further conditions on his freedom.[134]

In a phone interview with the Agence France-Presse (AFP) Watson told them that he was under house arrest and had to report to the police twice a day.[135] Watson argued in the interview that this was an attempt by his enemies to 'get him out of the way' and 'shut down our operations'. Watson maintained he was more than willing to: 'serve as a symbol of resistance to the destruction of our oceans from inside a prison cell'.[136] Watson alleged that this was a conspiracy by the Costa Rican shark-fin mafia. He stated:

> Although I have no reason to believe that the Costa Rican legal system would not give me a fair trial, my concern is not for the judicial system, but for the reality that the shark fin mafia of Costa Rica has a price on my head and a Costa Rican prison would provide an excellent opportunity for someone to exercise this lethal contract against me,' he said. We have cost the shark finners a great deal of money over the last two decades and they want their revenge. I would need absolute assurance that the Costa Rican authorities would not place me in a position to jeopardise my safety when I return to Costa Rica to prove my innocence in court.[137]

Watson claimed in an interview with Fairfax media that he felt fear for his life if he was extradited.[138] Further, he used this perceived threat to argue to the German authorities that he should not be extradited to Costa Rica.[139] However, the Costa Rican president, Laura Chincilla, maintained that Costa Rica had a completely independent judiciary and that Paul Watson would receive a fair trial.[140]

Watson also found the timing of the extradition order suspicious. He claimed that the extradition order was enacted in October 2011 at the same time the Japanese were suing him in a Seattle court.[141] Watson in the same interview expressed concern that the Japanese government was putting pressure on the German government to carry out the extradition. He argued: 'It may be more than coincidental that the extradition order was put out in October 2011 at around the same time that the Japanese brought civil charges against us – and lost – in a Seattle court.'[142] Watson claims that it is abnormal that an extradition order would be asked for in the case of 'a relatively minor offence, where no one was injured and no property damaged'.[143] He also has noted that: 'Germany does not have an extradition treaty with Costa Rica but insists they can extradite to Costa Rica if they decide to do so.'[144] The SSCS has publicly doubted that Paul

Watson would get a fair trial and urged their supporters to write to German officials protesting their actions.[145]

The Sea Shepherd spokesman, Peter Hammarstedt, stated that a General Public Prosecutor to the German Higher Regional Court had formally requested a preliminary extradition arrest warrant against Paul Watson based on the Costa Rica warrant and request for extradition. However, and unusually, the spokesman claimed the Public Prosecutor stated that the German Ministries of Justice and Foreign Affairs have the power to issue proceedings on political grounds, if they wish. The Sea Shepherds were waiting on a decision from the closed court hearing, but if extradition was allowed Costa Rica would have 90 days to file papers to complete the process. Failure to do so would see Watson freed.[146]

Paul Watson Skips Bail

On 26 July it was reported that Watson's lawyer told the Frankfurt court that Watson had fled Germany for an 'unknown destination'.[147] The catalyst for his flight appears to be Japan requesting Germany to arrest Watson. According to the SSCS German lawyer Oliver Wallasch, the Japanese Embassy had requested on 19 July 2012 to extradite Watson to Japan.[148] Lamya Essemlali, the president of the SSCS in France, stated that Japan had been trying to extradite Watson and, further, Japan has entered into an agreement with Costa Rica to work together against 'terrorism'.[149]

Paul Watson went on to claim in a letter to supporters that Germany and Japan were conspiring against him:

> 'The German government said I betrayed their trust by leaving Germany, yet they had already betrayed my trust,' he stated. 'The German politicians had made up their minds politically before the German court had made a decision, and during the time I was held in Germany, the Japanese negotiated with Germany to file for an extradition order to Japan on fabricated evidence provided by former Sea Shepherd Crewmember, Peter Bethune.[150]

Japan subsequently admitted that it had sought the arrest and extradition of Paul Watson, essentially confirming the details supplied by Watson's German lawyer. The Japanese Coast Guard requested that Watson be detained by the German authorities with the aim of extraditing him to Japan.[151] Watson accuses Japan of seeking revenge for past acts by him and his organization. He said in a message to his followers: 'I am very disappointed with the German government. For me it is obvious that the German government conspired with Japan and Costa Rica to detain me so that I could be handed over to the Japanese.'[152]

Watson said of his whereabouts: 'I am presently in a place on this planet where I feel comfortable, a safe place far away from the scheming nations who have turned a blind eye to the exploitation of our oceans.'[153] Following Paul Watson's escaping Germany the higher regional court in Frankfurt has resumed extradition proceedings against him to send him to Costa Rica to face pending charges. The court stated: 'Since by fleeing, Watson has shown that he can not justify the trust placed in him, the extradition process has been restarted.'[154]

An Interpol Red Notice has now been activated, which requested all 190 member states to consider enforcing the warrant issued by Costa Rica for Watson's arrest and to detain or arrest him so he can be extradited to Costa Rica. However, a Red Notice is framed as a request since Interpol does not have the authority to issue an arrest warrant nor can Interpol demand that a state arrest anyone.[155] As Watson's lawyer, Oliver Wallasch has pointed out that such a Red Notice merely means that police in a state that Watson is visiting should be aware that he is wanted in Costa Rica. However, it is their call if they wish to act on this local arrest warrant and detain Watson for extradition.[156]

The Sea Shepherd's German lawyer is on the record arguing that under German law (as opposed to US law, for example) skipping bail is not considered a crime. Paul Watson leaving Germany is considered to be a local matter (with a local arrest warrant issued by the German Higher Regional Court) and the forfeiture of the bail. At this time he claims that, due to this being an extradition matter, Germany is not actively searching for Watson.[157]

A Facebook posting by Watson alleges that: 'the German court has withdrawn their arrest warrant for me citing failure from Costa Rica to cooperate in answering their questions concerning my case. I guess the Costa Ricans failed to get their instructions from Japan in time. I am no longer wanted in Germany.'[158] Watson argues that this is because the Costa Rica government had failed to meet the: 'February 27 deadline set by the German court to explain why there was a warrant for his arrest'.[159] Watson has argued, however, that he is still: 'on an Interpol red list usually reserved for "serial killers and war criminals"'.[160] Watson will continue to remain on the high seas unless he receives assurances from the Australian government that if he enters Australia's jurisdiction he will not be sent to Japan.[161]

INJUNCTION LEVIED ON PAUL WATSON AND THE SSCS

Initially, in February 2012, the ICR lost a preliminary injunction they brought against Sea Shepherd US to prevent them interfering with the Japanese whale hunt.[162] However, in a blow to the SSCS, a US Court of Appeals for the Ninth Circuit in Washington State decision overturned the prior ruling in the group's favour by US District Judge Richard Jones and issued a preliminary injunction against the group.[163] The injunction enjoined the SSCS from physically confronting any vessel or any person on any vessel engaged by the plaintiffs, the ICR, in the Southern Ocean, and that they must not navigate in a manner that is likely to endanger the safe operation of any such vessel. It also mandates that the defendants shall not approach the plaintiffs any closer than 500 yards when defendants are navigating on the open sea. The preliminary injunction states that:

> Defendants Sea Shepherd Conservation Society and Paul Watson, and any party acting in concert with them (collectively 'defendants'), are enjoined from physically attacking any vessel engaged by Plaintiffs the Institute of Cetacean Research, Kyodo Senpaku Kaisha, Ltd., Tomoyuki Ogawa or Toshiyuki Miura in the Southern Ocean or any person on any such vessel (collectively 'plaintiffs'), or from navigating in a manner that is likely to endanger the safe navigation of any such vessel. In no event shall defendants approach plaintiffs any closer than 500 yards when defendants are navigating on the open sea.[164]

The injunction is to remain in place until the court issues an opinion on the merits of the appeal filed by the ICR.[165] The SSCS has publicly vowed that the injunction will not deter them from their mission since it is operational only to Sea Shepherd Conservation Society US and its founder, Paul Watson, not to other states that host Sea Shepherd groups, which are separate legal entities.[166] However, it does clear the way for Japan to bring more legal actions against the group.[167] Watson has publicly stated that since he was personally named in the injunction he believes he must step down as leader of the SSCS in order to avoid criminal charges for any of his actions.[168]

Paul Watson, though Canadian born, holds dual Canadian–US citizenship and has stated he would respect the court's decision and not violate the temporary injunction.[169] However, later he did admit that he was aboard the *Steve Irwin* as an observer and was present during Operation Zero Tolerance, the 2012–13 campaign to thwart Japanese whaling, which potentially puts him in breach of the injunction.[170] The SSCS's lawyers have asked the US Supreme Court to lift the injunction.[171] The attorneys for SSCS (US) filed a motion with the court against the ICR seeking relief arguing that the Ninth Circuit Court incorrectly issued the injunction, without any party filing a motion requesting such an outcome, and ignoring the earlier (they argue superior) decision of the District Court in February.[172]

OPERATION ZERO TOLERANCE

As discussed above, the Appeal Court's decision specifically named Watson so it severely curtailed his ability to lead the fight against Japanese whaling. Consequently Watson decided to resign as president of the SSCS in both the USA and Australia, and as executive director in the USA.[173] Watson stated on the SSCS website: 'I will hold no paid position with Sea Shepherd anywhere Sea Shepherd is registered and operates as a non-profit organization in any nation.'[174] However, Watson remained aboard one of the SSCS vessels as an observer and as an advisor but rejected the claim that the leadership restructure was merely a cosmetic change.[175] Despite their publicly stated position, and potentially infringing on the injunction issued by the Washington court, Peter Hammarstedt (captain of the *Bob Barker*) stated: 'it is expected Captain Watson would appear in command of one of the vessels when the action begins'.[176]

On 5 November 2012 the SSCS flotilla left Australia to commence Operation Zero Tolerance, its ninth Antarctic Whale Defence Campaign.[177] For the 2012–13 whaling season Japan's ICR has 'set itself a quota of 850 minke and 50 fin whales to be culled'.[178] However, the SSCS intended to pursue a new strategy for this campaign. As Captain Hammerstedt explains, the SSCS wanted to take the fight up to Japan itself by targeting the whaling vessels in the North Pacific rather than waiting for the whaling fleet to enter Antarctic waters.[179] As Watson stated: 'it's time to bring intervention north and show Japan we intend to ensure there are no whales killed. We have never been stronger, and the Japanese have never been weaker, so we need to take advantage of that.'[180]

On 15 February 2013, the *Bob Barker* caught up with the *Nisshin Maru* and the *Yushin Maru No. 2*.[181] A female minke whale was killed and eventually brought aboard the *Nisshin Maru* for processing, despite a tense five-hour blockade initiated by the *Bob Barker*.[182] The captain of that vessel claimed that the *Yushin Maru No. 2* attempted to block the SSCS ship: 'by dangerously criss-crossing the bow of the *Bob Barker*, coming as close as 600 yards and threatening to deploy prop fouling devices', forcing him to heave-to to avoid ramming the Japanese vessel.[183]

The SSCS also accused that their ships, the *Bob Barker* and the *Steve Irwin* were rammed by the Japanese whaling fleet's massive factory vessel, the *Nisshin Maru*.[184] The vessel was attempting to obtain fuel from the *Sun Laurel* when it hit the *Bob Barker* in the stern, effectively disabling it and pushing it into the side of the tanker as well as hitting the *Steve Irwin* a number of times.[185] Watson alleged that: 'the Japanese boat deliberately rammed the Sea Shepherd boats to try to move them aside and get to the re-fuelling tanker'.[186] However, the crew of the *Bob Barker* eventually got the situation under control and was able to continue with its mission.[187]

According to Paul Watson the *Nisshin Maru* deliberately rammed the *Bob Barker*. However, Japan's ICR accused 'several Sea Shepherd boats of slamming into the *Nisshin Maru* as the vessel attempted to refuel with her supply tanker the *Sun Laurel*'.[188] The Japanese whaling ship eventually was forced to quit trying to refuel after allegedly being hit five times by SSCS vessels determined to stop it refuelling.[189]

Both sides released video of the incident purporting to show their version of events.[190] The Japanese released a media statement that: 'the sabotage is not only malicious but inconceivably obstructive actions. Thus it threatens safety of our research ships and lives of crews on them and is therefore completely unacceptable.'[191] The Japanese government stated that it was mulling over filing a third claim in a US court for the SSCS actions, alleging they constitute an insult to the court's authority.[192]

According to SSCS Australia, for the 2012–13 whaling season Japan only managed to kill no more than 103 whales, possibly the lowest catch in the history of Japanese Antarctic whaling expeditions.[193] The SSCS's successes can be attributed to a number of factors: they pre-empted the Japanese whaling fleet arriving in Antarctic waters; used smaller more nimble boats to prevent whalers getting to their target; they tried to prevent the harpoon ship from meeting up with the factory ship; and they targeted the refuelling ship to, in effect, starve the fleet of vital fuel.[194]

Paul Watson: International Fugitive?

However, the successful campaign has come at a price. At the end of the campaign Watson was cautious about coming ashore in Australia as he traditionally did, since he fears the possibility of being arrested by the Australian Federal Police on the outstanding Interpol warrant. Australian National University law academic Don Rothwell argues that Japan could request the Federal Police to act, and since Watson is currently subject to an Interpol Red Notice he faces being arrested if Japan requests his extradition.[195] Watson claims he has been given a business entry visa to Australia by the Australian Embassy in Washington.[196] The Australian Environment Minister Tony Burke stated that the Australian government has no plans to arrest Watson if he comes ashore.[197] Current leader of the expedition Bob Brown stated, 'a key job in his new role as a Sea Shepherd Australia director was to ensure that Mr Watson could come ashore safely, and warned an arrest would bring an uproar'.[198]

The situation was heightened when it appeared that New Zealand (NZ) officials were searching for Watson, who evaded them by switching ships at sea and he was not on board when the ship docked in NZ. Watson professed that he was 'pretty shocked' that the NZ authorities were willing to acquiesce to the Japanese on this issue.[199] According to Makoto Ito (the spokesman for the company that owns Japan's whaling fleet), he hoped Paul Watson would be: 'arrested and brought to justice this year' since Watson poses a serious threat to whaling crews.[200]

The violent encounters with Japanese whalers continue. In early February 2014 the SSCS alleged again that their ship the *Bob Bark*er was struck by the *Yushin Maru No. 2* in Antarctica. They also alleged that the whaling vessels tried to tangle the propellers of the SSCS vessels and threw projectiles at their ships.[201]

ARE THE SSCS METHODS COUNTERPRODUCTIVE?

Over the last few years the SSCS has met one of its key objectives: the putting of economic pressure on the Japanese whaling industry through its harassing tactics. The 2012–13 whaling season saw possibly the lowest catch on record, continuing a trend of the last few years.[202] Watson has frequently stated that the primary objective of the Sea Shepherd had always been to 'sink the Japanese whaling fleet economically – to bankrupt them, and it is a strategy that appears to be working'.[203] He believes that Japanese consumer demand for whale meat is down, leading to a surplus of whale meat being required to be frozen in refrigerated warehouses at great cost.[204] It is true that the Japanese appetite for whale meat has diminished radically.[205] Further, a Greenpeace analysis has revealed that the Japanese whaling industry currently sells such small amounts of whale meat that the industry is totally reliant on government subsidies to function.[206] Also, the ICR has revealed that SSCS actions are taking a financial toll on the whaling fleet. In the 2010–11 season the whalers lost US $25.2 million since they were only able to catch 17 per cent of their declared quota that season and 26 per cent in 2011–12.[207]

While the SSCS has forsaken sinking vessels through the use of explosives, it continues to ram vessels and allow personnel to board vessels with the attendant risks that such tactics engender. The Sea Shepherd organization's violent tactics have appalled some fellow anti-whaling advocates and are seen by many as counterproductive. Dr Sidney Holt, one of the architects of the 1986 moratorium, believes that Watson and his group's actions are an 'absolute disaster' in terms of convincing Japan to stop whaling. Dr Holt insists that: 'Almost everything [Watson] has been doing has had blowback for those who want to see an end to whaling. In too many cases, playing piracy on the ocean, and creating danger for other ships, is simply not liked.'[208]

Although the Sea Shepherd group claims to be enforcing IWC rules, the IWC members have publicly condemned their direct action campaign.[209] Due to Paul Watson's actions in sinking two ships in Iceland in 1986 he is no longer allowed to attend IWC meetings because many conservationists believe that his actions have actually turned sympathy away from anti-whaling nations, denying him a voice to make his case in a less direct manner.[210]

NOTES

1. 'Sea Shepherd history' (1983) *Sea Shepherd Log* (winter), p. 4.
2. Ibid.
3. Ibid.
4. Ibid.
5. Pirate whaling continued to operate despite the edicts of the IWC to the contrary and refused to curtail whaling operations. Such ships flew flags of convenience from Spain, Peru and Taiwan and were financed by whaling nations such as Norway and Japan. The *Sierra* had a Norwegian national as a captain and was crewed primarily by Japanese sailors. It was 75 per cent owned by the Taiyo Fishery Company of Japan and 25 per cent by the Foreningsbanken of Norway. See Rex Weyler (2004) *Greenpeace: An Insider's Account*, pp. 542–3. Reportedly, the whaler was: 'the worst offender in a dirty business. Barred from ports around the world for violating international conventions on whaling and endangered species, and for not paying bills for fuel and provisions, it roved over the globe taking every whale it came across.' See Peter Heller, *The Whale Warriors: On Board a Pirate Ship in the Battle to Save the World's Largest Mammals* (New York: Free Press), pp. 34–5. The *Sierra* hunted and took 1,676 whales during a three-year period and then sold the meat in Japan. Despite many attempts to stop its whaling the ship was considered untouchable by the IWC or any other agency. See Rik Scarce (2006) *Eco-Warriors: Understanding the Radical Environment Movement* (updated edn) (California: Left Coast Press), p. 97.
6. Ibid., pp. 97–8.
7. Ibid., p. 98; Rex Weyler (2004) *Greenpeace: An Insider's Account* (London: Rodale International), p. 543.

8. Paul Watson (1982) *Sea Shepherd: My Fight for Whales and Seals* (New York and London: W.W. Norton and Company), p. 211.
9. Ibid., pp. 226–7.
10. Scarce, *Eco-Warriors: Understanding the Radical Environment Movement*', p. 98.
11. Ibid.
12. Ibid., p. 99.
13. Andrew Darby (2006) 'Hunters and protectors', *The Age*, 15 November, p. 15.
14. Watson, *Sea Shepherd: My Fight for Whales and Seals*, pp. 230–31.
15. Ibid., p. 233.
16. Scarce, *Eco-Warriors: Understanding the Radical Environment Movement*, p. 99; Weyler, *Greenpeace: An Insider's Account*, p. 543.
17. Watson, *Sea Shepherd: My Fight for Whales and Seals*, p. 233.
18. Scarce, *Eco-Warriors: Understanding the Radical Environment Movement*, p. 99, Weyler, *Greenpeace: An Insider's Account*, p. 543.
19. 'Sea Shepherd history', *Sea Shepherd Log*, p. 4.
20. Scarce, *Eco-Warriors: Understanding the Radical Environment Movement*, p. 99; Weyler, *Greenpeace: An Insider's Account*, p. 544.
21. Paul Watson (1994) *Ocean Warrior: My Battle to End the Illegal Slaughter on the High Seas* (Toronto: Key Porter Books), p. 6.
22. 'Sea Shepherd history', *Sea Shepherd Log*, p. 4.
23. Scarce, *Eco-Warriors: Understanding the Radical Environment Movement*, p. 99.
24. Watson, *Ocean Warrior: My Battle to End the Illegal Slaughter on the High Seas*, pp. 25–6.
25. 'Sea Shepherd history', *Sea Shepherd Log*, p. 4.
26. Watson, *Ocean Warrior: My Battle to End the Illegal Slaughter on the High Seas*, p. 30.
27. Scarce, *Eco-Warriors: Understanding the Radical Environment Movement*, p. 101.
28. Ibid., p. 100.
29. Watson, *Sea Shepherd: My Fight for Whales and Seals*, p. 247.
30. Peter Heller (2007) *The Whale Warriors: On Board a Pirate Ship in the Battle to Save the World's Largest Mammals* (New York: Free Press), p. 35.
31. Watson, *Ocean Warrior: My Battle to End the Illegal Slaughter on the High Seas*, p 21.
32. Gerry Nagtzaam and Peter Lentini (2008) 'Vigilantes on the high seas?: The Sea Shepherds and political violence', *Terrorism and Political Violence*, **1**, p. 123.
33. Raffi Khatchadourian (2007) 'Neptune's Navy: Paul Watson's wild crusade to save the oceans', *The New Yorker*, 5 November, p. 65.
34. Ibid.
35. Ibid., p. 66.
36. 'Sea Shepherds Record of Violence', *The High North News*, **7**, 10 April 1994, http://www.highnorth.no/library/movements/Sea_Shepherd/se-sh-re.htm.
37. Watson, *Ocean Warrior: My Battle to End the Illegal Slaughter on the High Seas*, p. 34.
38. Ibid., p. 34.
39. Peter C. List, (1993) *Radical Environmentalism: Philosophy and Tactics* (Belmont, CA: Wadsworth, Inc.), pp. 177–-179.
40. Iceland has a somewhat 'chequered history' with whaling that continues to this day. The country joined the IWC moratorium in 1989, then left the IWC in 1992 only to rejoin in 2002. See Teale Phelps Bondaroff (2008) 'Throwing a wrench into things: the strategy of radical environmentalism', *Journal of Military and Strategic Studies*, **10** (4), p. 16; 'Iceland bids to resume whaling', *BBC News*, 22 March 2007, http://www.news.bbc.co.uk/1/hi/sci/tech/2910655.stm.
41. 'Sea Shepherds Record of Violence', http://www.highnorth.no/library/movements/Sea_Shepherd/se-sh-re.htm.
42. List, *Radical Environmentalism: Philosophy and Tactics*, p. 172. In the same letter (regarding the raid on Reykjavik) Watson describes that it was Rod Coronado's idea to commit a commando-style action in Iceland. Initially Coronado and David Howitt got jobs in Iceland in the local fish processing plant and then for three weeks scouted the

sites to work out the security watches. 'Letter from Paul Watson', *Sea Shepherd Conservation* (November 1986), p. 1. List, *Radical Environmentalism: Philosophy and Tactics*, pp. 174–5.

43. 'Letter from Paul Watson', p. 1.
44. Ibid.
45. List, *Radical Environmentalism: Philosophy and Tactics*, pp. 174–5.
46. 'What did we accomplish in 1987?', *Sea Shepherd Log* (December 1987), p. 1.
47. Dean Kuipers (2009) *Operation Bite Back: Rod Coronado's War to Save the American Wilderness* (New York: Bloomsbury), p. 33.
48. 'Letter from Paul Watson', p. 2.
49. 'Sea Shepherds Record of Violence', http://highnorth.no/library/movements/Sea_Shepherd/se-sh-re.htm.
50. Christopher Manes (1990) *Green Rage: Radical Environmentalism and the Unmaking of Civilization* (Boston, Toronto: Little Brown and Company), p. 117.
51. Bondaroff, 'Throwing a wrench into things: the strategy of radical environmentalism', p. 16; Dale McLuhen (1996) *Children: The Greenpeace Message and the Media,* (Toronto: Between the Lines), p. 182.
52. 'Sea Shepherds Record of Violence', http://www.highnorth.no/library/movements/Sea_Shepherd/se-sh-re.htm.
53. Raffi Khatchadourian, 'Neptune's Navy: Paul Watson's Wild Crusade to Save the Oceans', p. 59.
54. 'Sea Shepherds Record of Violence', url: http://www.highnorth.no/library/movements/Sea_Shepherd/se-sh-re.htm.
55. 'Costa Rica', http://www.seashepherd.org/news-and-media/2012/05/13/captain-paul-watson-arrested-in-frankfurt-germany-on-warrant-issued-by-costa-rica-1374.
56. *Sharkwater* (2006) directed and produced by Rob Stewart (Canada: Alliance Films), DVD, 33-minute mark.
57. Ibid.
58. Ibid.
59. Ibid., 34-minute mark.
60. Ibid., 42-minute mark.
61. Ibid., 42-minute mark.
62. Ibid., 44-minute mark.
63. In the DVD it is recounted that the Costa Rican authorities initially charged the Sea Shepherd crew with seven counts of attempted murder. *Sharkwater*, 53-minute mark.
64. Shiv Malik (2012) 'Paul Watson, anti-whaling campaigner, held in Germany over 2002 incident', *The Guardian*, 14 May, http://www.guardian.co.uk/environment/2012/may/14/paul-watson-arrested-germany-sea-shepherd.
65. Don Freeman (2012) 'Can Paul Watson get a fair trial in Costa Rica?' 26 May, http://news.co.cr/can-paul-watson-get-a-fair-trial-in-costa-rica/7193/.
66. *Sharkwater*, 55-minute mark.
67. See the section entitled 'Paul Watson arrested', for further details of the Costa Rican authorities' attempts to extradite Paul Watson over this issue.
68. 'Japanese media report arrest warrant issued for Sea Shepherd leader Paul Watson', *Los Angeles Times*, 30 April 2010, http://latimesblogs.latimes.com/unleashed/2010/04/japanese-media-reports-arrest-warrant-issued-for-sea-shepherd-leader-paul-watson.html.
69. Thomas Hunter (2010) 'Whaling fleet more violent than ever: Sea Shepherd', *The Age*, 7 January, http://www.theage.com.au/action/printArticle?id=1019080.
70. 'Japanese media report arrest warrant issued for Sea Shepherd leader Paul Watson'.
71. Ibid.
72. Ibid. For example, on 9 February 2007 the Sea Shepherd's *Farley Mowat* and *Robert Hunter* engaged with the Japanese factory ship *Nisshin Maru*. According to the organization's news releases, Sea Shepherd crew conducted attacks in which they: 'delivered six liters of butyric acid onto the flensing deck of the *Nisshin Maru*. This "bitter acid" is a non-toxic obnoxious smelling substance. The foul smell … cleared the

flensing deck and stopped all work of cutting up whales.' Sea Shepherd, 'Whalers activities disrupted by Sea Shepherd', *Sea Shepherd News*, 8 February 2007, http://www.seashepherd.org/news/media_070208_2p.html. The Japanese contend that the Sea Shepherds also threw smoke bombs (and this was later confirmed on video tape) on the *Nisshin Maru*'s deck, and the Institute for Cetacean Research's Hatanaka said bottles of butyric acid hit two crewmen. In a statement he claimed: 'One of our crewmen is having difficulty opening his eye because of the acid, but the full extent of his injuries has yet to be determined.' Andrew Darby, 'Sea Shepherd leaves its mark'; Andrew Darby (2007) 'Film shows attempts to stop whalers', *The Age*, 12 February, p. 6.

73. 'Sea Shepherd crew remain hostages on the Japanese whaling ship, http://www.seashepherd.org/news-and-media/news-releases/Page-1.html.
74. *Whale Wars*, Season 1, produced by Animal Planet, 2009.
75. http://www.seashepherd.org/news-and-media/news-releases/Page-1.html.
76. Andrew Darby (2010) 'Japanese ship destroys whale protest boat Ady Gil', *The Age*, 6 January, http://www.theage.com.au/action/printArticle?id=1018264.
77. Andrew Darby and J. Pearlman (2010) 'Whaling war set to worsen after crash', *Sydney Morning Herald*, 8 January, http://www.smh.com.au/action/printArticle?id=1019179.
78. Thomas Hunter (2010) 'Whaling fleet more violent than ever: Sea Shepherd', *The Age*, 7 January, http://www.theage.com.au/action/printArticle?id=1019080.
79. 'Ady Gil sinks after collision', *The Age*, 8 January 2010, http://www.theage.com.au/actions/printArticle?id=1019084.
80. Cortlan Bennett (2010) 'Ady Gil captain tells of ramming at sea', *Sydney Morning Herald*, 28 January, http://news.smh.com.au/action/printArticle?id=1073407.
81. 'Sea Shepherd vessel Ady Gil sinking after being hit by Japanese whaler', http://www.japantoday.com/category/national/view/sea-shepherd-obstructs-japans-whaling-operations-for-4th-time.
82. 'Ady Gil sinks after collision'.
83. 'Sea Shepherd vessel Ady Gil sinking after being hit by Japanese Whaler'.
84. Mark McDonald (2010) 'Ships collide in war of nerves over whaling', *The New York Times*, 7 January, A12.
85. Darby, 'Japanese ship destroys whale protest boat Ady Gil'.
86. Darby and Pearlman, 'Whaling War Set to Worsen After Crash'.
87. 'Sea Shepherd activist boards whaling ship to "arrest" captain', http://www.japantoday.com/category/national/view/sea-shepherd-activist-boards-whaling-ship-to-arrest-captain.
88. Cathy Alexander (2010) 'Protester boards Japanese whaling vessel', *Sydney Morning Herald*, 15 February, http://www.news.smh.com.au/action/printArticle?=1121105.
89. James Murray and Chris Whitworth (2010) 'Citizen's arrest attempted on Japanese whaling captain', *3-News*, 15 February, http://www.3news.co.nz/Citizens-arrest-attempted-on-Japanese-whaling-captain/tabid/417/articleID/141811.Default.aspx. Bethune gave the captain papers, which detailed the arrest of the captain (of the *Shonan Maru 2* for 'attempted murder' charges, following the collision and sinking of the *Ady Gil*) and a bill for US $3 million, the amount to replace the sunken vessel. See Murray and Whitworth, 'Citizen's arrest attempted on Japanese whaling captain'.
90. Alexander, 'Protester boards Japanese whaling vessel'.
91. http://www.breitbart.com/article.php?id=D9ED0OCO2&show_article=1.
92. Andrew Darby (2010) 'Activist boards Japanese whaler and demands $3.4m for sunken boat', *The Age*, 16 February, http://www.theage.com.au/environment/whale-watch/activist-boards-japanese-whaler-and-demands-34m-for-sunken-boat-20100215-o2wt.html.
93. Andrew Darby (2010) 'Protester may face charges in Japan', *The Age*, 17 February, http://www.theage.com.au/environment/whale-watch/protester-may-face-charges-in-japan-20100216-o915.html.
94. Ibid.
95. Ibid.

96. 'Japan to arrest anti-whaling activist', *The Age*, 12 March 2010, http://news.theage.com.au/breaking-news-world/japan-to-arrest-antiwhaling-activist-20100312-q204.html.
97. Ibid.
98. Mari Yamaguchi (2010) 'Japan court convicts NZ anti-whaling activist', *Associated Press*, 7 July.
99. Ibid.
100. 'Activist lashes out at Sea Shepherd', *NZPA*, 7 October 2010, http://www.stuff.co.nz/the-press/news/4206365/Activist-lashes-out-at-Sea-Shepherd.
101. Mari Yamaguchi, 'Japan Court Convicts NZ anti-whaling Activist'.
102. 'Forest Rescue men go out on a limb for Sea Shepherd, commentary by Captain Paul Watson, 7 January 2012, http://www.seashepherd.org/commentary-and-editorials/2012/01/07/forest-rescue-men-go-out-on-a-limb-for-sea-shepherd-502.
103. Ibid.
104. Ibid.
105. 'The bullshit politics of betrayal: commentary by Captain Paul Watson', 8 January 2012, http://www.seashepherd.org/commentary-and-editorials/2012/01/08/the-bullshit-politics-of-betrayal-503.
106. On 9 January 2012, '32° 57' 48' South and 115° 20' 24' East – this is the position of the *Shonan Maru 2* when it was boarded by the three brave activists from Forest Rescue at 0430 hours on 8 January': http://www.seashepherd.org/news-and-media/2012/01/09/32-57-48-south-and-115-20-24-east-1310.
107. On 9 January 2012, 'Our sincere apologies, prime minister: commentary by Captain Paul Watson', http://www.seashepherd.org/commentary-and-editorials/2012/01/09/our-sincere-apologies-prime-minister-504.
108. On 9 January 2012, 'Australian whale defenders on their way to Antarctica against their will' http://www.seashepherd.org/news-and-media/2012/01/09/australian-whale-defenders-on-their-way-to-antarctica-against-their-will-1311.
109. On 10 January 2012, 'Heroes of forest and sea to be freed', http://www.seashepherd.org/commentary-and-editorials/2012/01/10/heroes-of-forest-and-sea-to-be-freed-505; on 15 January 2012, 'Focusing attention on things that matter is always positive: commentary by Captain Paul Watson', http://www.seashepherd.org/commentary-and-editorials/2012/01/15/focusing-attention-on-things-that-matter-is-always-positive-508.
110. 'Australian protesters safely transferred to ACV Ocean Protector', 13 January 2012, http://www.seashepherd.org/news-and-media/2012/01/13/australian-protesters-safely-transferred-to-acv-ocean-protector-1317; on 16 January 2012, 'Home from the sea; home to the trees: forest activist heroes return home, report by Jeff Hansen, http://www.seashepherd.org/news-and-media/2012/01/16/home-from-the-sea-home-to-the-trees-1318.
111. Andrew Darby (2010) 'Sea Shepherd bans activist Bethune from protests', *The Age*, 9 June.
112. 'Activist lashes out at Sea Shepherd', *NZPA*, 7 October 2010, http://www.stuff.co.nz/the-press/news/4206365/Activist-lashes-out-at-Sea-Shepherd.
113. Yamaguchi, 'Japan court convicts NZ anti-whaling activist'.
114. 'Green Group accused of sinking ship for a stunt', *Sydney Morning Herald*, 8 October 2010, http://www.smh.com.au/environment/whale-watch/green-group-accused-of-sinking-ship-for-a-stunt-20101007-169u7.html.
115. Ibid.
116. 'Activist lashes out at Sea Shepherd', *NZPA*, 7 October 2010, http://www.stuff.co.nz/the-press/news/4206365/Activist-lashes-out-at-Sea-Shepherd.
117. Ibid.
118. 'Green Group accused of sinking ship for a stunt'.
119. Ibid. In a setback for the SSCS Ady Gil, the businessman and long-time supporter of the group, has stated he is suing the organization for US$5 million over the sinking of the boat named after him. He is basing his claim on the information provided by former SSCS captain Pete Bethune that he was ordered to sink the vessel. Gil contends that the

sinking was: 'an opportunity to spin the incident into a major publicity and money maker'. Bethune is also currently suing the SSCS for US $500,000 for its share in purchasing the vessel from him. Watson has denied the charges and describes the lawsuit as 'frivolous', denying he ordered the sinking and he denies ever ordering Bethune to scuttle the vessel. See Kim Choe (2013) 'Ady Gil sues Sea Shepherd over Antarctic sinking', *3 News*, 10 January, http://www.3news.co.nz/Ady-Gil-sues-Sea-Shepherd-over-Antarctic sinking/tabid/417/articleID/282601/Default.aspx.

120. Ibid.
121. 'Activist Lashes Out at Sea Shepherd'. Bethune now operates his own group Earthrace, dedicated to ending poaching and deforestation and has his own TV show, *The Operatives*, airing in nine countries. See Caty Enders (2015) 'Can Sea Shepherds survive their own success?', *The Guardian*, 5 June, http://www.theguardian.com/environment/2015/jun/05/sea-shepherd-whale-wars-animal-planet.
122. Michael Destries (2010) 'Sea Shepherd emails that started online "war of words" released', *Ecorazzi*, 6 October, http://www.ecorazzi.com/2010/10/06/sea-shepherd-emails-that-started-online-war-of-words-released/.
123. Mike Willacy (2010) 'Sea Shepherd's Watson on Interpol's Wanted List', *Australian Broadcasting Company*, 27 June.
124. Ibid.
125. Don Freeman (2012) 'Can Paul Watson get a fair trial in Costa Rica?' 26 May, http://news.co.cr/can-paul-watson-get-a-fair-trial-in-costa-rica/7193/; Interpol statement to clarify the record concerning Paul Watson of the Sea Shepherd Conservation Society, 14 May 2012, N20120514/2012/News & media releases/News and media/Internet/Home – Interpol. With a Red Notice police forces are asked: 'to seek the location and arrest of wanted persons with a view to extradition or similar lawful action', while a blue notice requires national police forces: 'to collect additional information about a person's identity, location or activities in relation to a crime'. Further, 'in the case of Red Notices, the persons concerned are wanted by national jurisdictions for prosecution or to serve a sentence based on an arrest warrant or court decision. Interpol's role is to assist the national police forces in identifying and locating these persons with a *view to their arrest and extradition* or similar lawful action.' Interpol, http://www.interpol.int/INTERPOL-expertise/Notices, 18 February 2013.
126. Michael Destries (2015) 'Judge rules Sea Shepherd wrongfully sank crippled "whale wars" vessel', *Ecorazzi*, 25 September, http://www.ecorazzi.com/2015/09/25/judge-rules-sea-shepherd-wrongfully-sank-whale-wars-vessel/.
127. Andrew Darby (2012) 'Attempted murder probe: anti-whaling skipper faces deportation', 14 May, *The Age*, http://www.theage.com.au/environment/whale-watch/attempted-murder-probe-antiwhaling-skipper-faces-deportation-20120514-1ylpf.html This is not the first time Paul Watson had been arrested on an extradition warrant. In 1997 Paul Watson was picked up in the Netherlands pursuant to a Norwegian arrest warrant and placed in jail. An Oslo court had convicted him in absentia to 120 days of jail over the Sea Shepherds sinking a ship in 1994. After several months of court proceedings and a global outcry spearheaded by celebrities such as Pierce Brosnan and Jane Seymour he was eventually released. *AFP* (2011) 'Sea Shepherd hit by legal harpoon', 9 December, http://www.couriermail.com.au/ipad/sea-shepherd-hit-by-legal-harpoon/story-fn6ck55c-1226218642187.
128. Andrew Darby (2012) 'Activist arrested', 15 May, *The Age*, http://www.theage.com.au/environment/whale-watch/activist-arrested-20120514-1yn1b.html. The offence Paul Watson is alleged to have committed falls under Article 251 of the Costa Rican Penal Code whereby: 'Anyone who knowingly perpetrates an act that endangers the safety of a ship, floating structure or airplane shall be punished with imprisonment of 2–6 years. If the act results in a shipwreck, stranding or air disaster, the penalty is 6–12 years imprisonment. If the accident injures someone, the penalty is 6–15 years imprisonment and if, thereby, death occurs, imprisonment is from 8–18 years'. See 'Watson prepares defense in Costa

Rica', *Tico Times* (Costa Rica), 16 May 2012, http://www.ticotimes.net/Current-Edition/News-Briefs/Paul-Watson-prepares-defense-in-Costa-Rica_Wednesday-May-16-2012.

129. 'Watson prepares defense in Costa Rica'.
130. Andrew Darby (2012) 'Costa Rica confirms Watson extradition demand', *The Sydney Morning Herald*, 16 May, http://www.smh.com.au/environment/whale-watch/costa-rica-confirms-watson-extradition-demand-20120516-1yqmo.html.
131. Darby, 'Attempted murder probe: anti-whaling skipper faces deportation'.
132. AFP (2012) 'Anti-whaling leader freed on bail while extradition decided', 18 May, http://www.google.com/hostednews/afp/article/ALeqM5iJNfm-bWp3R...fkm4BYty0VCIEA?docId=CNG.0d8e1a34f8eed2b6a7343577531cf5e3.5f1.
133. Etienne Barker (2012) 'Anti-whaling group leader ordered held in Germany', *AFP*, 13 May, http://www.google.com/hostednews/afp/article/ALeqM5jDGUY_Py2v5...j4OGnenluS7cew?docId=CNG.cb81ca0cd4215a702104ce7afde58aba.181.
134. AFP, 'Anti-whaling leader freed on bail while extradition decided'.
135. AFP (2012) 'Anti-whaling leader says extraditing him won't halt campaign, 23 May, http://news.asiaone.com/News/Latest%2BNews/World/Story/A1Story20120523-347755.html.
136. Ibid.
137. AFP, 'Anti-whaling leader says extraditing him won't halt campaign'.
138. 'Sea Shepherd leader fears for his life', 17 May 2012, http://www.theage.com.au/environment/whale-watch/sea-shepherd-leader-fears-for-his-life-20120517-1ys4h.html.
139. Siobhán Dowling (2012) 'Veteran anti-whaling activist Paul Watson to be released on bail: Sea Shepherd group vows to fight founder's possible extradition from Germany to Costa Rica over 2002 incident at sea', *The Guardian*, 18 May, http://www.guardian.co.uk/environment/2012/may/18/anti-whaling-activist-paul-watson.
140. AFP (2012) 'Costa Rica assures fair trial for anti-whaling crusader', 17 June, http://www.expatica.com/de/news/german-news/costa-rica-assures-fair-trial-for-anti-whaling-crusader_229293.html.
141. 'Sea Shepherd boss blames Japan for arrest', 22 May 2012, http://www.theage.com.au/environment/whale-watch/sea-shepherd-boss-blames-japan-for-arrest-20120522-1z2ta.html; see section entitled 'Injunction levied on Paul Watson and the SSCS' for further details of the court case.
142. AFP, 'Anti-whaling leader says extraditing him won't halt campaign'.
143. Agence France-Presse (2012) 'Anti-whaling crusader Paul Watson will receive a fair trial, says Costa Rica's president', 23 May, http://news.nationalpost.com/2012/05/23/anti-whaling-crusader-paul-watson-will-recieve-a-fair-trial-says-costa-ricas-president/.
144. Paul Watson (2012) 'The law takes precedence over justice in Germany', 24 May, http://www.seashepherd.org/commentary-and-editorials/2012/05/29/the-law-takes-precedence-over-justice-in-germany-540.
145. 'Bail set for "Whale Wars" star in extradition fight', 18 May 2012, http://news.blogs.cnn.com/2012/05/18/bail-set-for-whale-wars-star-in-extradition-fight/?hpt=hp_c2.
146. 'Sea Shepherd leader fears for his life', 17 May 2012, http://www.theage.com.au/environment/whale-watch/sea-shepherd-leader-fears-for-his-life-20120517-1ys4h.html.
147. BBC News Europe (2012) 'Sea Shepherd founder Paul Watson "flees Germany"', 26 July, http://www.bbc.co.uk/news/world-europe-18996972.
148. Paul Everest (2012) 'Fugitive whale wars star's brother battling Stage 4 cancer; hopes Paul Watson makes it to London soon', 27 July, http://www.londoncommunitynews.com/2012/07/battling-stage-4-can...ugitive-whale-wars-star-hopes-paul-watson-comes-to-london-soon/.
149. Laura Stone (2012) Canadian anti-whaling activist Paul Watson flees Germany after Japan issues extradition request, 26 July, http://www.thestar.com/news/world/article/1232562–canadian-anti-w...t-paul-watson-flees-germany-after-japan-issues-extradition-request.

150. Miguel Llanos (2012) NBC News, 'Fugitive anti-whaling activist accuses former crew member of betraying him to Japan', 31 July, http://worldnews.nbcnews.com/_news/2012/07/31/13052889-fugitive…g-activist-accuses-former-crew-member-of-betraying-him-to-japan; 'Captain Paul Watson sends first message to supporters since departing Germany', 30 July 2012, http://www.seashepherd.org/news-and-media/2012/07/30/captain-pau…pherd-first-message-for-supporters-since-departing-germany-1413.
151. AFP (2012) 'Japan admits asking Germany to arrest, extradite Sea Shepherd chief', 28 July, http://www.japantimes.co.jp/text/nn20120728b6.html.
152. AFP (2012) The West Australian, 'Japan is after revenge: Watson', 31 July, http://au.news.yahoo.com/thewest/a/-/breaking/14417081/japan-is-after-revenge-watson/.
153. John R. Kennedy (2012) 'Canadian activist Paul Watson named on Interpol's notice', 8 August, http://www.globalnews.ca/canadian+activist+paul+watson+named+on+interpols+notice/6442693600/story.html.
154. AFP (2012) 'German court wants fugitive activist Paul Watson extradited', 25 July, http://news.yahoo.com/german-court-wants-fugitive-activist-paul-watson-extradited-111146440.html.
155. John R. Kennedy (2012) Global News (CAN), 'Canadian activist Paul Watson named on Interpol's notice', 8 August, http://www.globalnews.ca/canadian+activist+paul+watson+named+on+interpols+notice/6442693600/story.html; Interpol statement to clarify the record concerning Paul Watson of the Sea Shepherd Conservation Society, 14 May 2012, N20120514/2012/News & media releases/News and media/Internet/Home – Interpol.
156. 'Setting the record straight on Paul Watson's legal status: Sea Shepherd addresses the impact of Interpol 'Red Notice' on Captain Watson and the organization's operations, 11 August 2012, w.seashepherd.org/news-and-media/2012/08/11/setting-the-record-straight-on-paul-watsons-status-1425.
157. Ibid.
158. 'Germany drops arrest warrant for Sea Shepherd founder', *Environment News Service*, http://ens-newswire.com/2013/03/08/germany-drops-arrest-warrant-for-sea-shepherd-founder/.
159. Ibid.
160. Ibid.
161. Ibid.
162. 'Sea Shepherd Australia to lead Antarctic whale defense campaign', *Sea Shepherd Australia*, http://www.seashepherd.org.au/news-and-media/2013/01/07/sea-shepherd-australia-to-lead-antarctic-whale-defense-campaign-1477.
163. 'US court order to prevent clashes between Japanese Whalers and Sea Shepherd vessels', *The Australian*, 19 December 2012, http://www.theaustralian.com.au/news/world/us-court-order-to-prevent-clashes-between-japanese-whalers-and-sea-shepherd-vessels/story-e6frg6so-1226540130562; Laura Petersen (2013) 'OCEANS: Sea Shepherd takes fight against Japanese whalers to Supreme Court', *Sea Shepherd Australia*, 12 February, http://www.seashepherd.org.au/news-and-media/2013/02/12/oceans-sea-shepherd-takes-fight-against-japanese-whalers-to-supreme-court-1493; 'Paul Watson quits Sea Shepherd over US court order', *CBCNews*, 8 January 2013, http://www.cbc.ca/news/world/story/2013/01/08/canada-paul-watson-sea-shepherd-conservation-society-president.html.
164. Institute of Cetacean Research; Kyodo Senpaku Kaisha Ltd; Tomoyuki Ogawa; and Toshiyuki Muira v. Sea Shepherd Conservation Society and Paul Watson, United States Court of Appeals Ninth Circuit, No, 12-35266, Order, (17/12/12), http://cdn.ca9.uscourts.gov/datastore/opinions/2012/12/17/12-35266.pdf.
165. 'US court tells Sea Shepherd to stay away from Japan's whaling fleet in Southern Ocean', *MercoPress*, 19 December 2012, http://en.mercopress.com/2012/12/19/us-court-tells-sea-shepherd-to-stay-away-from-japan-s-whaling-fleet-in-southern-ocean. 'Sea Shepherd Australia to lead Antarctic whale defense campaign', *Sea Shepherd Australia*, 7 January 2013, http://www.seashepherd.org.au/news-and-media/2013/01/07/sea-shepherd-australia-to-lead-antarctic-whale-defense-campaign-1477.

166. Petersen, 'OCEANS: Sea Shepherd takes fight against Japanese whalers to Supreme Court'; 'US Court tells Sea Shepherd to stay away from Japan's whaling fleet in Southern Ocean', *MercoPress*, 19 December 2012, http://en.mercopress.com/2012/12/19/us-court-tells-sea-shepherd-to-stay-away-from-japan-s-whaling-fleet-in-southern-ocean.
167. David Kirby (2013) 'Sea Shepherd's Paul Watson mocks court's 'pirate' ruling', *takepart.com*, 28 February, http://www.takepart.com/article/2013/02/28/us-court-calls-sea-shepherd-pirates.
168. 'Paul Watson resigns as leader of anti-whaling organisation Sea Shepherd', *The Globe and Mail*, 8 January 2013, http://www.theglobeandmail.com/news/british-columbia/paul-watson-resigns-as-leader-of-anti-whaling-organisation-sea-shepherd/article7039373/.
169. 'Paul Watson quits Sea Shepherd over US court order', *CBCNews*, 8 January 2013, http://www.cbc.ca/news/world/story/2013/01/08/canada-paul-watson-sea-shepherd-conservation-society-president.html.
170. 'Sea Shepherd has intercepted the whale poachers before a single whale is killed', *Sea Shepherd Australia*, 29 January 2013, http://www.seashepherd.org.au/news-and-media/2013/01/28/sea-shepherd-has-intercepted-the-whale-poachers-1482.
171. Petersen, 'OCEANS: Sea Shepherd takes fight against Japanese whalers to Supreme Court'. The SSCS attorney, Charles Moore, has argued that: 'the injunction surprised the group because it was issued without warning or a chance to argue in front of the judges and without being requested by Japan's Institute for Cetacean Research … the court issued the preliminary injunction *sua sponte* or "of its own accord".'
172. 'Sea Shepherd takes battle against ICR to US Supreme Court', 13 February 2013, http://www.seashepherd.org.au/news-and-media/2013/02/13/sea-shepherd-takes-battle-against-icr-to-us-supreme-court-1497.
173. Adam Westlake (2013) 'Paul Watson steps down as Sea Shepherd leader, Australian Greens' Bob Brown takes over', *The Japan Daily Press*, 8 January, http://japandailypress.com/paul-watson-steps-down-as-sea-shepherd-leader-australian-greens-bob-brown-takes-over-0821046; 'Eco=Fugitive Paul Watson resigns From Sea Shepherd', *The Toronto Sun*, 8 January 2013, http://www.torontosun.com/2013/01/08/eco-fugitive-paul-watson-resigns-from-sea-shepherd.
174. 'Eco=Fugitive Paul Watson Resigns From Sea Shepherd'.
175. Ibid.; Westlake, 'Paul Watson steps down as Sea Shepherd Leader, Australian Greens' Bob Brown Takes Over'.
176. AFP (2012) 'Sea Shepherds Wanted Watson to join anti-whaling fight', 2 November, http://www.google.com/hostednews/afp/article/ALeqM5ihUXk4B_swixfswA3yY7ZGrgbKwA?docId=CNG.8b9ff8e613fe19f3f1f5c2ac5c34d3c6.11.
177. 'Sea Shepherd launches Operation Zero Tolerance', *Sea Shepherd Australia*, 5 November 2012, http://www.seashepherd.org.au/news-and-media/2012/11/05/sea-shepherd-launches-operation-zero-tolerance-1462. Australian SSCS Director Jeff Hansen maintains that this is the largest flotilla to date, comprising four vessels and over 100 crew members drawn from 23 nations.
178. Adam Westlake (2012) 'Japan's whaling industry looks forward to arrest of Sea Shepherd's Watson', *The Japan Daily Press*, 5 November, http://japandailypress.com/japans-whaling-industry-looks-forward-to-arrest-of-sea-shepherds-watson-0517837; Locky MacLean (2012) 'The SSS Sam Simon is unveiled in Hobart, Tasmania', *Sea Shepherd Australia*, 10 December, http://www.seashepherd.org.au/news-and-media/2012/12/10/the-sss-sam-simon-is-unveiled-in-hobart-tasmania-1471.
179. 'Sea Shepherd launches Operation Zero Tolerance'.
180. Neil Reid (2012) 'The Sea Shepherd extends battlefield', *stuff.co.nz*, 28 October, http://www.stuff.co.nz/national/7873346/The-Sea-Shepherd-extends-battlefield.
181. 'Sea Shepherd ship Bob Barker is on the slipway of the Nisshin Maru', *Sea Shepherd Australia*, 15 February 2013, http://www.seashepherd.org.au/news-and-media/2013/02/15/sea-shepherd-ship-bob-barker-is-on-the-slipway-of-the-nisshin-maru-1495.

182. Andrew Darby (2013) 'Whale taken onto factory ship after five-hour standoff', *The Age*, 16 February, http://www.theage.com.au/environment/whale-watch/whale-taken-onto-factory-ship-after-fivehour-standoff-20130216-2ejjh.html.
183. Ibid.; 'Sea Shepherd ship Bob Barker is on the slipway of the Nisshin Maru'.
184. 'Japanese whale poaching vessel, *Nisshin Maru*, rams South Korean fuel tanker, Sea Shepherd ships *Sam Simon, Steve Irwin* and *Bob* Barker', Sea Shepherd Australia, 20 February 2013, http://www.seashepherd.org.au/news-and-media/2013/02/20/japanese-whale-poaching-vessel-nisshin-maru-rams-s-korean-fuel-tanker-sea-shepherd-ships-sam-simon-s-1501.
185. 'Japanese whaling ship rams Sea Shepherd protesters', *The Australian*, 20 February 2013, http://www.theaustralian.com.au/news/nation/japanese-whaling-ship-rams-sea-shepherd-protesters/story-e6frg6nf-1226582013026; Andrew Darby (2013) 'Ships collide in Antarctic whaling protest', *The Brisbane Times*, 20 February, http://www.brisbanetimes.com.au/environment/whale-watch/ships-collide-in-antarctic-whaling-protest-20130220-2eqyg.html.
186. 'Activists say 4 boats collide near Antarctica in dustup over whaling', *The Vancouver Sun*, 20 February 2013, http://www.vancouversun.com/news/Activists+Japanese+whaling+boat+collides+with+antiwhaling/7988129/story.html. The SSCS accused the *Nisshin Maru* of damaging the portside life-raft, preventing its release in an emergency, and destroying the davit to launch the other life raft. They state that due to the ramming the *Bob Barker* lost all power and issued a distress call. Andrew Darby (2013) 'Ships collide in Antarctic whaling protest', *The Brisbane Times*, 20 February, http://www.brisbanetimes.com.au/environment/whale-watch/ships-collide-in-antarctic-whaling-protest-20130220-2eqyg.html; Japanese whale poaching vessel, *Nisshin Maru*, rams South Korean fuel tanker, Sea Shepherd ships *Sam Simon, Steve Irwin* and *Bob Barker*'.
187. 'Activists say 4 boats collide near Antarctica in dustup over whaling'.
188. 'Ram claims as Japanese whalers, Sea Shepherd protesters clash', *The Australian*, 26 February 2013, http://www.theaustralian.com.au/news/nation/ram-claims-as-japanese-whalers-sea-shepherd-protesters-clash/story-e6frg6nf-1226586174246.
189. Cherrie Lou Billones (2013) 'New video show Sea Shepherd ramming Japanese whaling ships', *Japan Daily Press*, 26 February, http://japandailypress.com/new-video-shows-sea-shepherd-ramming-japanese-whaling-ships-2624082.
190. Ibid. The SSCS also alleged that the *Nisshin Maru* used high-powered water cannons against the *Steve Irwin, Bob Barker* and *Sam Simon*, in an attempt to flood their engine room but were unsuccessful. 'Tensions rise in clash with the Japanese whalers', *Sea Shepherd Australia*, 25 February 2013, http://www.seashepherd.org.au/news-and-media/2013/02/25/tensions-rise-in-clash-with-the-japanese-whalers-1504. Watson further accused the Japanese Coast Guard personnel on board of utilizing 'flash bang' concussion grenades against the *Bob Barker* during the incident where the vessel was rammed by the *Nisshun Maru* into the *Sun Laurel*. See Andrew Darby (2013) 'Sea Shepherd claims whalers using stun grenades', *The Age*, 25 February, http://www.theage.com.au/environment/sea-shepherd-claims-whalers-using-stun-grenades-20130225-2f1is.html; Justin McCurry (2013) 'Sea Shepherd activists clash with Japanese whaler in Southern Ocean', *The Guardian*, 20 February, http://www.guardian.co.uk/world/2013/feb/20/anti-whaling-clash-japan-australia. The Japanese Fishery Agency denied the use of the weapon but admitted that the *Nisshin Maru* had rammed two Sea Shepherd ships. 'Whaling no risk to relationship with Australia: Japan', *ABC News*, 22 February 2013, http://www.abc.net.au/news/2013-02-22/whaling-no-risk-to-relationship-with-australia-japan-says/4535064.
191. Jonathon Gul and Emily Bryan (2013) 'Japanese whaling vessel "rammed" by Sea Shepherd fleet', *ABC News*, 26 February, http://www.abc.net.au/news/2013-02-26/japanese-whaling-vessel-being-rammed-by-sea-shepherd-fleet/4539718; Cherrie Lou Billones (2013) 'New video show Sea Shepherd ramming Japanese whaling ships', *Japan Daily Press*, 26 February, http://japandailypress.com/new-video-shows-sea-shepherd-ramming-japanese-whaling-ships-2624082.

192. Jethro Mullen and Mark Morgenstein (2013) 'Anti-whaling activists say they were attacked by Japanese ships', *CNN.com*, 26 February, http://edition.cnn.com/2013/02/20/world/asia/australia-japan-whaling/index.html.
193. AAP (2013) 'Japanese whalers have "worst catch" ever', *The Age*, 6 April, http://www.theage.com.au/environment/whale-watch/japan-whalers-haveworst-ever-catch-20130406-2hed5.html; 'Japanese whalers "quit hunting ground"', *Sydney Morning Herald*, 2 March 2013, http://www.smh.com.au/environment/whale-watch/japanese-whalers-quit-hunting-ground-20130302-2fcy7.html. The actions of the Sea Shepherd organization also forced an early end to the hunt in the 2011–12 whaling season, meaning that the Japanese only caught 266 whales out of a planned 900. For the second year in a row Sea Shepherd harassment had forced an early end to Japanese whaling and a reduced catch (in 2010–11 only approximately 166 whales were caught), which would again put financial pressure on Japanese whaling. See Rick Wallace (2012) 'Japanese whalers return to port', *The Australian*, 10 March, p. 13.
194. Nick Bryant (2013) 'Politics at play in Sea Shepherd–Japan whaling wars', *BBC News*, 1 March, http://www.bbc.co.uk/news/world-asia-21612740.
195. 'Sea Shepherd ships set to be raided by Australian Federal Police', *Perth Now*, 3 March 2013, http://www.perthnow.com.au/news/national/sea-shepherd-fleet-set-to-be-raided-by-australian-federal-police/story-fndor8bb-1226589262705.
196. Andrew Darby (2013) 'Anti-whaling skipper poses problem over arrest notice', 1 January, http://www.smh.com.au/environment/whale-watch/antiwhaling-skipper-poses-problem-over-arrest-notice-20121231-2c2q1.html.
197. Ibid.
198. Ibid.
199. Georgina Stylianou (2013) 'High-seas protester slips past Kiwi search', *stuff.co.nz*, 7 January, http://www.stuff.co.nz/the-press/news/8148473/High-seas-protester-slips-past-Kiwi-search.
200. Adam Westlake (2012) 'Japan's whaling industry looks forward to arrest of Sea Shepherd's Watson', *The Japan Daily Press*, 5 November, http://japandailypress.com/japans-whaling-industry-looks-forward-to-arrest-of-sea-shepherds-watson-0517837.
201. Andrew Darby (2014) 'Japanese whaling ship "attacks" Sea Shepherd boat', *Sydney Morning Herald*, 2 February, http://www.smh.com.au/environment/whale-watch/japanese-whaling-ship-attacks-sea-shepherd-boat-20140201-31uni; Rebecca Quilliam (2014) 'Sea Shepherd reportedly rammed by whaling ship', *New Zealand Herald*, 2 February, http://www.nzherald.co.nz/world/news/article.cfm?c_id=2&objectid=11195745.
202. AAP, 'Japanese whalers have "worst catch" ever'.
203. Paul Watson (2011) 'Will this be the Sea Shepherd's last Antarctic campaign?', 28 January.
204. Ibid.
205. UPI (2012) 'Japan plans wider sales of whale meat', 7 November, http://www.upi.com/Top_News/World-News/2012/11/07/Japan-plans-wider-sales-of-whale-meat/UPI-70471352314575/. A survey of 1,200 people by the International Fund for Animal Welfare and completed by Nippon Research Centre (which included 1,200 people) showed that: 'almost 90 per cent of respondents said they had not bought whale meat in the past year'. Of those that had bought whale meat most had only done so once. Only 27 per cent of those surveyed supported the ongoing funding of the scientific whaling' programme, while 87 per cent opposed it. See Kieran Mulvaney (2012) 'Japanese public on whale meat: "Meh"', *Discovery News*, 27 November, http://news.discovery.com/earth/japanese-public-on-whaling-whale-meat-meh-121127.htm. To try to overcome the lack of interest in whale meat, the Japan's Fisheries Agency has announced plans to publicly sell whale meat to the general public to recoup costs of around $60 million a year. Starting in 2013 individuals will be able to get whale meat via mail order, the school lunch system will receive more whale meat and it will also be sold to restaurants as opposed to the current scheme whereby whale meat was only made to wholesale distributors. 'Japan plans wider

sales of whale meat', *UPI*, 7 November 2012, http://www.upi.com/Top_News/World-News/2012/11/07/Japan-plans-wider-sales-of-whale-meat/UPI-70471352314575/.

206. Andrew Darby (2012) 'Japan props up floundering whale business', *The Age*, 21 December, http://www.theage.com.au/environment/whale-watch/japan-props-up-floundering-whale-business-greenpeace-20121220-2bpg5.html.
207. Neil Reid (2012) 'The Sea Shepherd extends battlefield', *stuff.co.nz*, 28 October, http://www.stuff.co.nz/national/7873346/The-Sea-Shepherd-extends-battlefield.
208. Andrew Hoek (2010) 'Sea Shepherd Conservation Society v. Japanese Whalers, the Showdown: who is the real villain?', *Stanford Journal of Animal Law and Policy*, **3**, p. 182.
209. 'Sea Shepherds record of violence', http://www.highnorth.no/library/movements/Sea_Shepherd/se-sh-re.htm.
210. Amanda M. Caprari (2010) 'Lovable pirates? 'The legal implications of the battle between environmentalists and whalers in the Southern Ocean', *Connecticut Law Review*, **42** (5), p. 1507.

8. Vigilante justice: the Sea Shepherd Conservation Society and the law

Sea Shepherd is to terrorism what Groucho was to Marxism.

Paul Watson

INTRODUCTION

Paul Watson and the SSCS have continually claimed that their actions are permissible at international law. This chapter critically analyses this claim through an analysis of the relevant international law pertaining to marine life. For example, Watson has cited that his group is entitled to act due to a failure of the International Whaling Commission to act on its own resolutions and the World Charter for Nature. This section will critically evaluate those claims to see if they stand up to scrutiny. Lastly, the SSCS's opponents, in particular the Japanese government, has labelled the organization as 'pirates' (a label the group wears proudly) and/or vigilantes.[1] This chapter will analyse these claims and determine if they can be considered so at international law and, if so, what might be the consequences for the group. The conclusion and analysis section will critically examine the organization in the light of the proposed radicalization theories, determining their applicability to the SSCS.

The Sea Shepherd organization considers itself to be a 'navy (or) policing force' whose purpose is to protect sentient animals and confront criminals/criminal activities.[2] Watson has long criticized many international laws, such as UNCLOS, which declared that the powers of enforcement are wielded by states alone.[3] Moreover, despite the clear intent of the UNCLOS signatories, the SSCS still appears to see its role as being an enforcement agency, since they argue no other state or international institution will take on that role. Watson ignores the regulations when he believes they are unjust – and enforces his own.[4] The SSCS has attempted to justify its ongoing activities by claiming that the Japanese whalers are breaking international law and regulations. Specifically they cite as authority for their actions that the Japanese whalers are violating the IWC whaling moratorium that bans commercial whaling and that the SSCS is empowered to act under the UN World Charter for Nature.[5]

Scientific Whaling

The SSCS argues that the claimed Japanese scientific research is merely a pretext for ongoing commercial whaling and that if the IWC member states will not act then SSCS will, as they are empowered to do so under international law.[6] Watson argues: 'our intention is to stop the criminal whaling. We are not a protest organization. We are here to enforce international conservation law. We don't have banners. We intervene.'[7]

Problematically, current maritime international law as regards whaling is complex, engendered by decades-old political compromises and a lack of foreseeability on the part of the IWC negotiators. Thus both whaling states and the SSCS have sought to pick and choose which laws to follow that suit them.[8] Further, both groups claim to have the legal right to their actions. The Japanese whalers cite that under the IWC exemption for research activities their whale hunt is legitimate, while the SSCS demurs, arguing that the UN World Charter for Nature gives them the authority to enforce that document by any means.[9]

According to Paul Watson and the SSCS the Japanese scientific research programme is 'bogus research' that must be stopped.[10] Since the IWC member states will not, or cannot, act to stop scientific whaling, which the SSCS regards as a travesty, the SSCS believes it has little choice but to militantly act to prevent ongoing whaling.[11] However, in a blow to the SSCS argument that scientific whaling is illegitimate, the United States Court of Appeals Ninth Circuit decreed that the USA allows scientific whaling pursuant to the Whaling Convention Act and the Marine Mammal Protection Act, and they determined that the whaler's activities were consistent with US Congressional policy as regards the marine ecosystem.[12]

On 31 March 2014, the International Court of Justice (ICJ) handed down the decision examining the legality of Japanese whaling in Antarctic waters. Australia brought a suit against Japan, after several decades of failing to limit ongoing Japanese scientific whaling under special permit, at the International Whaling Commission (IWC). The ICJ determined that the scope of the current Japanese Whale Research Programme under Special Permit in the Antarctic (JARPA II) was too broad and that the programme, which the SSCS had been fighting for decades, should be terminated.[13]

However, the decision did not end the possibility of whaling in Antarctica because the judges stated explicitly that there was nothing in international law that forbids the killing of whales as part of a scientific research programme. The issue the judges had was that the JARPA II programme was not scientifically valid due to the size of the hunt (over 900 whales on average annually) and the lack of legitimate scientific research from the programme. Whilst the decision took away the legal underpinnings of the JARPA II programme, it specifically leaves the door ajar for Japan to continue scientific whaling if the programme is redesigned with the court's caveats in mind.[14]

Due to the ICJ ruling Japan did not whale in the 2014–15 season but announced in December 2015 that it will be back whaling for the 2015–16 season in defiance of the ICJ decision. Japan argues that a new whaling programme (NEWREP-A) conforms with the whaling moratorium and it plans to take 4,000 whales over a 12-year period (but reserves the right to change the sample size at any time). In response the SSCS announced it would once again be sending its ships to harass the Japanese whaling ships.[15]

The UN World Charter for Nature

Watson and the SSCS allege that their actions to prevent ongoing Japanese whaling from occurring are justified under the United Nations World Charter for Nature (World Charter, 9 November 1982), a claim they have made repeatedly and in different forums.[16] Paul Watson argued in a radio interview in 2007:

> We intervene against illegal activities, and we are simply upholding international conservation law, and the United Nations World Charter for Nature allows for us to do that. It says that any nongovernmental organization, or individual, is empowered to uphold international conservation law. That's why I've sunk ten whaling ships and destroyed tens of millions of dollars' worth of illegal fishing gear, and I'm not in jail.[17]

The SSCS's claims to protection under the World Charter are extremely dubious. Even if it is accepted that Japan is whaling illegally this does not provide legal cover for ramming vessels. Further, the World Charter was deliberately created to be non-binding and was crafted to foster state protection of the environment by setting forward moral principles as to how states should act.[18] Caron, a law of the sea expert, emphatically argues that the SSCS arguments are incorrect as a matter of law and that there is no ambiguity as regards the World Charter as to what is or is not legitimate action.[19] Watson's claim that private individuals may take direct action to safeguard the World Charter is nonsensical since the Charter makes no mention of enforcement, allowances for direct action or penalties, let alone empowering a non-state actor such as the SSCS to carry out its mandate. Furthermore, the United Nations (UN) resolution is considered to have less legal effect than multilateral conventions such as the United Nations Convention on the Law of the Sea (UNCLOS) and the United Nations Convention for the Suppression of Unlawful Acts Against the Safety of Maritime Navigation (SUA) that are critical of the group's direct approach.[20] As Anton puts it: 'One cannot bootstrap private enforcement to this striving if it cannot be located elsewhere in the law.'[21] States do not consider the activities of the SSCS such as ramming or scuttling whaling ships as legal behaviour.[22]

CONVENTION FOR THE SUPPRESSION OF UNLAWFUL ACTS AGAINST THE SAFETY OF MARITIME NAVIGATION

The Japanese government has argued that the SSCS actions almost certainly transgress the United Nations Convention for the Suppression of Unlawful Acts Against the Safety of Maritime Navigation (SUA).[23] Legal scholars such as Moffa and Caprari have supported the Japanese position, arguing that violating SUA can constitute marine terrorism.[24] Caprari argues that the SSCS has violated SUA articles 3(1)(c) and (3)(2)(a) in that the group may have attempted to: 'cause[] damage to a ship … which is likely to endanger the safe navigation of that ship'.[25] Watson and the SSCS have been involved over the years in a number of incidents that fit under that rubric, including the ramming of the *Sierra*, the *Yushin Maru No. 2* and many other vessels that would potentially render them liable. However, Caprari argued that it would also be inappropriate to prosecute the Sea Shepherds as pirates when SUA was enacted in part to prosecute environmental terrorists who are politically motivated and who traditionally fall outside of the definition of piracy under UNCLOS.[26]

The Ninth Circuit Court of Appeals examined the issue of SUA in its judgement. It found that the Japanese whalers offered uncontradicted evidence by SSCS that their tactics could impede its ability to navigate. It further dismissed the District Court approach that since the SSCS had not yet disabled any of the whaler's ships, it would be unlikely to do so in the future. The Appeals Court examined the SUA Convention's language that prohibited: 'endanger[ing]' safe navigation. That test to be applied under the SUA Convention requires only that the SSCS creates dangerous conditions and, given their record of ramming and sinking vessels, is clearly met. The Appeals Court went on to find that the SSCS had indeed attempted to endanger the navigation of the whaling ships.

At the very least, the Appeals Court determined that attempting to endanger the navigation of the Japanese whaling ships is sufficient to activate the SUA Convention, even if held ultimately to be unsuccessful under the Convention. The Appeals Court rejected the SSCS's claim that its actions were merely 'symbolic' and designed for maximum safety, finding that SSCS vessels were often dangerously close to the whaling ships. The Appeals Court further argued that the initial district court's decision that the whalers would not be likely to succeed under SUA would be erroneous if an action was brought in the future.[27]

ARE THE SSCS PIRATES?

Japan has in the past also claimed that Watson and the SSCS are pirates, particularly where the militant direct actions undertaken include boarding Japanese ships while at sea.[28] Watson himself has done nothing to deny this charge, often appearing to revel in the appellation on a number of occasions. Watson has stated publicly that: 'if they want us to be pirates, th[e]n we will be damn pirates'.[29] In a media interview in Canada he stated: 'sometimes it takes a pirate to stop a pirate. Call me a pirate if you like, but remember, it was a pirate that stopped piracy in the Caribbean in the seventeenth century. The Royal Navy couldn't do it.'[30]

Defining Piracy

The Japanese government argues that because incidents such as the boarding of ships by SSCS personnel take place on the high seas that the UNCLOS provisions relating to piracy apply.[31] First, it should be pointed out that at international law, all states are obliged to act to prevent acts of piracy on the high seas.[32] The UNCLOS (1982), Article 101 defines piracy as:

> (a) any illegal acts of violence or detention, or any act of depredation, committed for private ends by the crew or the passengers of a private ship or a private aircraft, and directed;
>   (i) on the high seas, against another ship or aircraft, or against persons or property on board such ship or aircraft;
>   (ii) against a ship, aircraft, persons or property in a place outside the jurisdiction of any State;
>
> (b) any act of voluntary participation in the operation of a ship or of an aircraft with knowledge of facts making it a pirate ship or aircraft;

(c) any act of inciting or of intentionally facilitating an act described in subparagraph (a) or (b).

UNCLOS Article 103 defines a pirate ship as one utilized by the person in dominant control of the vessel to commit one of the above acts in Article 101.[33] Young and Valencia define piracy acts as ranging from activities such as in-port pilfering, hit-and-run attacks, to temporary and permanent seizure of ships. However, their definition of hit-and-run attacks (the most applicable to the SSCS) appears limited to actors clandestinely boarding ships to steal what they can and is not applicable to the SSCS, which is carrying out politically motivated acts.[34]

Likelihood of Being Charged and Convicted for Piracy

Paul Watson has stated previously that he hoped his adversaries would charge him with piracy and take him to court. At present, the Japanese authorities have declined to do so.[35] While Japan could potentially bring claims of piracy against Watson and the SSCS and the volunteers, they would likely fail.[36] There are several problems with successfully convicting the SSCS on a charge of piracy. First, the vagueness of the UNCLOS law regarding piracy has to date allowed the SSCS, by mostly operating outside of the territorial waters of states, to avoid legal consequences. For example, the UNCLOS Convention does not properly define the term 'illegal acts', leaving the term ambiguous. The term can have different meanings under different national laws to that which is expressed in UNCLOS.[37]

Second, states such as Australia appear extremely reluctant to bring piracy charges against the SSCS since they are opposed to the Japanese continued utilizing of the scientific research-programme loophole.[38] Third, enforcing piracy under the UNCLOS categorization has proven extremely difficult in the past. Nations are hesitant to prosecute pirates under international laws in their municipal courts because piracy has traditionally been viewed as a domestic problem.[39] Fourth, UNCLOS is not applicable to actions within a state's territorial waters such as the damaging and subsequent sinking of the *Sierra* and other whaling ships in harbour.[40] It is a matter for the individual state if they wish to pursue it and, as we have seen, most have been reluctant to do so for fear of handing Watson and the SSCS a media *cause célèbre*.

Private Ends

Perhaps the major problem with the UNCLOS definition of piracy is what can be understood by the term 'private ends'. Problematically it is not defined in the UNCLOS Convention but Caprari argues it would exclude political activities that would preclude maritime terrorism from being covered by the statute.[41] Arguably, as per Jesus, it could be extended to incorporate violent acts with the intent to plunder or acts of personally motivated hatred or sheer vengeance.[42] However, this attempted extension of 'private ends' does not appear applicable in the case of the SSCS. Caprari argues persuasively that a pirate is generally defined as: 'a private individual whose heinous acts are aimed towards achieving some personal economic benefit'. Thus it can be inferred that 'private ends' encompasses an act done for economic gain, which is not the SSCS motivation.[43]

Only once has an environmental group been prosecuted under the UNCLOS piracy laws: the Belgian case of *Castle John and Nederlandse Stichting Sirius v. NV Mabeco and NV Parfin*. In that case the Belgian Court of Cassation held that Greenpeace had committed piracy when two of its members disrupted two ships illegally dumping waste in the ocean. The court determined that the acts were for 'private ends' because the aim was to achieve stated Greenpeace goals and thus was a private act, subject to UNCLOS privacy laws. However, the case has traditionally not been ascribed much weight and there have been no further similar prosecutions of green groups under this provision.[44]

However, and worryingly for the future of the SSCS, the Ninth Circuit Court of Appeals Judges in *Institute of Cetacean Research*; *Kyodo Senpaku Kaisha Ltd*; *Tomoyuki Ogawa*; and *Toshiyuki Muira v. Sea Shepherd Conservation Society and Paul Watson* were willing to ascribe the 'pirate' tag to SSCS.[45] Judge Alex Kozinski asserted that the group's 'aggressive and high-profile attacks' are 'the very embodiment of piracy'.[46] He stated: 'you don't need a peg leg or an eye patch. When you ram ships; hurl glass containers of acid; drag metal-reinforced ropes in the water to damage propellers and rudders; launch smoke bombs and flares with hooks; and point high-powered lasers at other ships, you are, without a doubt, a pirate, no matter how high-minded you believe your purpose to be.'[47] Circuit Judge M. Smith added: 'even if one believes it is barbaric to harvest whales for any purpose at the beginning of the 21st century, as practiced by Cetacean, it is clearly permitted under international law … The Sea Shepherds are pirates. Period.'[48]

The Court Of Appeals maintains that acts such as ramming ships, fouling propellers and hurling fiery and acid-filled projectiles are violent activities, even if directed only at inanimate objects, since they could injure crew or cause damage to ships that could sink. Such acts are thus violent acts for private ends, which is the essence of piracy.[49]

The Appeals Court noted that the Belgian case was the only court to date to examine this issue that had ruled that environmental activism should be considered a 'private end'. They dismissed arguments made by the SSCS that because they saw themselves as serving a public did not render their ends public.[50] They further criticized 'Judge Jones for arguing that the SSCS tactics were non-violent because the SSCS only targeted ships and equipment'.[51] The Appeals Court argued that enjoining piracy has nothing to do with whaling but rather sends the message that piracy is not to be tolerated. Refusing to issue an injunction would tell the world that the USA tolerates 'violent vigilantism'.[52]

Choosing to flee the Austrian jurisdiction has left Watson an international fugitive who can be arrested pursuant to the Interpol notice by any government willing to do so. Rather than risk being arrested in previously friendly states such as Australia and New Zealand Watson has chosen to stay aboard the SSCS flotilla in international waters.[53] After 15 months at sea, Watson finally came ashore in the US city of Los Angeles in late 2013 to face court in Seattle and was not arrested.[54]

He had not been back to the USA since the Interpol notice was issued and he maintained at the time that the notice had been rescinded (although the Japanese request is still active). However, after one week of Watson being in the USA, Costa Rican judicial officials from the First Circuit Penal Court of San Jose formally requested that Watson be extradited to Costa Rica to stand trial over the 2002 offences. Watson's Costa Rican lawyer Federico Morales understood that the Costa Rican authorities had reactivated the Interpol arrest warrant that had been conveyed to US authorities. To date the US has not officially responded and Watson has not been arrested.[55] Watson claimed on Facebook that the Costa Rica Interpol Red Notice had been dropped and this appears true, though the red alert issued by Japan remains active.[56] Japan is still trying to have Watson extradited to face charges for obstructing the Japanese 'research whaling' programme.[57]

In December 2014 the SSCS was found guilty of contempt of court by the Ninth US Circuit Court of Appeals for continuing to throw butyric acid and smoke bombs at Japanese whaling ships during their annual Antarctic hunt. A commissioner was appointed to assess compensation with the whalers demanding AUD$2.16 million and costs.[58] The Ninth Circuit Court had previously ruled in February 2013 that the transfer of assets and control of the SSCS to other state arms of the entity did not obviate the initial 2012 order to cease its ongoing harassment of the

Japanese whaling fleet. Australia and other countries did not change their 2012 order to the group to cease its dangerous activities.[59] The SSCS eventually agreed to pay the Institute of Cetacean Research and Kyodo Senpaku US$2.55 million to resolve civil contempt charges for breaching a court-imposed injunction to stay clear of whaling vessels in the Antarctic Ocean.[60] The SSCS is still seeking to overturn the injunction preventing it from interfering with the Japanese Antarctic whaling fleet and has filed a certiorari petition with the US Ninth Circuit Court of Appeals.[61]

The SSCS claims for their actions utilizing international law cannot be justified via even a cursory examination of the relevant international law. The group's claims regarding scientific research whaling, and their role in enforcing what the IWC will not, has no legal validity given the strictures imposed on the IWC by the current version of the International Convention on the Regulation of Whaling. Further, the US Court of Appeals found that the use of the exception was valid under US law. It is up to the IWC members to resolve this issue, and outside pressure of the sort used by the SSCS appears counterproductive to the cause of ending global whaling: the group's stated objective. Similarly, the issue of Exclusive Economic Zone (EEZ) enforcement is one for individual states to determine how best to defend their sovereignty. The UN World Charter for Nature, quoted often by Watson as the legal justification for his group's action, also provides no succour. The Charter is non-binding; does not allow for private actors to take action as is so often claimed in the group's communications; does not mention enforcement; and requires all actions undertaken to be lawful.

Rather, given the recent US Court of Appeals judgement, there is validity to the proposition that international law may be utilized in the future to attack the SSCS. The willingness of the US Appeals Court to follow Belgian precedent regarding 'private ends' and being willing to brand the SSCS as pirates is also problematic for the group, opening them up to a plethora of similar legal cases by their opponents who now have a greater likelihood of success. Bringing such actions is of course contingent upon states being willing to do so, but given Japan's recent aggressive legal actions, it appears clear that they have a strategy to go after Paul Watson and the SSCS through the courts and will no doubt continue to bring further legal actions.

ANALYSIS AND CONCLUSION

In many ways the SSCS is at the zenith of its powers. It has grown exponentially since its inception, with a large operating budget; enormous charitable donations; dozens of paid staff; thousands of supporters globally; and a flotilla of ships to achieve their goals. The group has evolved into a global entity with national chapters staffed by eager volunteers desiring to force an end to global whaling through the mechanism of direct action. The SSCS is now evolving past whaling to encompass other marine species under threat. They are altering targets and expanding operations to go after toothfish poachers,[62] trying to prevent shark culling,[63] and illegal fishing in West Africa.[64] Further, in the past five years the SSCS has been incredibly successful in preventing Japanese whaling in Antarctic waters. In that period the SSCS has limited the Japanese whale-take to 10 per cent of what the Japanese wish to harvest.[65]

The SSCS in 2015 experienced record fund-raising and have a $12 million award from a Dutch national charity to build a new custom-built, super-fast 'dream ship', and have also bought two decommissioned Coast Guard vessels. The legal attacks on the organization have helped their public profile to grow globally, aided by a canny media strategy by Watson, who has always understood the power of the camera lens.[66]

The SSCS has, from the beginning, been fuelled by Watson's vision and his authoritarian manner to continue until all exploitation of marine life is ended. To achieve that goal the SSCS has engaged a multipurpose strategy that utilizes diplomacy, economic threats and damage coupled with media-savvy direct actions. It is their use of the global media apparatus to achieve their goals that truly sets the SSCS apart. Watson's media training has enabled him to create a drama where his group is the heroic underdog fighting on behalf of the planet against evil Japanese whalers who, he argues, are acting contrary to international law and Western mores. The group's bold direct actions are designed for a global media audience.

Watson understands that more media coverage means more donations, and a bigger organization able to carry out its mission. He has constantly dared the whaling states to put him on trial, knowing that such an act will draw the spotlight of the world's media to his cause. Until recently states had not been willing to fall for this 'Brer Rabbit' ploy but it appears that Japan now has gambled that calling his bluff may be necessary to rid themselves of Watson.

Of the groups examined here the SSCS appears to be the best placed to continue on in the short term, because of their resources and funding strength. However, in the long term they are vulnerable because their hierarchical structure is dominated by their charismatic leader Paul Watson. If he dies or is jailed the organization may not survive his loss, given there appears to be no strong heir apparent. Further, if jailed as Japan clearly hopes to do this would make him a martyr, which may boost his cause, bur despite his claims in the past to be willing to be jailed (or die) for the cause Watson clearly does not want that role.

While there is some evidence that members join the SSCS for excitement the primary reason they join is, as per Einwohler's insights, that they have formed emotional attachments to the marine animals they are seeking to protect – but this has become allied with a strong belief that marine creatures need to be protected from depredations that the members are willing to act upon. Members are recruited or volunteer from across the globe to be part of the SSCS and it is clear that many do not know each other before they enlist. Rather they are driven by their passion to protect marine life and their admiration of Paul Watson and his life story.

There is also evidence that Neumann and Rogers's radicalization theory is correct, because SSCS clearly can provide people with a mission in life (Watson, his long-time crew members but also many volunteers) and clearly some members do feel a sense of superiority over others, particularly in their perceptions of individuals who can allow the harvesting of marine resources to continue, but particularly there is contempt for Greenpeace's merely witnessing of the slaughter of whales. However, Sageman's 'band of guys' radicalization analysis is clearly not applicable to the SSCS. Women play a number of key roles (legal counsel, for example) and are accepted as volunteers in large numbers to go on missions.[67]

The SSCS currently finds itself beset on all sides by legal actions designed to limit its effectiveness. What impact all of the recent legal issues will have on the viability of the group remains to be seen. The Japanese state now appears to be targeting Watson and his group through the courts in order to remove a perennial thorn in their side. Japan now seems willing to use the US court system to prevent ongoing direct SSCS actions against its annual Antarctic whaling operations. They further appear to have instigated a programme to have Watson extradited to face charges in Japan and have sought an injunction from US courts to curtail the group's activities.

The US Ninth Circuit Court of Appeals' decision to grant a preliminary injunction against Watson and the SSCS weakens their ability to operate unhindered and opens them up to contempt of court proceedings if they are deemed to have contravened the injunction.[68] Further, the court action has forced Watson to step down as the public face of the group in order to avoid facing criminal charges for SSCS operations, but he still appears to wield a great deal of influence.[69]

Unlike the other groups examined here that are structured in affinity cells, the SSCS has always been a top-down organization, led by a charismatic leader in Paul Watson. The autocratic approach favoured by Watson, where all major decisions are decided by him, runs the risk of fatally weakening the organization if he is not at the helm. His potential imprisonment by Costa Rica or Japan, or limiting him to operating only on the high seas, could lead to the collapse of the organization without its totemic head. Or it might lead to an invigoration of the SSCS, with Paul Watson as a martyr languishing in jail and using a global megaphone to promote both his plight and his cause while others assume the mantle of leadership. Given the current reach and stability of the group Watson has built, it may very well be able to exist without his leadership; but given how the organization relies on his presence for fund-raising and media presence, its future without a Watson at the helm is uncertain.

Watson's leaving Greenpeace in dubious circumstances left him free to go on to create his own organization, free of the strictures of the Greenpeace ethos to merely 'bear witness' and instead to be able to take on his 'enemies' in a direct fashion. For Watson, change through non-violent means has historically been mostly a failure. He argues that the modern environmental movement, faced with violence against humans, animals and the planet, has been overly passive. Rather he argues there are times when it is necessary to break the law in defence of larger objectives. The group's direct action strategies and tactics inherently contain the seeds of the group's destruction as well. The group's use of violence remains problematic, and even if only utilized against property or in 'self-defence' involves an element of risk that life could be lost on both sides.

The SSCS has met one of its key objectives in recent years – that of harassing the Japanese Antarctic whaling fleet to reduce the numbers of whales caught. But how well is the group doing in its broader goal to end Japanese whaling via economic means? While it is true that the consumption of whale meat in Japan is down and that the activity is uneconomic, there appears no signs that Japan is willing to end the annual hunt. Rather the Japanese state appears to view Western disapproval of the whale hunt as a form of 'Western cultural imperialism' and they are determined to continue scientific research whaling.[70]

The Japanese government appears adamant not to be seen as giving in to this type of pressure, so ongoing SSCS operations may be counterproductive. Thus, the SSCS appears unlikely to achieve its stated goal of the economic ruin of Japan's whaling fleet, since Japan seems determined to support the ongoing whale hunt no matter how uneconomic or how little the Japanese public desires whale meat as a staple of their diet.

Further, the SSCS is highly unlikely through its actions to force change at the IWC. Rather, for many member-states and commentators their approach is seen as counterproductive to bringing about a negotiated end to non-commercial whaling. The IWC members perceive the SSCS operations as detrimental to convincing Japan to stop whaling. Actions such as ramming ships do not endear the group to other, even non-whaling nations.[71]

As the figurehead of the group, Paul Watson's zeal and energy has built a force to be reckoned with: not only by the Japanese whaling industry but also by the international law infrastructure itself. Up until recently there had been few legal consequences for Watson and his crew from his aggressive activities.[72] Opaque, weak and confusing international laws, combined with the problematic nature of enforcing international law, has allowed the SSCS to operate to a degree once thought unheard of by a non-state actor.[73]

The fig leaf of the group's claimed international law imprimatur for their activities is now well revealed to be false. While the SSCS has likened itself to Gaia's Navy, whose mission is to protect sentient marine creatures, their claims did stand up to critical scrutiny. The SSCS's arguments that they act on behalf of the IWC since they 'refuse' to act cannot be made out legally, as only that entity can act on its own behalf – if it chooses. The group's oft-mounted claims that their methods are sanctioned under the UN World Charter for Nature are also fallacious. The Charter was deliberately designed to be non-binding, makes no mention of enforcement and was meant, rather, to foster state protection of the environment, not direct actions by individual actors.[74]

An analysis of the relevant international law pertaining to SSCS activities reveals that, despite not being held to account for their actions to date, they are at risk if states are minded to pursue legal action against them. There have been numerous breaches by the SSCS of Section Two of COLREGS, requiring captains of vessels to operate their ships in line with the precepts of 'good seamanship'.[75] The US District Court of Appeal also determined that the SSCS breached the section in deliberately steering their vessels close to Japanese whaling ships.[76]

Moffa and Caprari mount persuasive cases that the SSCS has also violated the marine terrorism provisions of SUA.[77] Further, the Ninth

Circuit Court of Appeals highlighted that Japanese claims that SSCS tactics could impede their ship's ability to navigate went unchallenged by the organization. The Appeals Court determined that at the very least SSCS's endangering of Japanese ships was enough to activate the UNCLOS Convention, even if an adverse finding under the Convention was not obtained.[78]

There is a possibility that the Sea Shepherds may have conducted an attack on persons in the 2007 campaign that could be considered an act of terrorism. As indicated previously, both the Sea Shepherds and the Japanese whalers acknowledge the use of butyric acid in the clash with the *Nisshin Maru*. The Japanese claim it was thrown at the men or squirted in their eyes, and that at least two men were affected and one's eyesight has been affected. Watson, on the other hand, claims that the acid is non-toxic, it was thrown on the decks, and that it was thrown in bottles that broke on impact, and could not have been squirted in the whalers' eyes.[79]

Nevertheless, the use of butyric acid has been linked to convicted anti-abortion terrorists. According to Philip Jenkins: 'Rachelle "Shelley" Shannon earned celebrity for a 1994 murder attempt on a clinic doctor in Wichita, and was also convicted of firebomb and butyric acid attacks on clinics in 1992 and 1993 … The Federal Judge at her 1995 trial described her concisely as a terrorist.'[80] These examples suggest that these tactics – destroying property and butyric acid attacks – are within terrorists' playbooks and that there have been instances in which there have been successful convictions when individuals or groups have conducted them on land, within a country's jurisdiction, in both cases above, in the USA.

In these respects, it may be possible to question whether in the Sea Shepherds' case they constitute a blind spot in the scholarly literature on terrorism and political violence or whether individual states, several states, or the international community may be turning a blind eye to anti-terrorism legislation because of reluctance or inability to enforce legislation. It therefore begs a question of whether under different circumstances the Sea Shepherds might be considered terrorists.

Nevertheless, the question of whether the Sea Shepherds intended to harm humans is significant. It has already been established that the SSCS purports that it is not interested in harming humans. Moreover, in the case at hand Watson claimed that they used a non-toxic form of acid. However, at least one other instance suggests that Watson and his colleagues were concerned for human lives. After the *Robert Hunter* collided with the *Kaiko Maru*, and the Japanese vessel issued a distress signal, Watson offered his assistance, which the whalers declined. It is true that not all forms of terrorism are lethal. Indeed, many hostages have walked away from their long-term captors and their kidnappers following negotiations and payments (and sometimes both).

However, incidents like offering assistance to the crew of the *Kaiko Maru* suggest that they had been acting somewhat consistently with their philosophies and guidelines. It will be recalled that Sprinzak considers a dehumanization of opponents as an important component of his model's crisis of legitimacy (terrorism) stage.

Offering to assist whalers, whose lives may have been in danger, can hardly be considered dehumanizing the enemy. However, as indicated earlier, despite the SSCS's intentions not to harm humans there is a distinct possibility in virtually every one of their actions that they may cause some injuries or perhaps even deaths, and they therefore consistently put lives at risk through their actual or implied use of violence for political purposes. To use a colloquialism: their normal operations may be a lethal terrorist act waiting to happen.

Certainly, and unlike what Sprinzak's analysis would suggest, their attacks have not become more violent. Butyric acid attacks are still part of their repertoire but have not escalated into more vicious assaults on Japanese whalers. If anything they have lessened after the bombing of the whaling ships carried out by those allegedly inspired by the SSCS fight. This may well be due to the fact that their current campaigns and tactics have proven relatively efficacious in limiting whale killings and training a media spotlight on the issue of marine life destruction. Their successes appear to have been enough to prevent them from adopting terrorist actions, given that their primarily militant actions and concomitant publicity is working quite well.

However, most worryingly for the SSCS's continued functioning is whether the appellation of piracy can be applied to their actions. During the 2007 campaign both the *Farley Mowat* and the *Robert Hunter* were deregistered ships, which makes them pirate ships. Under international law they can be interdicted by any navy or official ship of another state.[81] While this could potentially be an issue that complicates the organization's activities, it is relatively simple to register a ship, and it is unlikely that the Sea Shepherds will permanently lose possession of their ships.

The Japanese government has long argued that incidents such as the SSCS boarding their vessels on the high seas mean that the UNCLOS piracy provision should be levied on the organization. To date, the piracy provisions have not been applied to the SSCS for a variety of factors: the relevant section is vaguely worded; states such as Australia have been reluctant to charge the SSCS for their actions; historically enforcing the provisions has proved problematic; the provisions cannot be applied inside territorial waters where some SSCS direct actions have occurred;[82] and the definition of 'private ends', with its connotations of economic gain incorporated within the UNCLOS Convention, was not seen as applicable to the SSCS, which is motivated by other goals.[83]

However, Judge Alex Kozinski of the US Ninth Circuit Court of Appeals was willing to assert that the actions of the SSCS fit within the rubric of piracy. His finding was based on broadening the definition of 'private ends' to include environmental protest.[84] This potentially opens up the SSCS to a raft of legal suits for its ongoing activities and threatens the viability of the organization in the long term if the ruling is allowed to stand.

The argument and narrative presented above suggest that like other forms of political violence, the Sea Shepherds' actions – from what would be considered environmental protest when Watson was a Greenpeace member to its present incarnation – was an incremental process. Watson and the Sea Shepherds' other members turned towards more robust forms of protest following their belief that working within the system would not permit them to achieve their objectives. In this respect, it is possible to claim that the Sea Shepherds' actions conform somewhat to Sprinzak's delegitimization model. However, the question remains whether they transcended from the conflict of legitimacy stage to the crisis of legitimacy stage (terrorism).

It will be recalled that some terrorism definitions not only claim that the act constitutes violence or the threat of violence against noncombatants to achieve political goals, but also targeting property for the same intentions. In many instances, the Sea Shepherds have committed politically motivated violent acts against property in order to induce fear into the whalers to force them to prevent the killing of the maritime mammals.

Above it was argued that the process by which the Sea Shepherds adopted more violent means corresponded with a delegitimization process. Indeed, they claim to have acted because they felt either that individual states or the international community could not or would not uphold international law pertaining to whaling. Such instances suggest that the Sea Shepherds felt that these entities lost their legitimacy, and the SSCS acted to enforce existing laws. Following the altercation with the *Kaiko Maru*, Watson asked: 'Do whale defenders have to die down here for the world to take notice and take action against the criminal actions of the Japanese whalers?'[85]

For Sprinzak the culminating crisis of legitimacy stage has a terrorist group considering all people associated with the suspect political order to be depersonalized, dehumanized and virtually subhuman, allowing members to commit heinous actions, up to and including murder. Such a disposition can be first observed in the language that a group's members use towards others, such as referring to them as 'dogs' or 'things', and second, in their outward acceptance of inflicting harm on them.[86]

It would appear that this does not occur in the Sea Shepherds' public statements. As recently as January 2007 Watson argued that the group's activities would be confined to inflicting damage to any whaling vessel – of sufficient magnitude to force it to comply with safety regulations and return to dock to be repaired, rather than committing physical violence against persons.[87]

The Japanese, however, consider the Sea Shepherds as terrorists and – following a telephone conversation between Watson and then-Australian Environment Minister Senator Ian Campbell, and his caution to the Japanese authorities that the whaling crews should not use water cannons against the Sea Shepherds – implied that the Australian government was supporting terrorists.[88]

Director General of the Institute for Cetacean Research Hiroshi Hatanaka, following the Sea Shepherds' altercations with the Japanese factory ship *Nisshin Maru* and the spotter ship *Kaiko Maru* in Antarctic waters in February 2007, claimed: 'Sea Shepherd is not an environmental group. It is a terrorist vigilante group that operates outside the law.'[89]

Although probably calling them 'vigilantes' pejoratively, Hatanaka was somewhat accurate in his assessment. It will be recalled that Sprinzak argues that vigilantes do not consider themselves to be violating the law. In fact, they view themselves as upholding the law, and regard themselves as only acting in such a manner because the status quo is unable to maintain the proper legal order. Nevertheless, there needs to be some clarification in regard to the Sea Shepherds as a vigilante group. Sprinzak's comments are intended to reflect the politics of right-wing vigilante groups. Clearly, the SSCS is more left-wing in orientation.

Moreover, usually left-wing groups intend to overthrow, not uphold the social order. Additionally, Sprinzak also claims that vigilante groups tend not to offer a new social vision. On this matter the SSCS is clearly in status quo maintenance-mode regarding legislation. However, as suggested previously, they might be offering an alternative blueprint for society by advocating that whales and other non-human species have equal rights with humans, especially the right to life, and basing their political actions on these principles. In some respects, therefore, it may be possible to consider the Sea Shepherds a new type of vigilante group. This may prompt analysts to broaden their conventional understandings of vigilantism, which can commit terrorist acts in support of their goals.

It is clear, however, that the SSCS, despite the threat of ongoing legal action and the loss of their figurehead, remains determined to end whaling through direct and, if needed, militant action.[90] While the role of Watson in the SSCS remains unclear and the organization faces an uncertain legal future, one outcome is definite: while marine life is threatened, Paul Watson and the group he founded will continue their self-imposed mission to protect aquatic life.

NOTES

1. Amanda M. Caprari (2010) 'Lovable pirates? The legal implications of the battle between environmentalists and whalers in the Southern Ocean', *Connecticut Law Review*, **42** (5), July, p. 1507.
2. Paul Watson (1991) 'Sea Shepherd defense policy', *Earth Island Journal*, **6** (4), p. 42.
3. Article 224, UNCLOS: 'The powers of enforcement against foreign vessels under this Part may only be exercised by officials or by warships, military aircraft, or other ships or aircraft clearly marked and identifiable as being on government service and authorized to that effect', http://www.un.org/Depts/los/convention_agreements/texts/unclos/unclos_e.pdf, p. 113.
4. Raffi Khatchadourian (2007) 'Neptune's Navy: Paul Watson's wild crusade to save the oceans', *The New Yorker*, 5 November, p. 58.
5. Sea Shepherd (2007) 'Japanese whaling fleet forced to run from Sea Shepherd', *Sea Shepherd News*, 8 February, http://www.seashepherd.org/news/media_070208_1p.html.
6. Andrew Hoek (2010) 'Sea Shepherd Conservation Society v. Japanese Whalers, the showdown: who is the real villain?', *Stanford Journal of Animal Law and Policy*, **3**, pp. 178–9.
7. Peter Heller (2007) *The Whale Warriors: On Board a Pirate Ship in the Battle to Save the World's Largest Mammals* (New York: Free Press), p. 5.
8. Joseph Elliott Roeschke (2009) 'Ecoterrorism and piracy on the high seas: Japanese whaling and the rights of private groups to enforce international conservation law in neutral waters', *Villanova Environmental Law*, **20**, p. 101.
9. Caprari, 'Lovable pirates? The legal implications of the battle between environmentalists and whalers in the Southern Ocean', pp. 1495–6.
10. Heller, *The Whale Warriors: On Board a Pirate Ship in the Battle to Save the World's Largest Mammals*, p. 4.
11. Khatchadourian, 'Neptune's Navy: Paul Watson's wild crusade to save the oceans', p. 58; Anthony L.I. Moffa (2012) 'Two competing models of activism, one goal: a case study of anti-whaling campaigns in the Southern Ocean', *Yale Journal of International Law*, **37**, pp. 209–10.
12. *Institute of Cetacean Research; Kyodo Senpaku Kaisha Ltd; Tomoyuki Ogawa; and Toshiyuki Muira v. Sea Shepherd Conservation Society and Paul Watson*, United States Court of Appeals Ninth Circuit, No, 12-35266, Opinion, (25/2/13), http://cdn.ca9.uscourts.gov/datastore/general/2013/02/25/1235266.pdf, pp. 11–12.
13. Gerry Nagtzaam (2014) 'Righting the ship?: Australia, New Zealand and Japan at the ICJ and the barbed issue of "scientific whaling"', *Australian Journal of Environmental Law*, **1**, p. 71; *Whaling in the Antarctic (Australia v Japan: New Zealand Intervening)* Judgment, I.C.J. Reports, pp. 226–379, http://www.icj-cij.org/docket/files/148/18136.pdf.
14. Nagtzaam, 'Righting the ship?: Australia, New Zealand and Japan at the ICJ and the barbed issue of "scientific whaling"', pp. 88–93; *Whaling in the Antarctic (Australia v Japan: New Zealand Intervening)* Judgment, I.C.J. Reports, pp. 226–379, http://www.icj-cij.org/docket/files/148/18136.pdf.

15. Daniel Fliton and Andrew Darby (2015) 'Japan whale hunt tensions to flare as Australia considers court action', *The Age*, 8 December, http://www.theage.com.au/federal-politics/political-news/japan-whale-hunt-tensions-to-flare-as-australia-considers-court-action-20151207-glhag4#ixzz3ueHejSfy.
16. Khatchadourian, 'Neptune's Navy: Paul Watson's wild crusade to save the oceans', p. 66; Paul Watson (1993) 'Captain's Log', *Sea Shepherd Log* (second quarter), p. 2.
17. Roeschke, 'Ecoterrorism and piracy on the high seas: Japanese whaling and the rights of private groups to enforce international conservation law in neutral waters', p. 108.
18. Caprari, 'Lovable pirates? The legal implications of the battle between environmentalists and whalers in the Southern Ocean', p. 1510.
19. Khatchadourian, 'Neptune's Navy: Paul Watson's wild crusade to save the oceans', p. 66.
20. Moffa, 'Two competing models of activism, one goal: a case study of anti-whaling campaigns in the Southern Ocean', p. 211. The World Charter's language is one of generality. The *travaux* makes it clear that the Charter's drafters clearly did not want the Resolution to have any binding force nor sanctions. See Donald K Anton (2011) 'Protecting whales by hue and cry: is there a role for non-state actors in the enforcement of international law?', *Journal of International Wildlife Law and Policy*, **14** (2), p. 142.
21. Anton, 'Protecting whales by hue and cry: is there a role for non-state actors in the enforcement of international law?', p. 142.
22. Khatchadourian, 'Neptune's Navy: Paul Watson's wild crusade to save the oceans', p. 66.
23. The United Nations Convention for the Suppression of Unlawful Acts Against the Safety of Maritime Navigation, 10 March 1988, 1678 U.N.T.S. 201, http://treaties.un.org/doc/db/Terrorism/Conv8-english.pdfSUA. This was introduced to address the issue of terrorism at sea that was not auspiced under the UNCLOS piracy laws. The Convention drafters did not define terrorism, deeming it too difficult. Its focus is on creating extraditable offences in situations where there were intentional and unlawful threats, attempts or actual endangerment of the safe navigation of a vessel. The Convention states:

    Any person commits an offence if that person unlawfully and intentionally:

    (b) performs an act of violence against a person on board a ship if that act is likely to endanger the safe navigation of that ship; or
    (c) destroys a ship or causes damage to a ship or to its cargo which is likely to endanger the safe navigation of that ship.

    It focuses on the tenets of apprehension, conviction, and punishment rather than prevention and it does not apply to governments or state-sponsored terrorist organizations but only can be utilized against individuals. The Convention covers only ships operating beyond the outer limits of any state's territorial sea, since attacks within the territorial waters are covered by domestic law. See Caprari, 'Lovable pirates? The legal implications of the battle between environmentalists and whalers in the Southern Ocean', p. 1517.
24. Moffa, 'Two competing models of activism, one goal: a case study of anti-whaling campaigns in the Southern Ocean', pp. 210–11.
25. http://treaties.un.org/doc/db/Terrorism/Conv8-english.pdf; see Caprari, 'Lovable pirates? The legal implications of the battle between environmentalists and whalers in the Southern Ocean', p. 1519.
26. Caprari, 'Lovable pirates? The legal implications of the battle between environmentalists and whalers in the Southern Ocean, p. 1524.
27. Institute of Cetacean Research; Kyodo Senpaku Kaisha Ltd; Tomoyuki Ogawa; and Toshiyuki Muira v. Sea Shepherd Conservation Society and Paul Watson, United States Court of Appeals Ninth Circuit, No, 12-35266, Opinion, (25/2/13), http://cdn.ca9.uscourts.gov/datastore/general/2013/02/25/1235266.pdf, pp. 7–9.
28. Roeschke, 'Ecoterrorism and piracy on the high seas: Japanese whaling and the rights of private groups to enforce international conservation law in neutral waters', p. 128.
29. Hoek, 'Sea Shepherd Conservation Society v. Japanese Whalers, the showdown: who is the real villain?', p. 185.

30. Paul Watson (1994) *Ocean Warrior: My Battle to End the Illegal Slaughter on the High Seas* (Toronto: Key Porter Books Ltd), p. 22.
31. Roeschke, 'Ecoterrorism and piracy on the high seas: Japanese whaling and the rights of private groups to enforce international conservation law in neutral waters', p. 128.
32. Caprari, 'Lovable pirates? The legal implications of the battle between environmentalists and whalers in the Southern Ocean', p. 1511; Hoek, 'Sea Shepherd Conservation Society v. Japanese Whalers, the showdown: who is the real villain?', p. 186.
33. http://www.un.org/Depts/los/convention_agreements/texts/unclos/part7.htm.
34. Adam J. Young and Mark J. Valencia (2003) 'Conflation of piracy and terrorism in Southeast Asia: rectitude and utility'', *Contemporary Southeast Asia,* **25**, p. 2.
35. Alston Chase (1992) 'Sea Shepherds may give piracy a good name', *Sea Shepherd Log* (third quarter), p. 9.
36. Roeschke, 'Ecoterrorism and piracy on the high seas: Japanese whaling and the rights of private groups to enforce international conservation law in neutral waters', p. 128.
37. Caprari, 'Lovable pirates? The legal implications of the battle between environmentalists and whalers in the Southern Ocean', p. 1512.
38. Ibid., p. 1513.
39. Ibid., p. 1512.
40. H.E. Jose Luis Jesus (2003) 'Protection of foreign ships against piracy and terrorism at sea: legal aspects', *The International Journal of Marine and Coastal Law*, **18**, (3), pp. 377–8.
41. Caprari, 'Lovable pirates? The legal implications of the battle between environmentalists and whalers in the Southern Ocean', p. 1512.
42. Jesus, 'Protection of foreign ships against piracy and terrorism at sea: legal aspects', pp. 377–8.
43. Caprari, 'Lovable pirates? The legal implications of the battle between environmentalists and whalers in the Southern Ocean', p. 1512.
44. Ibid., p. 1514; Moffa, 'Two competing models of activism, one goal: a case study of anti-whaling campaigns in the Southern Ocean, *Yale Journal of International Law*, **37** (201), p. 210.
45. 'Ninth Circuit Court of Appeals hands down ruling in favor of Japanese whale poachers', *Sea Shepherd Australia*, 27 February 2013, http://www.seashepherd.org.au/news-and-media/2013/02/27/ninth-circuit-court-of-appeals-hands-down-ruling-in-favor-of-japanese-whale-poachers-1507.
46. Institute of Cetacean Research; Kyodo Senpaku Kaisha Ltd; Tomoyuki Ogawa; and Toshiyuki Muira v. Sea Shepherd Conservation Society and Paul Watson, United States Court of Appeals Ninth Circuit, No, 12-35266, Opinion, (25/2/13), http://cdn.ca9.uscourts.gov/datastore/general/2013/02/25/1235266.pdf, p. 2; Nick Bryant (2013) 'Politics at play in Sea Shepherd–Japan whaling wars', *BBC News*, 1 March, http://www.bbc.co.uk/news/world-asia-21612740.
47. Mike Schuler (2013) 'Paul Watson and Sea Shepherd are pirates, US court says', *gcaptain.com*, 27 February, http://gcaptain.com/paul-watson-and-shepherd-pirates-us-court-rules/.
48. Institute of Cetacean Research; Kyodo Senpaku Kaisha Ltd; Tomoyuki Ogawa; and Toshiyuki Muira v. Sea Shepherd Conservation Society and Paul Watson, United States Court of Appeals Ninth Circuit, No, 12-35266, Opinion, (25/2/13), http://cdn.ca9.uscourts.gov/datastore/general/2013/02/25/1235266.pdf,p. 2; Schuler, 'Paul Watson and Sea Shepherd are pirates, US court says'.
49. Institute of Cetacean Research; Kyodo Senpaku Kaisha Ltd; Tomoyuki Ogawa; and Toshiyuki Muira v. Sea Shepherd Conservation Society and Paul Watson, United States Court of Appeals Ninth Circuit, No, 12-35266, Opinion, (25/2/13), http://cdn.ca9.uscourts.gov/datastore/general/2013/02/25/1235266.pdf,p. 6; Schuler, 'Paul Watson and Sea Shepherd are pirates, US court says.
50. Institute of Cetacean Research; Kyodo Senpaku Kaisha Ltd; Tomoyuki Ogawa; and Toshiyuki Muira v. Sea Shepherd Conservation Society and Paul Watson, United States

Court of Appeals Ninth Circuit, No, 12-35266, Opinion, (25/2/13), http://cdn.ca9.uscourts.gov/datastore/general/2013/02/25/1235266.pdf, p. 5, David Kirby (2013) 'Sea Shepherd's Paul Watson mocks court's 'pirate' ruling', *takepart.com*, 28 February, http://www.takepart.com/article/2013/02/28/us-court-calls-sea-shepherd-pirates.

51. Kirby, 'Sea Shepherd's Paul Watson mocks court's 'pirate' ruling'.
52. Institute of Cetacean Research; Kyodo Senpaku Kaisha Ltd; Tomoyuki Ogawa; and Toshiyuki Muira v. Sea Shepherd Conservation Society and Paul Watson, United States Court of Appeals Ninth Circuit, No, 12-35266, Opinion, (25/2/13), http://cdn.ca9.uscourts.gov/datastore/general/2013/02/25/1235266.pdf, p. 12.
53. AFP (2013) 'Activist Watson gets Australian visa', 3 November, http://www.japantimes.co.jp/news/2013/11/03/asia-pacific/activist-watson-gets-australian-visa/#.UvGer1uPjCp.
54. Agence France-Presse (2013) 'At sea for months, Sea Shepherd fugitive founder disembarks', 1 November, http://www.globalpost.com/dispatch/news/afp/131031/at-sea-months-sea-shepherd-fugitive-founder-disembarks.
55. 'CR wants Sea Shepherd's Captain Watson', *The Tico Times*, http://www.ticotimes.net/2013/11/13/costa-rica-seeks-arrest-extradition-from-us-of-sea-shepherd-s-paul-watson;,http://www.costaricantimes.com/costa-rica-wants-shepherds-captain-watson/22547.
56. David Boddiger (2013) 'Costa Rica seeks arrest, extradition from US of Sea Shepherd's Paul Watson', *Tico Times*, 12 November, http://www.ticotimes.net/2013/11/13/costa-rica-seeks-arrest-extradition-from-us-of-sea-shepherd-s-paul-watson.
57. 'Japan asks France to hand over Sea Shepherd founder', *Japan Times*, 20 April 2015, http://www.japantimes.co.jp/news/2015/04/20/national/japan-asks-france-to-hand-over-sea-shepherd-founder/#.Vl0f-ICSwi5.
58. Paul Elias (2014) 'Sea Shepherd found in contempt of court in US', *Sydney Morning Herald*, 20 December, http://www.smh.com.au/environment/sea-shepherd-found-in-contempt-of-court-in-us-20141220-12bfft.html#ixzz3t2TP4GKh.
59. Ibid.
60. AFP (2015) Sea Shepherd agrees $2.55m payment to Japanese whalers for injunction breach', *The Guardian*, 10 June, http://www.theguardian.com/environment/2015/jun/10/sea-shepherd-payment-japanese-whalers-breaching-injunction.
61. Matt Reynolds (2015) 'Sea Shepherd takes whalers to High Court, Courthouse News Service', 4 May, http://www.courthousenews.com/2015/05/04/sea-shepherd-takes-whalers-to-high-court.htm.
62. Bruce Einhorn (2015) 'In whale war ceasefire, activists hunt a new target: with a halt to Japanese whaling in the Antarctic, the conservation group Sea Shepherd has started hunting toothfish poachers', *Bloomburg Business*, 3 February, http://www.bloomberg.com/news/articles/2015-02-02/in-whale-war-ceasefire-activists-hunt-a-new-target.
63. Michael Safi (2014) 'Shark cull in Western Australia may be halted after Sea Shepherd court ruling', *The Guardian*, 5 March, http://www.theguardian.com/environment/2014/mar/05/shark-cull-may-be-called-off-after-sea-shepherds-court-challenge-in-wa.
64. Caty Enders (2015) 'Can Sea Shepherds survive their own success?', *The Guardian*, 5 June, http://www.theguardian.com/environment/2015/jun/05/sea-shepherd-whale-wars-animal-planet.
65. AAP (2013) 'Japanese whalers have "worst catch" ever', *The Age*, 6 April, http://www.theage.com.au/environment/whale-watch/japan-whalers-haveworst-ever-catch-20130406-2hed5.html.
66. Enders, 'Can Sea Shepherds survive their own success?'.
67. *Whale Wars* DVD, Season 1–4.
68. Institute of Cetacean Research; Kyodo Senpaku Kaisha Ltd; Tomoyuki Ogawa; and Toshiyuki Muira v. Sea Shepherd Conservation Society and Paul Watson, United States Court of Appeals Ninth Circuit, No, 12-35266, Opinion (25/2/13), http://cdn.ca9.uscourts.gov/datastore/general/2013/02/2 5/1235266.pdf, p. 2.

69. AFP (2013) 'Activist Watson gets Australian visa', 3 November, http://www.japantimes.co.jp/news/2013/11/03/asia-pacific/activist-watson-gets-australian-visa/#.UvGer1uPjCp.
70. Martin Fackler (2010) Uncertainty buffets Japan's whaling fleet', *New York Times*, 15 May, http://www.nytimes.com/2010/05/16/world/asia/16whaling.html.
71. Hoek, 'Sea Shepherd Conservation Society v. Japanese whalers, the showdown: who is the real villain?'
72. Caprari, 'Lovable pirates? The legal implications of the battle between environmentalists and whalers in the Southern Ocean, p. 1509; Hoek, 'Sea Shepherd Conservation Society v. Japanese Whalers, the showdown: who is the real villain?', p. 162.
73. Hoek, 'Sea Shepherd Conservation Society v. Japanese Whalers, the showdown: who is the real villain?', pp. 183–4; Roeschke, 'Ecoterrorism and piracy on the high seas: Japanese whaling and the rights of private groups to enforce international conservation law in neutral waters', p. 108.
74. Moffa, 'Two competing models of activism, one goal: a case study of anti-whaling campaigns in the Southern Ocean', p. 211.
75. Craig H. Allen (2005) *Farwell's Rules of the Nautical Road* (8th edn) (Annapolis, MD: Naval Institute Press); United Nations Convention on the International Regulations for Preventing Collisions at Sea, supra note 564.
76. Institute of Cetacean Research; Kyodo Senpaku Kaisha Ltd; Tomoyuki Ogawa; and Toshiyuki Muira v. Sea Shepherd Conservation Society and Paul Watson, United States Court of Appeals Ninth Circuit, No, 12-35266, Opinion (25/2/13), http://cdn.ca9.uscourts.gov/datastore/general/2013/02/2 5/1235266.pdf, p. 2.
77. See Moffa, 'Two competing models of activism, one goal: a case study of anti-whaling campaigns in the Southern Ocean', pp. 210–11; Caprari, 'Lovable pirates? The legal implications of the battle between environmentalists and whalers in the Southern Ocean, p. 1517.
78. Institute of Cetacean Research; Kyodo Senpaku Kaisha Ltd; Tomoyuki Ogawa; and Toshiyuki Muira v. Sea Shepherd Conservation Society and Paul Watson, United States Court of Appeals Ninth Circuit, No, 12-35266, Opinion (25/2/13), http://cdn.ca9.uscourts.gov/datastore/general/2013/02/2 5/1235266.pdf, p. 2.
79. Sea Shepherd (2007) 'Japanese claims of injuries are bogus', *Sea Shepherd News*, 9 February, http://www.seashepherd.org/news/media_070209_1.html.
80. Philip Jenkins (2003) 'Fighting terrorism as if women mattered: anti-abortion violence as unconstructed terrorism', in Pamala L. Griset and Sue Mahan (eds), *Terrorism in Perspective* (London: Sage), p. 114.
81. Paul Watson cited in Andrew Darby (2007) 'Anti-whaling "pirates" get more muscle for Antarctic skirmish', *The Age*, 10 January, p. 7.
82. Jesus, 'Protection of foreign ships against piracy and terrorism at sea: legal aspects', pp. 377–8.
83. Caprari, 'Lovable pirates? The legal implications of the battle between environmentalists and whalers in the Southern Ocean, p. 1512.
84. Institute of Cetacean Research; Kyodo Senpaku Kaisha Ltd; Tomoyuki Ogawa; and Toshiyuki Muira v. Sea Shepherd Conservation Society and Paul Watson, United States Court of Appeals Ninth Circuit, No, 12-35266, Opinion (25/2/13), http://cdn.ca9.uscourts.gov/datastore/general/2013/02/2 5/1235266.pdf, p. 2.
85. Andrew Darby (2007) '"Vigilantes" hit Japanese whaling fleet', *The Age*, 13 February, p. 2.
86. Ehud Sprinzak (1998) 'The psychopolitical formation of extreme left terrorism in a democracy: the case of the Weathermen', in Walter Reich (ed.) *Origins of Terrorism: Psychologies, Ideologies, Theologies, States of Mind* (Washington, DC: Woodrow Wilson Center Press), p. 82.
87. Andrew Darby (2006) 'Attack plan on Japan's whale ships: Sea Shepherd brings faster vessel', *The Age*, 27 December, p. 7.

88. Peter Alford (2006) 'Campbell backing eco-terrorists: whalers', *The Australian*, 15 December; Darby, 'Attack plan on Japan's whale ships: Sea Shepherd brings fastervessel, p. 7; Andrew Darby (2007) 'Satellite claim in whaler search', *The Age*, 18 January, p. 12.
89. Andrew Darby (2007) 'Sea Shepherd leaves its mark on Japanese whalers', *The Age*, 17 February, p. 11.
90. Clashes continued between the Japanese and the SSCS during the 2013–14 Antarctic whaling season, with Japanese and SSCS ships colliding and the SSCS claiming that their vessel was damaged by the actions of the Japanese boat. 'Sea Shepherd releases raw footage: *Yushin Maru No. 3* hits the *Bob Barker*', Sea Shepherd Australia, 2 February 2014, http://www.seashepherd.org.au/relentless/videos/raw-footage-japanese-whaling-fleet-attacks-sea-shepherd-hits-bob-barker.html.

Conclusion

The notion of using radical and violent methods within the environmental and animal rights movements began in one country and has widened out to the entire world. Adherents argue that this is due to being increasingly frustrated at society's inability to properly protect animals and the environment.[1] For radical environmentalists political violence is recognized as a key way forward to achieve the group's goals by bypassing democratic processes and centralized power structures.[2]

For all the radical environmental groups examined here: 'Nature is seen as benevolent and representative of a higher morality. In contrast, mere human morality is seen as tarnished or corrupt. As protesters are adhering to a higher morality – the preservation of the natural world – breaking human laws is deemed to be justifiable.'[3] In order to fully understand the actions of radical environmentalists, it is thus necessary to realize that all such adherents are 'driven by an intuitive *ecological consciousness* which serves as the movement's soul force'.[4]

A key factor in the development of these radical environmental groups was their perception that mainstream environmental groups were insufficient to protect the environment. Peter Borrelli (editor of *The Amicus Journal*) argues that, 'particularly during the 1980s, many activists became increasingly disenchanted and alienated from mainstream environmental organizations. They were discouraged by the compromising attitude of mainstream groups, by the bureaucratization of the groups, by the professionalization of leaders and their detachment from the emerging concerns of grassroots supporters, and by the lack of success of mainstream organizations.'[5] Bureaucratized environmental groups were branded as 'sellouts', were unable or unwilling to lead radical protest as demanded by some frustrated activists, and saw the torch passed to groups such as Earth First!, the ELF, the ALF and the SSCS.[6]

What is clear is that, for many radical environmentalists, a breakdown of the democratic process has occurred, which has proponents believing that their actions are morally justifiable in the face of a perceived global environmental crisis.[7] The most important belief within all radical environmental groups is the acceptance that an 'environmental apocalypse is imminent' that requires immediate radical action to 'hasten the downfall of modern civilization so as to realize a better world where man will live in harmony with the natural world'.[8] According to Manes, ecoterrorists realize that:

> The significance of radical environmentalism … is based on one simple but frightening realization: that our culture is lethal to the ecology that it depends on and has been so for a long time, perhaps from the beginning. The validity of the radical environmentalism movement rises or falls depending on the accuracy of this perception.[9]

In this concluding chapter we come back to the research questions posed in the Introduction. Further, the analysis of the case studies undertaken here have yielded a number of observations about the role played by leadership; radical environmentalists' use of media to achieve their goals; and radical environmental groups' treatment of philosophy, which need to be examined in greater detail. Lastly, this conclusion will outline the lessons that can be learned for the broader study of radicalization, by having undertaken the study of the hard case of radical environmental groups.

HAVE 'ECOTERRORIST' GROUPS GROWN STRONGER OR WEAKER?

Debate continues regarding whether or not the radical environmental phenomenon is 'a growing and widespread problem'.[10] It needs to be recalled that as late as 2005 the FBI Deputy Assistant Director John Lewis announced that the ALF/ELF was the 'number one domestic terrorism threat' in the USA.[11] However, have these groups and the SSCS proved to be a credible threat both in the USA and worldwide?

Certainly the geographic reach of the ALF and the ELF affinity cells have grown over time, with evidence of cells operating at one time or another in most Western countries and some developing states: for example, Canada, France, the Netherlands, Poland and South Africa.[12] Similarly, the SSCS has set up chapters in many US states and a number of other jurisdictions, including Australia and Canada.[13]

A problem for the researcher that is yet to be resolved, however, is to determine how many ecoterrorist actions are carried out globally, given methodological issues and a paucity of accurate statistic recording by law enforcement. Many such actions are easily conflated with vandalism or not reported since they are not perceived as ecoterrorist acts, thus leading to potentially high underreporting of such incidents.[14]

For example, the FBI's statistical reporting guidelines do not take motive into account when recording crimes. Thus figures are often inaccurate since they could deliberately include vandalism with an intention of inflaming public sentiment against the broader environmental movement.[15] Further, it is often extremely difficult to determine whether an attack is 'ecoterrorist' in nature or an act of petty, non-political vandalism, particularly where no public claim was made.[16] Others maintain that the figures are underreported because the police do not treat them seriously, concerned they could be copycat crimes, reprisal attacks or concern that any publicity would lower customer confidence in the victims' organizations.[17]

Despite these methodological problems we can glean at least some insights as to the ongoing strength of the 'ecoterrorist' phenomenon from existing figures. A survey of the currently available but incomplete terrorist literature reveals that nationalist and separatist groups have conducted the most terrorist acts in nearly 40 years (4,561). However, in terms of lethality, religious terrorists have generated the highest number of injuries (36,570) and fatalities (13,113).[18] Environmental terrorism, by contrast, has occurred relatively infrequently. Moreover, it is a relatively recent phenomenon.[19]

An authoritative study by Young argues that between 1993 and 2003 there were over 1,400 ecoterrorist actions reported in the news media. In 2004, a study found that news wire reports noted over 1,1400 incidents of ecoterrorism between 1993 and 2003. Out of those attacks committed since 1980 only about 100 would be considered 'major' incidents.[20]

Overall, research suggests that incidents of ecoterrorism and direct action by groups such as Earth First!, the Earth Liberation Front (ELF), the Animal Liberation Front (ALF), the Animal Rights Militia (ARM) and Stop Huntingdon Animal Cruelty (SHAC) have decreased between 2000 and 2015, with the number of incidents significantly fewer after a high peak of 572 (worldwide) in 2008. However, it is not simply these few groups that have disbanded or ceased activity. Over the same 15-year period the pattern of decreased activity remains steadfast for incidents in which no one claimed responsibility and actions in which the above groups had no involvement.[21]

Carson et al.'s work demonstrates that attacks on property by radical environmental groups in the USA in the 1970s were quite rare but increased from the early 1980s to peak in 1989 (39 incidents). There was a small decline in 1989 but this increased throughout the 1990s (50 attacks in 1997; 90 in 2000) before peaking in 2001 with 159 events. From 1991 to 2001, total attacks increased by 90 per cent, but after 2001 there was an aggregate drop of 79 per cent through to 2007.[22] Their choice of targets suggests that they prefer to attack private property and businesses, rather than government offices.[23]

In 1993 the US Departments of Justice and Agriculture issued a report assessing the activities of radical environmental groups from 1977 to 30 June 1993. It noted that most actions were acts of 'minor vandalism' on a small scale carried out haphazardly. The report noted a total of 313 incidents, peaking in 1987, with most committed by ALF affiliated entities. In 2008 a report by the Department of Homeland Security stated that 'ecoterrorists have perpetrated more illegal acts commonly associated with terrorism on U.S. soil than any other known group' and that 'the economic cost of these acts exceeds $100 million and is likely to grow in the future'. Again, the report notes that the majority of attacks undertaken were vandalism (45 per cent).[24] The FBI asserts that between 1979 and 2008 radical environmental groups committed more than 2,000 criminal acts and caused US $110 million in damages.[25]

In terms of attacks on humans, however, beginning in the mid-1990s attacks that targeted humans rose steadily until 2005 (the high point was in 2000 with almost 120 attacks). It then fell off by about 58 per cent by 2007 when there were still over 20 attacks. In that time period incomplete records note that such attacks carried out by 'ecoterrorist' groups injured 42 people and killed three. During 1985 a group calling themselves the 'Peace Conquerors' claimed responsibility for a bombing attack on a Bayer factory in Brussels, as well as an airport in Frankfurt that killed three people. Additionally it is believed that they conducted a bombing on a Union Carbide factory in Sydney during the same year, in response to the Bhopal tragedy in India.[26]

Carson et al. note that in over 1,000 physical incidents linked to the major groups studied here there has been only one fatality. On 8 February 1990, Dr Hyram Kitchen, the Dean of the Veterinary School of the University of Tennessee, was shot and died in his home driveway. While no group claimed responsibility for the attack it did occur one month prior to animal rights groups making several threats to kill one veterinary dean every month for 12 months.[27]

While the data clearly suggests that the activities of Earth First!, the ALF and ELF have waned over the past 15 years, it is important to note that the accuracy of this information remains uncertain. What is clear from the limited information we have is that animal rights proponents are more likely than the other examined 'ecoterrorist' groups to target people. Incidents involving both the ALF and the ELF have decreased since its peak in the early 2000s.[28] Hasan argues that the subsequent decline in activity that can be observed in 2006 and 2007 would most likely be due to FBI arrests and, similarly, in the UK in 2007 arrests by the authorities led to a diminution in actions.[29]

Thus one possible explanation for why the influence of Earth First!, the ALF and the ELF has waned is that many adherents fear being arrested and that legal sanctions could impinge adversely on their future prospects, and they did not see that the benefits of proposed actions outweighed the personal costs to themselves. Rather activists were more wedded to legal options such as lobbying to achieve environmental goals.[30] If activists believe they can effect change within the system there is no need to risk legal consequences to achieve environmental goals.

Further, as Liddick argues, correctly, those groups that utilize radical methods like arson or who physically attack scientists have an 'insurmountable image problem with average citizens'.[31] Such an extremist limits the size of the activist's pool where potential adherents can be drawn from. It is also important to note that as the Western governments have increased their resources to battle these organizations, the number of arrests and convictions of activists have increased. Further, private industry – loggers, miners, animal industries and the biomedical research community – have attempted to discredit radical environmental groups via education, advertising and political lobbying and to a large extent have succeeded.[32]

While the land-based radical environmental groups have struggled, the water-based SSCS has flourished by comparison. In terms of fundraising, scale of operations and increased numbers of volunteers the SSCS continues to expand. The number of operations the SSCS has been able to mount, both in terms of numbers and breadth, has also increased. It continues to go to Antarctica but has expanded the reach of its operations to tackle such issues as whaling in the Faroe Islands, the overexploitation of fishing stocks and the killing of marine animals. The reasons why the SSCS has been so comparatively successful is that the group operates in international waters limiting law enforcement; whaling as an action remains deeply unpopular in the Western world and any action to protest against it is well-received; also the SSCS's employment of media strategies, particularly the television show *Whale Wars*, has led to it having an unusually high profile for a radical environmental group.

However, the SSCS faces a number of issues that threaten its ongoing viability. It is currently facing multiple lawsuits that have the capacity to ruin the organization. Given the hierarchical structure of the SSCS and the overreliance on the leadership of Watson, if he is extradited to Japan and unable to lead, without there being a succession plan in place such a loss could cripple the SSCS. Further, the organization is currently facing potentially ruinous legal bills or penalties from a number of legal actions brought against it. Its being declared a pirate organization not only threatens Watson's ability to freely operate but also endangers the entire SSCS's ability to function, which is why it has devolved some powers to other groups to continue operations such as protesting Japanese Antarctic whaling.

The FBI does not see an end to these organizations or their radical tactics, stating: 'It is believed these trends will persist, as extremists within the environmental movement continue to fight what they perceive as greater encroachment of human society on the natural world.'[33] Despite the evidence of the downturn in ecoterrorism activity an assessment completed by the FBI in 2010 still rated ecoterrorists as one of the most credible domestic terrorist threats in the USA, since their tactics are 'becoming increasingly violent, with threats to life, not just to property'.[34] However, the UK no longer sees them as a viable threat at this stage, going so far as to reject the label 'ecoterrorism', with the Ministry of Justice regarding such activity as mere criminal damage as opposed to terrorism.[35]

Liddick argues that the future does not look bright for radical environmental groups, as evidenced by the fact that 'changes in societal use of animals and environmental protection have been incremental and slight'.[36] However, that is when you are more likely to see a more robust radical environmental movement, in whatever guise springs up. As Darryl Cherney (Earth First!) explains, 'As the Earth's condition gets worse, radical environmentalists will become more aggressive in defense of the planet', but there is currently no evidence of this happening.[37]

Thus there is a need to improve the empirical evidentiary foundations of the phenomenon of radical environmental action. There is a lack of reliable data for a rigorous study of violent environmental radicalization. Greater colouration amongst researchers in terms of data organization (an open access database tracking incidents and group activities) would also be welcome.[38]

Without a dedicated database, one that can be contributed to by law enforcement and government officials worldwide, it will always be impossible to have an accurate and up-to-date account of activities undertaken by such clandestine groups. With a countless number of unclaimed incidents, offshoot groups and individuals and active cells in countries worldwide, a centralized database is not only necessary but the only way to track accurately the actions and status of such groups. Thus there is a need to generate more empirical studies of this ongoing phenomenon.[39]

PHILOSOPHY AND RADICAL ENVIRONMENTAL GROUPS

The role played by philosophy and its impact on radical environmental groups is an intriguing one. All the groups examined here broadly subscribe to the concept that nature is intrinsically valuable in and of itself (ecocentric) and should be protected. Earth First! and the ELF have been influenced by such diverse philosophies as anarchist thought; anti-capitalist and anti-technological approaches; misanthropic beliefs; and deep ecology. ALF adherents drew from animal rights writings by Singer and Regan as to the moral worth of animals and how humans should interact with them.

However, unlike many other radical groups historically, the majority of 'ecowarriors' examined here appear to have 'no interest in a well-conceived philosophy or in any other explicit guideposts to tell them how to live their lives'.[40] As Watson has argued – in a view that neatly encapsulates what many radical environmentalists believe – an individual can make a difference but their fervour can only be expressed through action.[41] Given the belief that an unparalleled biotic extinction event is currently under way, radical environmental adherents insist that the use of direct action was the 'real focus of their involvement in environmentalism, and environmental philosophy was more like window dressing'.[42] Arguably therefore, for the majority of adherents, philosophy is always subservient to a practical commitment to action.[43]

However, it can be observed that the overarching philosophical commitment to protecting nature appears to have an ameliorating effect on Earth First!, the ELF and the SSCS's actions in that they seek not to injure anyone in the furtherance of their cause. The exception appears to be the ALF. While animal rights philosophy does not encourage the use of violence, ALF members appear to have co-opted a strand of animal rights thought to argue that moral equivalency allows for the use of physical violence in defence of others (in this case animals). Investigating the role that various ecocentric philosophies have played in influencing radical environmental action in different ways would be a fruitful line of inquiry for radicalization researchers, with potential implications for broader radicalization analysis.

Use of the Media

Given that the examined radical environmental groups are seeking to challenge societal norms and influence public opinion, they all recognize the vital role that the media plays in influencing public debate.[44] All the groups took advantage of the burgeoning internet to publicize their activities, record their successes and seek donations to their respective causes.

It is also clear that they understand how to use the media to achieve their goals and they do so in multifaceted ways. All the surveyed groups use the media to inform society (and individual communities in some cases) of threats to the environment.[45] For example, in an article published in *Earth First! Journal*, a member's letter argued that 'the bottom line here is that as a result of all this unfavorable coverage regarding spiking, people in the West Coast are acutely aware of the crisis that exists with our forests, and our role in trying to prevent it'.[46]

All the groups also clearly understand that to draw attention to their cause they need to undertake large-sale or dramatic actions that require people to pay attention.[47] Such an approach is problematic, however, since it can lead to a need to 'up the ante' over time to require a jaded public to acknowledge their cause.

One of the reasons in particular that the SSCS has been so successful has been their use of the media to promote themselves and their cause. Watson's media training has enabled him to directly play to a global audience, particularly through his own television show, which has increased the spotlight on his cause by presenting a morality play of noble ecowarriors standing up to evil whalers. Such an approach has enabled the SSCS to receive more donations, media exposure and public approval than the other radical environmental groups surveyed here.

The Relationship between Extremism and Mainstream Organizations

All the groups examined broke off from mainstream environmental groups since they perceived that such entities were failing in their primary duty to protect the environment sufficiently or quickly enough.[48] The radical environmental groups can be easily distinguished in a number of ways. They were willing to use direct action and in some instances political violence to achieve their goals. The groups Earth First!, the ELF and the ALF tended to be poorly resourced compared with mainstream groups such as Greenpeace or the Sierra Club. Even the SSCS, which is relatively well funded for a radical environmental group, does not have the financial reserves of mainstream environmental bodies. The radical environmental groups operate autonomously (again with the exception being the SSCS) in small groups where mainstream environmental organizations are hierarchically organized, similarly to companies in many cases. However, the key distinction is philosophical, with mainstream groups adopting an anthropogenic approach while the examined groups all have some version of biocentric beliefs towards nature. The adoption of biocentric philosophical underpinnings has impacted on the goals, strategies and tactics adopted by the groups.[49]

Has 'Ecoterrorism' had a Positive Impact on the Environment Movement?

The question of whether the radical environmental organizations and their use of political violence against both property and persons has had a positive or negative impact on the environmental movement has been hotly debated.[50] According to Kamieniecki et al., many argue that 'radical environmentalists play into the hands of development and economic-growth advocates by alienating average citizens as a result of their extreme appeals and actions'.[51] Jasper and Nelkin further argue that a radical approach can be a counterproductive one. Such an approach can 'undermine the ability to engage those with competing visions in the democratic conversation necessary to develop acceptable policies'.[52]

Others argue, however, that radical actions in the movement often have the effect of creating a niche for more moderate voices to be heard and acted on.[53] Many mainstream environmentalist organizations noted that their perceived 'moderation' enabled them to obtain a better hearing in stating their case from their opponents.[54] As Watson concludes, 'because of extremism, moderates can make progress. The underground troops are simply the shock troops for the movement armies of supporters.'[55]

Arguably, the opinions expressed and the endeavours undertaken by radical environmentalists can force states and business leaders to negotiate with 'moderate', mainstream environmental groups.[56] For example, as Adele Douglass of the American Humane Association states:

> I know for a fact that the 1985 amendments to the Animal Welfare Act would never have been passed without the PETA protests and all the stuff that they were doing. Because then – and it helps us I have to say from the perspective that we're at – when you have extremists and then we come in and where the extremists say 'we want research ended this afternoon', and we say 'we want the animal treated humanely', they pay attention to us because that's the other option … I don't think the laws since at least the 1980s would have ever gotten this far without those organizations.[57] (Interview, 1996)

Radical environmental actions can also bring about lengthy delays and increase costs, allowing mainstream groups time to bring legal proceedings or utilize political processes.[58] It should also be noted that, while radicals may engage in political violence, many adherents act in ways that support the activities of more mainstream environmental groups as well.[59]

Radical environmentalism can also serve as an outlet for the broader environmental movement's frustration. Closing the 'spigot' may lead to greater political violence since a form of outlet is needed.[60]

Haines, who has written widely on the concept of radicalization, argues that radical environmentalism could result in either a positive or negative outcome. However, he warns that where the effect is negative, 'the moderates get tainted with the same brush as the radicals; this was the media's reaction to the peaceful protests associated with the live animal export trade in the UK in the mid 1990s'.[61]

Mainstream environmental groups do not want to be tarred with the same brush and will not associate in any way with these groups. It is important to note that, while many mainstream organizations (such as Sierra Club and Wilderness Society) have renounced and condemned political violence tactics, others (including PETA) have actively cheered on their actions while vowing that their organizations take no active part in such activities.[62]

Failure to Become a Mass Movement

Despite working together on a number of issues none of the groups examined here have developed into a mass movement. As Vanderheiden has noted, and this study has demonstrated, while a small number of activists may be tempted to adopt radical actions it is unlikely to spawn a mass movement. Most mainstream environmentalists have been repelled by the criminal actions of the groups and have not been willing to commit political violence (either against property or people) in the furtherance of their goals.[63] Although it is cannot be stated with certainty that radical or violent action on behalf of the environment is dead, it does appear that the phenomenon has followed the 'increasing diffusion and nihilism of other militant groups' and become moribund as a force at this time.[64]

Several other factors prevented Earth First!, the ELF and the ALF from developing into a mass movement. As Lee pointed out in the case of the ALF, and applicable to Earth First! and the ELF, is that the limitations of the affinity cell model prevented its growth to the next level. Established cells were not willing to allow new members, in case they were law enforcement, thus inhibiting adherents who were not willing to start their own affinity cells. As such the ability to share experiences and training greatly retarded the growth of these cells.[65]

Second, law enforcement efforts, particularly as regards the ALF and the ELF, have been successful in limiting ongoing operations. Given that there appears to have only ever been approximately 100 adherents in each grouping willing to commit ecotage or physical attacks, jailing entire cells has the ability to seriously disrupt group activities and growth. Third, for many activists it has not been necessary to adopt radical methods, given the successful adoption of environmental norms such as vegetarianism, care for the land and a greater appreciation of the intrinsic worth of the environment throughout most of the world. Given this, many activists are not willing to risk legal consequences such as prison if they can achieve their objectives by other effective means.

Many mainstream ENGO members are happy to support militant ecotage but draw the line at physical attacks, which limits group growth. It cannot be a mass movement if potential adherents are turned off by such attacks. Further, because there have been outlets for environmental ideas within the mainstream system over the last few decades this has reduced the 'righteous anger' of most to save the environment through the use of political violence. Thus the appeal of such radical groups has tended to be at best avante garde and has yet to generate any sort of mass following for their approach.

Of the groups examined here the SSCS appears to be the best placed to continue on in the short term, because of their resources and funding strength. However, as noted earlier, in the long term they are vulnerable because their hierarchical structure is dominated by their charismatic leader Paul Watson. If he dies or is jailed the organization may not survive his loss, given that there appears to be no strong heir apparent. Further, if he is jailed, as Japan clearly hopes, this would make him a martyr, which may boost his cause but, despite his claims in the past to be willing to be jailed (or die) for the cause, Watson clearly does not want that role.

Despite the failure to individually or collectively develop into a mass movement there is a great deal of evidence that the groups have worked together when the goal has been the same. Given their similarities in both aims and structure it is not surprising that Earth First!, the ALF and the ELF have at times carried out missions together. An early Earth First! activist, who was also involved in the ALF organization said:

> A good way to approach the hunt saboteurs because they are already into [a] sort of direct action and it is quite easy to show them the links … if you are going to save the fox from the hunt why let it be killed by a contractor … the thing that really appealed to me initially was the deep ecology that I saw as an extension of the animal liberation idea.[66]

Law agencies in Europe believe that cells from both groups have staged strategically organized attacks dating back to at least 1990.[67]

Leader argues that since the ELF 'declared solidarity' in 1993 with the ALF, the two groups have been closely linked and have shared leaders, members, tactical knowledge, agendas and funding sources.[68] For example, following actions at the Great Lakes, there were a number of actions carried out by the two groups in concert.[69] On 14 March 1997, following the spiking of 47 trees in the Robinson Scott Clearcut area in Oregon, a communiqué was released by the 'Animal Liberation Front Eco-Animal Defense Unit', claiming the action was a joint campaign between the ELF and ALF and 'warned of more collaborative actions to come'. Several days later, the 'Bay Area Cell of the Earth and Animal Liberation Front' claimed joint responsibility for an arson attack on an animal research facility at the University of California.[70]

The ALF and ELF relationship has included activists (such as Rodney Coronado and Craig Rosebraugh) who actively participate in both groups and Coronado has also been linked to bombing campaigns of whaling ships carried out by the SSCS. Until 2003, the ALF and the ELF released official public statements through NAELFPRO. Philip Celetini (FBI special agent in the Domestic Terrorism Operations Unit) has said, '[radical environmentalism] is the most vexing and troublesome issue that the FBI investigates, [and] we don't think for a minute that these groups are entirely different sets of people'.[71]

However, despite the groups working together occasionally it needs to be understood that extreme 'ideological differences' remain and they are best understood as different 'distinct subcultures' and that perhaps a dozen adherents supported both groups.[72] While radical environmentalists seek to encourage an 'ecosystem-and-species-focused ethic', animal liberationists concentrate primarily on the 'well-being of individual, sentient animals'.[73] There is also little evidence that the ALF and ELF are or have been directly coordinating actions.[74]

While some activists who joined Earth First! had experience with 'militant animal rights networks', the two movements were more similar in the 1970s than in later decades. Violent acts of sabotage by the ALF were largely denounced and criticized in *Peace News* and many activists involved in the environmental movement believed the animal liberation movement was 'too single issue'.[75] These fundamental differences will, arguably, decrease the amount of future collaboration between the two groups.

RADICALIZATION THEORY AND RADICAL ENVIRONMENTAL GROUPS

Critics of radical environmental actions have freely utilized the term 'ecoterrorist' to impugn their opponents. However, the majority of radical environmental activists deny the notion that their actions equate to terrorism. They argue that, if the appellation 'ecoterrorist' must be used it is more suitable for despoilers of nature such as corporations.[76] Scholars examining this issue have also tended to fall into these two camps. Vanderheiden and Anster constituting one wing argue that such radical environmental groups should not be classified this way since they do not target humans. Similarly, Liddick argues they should not be considered so since they focus on causing property damage, not going after humans physically. On the other hand, Perlstein argues that they should be considered terrorists not the pranksters they seek to portray themselves as, since not doing so does a disservice to the true threat they pose.[77]

Watson attempts to thread this rhetorical needle by arguing that 'it depends on who is judging the actions. Accusations of terrorism are usually subjective.'[78] Liddick further points out that even the language and labels that are utilized to describe radical environmentalism are filled with biases both for and against. As an example, while activists refer to their acts as 'direct action', the government has labelled such behaviour as 'ecoterrorism'.[79]

The argument and narrative presented here suggests that, like other forms of political violence, 'ecoterrorist' actions are an incremental process. Members have turned towards more robust forms of protest following their belief that working within the system would not permit them to achieve their objectives. It will be recalled that some terrorism definitions not only claim that the act constitutes violence or the threat of violence against non-combatants to achieve political goals, but also targeting property for the same intentions.[80] In all instances, radical environmental groups have committed violent acts against property. In other countries, there are individuals who the state and its officials consider ecoterrorists (but have not *de jure* convicted them as such), who have been incarcerated for substantial periods for committing politically motivated violent acts for environmental causes. Such statements suggest that broader forms of environmental political violence may conform to Sprinzak's model.

History teaches that extremist-group violence tends to escalate if the group's approach does not bring about the desired results.[81] However, as Barcott points out, 'it's difficult to mark the exact moment when a radical advocate chooses to cross the line separating civil disobedience from violent crime'.[82] Using the modified Sprinzak analysis that focuses primarily on group dynamics but also examines individual behaviour can glean some important insights into both radical environmental violence and broader radicalization trends.

Are Such Groups Becoming More Violent?

According to a reporter, Stoner, there is solid proof that radical environmental groups were becoming more violent over time. He provided, as an example, a case in Virginia in which 'the ELF publicly made a statement that some of its followers will no longer hesitate to pick up the gun to implement justice'.[83] However, an examination of the statistics relating to the examined groups reveal a more complex picture than the one Stoner portrays. First there is the question of the number of incidents that are occurring globally. Secondly, are the groups targeting humans for more physical violence?

Hasan also argues that to demonstrate that radical environmental groups were utilizing increasingly violent approaches, several pieces of evidence can be considered. Certainly if we examine the early years of both the ALF and Earth First! their focus was small militant actions (the ALF with liberation operations and Earth First! with stunts and small acts of ecotage). By the mid-1980s ALF operatives had graduated to bombing campaigns against animal researchers and ELF operatives in the USA were committing large-scale arson attacks. Hasan's study indicates that the number of serious incidents (bombings, physical assaults) increased by a factor of two, led primarily by the Animal Rights Militia and Justice Department groups. He argues that from 2000 to 2007 'serious incidents increased triple the amount' of previous periods. For example, on 19 April 2000, in Dinah, France, a McDonald's employee was killed by a firebomb while in October 1999 Graham Hall, a journalist critical of the ALF, was kidnapped at gunpoint and branded with the letters 'ALF' on his back.[84]

Numerous other actions are put forth as evidence that the radical environmental groups are ready to institute mass killings. For example, a 1989 plot to destroy the Palo Verde nuclear facility; the 1991 threats to put rat poison into soft drinks as a protest over scientific and animal testing; and in 2000 the leaving of three jars of cyanide in Minneapolis to protest animal genetic engineering.[85] However, these incidents do not appear to be linked to the groups studied here.

The most extreme case with regards to the use of biological warfare relates to RISE, a small cell of ecological extremists who in 1972 had a plan to destroy humanity via the mechanism of infectious diseases. The group's ideology was very similar to current radical environmental groups (except its ideology was much more extreme) and the demography of RISE and the ELF were similar in comprising young, male adherents.[86]

In October 1994, a group called the David Organisation was involved in protesting 'clearcutting' in British Columbia, Canada. The group in a public letter threatened to 'poison the courts, the Crown Counsel and various forest companies, which mentioned using the ventilation system. The group also issued death threats against the Chief Justice.' The police later discovered 'harmless garden insecticides' in a planter at a forest company and on an elevator at the regional Crown Counsel offices.[87]

There is certainly evidence that certain cells or individuals linked to the ALF or the ELF were willing to commit political violence against their perceived enemies. Death threats (especially within the timber community) were common. According to Shep Tucker (spokesman for Louisiana Pacific, whose Cloverdale mill was the target of a failed bomb attack in 1990): 'many people received threats ... We've had bomb threats. People have been tailgated. They've phoned in the middle of the night.'[88] However, they were clear examples where cells or individuals were willing to go beyond threats. In 1980 ecosaboteurs tried to disrupt a desert motorcycle race from Barstow, California, to Las Vegas through the East Mojave. They placed railroad ties to block off a section of the course in a tunnel that the racers were using. If they had not been spotted it might have killed some riders.[89]

Fran Trutt of Queens, New York, wanted to kill Leon C. Hirsch, chairman and CEO of US Surgical (whose firm conducted animal research experiments), with a pipe bomb but was apprehended first. In 1990 someone planted a car bomb trying to kill Margaret Baskerville, a veterinary officer from the Ministry of Defense Porton Down chemical research centre who only escaped by 'diving out of her car window as it burst into flames'.[90] In April 2010 an 'Italian anarchist group' Il Silvestre, who were reportedly on a mission to blow up an unfinished IBM nanotechnology facility was stopped by police on the way to the operation. It was believed that the attempted attack was 'part of a new co-ordinated wave of eco-terror on the continent'. The group emerged in Tuscany, Italy and is considered one of the up-and-coming ecoterrorist groups in Europe, 'with a rigid cell structure, access to explosives, and a membership that supposedly has no qualms about killing to achieve its goals'.[91]

These examples demonstrate it is not inconceivable that radical environmental groups or individuals could utilize chemical or biological agents if they thought it would further their cause. However, to date there is no evidence that groups are seeking such agents, nor at present are there 'specific ideological imperatives *prescribing* their use' from any active group.[92]

On the other hand, Bron Taylor, who has to date carried out probably the most extensive ethnographic study of radical environmentalist groups, maintains they are unlikely to become more violent. He believes that the 'violent rhetoric of radical environmentalists tends to be exactly that – rhetoric, rather than reality – and often is inappropriately taken out of context by the movement's opponents'.[93] To date there is still little evidence of violence being utilized to cause injuries or death or create campaigns designed to elicit terror amongst the global public by the examined case studies (excepting the ALF and some rare occurrences).[94]

Explanatory Force of Radicalization Models

Sprinzak's delegitimation model mapped on to Wright-Neville's activist to militant to terrorist labels has proved useful in understanding how the groups evolved over time. To varying degrees they all have used political violence in the furtherance of their goals. The key issue has been whether they have moved from militant to terrorist. Of the radical environmental groups examined the ALF comes closest to hewing to Sprinzak's process theory expected outcomes, in what we can clearly observe. From Hunt Saboteurs activists only using non-violent direct action, through to adopting militant actions under the auspices of the Band of Mercy and the formation of the ALF and its 'offshoots' to carry out political violence culminating in a willingness to target humans, all fit the paradigm suggested by Sprinzak of how terrorist groups come into existence.

Further, we can observe that Lee and his followers did experience a crisis of confidence over society's attitude to animals. Lee and his adherents became frustrated at the slow pace of change and were determined to do something about it. They first engaged in small acts of ecotage and liberation raids before graduating to arson and then hoaxes against the general public and attacks on those deemed enemies of the cause. Some of the affinity cells travelled along the radicalization continuum to the point where, perceiving the world on only 'us and them' terms, they were willing to kill humans in the pursuit of their cause. For those adherents the world, as Sprinzak's model predicted, became a Manicheistic one of cosmic importance, with them as the good guys and their opponents as evil that could be spoken of in derogatory terms.[95] Their enemy became depersonalized and dehumanized as expressed through their epithets for them, to the point they were willing to target them since they were seen as having less moral worth than the animals they hurt and that the ALF adherents were determined to protect.[96] There is more than enough evidence to suggest that the ALF and its *nom de guerres* of ARM, JD and SHAC were, given their targeting of humans for harm, willing to carry out terrorist acts in pursuit of their goals. The purpose of terrorism is to instil fear, or to terrorize, and it is clear that ALF adherents under both their own name and other pseudonyms were willing to use personal violence to that end. This is evidenced not only by the reaction of their targets, but also by the response of the 'larger target audience'.[97]

The operating ALF philosophy, unlike the other group's viewpoints that equate human life with animal existence, allowed adherents to justify their political violence as 'defence of another'. Sprinzak's theory would tell us at this stage that followers would be willing to engage in other types of criminality or non-conventional sexual activity, but there is no evidence of this occurring.[98] Rather, most adherents appear to be members of the broader environmental community and ordinary, productive members of society, except due to their personal philosophy and political beliefs they are willing to carry out terrorist acts in defence of animals.

The application of Sprinzak's approach to the other groups examined here yields more nebulous results. In terms of Earth First! the Sprinzak approach holds up, at least initially. Earth First! initially only engaged in non-violent activities before engaging in ecotage (a militant action). The founders of Earth First! clearly suffered a crisis of confidence, experiencing a 'profound disenchantment' with current societal attitudes to the environment.[99] The group also adhered to the countercultural aspect of Sprinzak's model in their annual meetings (Roundups) and the rejection of prevailing cultural mores.[100] It also appears that initially they were seeking to challenge the current political system and its interactions with the biosphere, with the aim of changing human behaviour and human consciousness.[101]

They entered the conflict of legitimacy stage when offshoots like EMETIC began ecotage but the vast majority of cells remained committed to civil disobedience tactics or small acts of ecotage. Nor is there any evidence of small-scale physical violence happening at this time. The FBI rated Earth First! merely a 'soft core' terrorist group, so designated because it was not willing to deliberately kill.[102]

Generally Sprinzak's theory maintains that a radical group goes on through stages until it reaches the crisis of legitimacy stage. If it does not it is not considered to be a terrorist group. Here, though, there was a split within the organization with an Earth First! faction led by Judi Bari that did not wish to engage in ecotage; Earth First! members who wanted to commit political violence in the form of ecotage went on to found the ELF so that they could continue militant actions.

The ELF has been known to use derogatory language about their opponents,[103] and has dabbled in misanthropic statements and the need to winnow the human populace.[104] However, there is no evidence that adherents engaged in other forms of criminality or non-conventional sexual activity. Affinity cells have not been willing to threaten or use physical force against humans (except where protesters placed cyanide canisters at a genetic engineering conference) but have been willing to engage in arson. It is arguable therefore that a sustained arson campaign could well be characterized as sufficient for a group to enter Sprinzak's third stage. However, while the activities may well mean that that cell graduated to terrorist activities, the majority of ELF cells have merely engaged in smaller-scale ecotage that would not meet the criteria.

It is clear that the initial phase mapped out by Sprinzak also applies to the SSCS. Watson was originally a member of Greenpeace, dedicated to civil disobedience but finding the organization's strictures too rigorous. The SSCS was founded to engage in more militant action in the belief that the international system of marine protection, as currently configured, was incapable of protecting sealife (crisis of confidence). Thus we can easily observe that they entered into the conflict of legitimacy stage, but it is not clear they entered the crisis of legitimacy stage and engaged in terrorist acts.

There is no public evidence that SSCS members have engaged in derogatory language aimed at their opponents. Further, while they have engaged in butyric acid attacks on Japanese whaling ships, have been (most likely falsely) accused of the attempted murder of Costa Rican fishermen, and have sunk whaling ships in harbours they appear to do everything they can to avoid 'terrorist' acts. Watson has maintained that while he is willing to damage whaling ships to force them to return to dock he is not willing to commit direct physical violence against their opponents.[105] Nor is there any evidence of the group's members perceiving they are engaged in an apocalyptic battle against the forces of evil that would allow them to directly use physical force against their opponents. Thus it cannot be stated that the SSCS has fully entered into the crisis of legitimacy stage.

If we are seeking to understand the actions of the SSCS rather than use Sprinzak's approach they are better understood in the way that Director General of the Institute for Cetacean Research Hiroshi Hatanaka has publicly labelled them: vigilantes.[106] Vigilantes do not perceive themselves to be in principled conflict with the state or the law; they are not revolutionary nor are they trying to end government authority. Rather they believe that the government is failing to create or enforce their laws, thus requiring them to take on that role to effect justice.[107] As Sprinzak has noted, vigilantes do not consider themselves to be in violation of the law but rather are upholding the law. As noted previously, while their argument that they are upholding established international law is dubious there is no doubt that they are willing to press those claims in the service of their cause.

Although probably calling them 'vigilantes' pejoratively, Hatanaka was somewhat accurate in his assessment. It will be recalled that Sprinzak argues that vigilantes do not consider themselves to be violating the law. In fact, they view themselves as upholding the law, and are only acting in such a manner because the status quo is unable to maintain the proper legal order. Nevertheless, there needs to be some clarifications in regards to the Sea Shepherds as a vigilante group. Sprinzak's comments are intended to reflect the politics of right-wing vigilante groups. Clearly, the SSCS is more left-wing in orientation. Moreover, usually left-wing groups intend to overthrow, not uphold the social order.

Additionally, Sprinzak also claims that vigilante groups tend not to offer a new social vision. On this matter the SSCS is clearly in status quo maintenance mode regarding legislation. However, as mooted previously, they might be offering an alternative blueprint by introducing the notion of species equality. In some respects, therefore, it may be possible to consider the SSCS a new type of vigilante group.

Vigilantism should not generally be confused with terrorism, but under serious pressure vigilantes undergo a process of delegitimization that can push them towards terrorist acts.[108] Such groups, however, generally act out only against perceived lawbreakers unless sufficiently harassed by government agents to decide to confront the state.[109]

Sprinzak's analysis has been usually applied to right-wing vigilante groups but there is no reason they cannot apply to groups of a left-wing persuasion such as the SSCS, even though they do not, as left-wing groups usually do, desire to overthrow the existing social order. However, contrary to Sprinzak's claim that vigilante groups do not tend to offer an alternative and competing social vision, the SSCS does offer such with their vision of how humans should interact with marine life. Consequently the SSCS should not be considered an ecoterrorist group but perhaps a new type of vigilante.

In these respects, it may be possible to question whether the Sea Shepherds are a unique case in that they constitute a blind spot in the scholarly literature on terrorism and political violence, or whether individual states, several states or the international community may be turning a blind eye to anti-terrorism legislation because of reluctance or inability to enforce legislation. More research needs to be undertaken to better understand the interstices between conventional vigilante groups and the SSCS.

The Sprinzak analysis would suggest that attacks would become more violent but, except in the case of the ALF, there appears to be a ceiling in terms of the level of violence they are willing to commit. While in the case of the ELF individual cells have committed arson and there have been isolated threats made against those considered to be enemies, such tactics have not escalated in recent decades nor have the number of incidents increased. Similarly, while the SSCS has engaged in personal attacks, they have tended to be low-level incidents such as throwing butyric acid at Japanese whaling ships, which could potentially harm someone.

Why does there appear to be an upper limit to the violence that the SSCS and the ELF are willing to undertake, when the analysis would suggest that such groups tend to continue ratcheting up violence, as was the case with the ALF? In the case of the SSCS it might be because their current campaigns, and the publicity generated by their actions and tactics, have been quite effective. While the ELF has not been as effective in advancing its cause, the fear of law enforcement as well as successful campaigns carried out by the authorities and the achievement of environmental goals by other means may all have played a part.

For Earth First!, the ELF and the SSCS, it may well be that their operating philosophies that prioritize life and living in harmony with the world may have had an ameliorating effect on the vast majority of activists who do not wish to carry out the same tactics as their opponents. While there may be some willing to fight 'fire with fire' they appear to be in the minority at present.

Even the ALF, however, appears to have stepped back from its use of targeting of humans and has regressed to carrying out liberation raids and mostly smaller-scale arson. This is mostly due to the success that law-enforcement has had in successfully prosecuting the more violent cells, but also may be a tacit acknowledgement that such tactics do not work given the loss of public support engendered by such actions. Certainly any process model needs to account for why this has occurred.

It can certainly be observed that all groups examined have certainly reached the second stage predicted by Sprinzak in that committing small acts of violence is acceptable. In particular, all groups are comfortable with causing property damage but they all still insist that they minimize loss of life and injury to humans.

The question of whether the ecoterrorist groups *intend to harm humans* is significant. It has already been established that all groups purport that they are not interested in harming humans. However, as indicated earlier, despite their intentions not to harm humans there is a distinct possibility in virtually every one of their actions that they may cause some injuries or perhaps even deaths, and therefore consistently put lives at risk through the actual or implied use of violence for political purposes. To use a colloquialism: their normal operations may be a lethal terrorist act waiting to happen.

While publicly the ALF and the ELF promote non-violence towards human life there is always the possibility that some adherents may decide to escalate their attacks, which historically has occurred with occasional cells like the Family.[110] However, this is less likely to happen with the SSCS given its hierarchical structure and strong leadership, unless Watson himself chooses to escalate, which given current SSCS successes appears unlikely.

However, when examining where the next 'ecoterrorist' threat is likely to be, the danger is not so much from radical environmental groups but rather from lone wolves who have become progressively radicalized,[111] individuals such as the Unabomber, and James Lee who was involved in a hostage stand-off at Discovery Communication headquarters in Silver Spring before being killed. Lee wrote in an internet communiqué that 'humans are the most destructive, filthy, pollutive creatures around and are wrecking what's left of the planet with their false morals and breeding culture … and nothing is more important than saving animals: the lions, tigers, giraffes, elephants, froggies, turtles, apes, raccoons, beetles, ants, sharks, bears, and, of course, the squirrels'.[112] Predicting and tracking such individuals remains far more problematic for both law enforcement officials and radicalization researchers.

McCauley and Moskalenko note that radicalization is underwritten by a 'syndrome of beliefs' about the current state of the world. Generally radicals believe that: 'We are a special or chosen group (superiority) who have been unfairly treated and betrayed (injustice), no one else cares about us or will help us (distrust) and the situation is dire – our group and our cause are in danger of extinction (vulnerability).'[113] However, what is different about radical environmental groups is that the sense of being unfairly treated is not about themselves but rather on behalf of other species and the global environment.

However, it is not clear that ecoterrorism groups are displaying antinomian norms of behaviour as Sprinzak predicts they would. Activists do not appear to want to violently overthrow governments. Rather, the revolution they seek is rather creating a societal change in norms.

Further, the landlocked groups have, in many cases, focused on defeating corporate action. Only the Sea Shepherds have focused primarily on the actions of whaling states such as Japan and Norway with an aim to defeat state action.

Leaders and Radicalization

The leader is a key figure in the study of radicalization since they often recruit and radicalize members – and so it has proved here in the cases examined.[114] Foreman, Lee and in particular Watson have had an outsized impact on the groups they helped found, and in Watson's case continue to lead, and have often been described by their followers as charismatic. Peter Nesser's work argues that where the process of radicalization occurs there is usually a charismatic, idealistic leader keenly interested in politics and activism.[115] Can we see that occurring here?

Leaders of radical groups tend to be self-assured, eloquent and resourceful, and compared to their followers they tend to be better educated, slightly older and more knowledgeable about key issues. They are politically and ideologically conscious and tend to set the group's parameters on ideology and use of violence.[116] We can observe to varying degrees that the leaders of these radical environmental groups do conform to this description.

They have proven to be generally older (but not always) than their acolytes; confident, knowledgeable and eloquent in their vision for a better society that embraces environmental mores; resourceful; and university-educated (Watson being the only leader not to complete university study). They are also clearly well-read in both strategic thinking and philosophy as well as politically and ideologically aware. Where the description differs is in regards to the degree of control they exercise on their group's ideology and the use of political violence. While Watson does set the SSCS parameters for its operational ideology and use of political violence as a tactic, both Lee and Foreman helped formulate their respective group's philosophies and use of political violence but then refused to continue leading their groups, preferring to devolve such responsibilities to individual anarchic cells.

The question, though, is whether the key formative leaders of each group should be considered charismatic. When examining terrorism groups and their leaders, researchers have often fallen back on describing leaders as charismatic to help explain how a group has formed or become successful. However, to merely say a terrorist leader is charismatic is not analytically helpful.[117] Thus there is a need to understand what charisma is in relation to leadership and how it impacts on radicalization. While charismatic leadership is not present in every terrorist movement, it does appear to operate concurrently with an ongoing process of radicalization. However, the issue needs to be empirically investigated further and the environmentally radical groups examined here allow us to do so.[118]

Charisma is often used merely to describe that a leader is very popular or influential over their acolytes.[119] Hofmann and Dawson provide a more nuanced definition of charisma (while admitting that such a definition does not fully capture the complexity of the term) when they describe it as: 'a quality attributed to individuals who are thought to possess exceptional abilities, particularly to influence and inspire others, which are not available to the rest of us. *Charismatic authority* is the accepted power to lead and command others stemming from the recognition of this quality.'[120] Charismatic leaders can be distinguished from other types of leaders, 'by their ability to formulate and articulate an inspirational vision and by behaviors and actions that foster an impression that they and their mission are extraordinary'.[121]

However problematically, both Nesser and Slootman and Tillie's research does not explain the difference between a violent radical charismatic leader and those equally charismatic individuals who share the same sense of outrage but elect to work within the system.[122] All three leaders examined – Watson, Lee and Foreman – meet the simplest definition of a charismatic leader at least initially, but Dawson's analysis provides us a way to drill down and examine the role played by charismatic leaders. Do the three leaders here meet these criteria?

Dawson maintains that certain factors can be observed where true charismatic leaders exploit social crises to try to achieve their objectives. One, the crisis will be seen as 'acute' or 'chronic' and also as bringing about total and permanent change ('ultimate phase'). The role of the leader is to make others see that the crisis being faced fits in the ultimate category. Two, there needs to be a breakdown or threat of such an occurrence of the existing social order. Again, a leader can play a key part in promoting such a view. If society breaks down people become 'charisma hungry' as they search for solutions. Three, such leaders can more easily emerge in societies that welcome their appearance. Strategically, a charismatic leader's message must resonate with their intended mass audience if they are to effectively claim special authority. Lastly, the leader must believe that they hold the solution and can convince others this is so. Thus it has been observed that such individuals tend to verge on the messianic.[123]

All three leaders examined here fit the above criteria in their ability to utilize societal crises to try to enact their goals. All three have argued that there was an acute ecological crisis in the way humans interacted with the environment and that they could offer solutions. Their varying messages also deeply resonated with a portion of the populace that had come of age in societies that were already beginning to rethink their relationship with global ecological processes but were afraid that solutions were not being found quick enough to stave off an environmental catastrophe.

Charismatic leaders also need to both attain and manage power by demonstrating their strength. Dawson points out that all charismatic leaders face four structural challenges: (1) maintaining the leader's image; (2) moderating the psychological identification of the followers with the leader; (3) negotiating the routinization of charisma; and (4) achieving new successes. When applied to terrorist groups, Hofmann and Dawson argue, failure to meet these challenges may see a terrorist group – one that is heavily reliant on a charismatic leader – escalate or increase extreme violent acts.[124]

In terms of Watson though we have seen this occurring. For decades Watson has managed to remain tightly in control of the organization he founded, by arguing he was willing to die or go to jail for whales (not true) and articulating a vision that he and his group need to enforce international law when no state will. The SSCS is very reliant on their inspirational figurehead, but while violence against primarily property – and some physical attacks on a small scale – have occurred there is no evidence of an increase in violence. This is primarily because Watson has put a great deal of effort into burnishing his personal image and has had a number of key successes in stopping pirate whaling ships and effectively hindering Japanese Antarctic whaling operations.

Lee and Foreman are more complex cases. Rather than being leaders in the true sense, given the non-hierarchical nature of the organizations they created they might be better thought of as initial leaders that developed into figureheads for their respective organizations. Neither sought to retain power, as the Dawson model presupposes, at all costs and both left their respective groups in disillusionment: Foreman, when he believed Earth First! had lost its way; and Lee, when he believed the ALF could not become a mass movement in the mould he wished it to be.

Charismatic leaders, at least initially, were essential to the early success of such groups but with those leaders in the ALF and Earth First! refusing to take up the mantle as ongoing charismatic leaders, and the ELF never developing a leader, given its commitment to the affinity cell model, these groups appear unable to live up to the potential that their early leaders envisaged. The topic of charismatic leadership is also an area of study that would benefit from a more detailed examination of the concept and its impact on the radicalization of environmental groups.

WHAT TYPE OF PERSON BECOMES AN 'ECOTERRORIST'?

This study has shown that it is impossible to determine what 'type' of person becomes an 'ecoterrorist'. There are too many differing kinds of persons – genders, differing classes, occupations, ages, those who come from 'normal' homes who have joined the examined radical environmental groups. What can be discerned is that they tend to have no personal profit for their actions.[125] That is one of the strengths of radical environmentalism – it drew and continues to draw from a wide array of potential candidates.

This makes it almost impossible for researchers and law enforcement to generate any kind of profile of a 'typical ecoterrorist'. However, there are a few observations that can be made. It is clear from the case studies that while some members join for the excitement (particularly Earth First! and the ELF followers) most adherents feel a deep emotional attachment to the Earth, the biosphere or animals, or a combination of these factors.[126]

What is also clear is that they do, in line with radicalization theories, perceive themselves as being 'more aware' of ongoing environmental destruction, differing from the general public who lack such awareness and can be dismissive of those not on the 'inside' of the movement, tending to refer to them in derogatory terms.[127] Some members tend to see themselves as morally superior by engaging in their 'fight' and this can be a key to understanding their behaviours.

Further, many tend to see themselves as freedom fighters fighting a terrible enemy that needs to be defeated, which can lend itself to a Manicheistic outlook that can easily tip over into perceiving your opponents as an 'evil enemy' that needs to be defeated by any means necessary.[128] It can also be observed that for many followers, as per Neumann and Rogers's radicalization theory, becoming a radical environmentalist can provide people with a mission in life, though there is again evidence that some people do this for only a short time, while for others it is a life-long calling. According to Eric Hoffer:

> The burning conviction that we have a holy duty towards others is often a way of attaching our drowning selves to a passing raft. What looks like giving a hand is often a holding on for dear life. Take away our holy duties and you

> leave our lives puny and meaningless. There is no doubt that in exchanging a self-centered for a selfless life we gain enormously in self-esteem. The vanity of the selfless, even those who practice utmost humility, is boundless.[129]

Sprinzak's analysis maintains that members who become more militant tend to isolate themselves from the broader community, but there is scant evidence of this appearing here (outside of lone-wolf individuals).[130] Many are either involved with their local communities or the larger environmental movement. Further, the groups did not tend to impose on adherents a new set of behavioural and moral standards.

Analysis of the case studies indicates that most followers were committed to moral behaviour, such as vegetarianism, before becoming adherents. At best we can talk of a reinforcement of previous beliefs from being in a situation where others also share your beliefs regarding humanity's place in the world. Such cells or trips to Antarctica to confront Japanese whaling tend to forge a close group identity and an adherence to the overarching mission that can lead to the commitment of political violence.[131] However, these individual groupings, except in the case of some ALF cells, have not risen to the point where they perceive their struggle in such stark 'good guys versus bad guys' terms that they are willing to inflict personal violence against humans.

Sageman's 'band of guys' radicalization analysis is clearly not broadly applicable to the radical environmental movement. While Earth First! and the ELF have had a number of young men attracted to them, even they have had multiple women in positions of power and volunteering for ecotage missions, whilst the ALF and the SSCS have also seen women involved at all levels.[132]

What has been revealed by this study is that, while it has generated some insights, a more complete examination at the individual level, preferably a global survey approach of the various radical environmental group adherents, needs to be undertaken to understand what drives someone to become a radical environmentalist.

POLITICAL VIOLENCE AND THE PRACTICE OF ECOTAGE

The question of whether ecotage should be considered political violence is one that continues to vex analysts and adherents alike. The adoption of ecotage by the examined radical environmental groups has proved to be an effective tactic against those deemed environmental despoilers by making such destruction unprofitable.[133] It has also in some cases engendered public sympathy and awareness of a particular issue, leading to a cessation of environmental exploitation.[134] However, its use has led to an ongoing debate over whether such a strategy can be morally and operationally justified. Proponents like Foreman claim that ecotage is not a violent act. He contends that:

> [a]ctions against property ought to be judged in terms of broad political purposes and not on the moral distinction between violent and non-violent behavior. In other words, property's meaning is socially constructed, and actions resulting in its destruction need to be judged within a historical and political context.[135]

Further, according to Foreman, 'as long as no one is hurt, the practice is seen as consistent with the deep ecology axiom that diversity of life (including human) is more important than the integrity of inanimate objects that are used to diminish diversity of life'.[136] However, it is argued by critics of the practice that radical environmentalists cannot claim to be non-violent while engaging in ecotage, because of the risk of accidental injury or death.[137]

Vanderheiden argues that the conducting of ecotage, while objectionable, should not be classified as terrorism but rather should be considered to be on the spectrum between civil disobedience and terrorist acts.[138] Adopting such a distinction would see ecotage more consistent with militant acts rather than terrorism. While such an approach has much to recommend it, it does not allow for large-scale property attacks using arson or explosives that have been utilized by adherents linked to all groups and which should be considered in some cases more terrorist acts. Thus the proposed scale of actions needs to be amended to allow for the possibility that in certain circumstances and of sufficient scale, ecotage is not merely a militant act but a terrorist one.

In many ways 'ecoterrorism' is a hard case for students of radical behaviour. This is because it is clear that radical environmental groups are willing in some limited cases to use political violence that flows through to utilizing personal violence. However, groups have tended not to adopt officially such positions and in the majority of cases have not undertaken such attacks as opposed to terrorist groups such as Al Qaeda and the Weathermen. There are also some outstanding issues raised here, which radicalism researchers will have to come to terms with if they are to develop a robust theoretical model that can be applied successfully to radical environmental action.

Sprinzak's process theory of left-wing terrorist development, venerable as it may be, has had trouble – as this book has demonstrated – in accounting sufficiently for all the examined ecoterrorist groups' evolution. The assumptions built into the model seem unable to account for the ecoterrorist insistence on the need not to harm sentient beings and to focus on property damage rather than progressing in all cases to experiencing a crisis of legitimacy that presages political violence on a large scale or targeted against humans. Similarly, individual theories of the radicalization of adherents have also proved not terribly helpful when determining the types of people likely to join such groups, nor was it helpful when it came to understanding the gender politics at play.

While time will tell if Sprinzak's conception of political violence is correct and ecoterrorist groups will progress to the third 'crisis of legitimacy' stage, with the exception of the ALF there appears little evidence to date that the groups examined, except in isolated instances, have reached that threshold. Wright-Neville's activist to militant to terrorist nomenclature is useful as shorthand but does not fully capture the fluidity of the radicalization spectrum, particularly with the classification of large-scale ecotage. Either new stages need to be considered that more accurately reflect empirical evidence or the description needs to be abandoned in favour of more fluid, dynamic descriptors.

Radical environmentalism is at an interesting point in its history. For groups like Earth First!, the ELF and the ALF there appears to be an interregnum phase where they have lost societal support, adherents and appear unsure what strategies and tactics are best suited to achieve their goals. The more hierarchically structured group like the SSCS is currently going from strength to strength. If land-based radical environmental groups are to survive as a political force they would do well to examine the SSCS structure and perhaps seek to emulate some aspects such as its media strategy, fund-raising approach and its charismatic leadership model.

The gains made by the mainstream environmental movement appear to be enough to satiate the vast majority of environmental activists, robbing the radical environmental groups of a large enough pool from which to draw adherents. However, if activists come to believe that the survival of the planet is at stake, perhaps in the wake of a global environmental catastrophe or a perception that the problem of anthropomorphic climate change is not being suitably addressed, and despairing of mainstream political solutions, they may choose to adopt violence against fellow humans as a legitimate tactic.[139]

NOTES

1. Hasan T. Arslan (2008) 'The social and operational intersections of environmental extremism in North America and Europe' (PhD dissertation, Sam Houston State University, Huntsville, TX), pp. 1–2.
2. Derek Wall (1999) *Earth First! and the Anti-Roads Movement: Radical Environmentalism and Comparative Social Movements* (London and New York: Routledge), p. 154.
3. Jay Hasbrouck (2005) 'Primitive dissidents: Earth Liberation Front and the making of a radical movement' (PhD dissertation, University of Southern California, Los Angeles, CA), pp. 119–20.
4. Rik Scarce (2006) *Eco-Warriors: Understanding the Radical Environmental Movement* (updated edn) (California: Left Coast Press), p. 7.
5. Bill Devall (2014) 'Deep ecology and radical environmentalism', in Riley E. Dunlop and Angela G. Mertig (eds) *American Environmentalism: The U.S. Environmental Movement, 1970–1990* (London: Taylor & Francis), p. 55.
6. Donatella della Porta and Dieter Rucht (2002) 'The dynamics of environmental campaigns', *Mobilization: An International Journal*, **7** (1), p. 2.
7. B.R. Taylor (1995) 'Introduction: the global emergence of popular ecological resistance and chapter 1: Earth First! and global narratives of popular ecological resistance', in B.R. Taylor (ed.) *Ecological Resistance Movements: The Global Emergence of Radical and Popular Environmentalism* (Albany: State University of New York Press), p. 17.
8. Donald R. Liddick (2006) *Eco-Terrorism: Radical Environmental and Animal Liberation Movements* (Wesport, Connecticut: Praeger), p. 3.
9. Christopher Manes (1990) *Green Rage: Radical Environmentalism and the Unmaking of Civilization* (Boston, Toronto: Little Brown and Company), p. 22.
10. Mitchell Mobley (2002) 'The new wave of radical environmentalism: America's inaction and reaction to domestic ecoterrorism', *Appalachian Journal of Law*, 1 (1), p. 20.
11. Randall Amster (2006) 'Perspective on ecoterrorism: catalysts, conflations, and casualties', *Contemporary Justice Review*, **9** (September), p. 288.
12. Arslan, 'The social and operational intersections of environmental extremism in North America and Europe', p. 12.
13. Sea Shepherd Conservation Society Chapters, http://www.seashepherd.org/chapters/.
14. Colin J. Beck (2007) 'On the radical cusp: ecoterrorism in the United States, 1998–2005,' *Mobilization: An International Quarterly Review*, **12** (2), p. 163.
15. Mobley, 'The new wave of radical environmentalism: America's inaction and reaction to domestic ecoterrorism', p. 20.
16. Beck, 'On the radical cusp: ecoterrorism in the United States, 1998–2005', p. 163.
17. Mobley, 'The new wave of radical environmentalism: America's inaction and reaction to domestic ecoterrorism', p. 29.
18. MIPT Terrorism Knowledge Base, http://tkb.org.
19. Beck, 'On the radical cusp: ecoterrorism in the United States, 1998–2005', p. 163.
20. Ibid.
21. Contra Info, http://en.contrainfo.espiv.net; Bite Back Magazine, http://www.directaction.info; Global Terrorism Database, http://www.start.umd.edu/gtd/; North American Animal Liberation Press Office, http://animalliberationpressoffice.org/NAALPO/; 325, http://325.nostate.net.
22. Jennifer Varriale Carson et al. (2012) 'Terrorist and non-terrorist criminal attacks by radical environmental and animal rights groups in the United States, 1970–2007', *Terrorism and Political Violence*, **24** (2), p. 303.
23. Data has been derived from material that appears on the websites for the Animal Liberation Front (http://tkb.org/Group.jsp?groupID=14); the Earth Liberation Front (http://tkb.org/Group.jsp?groupID=41); Coalition to Save the Preserves (http://tkb.org/Group.jsp?groupID=3967); Peace Conquerors (http://tkb.org/Group.jsp?groupID=4192); Revolutionary Cells Animal Liberation Brigade (http://tkb.org/Group.jsp?groupID=4234); and Fighting Ecological Activism (http://tkb.org/Group.jsp?groupID=4369). One puzzling

anomaly in the data is that the Sea Shepherds have not been included among these groups and their activities, even in the maritime category.

24. Carson et al., 'Terrorist and non-terrorist criminal attacks by radical environmental and animal rights groups in the United States, 1970–2007', p. 299.
25. Sue Russell (2012) 'When Extreme Animal Rights Activists Attack', *Pacific Standards, Politics & Law*, 17 March, http://www.psmag.com/politics-and-law/when-extreme-animal-rights-activists-attack-40430.
26. MIPT Terrorism Knowledge Base, http://tkb.org.
27. Carson et al., 'Terrorist and non-terrorist criminal attacks by radical environmental and animal rights groups in the United States, 1970–2007', p. 303.
28. Ibid., p. 311.
29. Arslan, 'The social and operational intersections of environmental extremism in North America and Europe', p. 149.
30. Carson et al., 'Terrorist and non-terrorist criminal attacks by radical environmental and animal rights groups in the United States, 1970–2007', pp. 311–13.
31. Liddick, *Eco-Terrorism: Radical Environmental and Animal Liberation Movements*, p. 112.
32. Ibid., p. 100.
33. Scarce, *Eco-Warriors: Understanding the Radical Environmental Movement* (updated edn, 2006), p. 274.
34. Nick Harding (2010) 'Eco-anarchists: the new breed of terrorist', *The Independent (UK)*, 18 May.
35. Ibid.
36. Liddick, *Eco-Terrorism: Radical Environmental and Animal Liberation Movements*, p. 99.
37. Manes, *Green Rage: Radical Environmentalism and the Unmaking of Civilization*, p. 17.
38. Mohammed Hafez and Creighton Mullins (2015) 'The radicalization puzzle: a theoretical synthesis of empirical approaches to homegrown extremism', *Studies in Conflict and Terrorism*, **38** (11), p. 971.
39. Anja Dalgaard-Nielsen (2010) 'Violent radicalization in Europe: what we know and what we do not know', *Studies in Conflict & Terrorism*, **33** (9), p. 811.
40. Scarce, *Eco-Warriors: Understanding the Radical Environmental Movement* (updated edn, 2006), p. 31.
41. Paul Watson (1994) *Ocean Warrior: My Battle to End the Illegal Slaughter on the High Seas* (Toronto, Key Porter Books Ltd), p. xiii.
42. Peter C. List (1993) *Radical Environmentalism: Philosophy and Tactics* (Belmont, CA: Wadsworth Inc.), p. 7.
43. List, *Radical Environmentalism: Philosophy and Tactics*, pp. 7–8.
44. Sean P. Eagan (1996) 'From spikes to bombs: The rise of ecoterrorism', *Studies in Conflict and Terrorism*, **19** (1), p. 10.
45. Ibid.
46. Ibid.
47. Ibid.
48. Brian Doherty et al. (2000) 'Direct action in British environmentalism', in B. Seel et al. (eds), *Direct Action in British Environmentalism* (London and New York: Routledge), p. 1.
49. Anthony Vincent Silvaggio (2005) 'The Forest Defense Movement, 1980–2005: resistance at the point of extraction, consumption, and production' (PhD dissertation, University of Oregon), pp. 32–3.
50. Sheldon Kamieniecki et al. (1995) 'The effectiveness of radical environmentalists' in Bron Taylor (ed.), *Ecological Resistance Movements: The Global Emergence of Radical and Popular Environmentalism* (Albany, NY: State University of New York Press), p. 323.
51. Ibid.
52. J.M. Jasper and D. Nelkin (1992) *The Animal Rights Crusade: The Growth of a Moral Protest* (New York: Free Press), p. 176.

53. Lyle Munro (2005) *Confronting Cruelty: Moral Orthodoxy and the Challenge of the Animal Rights Movement* (Boston, Leiden: Brill), p. 135.
54. Robert Young (1996) '"Monkeywrenching" and the Processes of Democracy', in Freya Mathews (ed.), *Ecology and Democracy* (London: Frank Cass), p. 205.
55. Paul Watson (2004) 'ALF and ELF – terrorism is as terrorism does' in Steven Best and Anthony Nocella (eds), *Terrorists or Freedom Fighters: Reflections on the Liberation of Animals* (New York: Lantern Books), p. 285.
56. Kamieniecki et al., 'The effectiveness of radical environmentalists', pp. 324–5.
57. Munro, *Confronting Cruelty: Moral Orthodoxy and the Challenge of the Animal Rights Movement*, p. 135.
58. Kamieniecki et al., 'The effectiveness of radical environmentalists', p. 325.
59. Scarce, *Eco-Warriors: Understanding the Radical Environmental Movement* (updated edn, 2006), p. 6.
60. Steve Vanderheiden (2008) 'Radical environmentalism in an age of antiterrorism', *Environmental Politics*, **17** (2), p. 310.
61. Munro, *Confronting Cruelty: Moral Orthodoxy and the Challenge of the Animal Rights Movement*, p. 135.
62. Arslan, 'The social and operational intersections of environmental extremism in North America and Europe', p. 14.
63. Vanderheiden, 'Eco-terrorism or justified resistance? Radical environmentalism and the "war on terror"', p. 436.
64. Beck, 'On the radical cusp: ecoterrorism in the United States, 1998–2005', p. 173.
65. Carolyn Bailey (2010) 'Transcript of Ronnie Lee's ARZone live guest chat', 27 March at 7 p.m. Eastern DST, 11 p.m. UK time and 28 March 2010 at 9 a.m. Australian Eastern Standard Time, http://arzone.ning.com/profiles/blogs/transcript-of-ronnie-lees-live.
66. Derek Wall (2000) 'Snowballs, elves and skimmingtons?: Genealogies of environmental direct action', in B. Seel et al. (eds), *Direct Action in British Environmentalism* (London and New York: Routledge), p. 86.
67. Horacio R. Trujillo (2005) 'The radical environmentalist movement', *Aptitude for Destruction*, **2**, p. 162.
68. Gary Ackerman (2003) 'Beyond arson? A threat assessment of the Earth Liberation Front', *Terrorism and Political Violence*, **15** (4), p. 155; Stefan Leader and Peter Probst (2003) The Earth Liberation Front and environmental terrorism, *Terrorism and Political Violence*, **15** (4), p. 38.
69. Noel Molland (2006) 'A spark that ignited a flame: the evolution of the Earth Liberation Front' in Steven Best and Anthony Nocella (eds), *Igniting a Revolution: Voices in Defense of the Earth* (Oakland, CA: AK Press), p. 56.
70. Ibid.
71. Trujillo, 'The radical environmentalist movement', p. 161.
72. Bron Taylor (1998) 'Religion, violence and radical environmentalism: From Earth First! to the Unabomber to the Earth Liberation Front', *Terrorism and Political Violence*, **10** (4), p. 18.
73. Ibid., p. 20.
74. Trujillo, 'The radical environmentalist movement', p. 161.
75. A. Plows et al. (2004) 'Covert repertoires: ecotage in the UK', *Social Movement Studies*, **3** (2), p. 212.
76. Trujillo, 'The radical environmentalist movement', p. 145.
77. Carson et al., 'Terrorist and non-terrorist criminal attacks by radical environmental and animal rights groups in the United States, 1970–2007', p. 296.
78. Watson, 'ALF and ELF – terrorism is as terrorism does', p. 279.
79. Liddick, *Eco-Terrorism: Radical Environmental and Animal Liberation Movements*, p. 7.
80. Traditionally, terrorism is defined as: 'the calculated use of violence or threat of violence to attain goals that are political, religious or ideological in nature … through intimidation, coercion or instilling fear'. See Steve Vanderheiden (2005) 'Eco-terrorism or justified resistance? Radical environmentalism and the "war on terror"', *Politics and Society*, **33**

(3), pp. 427–8. As such, 'merely threatening violence may constitute terrorism, so long as the threat is sufficiently palpable and directed toward these public ends (as opposed to merely private gain, about which persons may be similarly terrorized but with different moral effect)'.

81. Mobley, 'The new wave of radical environmentalism: America's inaction and reaction to domestic ecoterrorism', p. 29.
82. Arslan, 'The social and operational intersections of environmental extremism in North America and Europe', p. 2.
83. Russell Lee Young (2004) 'A time series analysis of eco-terrorist violence in the United States: 1993–2003' (PhD dissertation, Sam Houston State University, Huntsville, TX), p. 61.
84. Arslan, 'The social and operational intersections of environmental extremism in North America and Europe', pp. 153–4; B. Bosworth (2002) 'America's homegrown terrorists', *The American Enterprise*, **13** (3) (April/May), p. 49.
85. Trujillo, 'The radical environmentalist movement', p. 166.
86. Ackerman, 'Beyond arson? A threat assessment of the Earth Liberation Front', pp. 158–9.
87. Ibid., p. 159.
88. Eagan, 'From spikes to bombs: the rise of ecoterrorism', p. 10.
89. Ibid.
90. Ibid.
91. Nick Harding (2010) 'Killing in the name of earth forms new breed of terrorist', *New Zealand Herald*, 23 May.
92. Ackerman, 'Beyond arson? A threat assessment of the Earth Liberation Front', p. 160.
93. Trujillo, 'The radical environmentalist movement', p. 167.
94. Taylor, 'Religion, violence and radical environmentalism: From Earth First! to the Unabomber to the Earth Liberation Front', p. 3.
95. Lee Hall (2006) *Capers in the Churchyard: Animal Rights Advocacy in the Age of Terror* (Darien, Connecticut: Nectar Bat Press), p. 66.
96. Ehud Sprinzak (1998) 'The psychopolitical formation of extreme left terrorism in a democracy: the case of the Weathermen', in Walter Reich (ed.), *Origins of Terrorism: Psychologies, Ideologies, Theologies, States of Mind* (Washington, DC: Woodrow Wilson Center Press), p. 82; 'Dutch ALF Communique', http://www.animalliberationfront.com/ALFront/Actions-Netherlands/DutchALF.htm; http://www.animalliberationfront.com/Saints/Authors/Quotes/ARQuotesLyrics.htm.
97. Rachel Monaghan (1999) 'Terrorism in the name of animal rights', *Terrorism and Political Violence*, **11** (4), p. 167.
98. Sprinzak, 'The psychopolitical formation of extreme left terrorism in a democracy: the case of the Weathermen', p. 83.
99. Ehud Sprinzak (1991) 'The process of delegitimation: towards a linkage theory of political terrorism', *Terrorism & Political Violence*, 3 (1), p. 54.
100. Ibid.
101. Martha F. Lee (1995) 'Violence and the environment: the case of 'Earth First!', *Terrorism and Political Violence*, **7** (3), pp. 120–21.
102. Douglas Long (2004) *Ecoterrorism: Library in a Book* (New York: Facts on File, Inc.), p. 35.
103. Sprinzak, 'The psychopolitical formation of extreme left terrorism in a democracy: the case of the Weathermen', p. 82.
104. Kamieniecki et al., 'The effectiveness of radical environmentalists', p. 326.
105. Andrew Darby (2006) 'Attack plan on Japan's whale ships: Sea Shepherd brings faster vessel', *The Age*, 27 December, p. 7.
106. Andrew Darby (2007) 'Sea Shepherd leaves its mark on Japanese whalers', *The Age*, 17 February, http://www.theage.com.au/news/national/sea-shepherd-leaves-its-mark-on-japanese-whalers/2007/02/16/1171405442617.html.
107. Ehud Sprinzak (1987) 'From messianic pioneering to vigilante terrorism: the case of the gush emunim underground', *Journal of Strategic Studies*, **10** (4), p. 211.

108. Ehud Sprinzak (1995) 'Right-wing terrorism in a comparative perspective: the case of split delegitimization', in Tore Bjørgo (ed.), *Terror From the Extreme Right* (London: Frank Cass & Co. Ltd), p. 29.
109. Ibid., p. 31.
110. Amster, 'Perspective on ecoterrorism: catalysts, conflations and casualties', p. 293.
111. Liddick, *Eco-Terrorism: Radical Environmental and Animal Liberation Movements*, p. 113.
112. Dan Morse et al. (2010) 'Man slain after taking hostages', *Washington Post*, 2 September.
113. Clark McCauley and Sophia Moskalenko (2008) 'Mechanisms of political radicalization: pathways towards terrorism', *Terrorism and Political Violence*, **20**, p. 416.
114. Dalgaard-Nielsen, 'Violent radicalization in Europe: what we know and what we do not know', p. 808.
115. Ibid., p. 806.
116. Ibid., p. 807.
117. David C. Hofmann and Lorne L. Dawson (2000) 'The neglected role of charismatic authority in the study of terrorist groups and radicalization', *Studies in Conflict and Terrorism*, **37** (4), p. 349.
118. Ibid., p. 361.
119. Ibid., p. 355.
120. Ibid., p. 349.
121. Jay A Conger et al. (2000) 'Charismatic leadership and follower effects', *Journal of Organizational Behavior*, **21**, p. 748.
122. Dalgaard-Nielsen, 'Violent radicalization in Europe: what we know and what we do not know', p. 808.
123. Hofmann and Dawson, 'The neglected role of charismatic authority in the study of terrorist groups and radicalization', pp. 352–3.
124. Ibid., p. 355.
125. Young, 'A time series analysis of eco-terrorist violence in the United States: 1993–2003', p. 142.
126. Rachel L. Einwohler (2002) 'Bringing the outsiders in: opponents' claims and the construction of animal rights activists' identity', *Mobilization: An International Journal*, **7** (3), p. 261.
127. Ibid.
128. Steven Best and Anthony Nocella (2004) 'Behind the mask: uncovering the Animal Liberation Front', in Steven Best and Anthony Nocella (eds) *Terrorists or Freedom Fighters: Reflections on the Liberation of Animals* (New York: Lantern Books), p. 23.
129. Liddick, *Eco-Terrorism: Radical Environmental and Animal Liberation Movements*, p. 96.
130. Gerry Nagtzaam and Pete Lentini (2008) 'Vigilantes on the high seas?: The Sea Shepherds and political violence', *Terrorism and Political Violence*, **1**, p. 118.
131. Sprinzak, 'The process of delegitimation: towards a linkage theory of political terrorism', p. 64.
132. *Whale Wars*, DVD Season 1–4.
133. Bron Taylor (1995) 'Earth First! and Global Narratives of Popular Ecological Resistance', in Bron Taylor (ed.), *Ecological Resistance Movements: The Global Emergence of Radical and Popular Environmentalism* (Albany, NY: State University of New York Press) p. 14.
134. Teale Phelps Bondaroff (2008) 'Throwing a wrench into things: the strategy of radical environmentalism', *Journal of Military and Strategic Studies*, **10** (4), p. 8.
135. Amster, 'Perspective on ecoterrorism: catalysts, conflations, and casualties', p. 289.
136. Young, 'A time series analysis of eco-terrorist violence in the United States: 1993–2003' p. 28; D. Foreman (191) *Confessions of an Eco-Warrior* (New York: Crown), p. 121.
137. Young, 'A time series analysis of eco-terrorist violence in the United States: 1993–2003', p. 28.

138. Vanderheiden, 'Eco-terrorism or justified resistance? Radical environmentalism and the "war on terror"', p. 432.
139. Taylor, 'Religion, violence and radical environmentalism: from Earth First! to the Unabomber to the Earth Liberation Front', p. 22.

Bibliography

AAP (2013) 'Japanese whalers have "worst catch" ever', *The Age*, 6 April

Abbey, Edward (1975) *The Monkey Wrench Gang* (New York: Avon)

ABC Newcastle, NSW (2012) 'Paul Watson: the man behind Sea Shepherd', 23 May, accessed 23 May 2012 at http://www.abc.net.au/news/2012-05-15/paul-watson-sea-shepherd-profile/4011498/?site=newcastle

Ackerman, G. (2003) 'Beyond arson? A threat assessment of the Earth Liberation Front', *Terrorism and Political Violence*, **15** (4), pp. 145–50

'Activist lashes out at Sea Shepherd', *NZPA*, accessed 7 October 2010 at http://www.stuff.co.nz/the-press/news/4206365/Activist-lashes-out-at-Sea-Shepherd

'Activists say 4 boats collide near Antarctica in dustup over whaling', *The Vancouver Sun*, accessed 20 February 2013 at http://www.vancouversun.com/news/Activists+Japanese+whaling+boat+collides+with+antiwhaling/7988129/story.html

'Activists threaten power plant CEO', *ABC News*, accessed 15 June 2009 at http://www.abc.net.au/news/2009-06-15/activists-threaten-power-plants-ceo/1713308

'Ady Gil sinks after collision', *The Age*, 8 January 2010

AFP (2013) 'Activist Watson gets Australian visa', 3 November, accessed 3 November 2013 at http://www.japantimes.co.jp/news/2013/11/03/asia-pacific/activist-watson-gets-australian-visa/#.UvGer1uPjCp

AFP (2012) 'Anti-whaling crusader Paul Watson will receive a fair trial, says Costa Rica's president', 23 May, accessed 23 May 2012 at http://news.nationalpost.com/2012/05/23/anti-whaling-crusader-paul-watson-will-recieve-a-fair-trial-says-costa-ricas-president/

AFP (2012) 'Anti-whaling leader freed on bail while extradition decided', accessed 18 May 2012 at http://www.google.com/hostednews/afp/article/ALeqM5iJNfm-bWp3R…fkm4BYty0VCIEA?docId=CNG.0d8e1a34f8eed2b6a7343577531cf5e3.5f1

AFP (2012) 'Anti-whaling leader says extraditing him won't halt campaign', accessed 23 May 2012 at http://news.asiaone.com/News/Latest%2BNews/World/Story/A1Story20120523-347755.html

AFP (2012) 'Costa Rica assures fair trial for anti-whaling crusader', 23 May, accessed 17 June 2012 at http://www.expatica.com/de/news/

german-news/costa-rica-assures-fair-trial-for-anti-whaling-crusader_229293.html

AFP (2012) 'German court wants fugitive activist Paul Watson extradited', 25 July, accessed 25 July 2012 at http://news.yahoo.com/german-court-wants-fugitive-activist-paul-watson-extradited-111146440.html

AFP (2012) 'Japan admits asking Germany to arrest, extradite Sea Shepherd chief', 28 July, accessed 28 July 2012 at http://www.japantimes.co.jp/text/nn20120728b6.html

AFP (2012) 'Japan is after revenge: Watson', 31 July, accessed 31 July 2012 at http://au.news.yahoo.com/thewest/a/-/breaking/14417081/japan-is-after-revenge-watson/

AFP (2011) 'Sea Shepherd hit by legal harpoon', 9 December, accessed 9 December 2011 at http://www.couriermail.com.au/ipad/sea-shepherd-hit-by-legal-harpoon/story-fn6ck55c-1226218642187

AFP (2012) 'Sea Shepherd's wanted Watson to join anti-whaling fight', 5 November, accessed 5 November 2012 at http://www.google.com/hostednews/afp/article/ALeqM5ihUXk4B_swixfswA3yY7ZGrgbKwA?docId=CNG.8b9ff8e613fe19f3f1f5c2ac5c34d3c6.11

Alexander, C. (2010) 'Protester boards Japanese whaling vessel', *Sydney Morning Herald*, 15 February

'ALF issues false press releases', *FCUSA*, 7 April 2010

Amster, R (2006) 'Perspectives on ecoterrorism: catalysts, conflations, and casualties', *Contemporary Justice Review*, **9** (September), pp. 287–301

Animal Liberation Front, 'Animal Rights Militia', accessed 12 December 2015 at http://www.animalliberationfront.com/ALFront/ARMilitia.htm

Animal Liberation Front, 'Complete U.S. diary of actions, the first 30 years', *United States: Voice of the Voiceless Communications*, 2010

Animal Liberation Front, 'SHAC', accessed 10 December 2015 at http://www.animalliberationfront.com/ALFront/SHAC.htm

Animal Liberation Fund.com, 'Worldwide news & information resource about the A.L.F.: funding your actions', accessed 1 December 2015 at http://www.animalliberationfront.com/ALFront/Activist%20Tips/LettersfromUnderground3.htm

'Animal research facility protection: hearing before the house subcommittee on department opinions, research and foreign agriculture and the subcommittee on livestock, dairy and poultry, of the Committee on Agriculture', 101st Congress, accessed 8 December 2015 at http://www.animaliberationfront.com/ALFront/alfusa.htm

Animal Rights Extremism, 'Violent extremism', accessed 12 December 2015 at http://www.animalrightsextremism.info/animal-rights-extremism/history-of-animal-rights-extremism/violent-extremism/

'Animal rights group ends 15-year campaign against experiments at Huntingdon: activists have changed their tactics due to an "onslaught of government repression"', accessed 2 December 2015 at http://www.independent.co.uk/news/uk/crime/animal-rights-group-ends-15-year-campaign-against-experiments-at-huntingdon-9687843.html

Animal Rights Militia Communiqué (1985) Animal Liberation Front Supporters' Group Newsletter, **17**

'Animal rights, terror tactics' *BBC News*, 30 August 2000, accessed 1 December 2015 at http://news.bbc.co.uk/2/hi/uk_news/902751.stm

'Animal rights, terror tactics', *BBC News*, 30 August 2000, accessed 1 December 2015 at http://news.bbc.co.uk/2/hi/uk_news/902751.stm

'Animal rights thugs' (2010) *ScienceBlogs*, 24 February, accessed 1 January 2016 at http://scienceblogs.com/insolence/2010/02/24/animal-rights-thugs-researchers-children/

Anton, Donald, K. (2011) 'Protecting whales by hue and cry: is there a role for non-state actors in the enforcement of international law?', *Journal of International Wildlife Law and Policy*, 14 (2), pp. 137–45

Anonymous Communique (2007) 'Will Novartis products ever be safe?', *Bite Back*, 8 October, accessed 1 December 2007 at http://www.animal liberationfront.com/ALFront/Premise_History/Biteback2007.htm

Anonymous, accessed 11 October 2015 at http://www.abolitionist-online.com/?f

Anonymous, About ALF, History, Animal Liberation Front.com, Worldwide News and Information Resource about the A.L.F., accessed 11 October 2015 at http://www.animalliberationfront.com/ALFront/Premise_History/30yearsofDirectAction.htm

Anonymous, About ALF, History, ALF 2003, Animal Liberation Front-.com, Worldwide News and Information Resource about the A.L.F., accessed 1 January 2016 at http://www.animalliberationfront.com/ALFront/Premise_History/2003_Chronicle_of_Direct_Actions.htm

Anonymous, *Bite Back*, 'News from the Frontline', 'Diary of actions, 2011–12', accessed 1 December 2015 at http://directaction.info/news.htm

Anonymous, *Bite Back*, 'News from the Frontline', accessed 1 December 2015 at http://www.directaction.info/news_nov10_14.htm

Anonymous, *Bite Back*, 'News from the Frontline', accessed 1 December 2015 at http://www.directaction.info/news_jan02_15.htm

Anonymous, *Bite Back*, 'News from the Frontline', accessed 1 December 2015 at http://www.directaction.info/news_jan03_08.htm

Anonymous, *Bite Back*, 'News from the Frontline', 'North American animal', accessed 13 December 2015 at http://www.directaction.info

Anonymous, *Bite Back*, 'News from the frontline', accessed 28 December 2015 at http://directaction.info/news_dec27_14.htm

Anonymous, *Bite Back*, 'News from the Frontline', accessed at http://www.directaction.info/news_jan27_14.htm

Anonymous, 'Ecoterrorism', *Sourcewatch*, accessed 10 March 2010 at http://www.spokeo.com/Ronnie+Lee+1

Anonymous, 'Ecoterrorism', *Sourcewatch*, accessed 10 March 2010 at http://www.sourcewatch.org/index.php?title=Eco-terrorism

Anonymous,'How old is Ronnie Lee?', accessed 10 March 2010 at http://howold.co/ronnie-lee

Anonymous, Quotes and Lyrics, Animal Liberation Front.com, World-wide News and Information Resource about the A.L.F., accessed 1 January 2016 at http://www.animalliberationfront.com/Saints/Authors/Quotes/ARQuotesLyrics.htm

Anonymous, 'The SHAC7', accessed 10 September 2016 at http://www.shac7.com

Anti-defamation League, 'Animal Rights Extremists Target the University of California', 12 May 2011, accessed 10 September 2016 at http://archive.adl.org/nr/exeres/fe4f2992-54b2-4e4e-84c5-4c6a9596a7de,db7611a2-02cd-43af-8147-649e26813571,frameless.html

Anti-Defamation League, 'Eco-terrorism: extremism in the animal rights and environmentalist movements', 2006, accessed 30 April 2014 at http://www.adl.org/learn/ext_us/Ecoterrorism.asp?LEARN_Cat=Extremism&LEARN_SubCat=Extremism_in_America&xpicked=4&item=eco

Arnold, Ron (1997) *Ecoterror: The Violent Agenda to Save Nature, The World of the Unabomber*, Bellevue: WA: Free Enterprise Press

Arslan, Hasan T. (2008) 'The social and operational intersections of environmental extremism in North America and Europe', PhD dissertation, Sam Houston State University, Huntsville, TX

'Australian protesters safely transferred to ACV ocean protector', 13 January 2012, accessed 10 September 2016 at http://www.seashepherd.org/news-and-media/2012/01/13/australian-protesters-safely-transferred-to-acv-ocean-protector-1317

'Australian whale defenders on their way to Antarctica against their will', 9 January 2012, accessed 10 September 2016 at http://www.seashepherd.org/news-and-media/2012/01/09/australian-whale-defenders-on-their-way-to-antarctica-against-their-will-1311

Author unknown (2011) 'Activists claim French arson', *Bite Back Magazine*, 21 January, accessed at http://directaction.info/news_jan21_11.htm

Author unknown (date unknown) 'A discussion of the Animal Enterprise Terrorism Act'

Author unknown (2010) 'ALF visit another fortress executive', *Bite Back Magazine*, 2 December

Author unknown (2010) 'Dove gets another chance at life', *Bite Back Magazine*, 8 February

Author unknown (2010) 'KFC bombed', *Bite Back Magazine*, 12 May

Author unknown (date unknown) 'Regulation of "eco-terrorism" in the United States'

Author unknown, 'Two pigs liberated, graffiti and a call to action', *Bite Back Magazine*, 24 October 2010

'Bail set for "Whale Wars" star in extradition fight', 18 May 2012, accessed 15 August 2016 at http://news.blogs.cnn.com/2012/05/18/bail-set-for-whale-wars-star-in-extradition-fight/?hpt=hp_c2

Bailey, Carolyn (2010) 'Transcript of Ronnie Lee's ARZone live guest chat', 27 March at 7 p.m. Eastern DST, 11 p.m. UK time and 28 March 2010 at 9 a.m. Australian Eastern Standard Time, available at http://arzone.ning.com/profiles/blogs/transcript-of-ronnie-lees-live

Bakker, E. (2006) *Jihad Terrorists in Europe*, The Hague: Cliengendael

Bandow, D. (2003) 'American terrorism, environment-style', *Human Events*, **59** (33), 29 September

Barker, E., AFP, 'Anti-whaling group leader ordered held in Germany', accessed 13 May 2012 at http://www.google.com/hostednews/afp/article/ALeqM5jDGUY_Py2v5...j4OGnenluS7cew?docId=CNG.cb81ca0cd4215a702104ce7afde58aba.181

Bartlett, J. and Miller, C. (2012) 'The edge of violence: towards telling the difference between violence and non-violent radicalization', *Terrorism and Political Violence*, **24** (1), pp. 1–21, pp. 13–16

BBC News Europe (2012) 'Sea Shepherd founder Paul Watson flees Germany', accessed 26 July 2012 at http://www.bbc.co.uk/news/world-europe-18996972

Beck, C. (2007) 'On the radical cusp: ecoterrorism in the United States, 1998–2005', *Mobilization: An International Quarterly Review*, **12** (2), pp. 161–76

Becker, Michael (2006) 'Rhizomatic resistance: the Zapatistas and the Earth Liberation Front', *Green Theory & Praxis: The Journal of Ecopedagogy*, **2** (2), pp. 2–21

'Becoming a Sea Shepherd onshore volunteer', accessed 30 November 2015 at http://www.seashepherd.org/get-involved/volunteer-onshore.html

Bennett, C. (2010) 'Ady Gil captain tells of ramming at sea', *Sydney Morning Herald*, 28 January

Bertlet, C. (1991) 'Hunting the "Green Menace"', *The Humanist* (July/August)

Best, Steven (2006) 'Rethinking the revolution: animal liberation, human liberation, and the future of the left', *International Journal of Inclusive Democracy*, **2** (3), pp. 5–6

Best, Steven (2007) 'The Animal Enterprise Terrorism Act: New, Improved and ACLU approved', *Journal for Critical Animal Studies*, 5 (1)

Best, Steven (2010) 'War against animals: time to stop playing nice', *The Scavenger*, blog, 10 July 2010, accessed 10 September 2016 at http://wwwthescavenger.net/animals/war-against-animals-time-to-stop-playing-nice-animal-liberation-95623-365.html

Best, Steven and Nocella, Anthony (2015) 'Behind the mask: uncovering the Animal Liberation Front', accessed 30 November 2015 at http://www.animalliberationfront.com/ALFront/Behind_The_Mask.pdf

Best, Steven and Nocella, Anthony (2004) 'Behind the mask: uncovering the Animal Liberation Front', in Steven Best and Anthony Nocella (eds), *Terrorists or Freedom Fighters: Reflections on the Liberation of Animals*, New York: Lantern Books

Billones, C.L. (2013) 'New video show Sea Shepherd ramming Japanese whaling ships', *Japan Daily Press*, 26 February

Black, J.M. (2012) 'Paul Watson: shining activist hero or psychopathic terrorist', blog, 17 June, accessed 10 September at http://news.co.cr/paul-watson-shining-activist-hero-or-psychopathic-terrorist-2/6967/

'Board of Advisors', accessed 30 November 2015 at http://www.seashepherd.org/who-we-are/board-of-advisors.html

'Board of Directors', accessed 20 November 2015 at http://www.seashepherd.org/who-we-are/board-of-directors.html

Bondaroff, T. P. (2008) 'Throwing a wrench into things: the strategy of radical environmentalism', *Journal of Military and Strategic Studies*, **10** (4)

Bondaroff, T.P. (2011) 'Sailing with the Sea Shepherds', *Journal of Military and Strategic Studies*, **13** (3), pp. 1–55

Borum, R. (2004) *Psychology of Terrorism*, Tampa: University of South Florida

Borum, R. (2011) 'Radicalization into violent extremis II: a review of conceptual models and empirical research', *Journal of Strategic Security*, **4** (4), pp. 37–62

Bosworth, Brandon (2002) 'Terror Watch: America's Homegrown Terrorists', *The American Enterprise*, **48**

Bryant, N. (2013) 'Politics at play in Sea Shepherd-Japan whaling wars', *BBC News*, 1 March

Button, M., John, T. and Brearley, N. (2002) 'New challenges in public order policing: the professionalisation of environmental protest and the emergence of the militant environmental activist', *International Journal of the Sociology of Law*, **30** (1), 17–32

'Campaigns from 1984–1986', *Sea Shepherd*, 1984, Summer

Campbell, C. (1991) 'Crisis plans leak smudges clorox', *Los Angeles Times*, 2 June, D8

Caprari, A.M. (2010) 'Lovable pirates? The legal implications of the battle between environmentalists and whalers in the Southern Ocean', *Connecticut Law Review*, **42** (5)

'Captain Paul Watson', accessed 19 August 2012 at http://www.seashepherd.org/who-we-are/captain-watsons-biography.html

'Captain Paul Watson sends first message to supporters since departing Germany', accessed 30 July 2012 at http://www.seashepherd.org/news-and-media/2012/07/30/captain-pau…pherd-first-message-for-supporters-since-departing-germany-1413

Carlson, Peter (1991) 'The great silver spring monkey debate', *The Washington Post Magazine*, 24 February

Carson, J.V., LaFree, G. and Dugan, L. (2012) 'Terrorist and non-terrorist criminal attacks by radical environmental and animal rights groups in the United States, 1970–2007', *Terrorism and Political Violence*, **24** (2), pp. 295–319

Case, Denise (2002) 'The USA Patriot Act: adding bite to the fight against animal rights terrorism?', *Rutgers Law Journal*, **187** (Fall)

Castells, Manuel (2000) 'Toward a sociology of the Network Society', *Contemporary Sociology*, **29** (5), pp. 693–9

Castree, Noel (2002) 'False antitheses? Marxism, nature and actor-networks', *Antipode*, **34** (1), pp. 111–46

Chalecki, E. (2002) 'A new vigilance: identifying and reducing the risks of environmental terrorism', *Global Environmental Politics*, **2** (1), pp. 46–64

Chase, A. (1992) 'Sea Shepherds may give piracy a good name', *Sea Shepherd Log*, third quarter

Choe, K. (2013) 'Ady Gil sues Sea Shepherd over Antarctic sinking', *3 News*, 10 January, accessed 10 January 2013 at http://www.3news.co.nz/Ady-Gil-sues-Sea-Shepherd-over-Antarcticsinking/tabid/417/articleID/282601/Default.aspx

Cohen, Adam (2010) 'Case study: can animal rights go too far?', *Time Magazine*, 14 July

Conger, Jay, Kanungo, A., Rabindra N. and Menon, Sanjay T. (2000) 'Charismatic leadership and follower effects', *Journal of Organizational Behavior*, **21**, pp. 747–67

Cooper, H.H.A. (1977) 'What is a terrorist: a psychological perspective', *Legal Medical Quarterly*, **1**, cited in Jonathan R. White (1998) *Terrorism: An Introduction*, 2nd edn, Elmont, CA: West/Wadsworth

Costa Rica (2012) 'Captain Paul Watson arrested in Frankfurt, Germany on warrant issued by Costa Rica', 13 May, accessed 13 May 2012 at http://www.seashepherd.org/news-and-media/2012/05/13/captain-paul-watson-arrested-in-frankfurt-germany-on-warrant-issued-by-costa-rica-1374

Cottee, S. and Hayward, K. (2011) 'Terrorist (e)motives: the existential attractions of terrorism', *Studies in Conflict & Terrorism*, **34** (12), pp. 963–86

Crelinsten, R.D. (1999) 'Analysing terrorism and counter-terrorism: a communication model', *Terrorism and Political Violence*, **14** (2) (Summer), pp. 77–122

Dalgaard-Nielsen, A. (2010) 'Violent radicalization in Europe: what we know and what we do not know', *Studies in Conflict & Terrorism*, **33** (9), pp. 797–814

Darby, A. (2012) 'Activist arrested', *The Age*, 15 May

Darby A. (2010) 'Activist boards Japanese whaler and demands $3.4m for sunken boat', *The Age*, 16 February

Darby A. (2007) 'Anti-whaling 'pirates' get more muscle for Antarctic skirmish', *The Age*, 10 January 2007

Darby, A. (2013) 'Anti-whaling skipper poses problem over arrest notice', 1 January

Darby, A. (2006) 'Attack plan on Japan's whale ships: Sea Shepherd brings faster vessel', *The Age*, 27 December

Darby, A. (2012) 'Attempted murder probe: anti-whaling skipper faces deportation', *The Age*, 14 May

Darby, A. (2012) 'Costa Rica confirms Watson extradition demand', *The Sydney Morning Herald*, 16 May

Darby A. (2007) 'Film shows attempts to stop whalers', *The Age*, 12 February

Darby, A. (2012) 'How Sea Shepherd stays afloat', 11 January, accessed 11 January 2012 at http://www.theage.com.au/national/how-sea-shepherd-stays-afloat-20120110-1ptu6.html#ixzz1lGmK69CU

Darby, A. (2006) 'Hunters and protectors', *The Age*, 15 November

Darby, A. (2012) 'Japan props up floundering whale business', *The Age*, 21 December

Darby, A. (2010) 'Japanese ship destroys whale protest boat Ady Gil', *The Age*, 6 January

Darby, A. (2014) 'Japanese whaling ship "attacks" Sea Shepherd boat', *Sydney Morning Herald*, 2 February, accessed 2 February at 2014, http://www.smh.com.au/environment/whale-watch/japanese-whaling-ship-attacks-sea-shepherd-boat-20140201-31uni

Darby, A. (2010) 'Protester may face charges in Japan', *The Age*, 17 February

Darby, A. (2010) 'Sea Shepherd bans activist Bethune from protests', *The Age*, 9 June

Darby, A. (2007) 'Sea Shepherd leaves its mark on Japanese whalers', *The Age*, 17 February

Darby, A. (2013) 'Ships collide in Antarctic whaling protest', *The Brisbane Times*, 20 February

Darby, A. (2013) 'Whale taken onto factory ship after five-hour standoff', *The Age*, 16 February

Darby, A., and Pearlman J. (2010) 'Whaling war set to worsen after crash', *Sydney Morning Herald*, 8 January

della Porta, Donatella and Rucht, Dieter (2002) 'The dynamics of environmental campaigns', *Mobilization: An International Journal*, **7** (1), pp. 1–14

Denson, B. and Long, J. (1999) 'Eco-terrorism sweeps the American West', *The Oregonian*, 26 September

Destries, M. (2010) 'Sea Shepherd emails that started online "war of words" released', *Ecorazzi*, accessed 6 October 2010 at http://www.ecorazzi.com/2010/10/06/sea-shepherd-emails-that-started-online-war-of-words-released/

Devall, Bill (2014) 'Deep ecology and radical environmentalism' in Riley E. Dunlop and Angela G. Mertig (eds), *American Environmentalism: The U.S. Environmental Movement, 1970–1990*, London: Taylor & Francis

Doherty, Brian, Paterson, Matthew and Seel, Benjamin (2000) 'Direct action in British environmentalism', in B. Seel, M. Paterson and B. Doherty (eds), *Direct Action in British Environmentalism*, London and New York: Routledge

Doosje, B., Loseman, A. and Bos, K. (2013) 'Determinants of radicalization of Islamic youth in the Netherlands: personal uncertainty, perceived injustice, and perceived group threat', *Journal of Social Issues*, **69** (3), pp. 586–604

Dowling S. (2012) 'Veteran anti-whaling activist Paul Watson to be released on bail: Sea Shepherd group vows to fight founder's possible extradition from Germany to Costa Rica over 2002 incident at sea', 18 May, accessed 18 May 2012 at http://www.guardian.co.uk/environment/2012/may/18/anti-whaling-activist-paul-watson

'Dutch ALF Communique' accessed 1 January 2016 at http://www.animalliberationfront.com/ALFront/Actions-Netherlands/DutchALF.htm

Eagan, Sean P. (1996) 'From spikes to bombs: The rise of ecoterrorism', *Studies in Conflict and Terrorism*, **19** (1), pp. 1–18.

'Eco-fugitive Paul Watson resigns from Sea Shepherd', *The Toronto Sun*, 8 January 2013, accessed 8 January 2013 at http://www.torontosun.com/2013/01/08/eco-fugitive-paul-watson-resigns-from-sea-shepherd

Einhorn, B. (2015) 'In whale war ceasefire, activists hunt a new target: with a halt to Japanese whaling in the Antarctic, the conservation group Sea Shepherd has started hunting toothfish poachers', *Bloomburg Business*, 2 February, accessed 3 February 2015 at http://www.bloomberg.com/news/articles/2015-02-02/in-whale-war-ceasefire-activists-hunt-a-new-target

Einwohler, R.L. (2002) 'Bringing the outsiders in: opponents' claims and the construction of animal rights activists' identity', *Mobilization: An International Journal*, **7** (3), pp. 253–68

Emel, Jody and Wolch, Jennifer (1998) 'Witnessing the animal moment', in J. Woch and J. Emel (eds), *Animal Geographies: Places, Politics and Identity in the Nature-Culture Borderlands*, London and New York: Verso

Enders, C. (2015) 'Can Sea Shepherds survive their own success?', *The Guardian*, 5 June, accessed 5 June 2015 at http://www.theguardian.com/environment/2015/jun/05/sea-shepherd-whale-wars-animal-planet

Enders, W. and Sandler, T. (2000) 'Is transnational terrorism: becoming more threatening? A time-series investigation', *Journal of Conflict Resolution*, **44** (3), pp. 307–32

Everest, P. (2012) 'Fugitive whale wars star's brother battling stage 4 cancer; hopes Paul Watson makes it to London soon', 27 July, accessed 27 July 2012 at http://www.londoncommunitynews.com/2012/07/battling-stage-4-can…ugitive-whale-wars-star-hopes-paul-watson-comes-to-london-soon/

'Extremism in America – updates, "Justice Department" claims responsibility for threats against UCLA animal researcher', accessed 5 December 2015 at http://archive.adl.org/learn/extremism_in_america_updates/movements/ecoterrorism/justice_department_ucla.html#.VmI_gGSGRHw

Fackler, M. (2010) 'Uncertainty buffets Japan's whaling fleet', *The New York Times*, 15 May

Ferry, Luc (1995) 'Animal liberation' or the rights of creatures', in Luc, F. (ed.), *The New Ecological Order*, Chicago and London: University of Chicago Press

Fiala, J. (2004) 'String of attacks: ALF targets universities', *The Newsmagazine of Veterinary Medicine* (May), accessed 10 May 2007 at http://www.swaebr.org/cfaar/newsletters/2004/July%202004%20news.pdf

Finsen, Lawrence and Finsen, Susan (1994) *The Animal Rights Movement in America: From Compassion to Respect*, New York: Twayne Publishers

Fliton, D. and Darby, A. (2015) 'Japan whale hunt tensions to flare as Australia considers court action' *The Age*, 8 December, accessed 8

December 2015 at http://www.theage.com.au/federal-politics/political-news/japan-whale-hunt-tensions-to-flare-as-australia-considers-court-action-20151207-glhag4#ixzz3ueHejSfy

Flynn, Jim (2005) 'Dear shit fer brains letters to the editors', *Earth First! Journal*, **25** (3), 1 March

'Focusing attention on things that matter is always positive: commentary by Captain Paul Watson', 15 January 2012, accessed 10 September 2016 at https://www.seashepherd.org.uk/news-and-commentary/commentary/focusing-attention-on-things-that-matter-is-always-positive.html

'For First Time in U.S. History – Animal Rights Extremist to go to Jail for A.L.F. Related Terror Activity', *PR Newswire*, 4 March 1995

Foreman, D., Wolke, H. and Koehler, B. (1983) 'The Earth First! Wilderness Preserve System', *Earth First!*, **3** (5), 21 June

Foreman, D. (1985) 'Ecodefense: a field guide to monkeywrenching' accessed 10 March 2010 at http://www.omnipresence.mahost.org/ch1 txt.htm

Foreman, D. (1991) *Confessions of an Eco-Warrior*, New York: Crown

'Forest Rescue men go out on a limb for Sea Shepherd, commentary by Captain Paul Watson', 7 January 2012, accessed 10 September 2016 at http://www.seashepherd.org/commentary-and-editorials/2012/01/07/forest-rescue-men-go-out-on-a-limb-for-sea-shepherd-502

Francione, Gary (2000) *Introduction to Animal Rights: Your Child or the Dog?*, Philadelphia, PA: Temple University Press

Freeman, D. (2012) 'Can Paul Watson get a fair trial in Costa Rica?', 26 May, accessed 26 May 2012 at http://news.co.cr/can-paul-watson-get-a-fair-trial-in-costa-rica/7193/

Gardham, Duncan (2011) 'University extremism: AR a bigger problem than Islamists', *The Telegraph* (UK), 18 February

Garner, Robert (1993) 'Political animals: a survey of the animal protection movement in Britain', *Parliamentary Affairs*, **46** (3), pp. 333–52

'Germany drops arrest warrant for Sea Shepherd founder', *Environment News Service*, 8 March 2013, accessed 8 March 2013 at http://ens-newswire.com/2013/03/08/germany-drops-arrest-warrant-for-sea-shepherd-founder/

Global Terrorism Database, accessed 12 December 2015 at http://www.start.umd.edu/gtd/; http://325.nostate.net

Gold-Biss, Michael (1994) The Discourse on Terrorism: Political Violence and the Subcommittee on Security and Terrorism 1981–1986, New York: Peter Lang

Government of Japan (2005) 'Plan for the second phase of the Japanese Whale Research Program under Special Permit in the Antarctic (JARPA II) – monitoring of the Antarctic eco-system and development of new management objectives for whale resources'

'Green group accused of sinking ship for a stunt', *Sydney Morning Herald*, 8 October 2010, accessed 8 October 2010 at http://www.smh.com.au/environment/whale-watch/green-group-accused-of-sinking-ship-for-a-stunt-20101007-169u7.html

Greenpeace (1991) 'Clorox company's public relations "crisis management plan" leaked to Greenpeace', press release, 10 May

Grubs, K. (2010) 'Saving lives or spreading fear: the terroristic nature of eco-extremism', *Animal Law*, **16**, p. 366

Gul, J. and Bryan, E. (2013) 'Japanese whaling vessel "rammed" by Sea Shepherd fleet', *ABC News*, 26 February

Hafez, Mohammed and Mullins, Creighton (2015) 'The radicalization puzzle: a theoretical synthesis of empirical approaches to homegrown extremism', *Studies in Conflict and Terrorism*, **38** (11), pp. 958–75

Hall, Lee (2006) *Capers in the Churchyard: Animal Rights Advocacy in the Age of Terror*, Darien, Connecticut: Nectar Bat Press

Hammond J. (2012) 'Absurd outcome for Sea Shepherd tax', *The West Australian*, 10 August, accessed 10 August 2012 at http://au.news.yahoo.com/thewest/a/-/breaking/14520935/absurd-outcome-for-sea-shepherd-tax/

Hansen Jeff (2012) 'Home from the sea; home to the trees: forest activist heroes return home', 16 January, accessed 10 September 2016 at http://www.seashepherd.org/news-and-media/2012/01/16/home-from-the-sea-home-to-the-trees-1318

Harding, N. (2010) 'Eco-anarchists: the new breed of terrorist', *The Independent (UK)*, 18 May

Harding, Nick (2010) 'Killing in the name of earth forms new breed of terrorist', *New Zealand Herald*, 23 May

Hasbrouck, J. (2005) 'Primitive dissidents: Earth Liberation Front and the making of a radical movement', PhD dissertation, University of Southern California, Los Angeles, CA

Heller, P. (2007) *The Whale Warriors: On Board a Pirate Ship in the Battle to Save the World's Largest Mammals*, New York: Free Press

Henshaw, David (1989) *Animal Warfare: The Story of the Animal Liberation Front*, London: Fontana

Hoek, A. (2010) 'Sea Shepherd Conservation Society v. Japanese whalers, the showdown: who is the real villain?', *Stanford Journal of Animal Law and Policy*, 3, p. 159

Hofmann, David C. and Dawson, Lorne L. (2000) 'The neglected role of charismatic authority in the study of terrorist groups and radicalization', *Studies in Conflict and Terrorism*, **37** (4), pp. 348–68

Hooley (2001) 'Plans for ecoterrorism legislation', *The Associated Press*, 7 July

Horgan, J. (2008) 'From profiles to *pathways* and roots to *routes*: perspectives from psychology on radicalization into terrorism', *The Annals of the American Academy of Political and Social Science*, 618.1, pp. 80–94

Hunter, R. (2011) *Warriors of the Rainbow: A Chronicle of the Greenpeace Movement from 1971 to 1979*, Amsterdam: Greenpeace Press

Hunter T. (2010) 'Whaling fleet more violent than ever: Sea Shepherd', *The Age*, 7 January

'If you don't fight, you've already lost', *Corporate Watch*, 17 April 2014, accessed 13 December 2015 at https://corporatewatch.org/news/2014/apr/17/if-you-don't-fight-you've-already-lost

Institute of Cetacean Research; Kyodo Senpaku Kaisha Ltd; Tomoyuki Ogawa; and Toshiyuki Muira v. Sea Shepherd Conservation Society and Paul Watson, United States Court of Appeals Ninth Circuit, No, 12-35266, Opinion, accessed 25 February 2013 at http://cdn.ca9.uscourts.gov/datastore/general/2013/02/25/1235266.pdf

Institute of Cetacean Research; Kyodo Senpaku Kaisha Ltd; Tomoyuki Ogawa; and Toshiyuki Muira v. Sea Shepherd Conservation Society and Paul Watson, United States Court of Appeals Ninth Circuit, No, 12-35266, Order, 17 December 2012

International Convention of the Regulation of Whaling (ICRW), 1946

Interpol, accessed 18 February 2013 at http://www.interpol.int/INTERPOL-expertise/Notices

'Iceland bids to resume whaling', *BBC News*, 22 March 2007, accessed 22 March 2007 at http://www.news.bbc.co.uk/1/hi/sci/tech/2910655.stm

'Japan plans wider sales of whale meat', *UPI*, 7 November 2012, accessed 7 November 2012 at http://www.upi.com/Top_News/World-News/2012/11/07/Japan-plans-wider-sales-of-whale-meat/UPI-70471352314575/

'Japan to arrest anti-whaling activist', *The Age*, 12 March 2010

'Japanese media report arrest warrant issued for Sea Shepherd leader Paul Watson', *Los Angeles Times*, 30 April 2010, accessed 30 April 2010 at http://latimesblogs.latimes.com/unleashed/2010/04/japanese-media-reports-arrest-warrant-issued-for-sea-shepherd-leader-paul-watson.html

Japanese whale poaching vessel, *Nisshin Maru*, rams South Korean fuel tanker, Sea Shepherd ships *Sam Simon, Steve Irwin* and *Bob Barker*', *Sea Shepherd Australia*, 20 February 2013, accessed 20 February 2013 at http://www.seashepherd.org.au/news-and-media/2013/02/20/japanese-whale-poaching-vessel-nisshin-maru-rams-s-korean-fuel-tanker-sea-shepherd-ships-sam-simon-s-1501

'Japanese whalers "quit hunting ground"', *Sydney Morning Herald*, 2 March 2013, accessed 2 March 2013 at http://www.smh.com.au/environment/whale-watch/japanese-whalers-quit-hunting-ground-20130302-2fcy7.html

'Japanese whaling fleet abandons harpoon vessel nearly empty on fuel, pressure Korean refuelling vessel to enter Australian Antarctic territory', *Sea Shepherd Australia*, 10 February 2013, accessed 10 February 2013 at http://www.seashepherd.org.au/news-and-media/2013/02/10/japanese-whaling-fleet-abandons-harpoon-vessel-nearly-empty-on-fuel-1491

'Japanese whaling ship rams Sea Shepherd protesters', *The Australian*, 20 February 2013

'Japan will never stop whaling: minister', *The Age*, 26 February 2013

'Japan will never stop whaling: minister', *The Herald Sun*, 26 February 2013

Jarboe, J.F. (2002) 'The threat of eco-terrorism', statement of James F. Jarboe, Domestic Terrorism Section Chief, Counter-Terrorism Division, Federal Bureau of Investigation, made before the House Resources Committee, Subcommittee on Forests and Forest Health, accessed 9 September 2014 at http://www.fbi.gov/congress/congress02jarboe021202.htm

Jasper, J.M. and Nelkin, D. (1992) *The Animal Rights Crusade: The Growth of a Moral Protest*, New York: Free Press

Jesus, H.E. (2003) 'Protection of foreign ships against piracy and terrorism at sea: legal aspects', *The International Journal of Marine and Coastal Law*, **18** (3), pp. 363–400

Joosse, Paul (2007) 'Leaderless resistance and ideological inclusion: the case of the Earth Liberation Front', *Terrorism and Political Violence*, **19** (3), pp. 351–68

'Justice Department – Animal Rights, Terrorism Research & Analysis Consortium', accessed 1 December 2015 at http://www.trackingterrorism.org/group/justice-department-animal-rights

Kamieniecki, Sheldon et al. (1995) 'The effectiveness of radical environmentalists' in Bron Taylor (ed.), *Ecological Resistance Movements: The Global Emergence of Radical and Popular Environmentalism*, Albany, NY: State University of New York Press

Karasick, P.J. (2009) 'Curb your ecoterrorism: identifying the nexus between state criminalization of ecoterror and environmental protection policy', *Environmental Law and Policy Review*, **33** (2), Winter

Kelly, Tom (2008) 'Guilty: animal terror gang who raised £1 million rattling tins on the high street', *The Daily Mail*, accessed 4 December

2015 at http://www.dailymail.co.uk/news/article-1100822/Guilty-Animal-terror-gang-raised-1million-rattling-tins-high-street.html, 24 December

Kennedy, J.R. (2012) 'Canadian activist Paul Watson named on Interpol's notice', 8 August, accessed 8 August 2012 at http://www.globalnews.ca/canadian+activist+paul+watson+named+on+interpols+notice/6442693600/story.html

Ketchum, 'Crisis Management Plan for the Clorox Company'

Khatchadourian, R. (2007) 'Neptune's Navy: Paul Watson's wild crusade to save the oceans', *The New Yorker*, 5 November

King, M. and Taylor, D.M. (2011) 'The radicalization of homegrown jihadists: a review of theoretical models and social psychological evidence', *Terrorism and Political Violence*, **23** (4), pp. 602–22

Kirby D., 'Sea Shepherd's Paul Watson mocks court's 'pirate' ruling', 28 February 2013, accessed 28 February 2013 at http://www.takepart.com/article/2013/02/28/us-court-calls-sea-shepherd-pirates

Koopmans, R. (1993) 'The dynamics of protest waves: West Germany, 1965–1989', *American Sociological Review*, **58** (5), pp. 637–58

Kruse, Corwin (2001) 'The movement and the media: framing the debate over animal experimentation', *Political Communication*, **18** (1), pp. 67–87

Kuipers, D. (1995) 'The tracks of the coyote', *Rolling Stone*, **70**, 1 June

Kuipers, Dean (2009) *Operation Bite Back: Rod Coronado's War to Save the American Wilderness*, New York: Bloomsbury

Kushner, H.W. (1998) *The Future of Terrorism: Violence in the New Millennium*, Thousand Oaks, CA: Sage Publications

Laurent, B. (2001) 'Eco-vandals put a match to "progress"', *Christian Science Monitor*, 5 July

Leader, Stefan and Probst, Peter (2003) 'The Earth Liberation Front and environmental terrorism', *Terrorism and Political Violence*, **15** (4), pp. 37–58

Lee, Martha F. (1995) 'Violence and the environment: the case of 'Earth First!', *Terrorism and Political Violence*, 7 (3), pp. 109–27

Lee, Ronnie (1983) 'Free the 4,344,843', *Peace News*, **2201**

Lee, Ronnie (1990) 'Animal Liberation But Not Too Much?', accessed 9 December 2015 at http://www.animalliberationfront.com/ALFront/Arkangel/Arkangel2.htm#nottoomuch, *Arkangel*

Lentini, P. (2003) 'Terrorism and its (re)sources: a review article', *The Australian and New Zealand Journal of Criminology*, **36** (3) (December), pp. 368–78

Lentini, P. (2008) 'The transference of Neojihadism: towards a process theory of transnational radicalisation', accessed 2 January 2016 at http://artsonline.monash.edu.au/gtrec/files/2012/08/gtrec-proceedings-2008-01-pete-lentini.pdf, pp. 8–9

Lentini, P. (2013) *Neojihadism*, Cheltenham, UK and Northampton, MA, USA: Edward Elgar Publishing

Letter from Paul Watson, Sea Shepherd Conservation (November 1986), p. 83

Lewis, J.L., Deputy Assistant Director, Counterterrorism Division Federal Bureau of Investigation, 'Congressional testimony before the Senate Judiciary Committee', Washington, DC (18 May 2004), accessed 17 April 2012 at http://www.fbi.gov/congress/congress04/lewis051804.htm

Liberation Press Office, accessed 12 December 2015 at http://animalliberationpressoffice.org/NAALPO/

Liddick, D.R. (2006) *Eco-Terrorism: Radical Environmental and Animal Liberation Movements*, Westport, Connecticut: Praeger

List, P.C. (1993) *Radical Environmentalism: Philosophy and Tactics*, Belmont, CA: Wadsworth, Inc.

Llanos, M. (2012) NBC News, 'Fugitive anti-whaling activist accuses former crew member of betraying him to Japan', 31 July, accessed 31 July 2012 at http://worldnews.nbcnews.com/_news/2012/07/31/13052889-fugitive…g-activist-accuses-former-crew-member-of-betraying-him-to-japan

Long, D. (2004) *Ecoterrorism: Library in a Book*, New York, Facts on File, Inc.

Lynch, M. (2003) 'Taking Arabs seriously', *Foreign Affairs*, **82** (5), September/October

MacLean L. (2012) 'The SSS Sam Simon is unveiled in Hobart, Tasmania', *Sea Shepherd Australia*, 10 December, accessed 10 December 2012 at http://www.seashepherd.org.au/news-and-media/2012/12/10/the-sss-sam-simon-is-unveiled-in-hobart-tasmania-1471

Malik S. (2012) 'Paul Watson, anti-whaling campaigner, held in Germany over 2002 incident', *The Guardian*, 14 May, accessed 14 May, 2012 at http://www.guardian.co.uk/environment/2012/may/14/paul-watson-arrested-germany-sea-shepherd

Manes, C. (1990) *Green Rage: Radical Environmentalism and the Unmaking of Civilization*, Boston, Toronto: Little Brown and Company

Mann, Keith (2008) *From Dusk 'til Dawn: An Insider's View of the Growth of the Animal Liberation Movement*, US: Voice of the Voiceless

Marine Wildlife Conservation (Circa 1984)

Marquis, J.K. and Weiss, D.M. (2005) 'Eco-terror: special interest terrorism', *Prosecutor*, Jan–Feb

McBride, M.K. (2011) 'The logic of terrorism: existential anxiety, the search for meaning, and terrorist ideologies', *Terrorism & Political Violence*, **23** (4), pp. 560–81

McCauley, C. and Moskalenko, S. (2008) 'Mechanisms of political radicalization: pathways towards terrorism', *Terrorism and Political Violence*, **20**, pp. 415–33

McDonald, M. (2010) 'Ships collide in war of nerves over whaling', *The New York Times*, 7 January

McLuhen D. (1996) *Children: The Greenpeace Message and the Media*, Toronto: Between the Lines

Melvin, D. (2011) *Tacoma News Tribune*, accessed 13 June 2011 at http://www.thenewstribune.com/2011/06/12/17029641/activists-searching-for-tuna-boats.html#ixzz1PMaVonDu

Mench, Joy A. and Bekoff, Mark (1998) *Encyclopedia of Animal Rights and Animal Welfare*, London: Greenwood Press

Midlarsky, M. (2011) *Origins of Political Extremism: Mass Violence in the Twentieth Century and Beyond*, Cambridge, UK: Cambridge University Press

MIPT Terrorism Knowledge Base, accessed 14 October 2006 at http://tkb.org

Mission Statement, accessed 15 August 2016 at http://www.animalliberationfront.com/ALFront/mission_statement.htm

Mobley, M. (2002), 'The new wave of radical environmentalism: America's inaction and reaction to domestic ecoterrorism', *Appalachian Journal of Law*, **1** (1), pp. 19–42

Moffa, A.L.I. (2012) 'Two competing models of activism, one goal: a case study of anti-whaling campaigns in the Southern Ocean, *Yale Journal of International Law*, **37**, p. 201

Moghaddam, F.M. (2005) 'The staircase to terrorism: a psychological exploration', *American Psychologist*, **60**, pp. 161–9

Molland, Noel, 'Thirty years of direct action', *No Compromise*, **18**, accessed 12 October 2015 at http://www.nocompromise.org/issues/18thirty_years.html

Molland, Noel (2006) 'A spark that ignited a flame: the evolution of the Earth Liberation Front' in Steven Best and Anthony Nocella (eds), *Igniting a Revolution: Voices in Defense of the Earth*, Oakland, CA: AK Press

Monaghan, Rachel (1997) 'Animal rights and violent protest', *Terrorism and Political Violence*, **9** (4), pp. 106–16

Monaghan, Rachel (1999) 'Terrorism in the name of animal rights', *Terrorism and Political Violence*, **11** (4), pp. 159–69

Monaghan, Rachel (2000) 'Single-issue terrorism: a neglected phenomenon?', *Studies in Conflict and Terrorism*, **23**, pp. 255–65

Monaghan, Rachel (2006) 'Animal rights and violent protest', *Terrorism and Political Violence, Liberation*, Westport, Connecticut: Praeger

Monaghan, Rachel (2007) 'Terrorism in the name of animal rights', *Terrorism and Political Violence*, 21 December, pp. 159–69

Monaghan, Rachel (2013) 'Not quite terrorism: animal rights extremism in the United Kingdom', *Studies in Conflict and Terrorism*, **36** (11), pp. 933–51

Morse, Dan, Vargas, Theresa and Euane, Michael (2010) 'Man slain after taking hostages', *Washington Post*, 2 September

Moskalenko, S. and McCauley, C. (2009) 'Measuring political mobilization: the distinction between activism and radicalism', *Terrorism and Political Violence*, **21** (2), pp. 239–60

Mullen, J. and Morgenstein, M. (2013) 'Anti-whaling activists say they were attacked by Japanese ships', *CNN.com*, 26 February, accessed 10 September 2016 at http://edition.cnn.com/2013/02/20/world/asia/australia-japan-whaling/

Mulvaney, K. (2012) 'Japanese public on whale meat: "meh"', *Discovery News*, 27 November, accessed 27 November 2012 at http://news.discovery.com/earth/japanese-public-on-whaling-whale-meat-meh-121127.htm

Munro, Lyle (1999) 'Contesting moral capital in campaigns against animal liberation', *Society & Animals*, **5** (2), pp. 43–4

Munro, L. (2005) *Confronting Cruelty: Moral Orthodoxy and the Challenge of the Animal Rights Movement*, Boston, Leiden: Brill

Munro, L. (2005) 'Strategies, action repertoires and DIY activism in the animal rights movement', *Social Movement Studies*, **4** (1), pp. 75–94

Murphy, D. (2010) 'Whale wars: the aggressive tactics of Sea Shepherd Paul Watson', *The Christian Science Monitor*, 6 January, accessed 6 January 2010 at http://www.csmonitor.com/World/Global-News/2010/0106/Whale-Wars-The-aggressive-tactics-of-Sea-Shepherd-Paul-Watson

Murray, J. and Whitworth C. (2010) 'Citizen's arrest attempted on Japanese whaling captain', *3-News*, 15 February

Nagtzaam, Gerry (2014) 'Righting the ship?: Australia, New Zealand and Japan at the ICJ and the barbed issue of "scientific whaling"', *Australian Journal of Environmental Law*, **1**, pp. 71–95

Nagtzaam, G and Lentini, P. (2008) 'Vigilantes on the high seas?: The Sea Shepherds and political violence', *Terrorism and Political Violence*, **20** (1), pp. 110–33

National Extremism Tactical Coordination Unit, *Domestic Extremism Tactics*, accessed 2008 at http://www.netcu.org.uk/protection/domesticextremisttactics.jsp

Neumann, P.R. (2013) 'The trouble with radicalization', *International Affairs*, **89** (4), pp. 873–93

Neumann, P.R. and Rogers, B. (2007) *Recruitment and Mobilisation for the Islamist Militant Movement in Europe*, London: Kings College, University of London

Neville, D.W. (2004) 'Dangerous dynamics: activists, militants and terrorists in Southeast Asia', *The Pacific Review*, **17** (1), pp. 27–46

Neville, D.W. (2006) 'Terrorism as the politics of dashed expectations', *Dialogue* (Academy of the Social Sciences in Australia), **25** (3), pp. 11–24

Newkirk, Ingrid (1992) *Free the Animals! The Amazing True Story of the Animal Liberation Movement*, Chicago: The Noble Free Press, Inc.

Nilson, C. and Burke, T. (2002) 'Environmental extremists and the eco-terrorism movement', *ACJS Today*, **24** (5), pp. 1–3

'Ninth Circuit Court of Appeals hands down ruling in favor of Japanese whale poachers', *Sea Shepherd Australia*, accessed 27 February 2013 at http://www.seashepherd.org.au/news-and-media/2013/02/27/ninth-circuit-court-of-appeals-hands-down-ruling-in-favor-of-japanese-whale-poachers-1507

Nocella, Anthony (2007) 'Unmasking the Animal Liberation Front using critical pedagogy: seeing the ALF for who they really are', *Journal for Critical Animal Studies*, **V** (1), pp. 1–10

North American Animal Liberation Press Office, accessed 1 December 2015 at http://animalliberationpressoffice.org/NAALPO/

O'Lear, S. (2003) 'Environmental terrorism: a critique', *Geopolitics*, **8** (3), pp. 127–50

'Our Sincere Apologies, Prime Minister: Commentary by Captain Paul Watson', 9 January 2012, accessed 10 September 2016 at http://www.seashepherd.org/commentary-and-editorials/2012/01/09/our-sincere-apologies-prime-minister-504

Pacheco, Alex and Francione, Anna (1985) 'The Silver Spring Monkeys' in Peter Singer (ed.), *In Defense of Animals*, New York: Basil Blackwell, pp. 135–47

Paris, S.E. (1995) 'Firebombing 'animal liberationist' given prison sentence for his terrorism', *Human Events*, **51** (33), p. 17

Parson, Sean (2008) 'Understanding the ideology of the Earth Liberation Front', *Green Theory & Praxis: The Journal of Ecopedagogy*, **4** (2), pp. 50–66

'Paul Watson quits Sea Shepherd over US court order', *CBCNews*, 8 January 2013, accessed 8 January 2013 at http://www.cbc.ca/news/world/story/2013/01/08/canada-paul-watson-sea-shepherd-conservation-society-president.html

'Paul Watson resigns as leader of anti-whaling organisation Sea Shepherd', *The Globe and Mail*, 8 January 2013, accessed 8 January 2013 at http://www.theglobeandmail.com/news/british-columbia/paul-watson-resigns-as-leader-of-anti-whaling-organisation-sea-shepherd/article7039373/

'Paul Watson tells Alex McClintock why he won't give up fighting for the whales', *Sydney Morning Herald*, 14 March 2010

'People and animals: also part of creation', *The Economist*, 19 August 1995, pp. 17–19

People for the Ethical Treatment of Animals (PETA), 'Activist Facts', accessed 1 December 2015 at https://www.activistfacts.com/organizations/21-people-for-the-ethical-treatment-of-animals/

'Peter Hammarstedt biography' accessed 30 November 2015 at http://seashepherd.org.au/relentless/bob-barker-crew/peter-hammarstedt.html

Petersen, L. (2013) 'OCEANS: Sea Shepherd takes fight against Japanese whalers to Supreme Court', *Sea Shepherd Australia*, accessed 12 February 2013 at http://www.seashepherd.org.au/news-and-media/2013/02/12/oceans-sea-shepherd-takes-fight-against-japanese-whalers-to-supreme-court-1493

Plows, Alexandra, Wall, Derek and Doherty, Brian (2001) 'From the Earth Liberation Front to universal dark matter: the challenge of covert repertoires to social movement research', Paper for the Workshop on Democracy and Extremism European Consortium for Political Research Joint Sessions Grenoble, 6–11 April

Plows, Alexandra, Wall, Derek and Doherty, Brian (2004) 'Covert repertoires: ecotage in the UK', *Social Movement Studies*, **3** (2), pp. 199–219

Porta, D. and Rucht, D. (1995) 'The dynamics of environmental campaigns', *Mobilization*, **7** (1), pp. 1–14

PR Newswire, 4 March 1995

Proussalidis, D. (2012) 'Germans search for eco-fugitive Paul Watson', *Toronto Sun*, 2 August, accessed 2 August 2012 at http://www.torontosun.com/2012/08/02/germans-search-for-eco-fugitive-paul-watson

Quillen, C. (2002) 'A historical analysis of mass casualty bombers', *Studies in Conflict and Terrorism*, **25** (5), pp. 279–92

'Ram claims as Japanese whalers, Sea Shepherd protesters cash', *The Australian*, 26 February 2013

'Reaching critical will, references to the definition of terrorism and the United Nations General Assembly Debate, Measures to Eliminate International Terrorism', 1 October to 5 October 2001, United Nations, New York, accessed at http://www.reachingcritical will.org/political/1com/terror.html

Regan, Tom (1989) 'The case for animal rights', in Tom Regan and Peter Singer (eds), *Animal Rights and Human Obligations*, 2nd edn, New Jersey: Prentice Hall, pp. 111–12

Reid, N. (2012) 'The Sea Shepherd extends battlefield', 28 October, accessed 28 October 2012 at http://www.stuff.co.nz/national/7873346/The-Sea-Shepherd-extends-battlefield

Rodney Coronado, accessed 1 December 2015 at http://www.targetofopportunity.com/coronado.htm

Roe, Nicholas (1988) 'Crusaders against cruelty: whether sabotaging hunts, fire-bombing or burgling, anti-vivisectionists are sure right is on their side', *London Independent*, 12 December

Roeschke, J.E. (2009) 'Ecoterrorism and piracy on the high seas: Japanese whaling and the rights of private groups to enforce international conservation law in neutral waters', *Villanova Environmental Law*, **20**, p. 99

Rosebraugh, C. (2004) *Burning rage of a dying planet: speaking for the Earth Liberation Front*, New York: Lantern Books

Rosenthal, D. (2012) 'High seas hijinks for Paul Watson', 22 May 2012, accessed 17 June 2012 at http://www2.macleans.ca/2012/05/22/high-seas-hijinks/

Rowan, Andrew N. (1984) *Of Mice, Models and Men: A Critical Evaluation of Animal Research*, New York: SUNY Press

Rowell, A. (1996) *Green Backlash: Global Subversion of the Environment Movement*, London, New York: Routledge, p. 150

Russell, Sue (2012) 'When extreme animal rights activists attack', *Pacific Standards, Politics & Law*, 17 March, accessed 1 December 2015 at http://www.psmag.com/politics-and-law/when-extreme-animal-rights-activists-attack-40430

Safi, M. (2014) 'Shark cull in Western Australia may be halted after Sea Shepherd court ruling', *The Guardian*, 5 March, accessed 5 March 2014 at http://www.theguardian.com/environment/2014/mar/05/shark-cull-may-be-called-off-after-sea-shepherds-court-challenge-in-wa

Sageman, M. (2004) *Understanding Terror Networks*, Philadelphia, PA: University of Pennsylvania Press

Sageman, M. (2008) 'A strategy for fighting international Islamist terrorists', *The Annals of the American Academy of Political and Social Science*, **618** (1), pp. 223–31

Sahagun, L. (2010) 'Whaling fight highlights two key donors', *Los Angeles Times*, 7 January

Sansone, K. (2010) 'Sea Shepherd attacks Maltese fishermen, two sent to hospital', *Times of Malta*, 18 June

Scarce, Rik (2006) *Eco-Warriors: Understanding the Radical Environmental Movement*, updated edn, California: Left Coast Press

Schmid, A.P. (2013) *Radicalisation, de-radicalisation, counter-radicalisation: a conceptual discussion and literature review*, ICCT Research Paper, March

Schnurer, Maxwell (2004) 'At the gates of hell: the ALF and the legacy of Holocaust resistance', in Steven Best and Anthony Nocella (eds), *Terrorists or Freedom Fighters: Reflections on the Liberation of Animals,* New York: Lantern Books

Schuler, M. (2013) 'Paul Watson and Sea Shepherd are pirates, US court says', 27 February, accessed 10 September 2016 at http://gcaptain.com/paul-watson-and-shepherd-pirates-us-court-rules/

Schwartz, D.M. (1998) 'Environmental terrorism: analyzing the concept', *Journal of Peace Research*, **35** (4), pp. 483–96

Sea Shepherd (2007) 'Japanese whaling fleet forced to run from Sea Shepherd', *Sea Shepherd News*, 8 February, accessed 10 February 2007 at http://www.seashepherd.org/news/media_070208_1p.html

Sea Shepherd (2007) 'Whalers activities disrupted by Sea Shepherd', *Sea Shepherd News*, 8 February

'Sea Shepherd Australia to Lead Antarctic whale defense campaign', *Sea Shepherd Australia*, 7 January, accessed 7 January 2013 at http://www.seashepherd.org.au/news-and-media/2013/01/07/sea-shepherd-australia-to-lead-antarctic-whale-defense-campaign-1477

'Sea Shepherd boss blames Japan for arrest', 22 May, accessed 22 May 2012 at http://www.theage.com.au/environment/whale-watch/sea-shepherd-boss-blames-japan-for-arrest-20120522-1z2ta.html

'Sea Shepherd confiscates Japanese drift net', *Sea Shepherd Log*, 1992, third quarter

Sea Shepherd Conservation Society Chapters, accessed 2 January 2016 at http://www.seashepherd.org/chapters/

'Sea Shepherd crew remain hostages on the Japanese whaling ship, accessed 16 January 2009 at http://www.seashepherd.org/news-and-media/news-releases/Page-1.html

'Sea Shepherd has intercepted the whale poachers before a single whale is killed', *Sea Shepherd Australia*, 29 January, accessed 29 January 2013 at http://www.seashepherd.org.au/news-and-media/2013/01/28/sea-shepherd-has-intercepted-the-whale-poachers-1482

'Sea Shepherd history' (1983) *Sea Shepherd Log* (winter)

'Sea Shepherd launches operation zero tolerance', *Sea Shepherd Australia*, 5 November 2012, accessed 5 November 2012 at http://www.seashepherd.org.au/news-and-media/2012/11/05/sea-shepherd-launches-operation-zero-tolerance-1462

'Sea Shepherd leader fears for his life', 17 May 2012, accessed 17 May 2012 at http://www.theage.com.au/environment/whale-watch/sea-shepherd-leader-fears-for-his-life-20120517-1ys4h.html

'Sea Shepherd severs fuel supply to the whaling fleet', *Sea Shepherd Australia*, 7 February 2013, accessed 7 February 2013 at http://www.seashepherd.org.au/news-and-media/2013/02/07/sea-shepherd-severs-fuel-supply-to-the-whaling-fleet-1489

'Sea Shepherd ship *Bob Barker* is on the slipway of the *Nisshin Maru*', *Sea Shepherd Australia*, 15 February 2013, accessed 15 February 2013 at http://www.seashepherd.org.au/news-and-media/2013/02/15/sea-shepherd-ship-bob-barker-is-on-the-slipway-of-the-nisshin-maru-1495

'Sea Shepherd ships intercept the *Nisshin Maru* – whale poachers on the run', *Sea Shepherd Australia*, 30 January 2013, accessed 30 January 2013 at http://www.seashepherd.org.au/news-and-media/2013/01/30/sea-shepherd-ships-intercept-the-nisshin-maru-1483

'Sea Shepherd ships set to be raided by Australian Federal Police', *Perth Now*, 3 March 2013

'Sea Shepherd takes battle against ICR to US Supreme Court', *Sea Shepherd Australia*, 13 February 2013, accessed 13 February 2013 at http://www.seashepherd.org.au/news-and-media/2013/02/13/sea-shepherd-takes-battle-against-icr-to-us-supreme-court-1497

'Sea Shepherd vessel *Ady Gil* sinking after being hit by Japanese whaler', accessed 5 January 2016 at http://www.japantoday.com/category/national/view/sea-shepherd-obstructs-japans-whaling-operations-for-4th-time

'Sea Shepherds record of violence', *The High North News Extra*, No. 7, 10 April 1994

Serious Organised Crime and Police Act 2005, accessed 13 December 2015 at http://www.legislation.gov.uk/ukpga/2005/15/contents

Sharkwater (2006) directed and produced by Rob Stewart, Canada: Alliance Films

'Shepherd fugitive to stay at sea', *The Age*, 2 September 2012, accessed 2 September 2012 at http://www.theage.com.au/environment/whale-watch/shepherd-fugitive-to-stay-at-sea-20120901-2573r.html

Silber, M.D., Bhatt, A. and Senior Intelligence Analysts (2007) *Radicalization in the West: The Homegrown Threat*, New York: Police Department

Silvaggio, A.V. (2005) 'The Forest Defense Movement, 1980–2005: resistance at the point of extraction, consumption, and production', PhD dissertation, University of Oregon

Silverstein, Helena (1996) *Unleashing Rights: Law, Meaning, and the Animal Rights Movement*, Detroit: University of Michigan Press

Singer, Peter (1990) *Animal Liberation*, New York: Random House

Smith, Brent L. (1994) *Terrorism in America: Pipe Bombs and Pipe Dreams*, Albany, NY: University of New York Press

Smith, C.M. (2006) 'From monkeywrenching to mass destruction: eco-sabotage and the American West', *Journal of Land Resources and Environmental Law*, **26**, p. 319

Smith, Phillip Andrew (2014) 'The axe without the handle: an exploratory analysis of eco-terrorism and its relationships to U.S. public policy towards terrorism: 1990–2010', PhD dissertation, Nova Southeastern University, 245 pages; 3646796, http://gradworks.umi.com/36/46/3646796.html

Smith, T. (date unknown) 'Whaling protester to be charged in Japan', *The Associated Press*

Snow, D., Rochford, E.B., Worden, S. and Benford, R. (1986) 'Frame alignment processes, micromobilization, and movement participation', *American Sociological Review*, **51**, pp. 461–81

Speaking of Research (2009) 'Grave robbing by animal rights extremists', 5 August, accessed 4 December 2015 at http://speakingofresearch.com/2009/08/05/graverobbing-by-animal-rights-extremists/

Sprinzak, Ehud (1987) 'From messianic pioneering to vigilante terrorism: the case of the gush emunim underground', *Journal of Strategic Studies*, **10** (4), pp. 194–216

Sprinzak, Ehud (1991) 'The process of delegitimation: towards a linkage theory of political terrorism', *Terrorism & Political Violence*, **3** (1), pp. 50–68

Sprinzak, E. (1995) 'Right-wing terrorism in comparative perspective: the case of split delegitimization', in Tore Bjørgo (ed.), *Terror From the Extreme Right*, London: Frank Cass & Co. Ltd, pp. 17–43

Sprinzak, Ehud (1990) 'The psychopolitical formation of extreme left terrorism in a democracy: the case of the Weathermen', in Walter Reich (ed.), *Origins of Terrorism: Psychologies, Ideologies, Theologies, States of Mind*, Washington, DC: Woodrow Wilson Center Press, pp. 65–85

Sprinzak, E. (1998) 'The psychopolitical formation of extreme left terrorism in a democracy: the case of the Weathermen', in Walter Reich (ed.), *Origins of Terror*, Baltimore, M.A.: John Hopkins University Press

Stallwood, Kim (2004) 'A personal overview of direct action in the United Kingdom and the United States', in Steven Best and Anthony Nocella (eds), *Terrorists or Freedom Fighters: Reflections on the Liberation of Animals*, New York: Lantern Books

Stone, L. (2012) 'Canadian anti-whaling activist Paul Watson flees Germany after Japan issues extradition request', 26 July 2012, accessed 26 July 2012 at http://www.thestar.com/news/world/article/1232562–canadian-anti-w…t-paul-watson-flees-germany-after-japan-issues-extradition-request

Stylianou, G. (2013) 'High-seas protester slips past Kiwi search', 17 January, accessed 7 January 2013 at http://www.stuff.co.nz/the-press/news/8148473/High-seas-protester-slips-past-Kiwi-search

Taylor, Bron (1995) 'Earth First! and global narratives of popular ecological resistance' in Bron Taylor (ed.), *Ecological Resistance Movements: The Global Emergence of Radical and Popular Environmentalism*, Albany, NY: State University of New York Press

Taylor, Bron (1998) 'Religion, violence and radical environmentalism: from Earth First! to the Unabomber to the Earth Liberation Front, *Terrorism and Political Violence*, **10** (4), pp. 1–42

Taylor, Bron (2003) 'Threat assessments and radical environmentalism', *Terrorism and Political Violence*, **15** (4), 173–82

Taylor, B.R. (1995) 'Introduction: the global emergence of popular ecological resistance and Chapter 1: Earth First! and global narratives of popular ecological resistance', in B.R. Taylor (ed.), *Ecological Resistance Movements: The Global Emergence of Radical and Popular Environmentalism*, Albany: State University of New York Press

'Tensions rise in clash with the Japanese whalers', *Sea Shepherd Australia*, 25 February 2013, accessed 25 February 2013 at http://www.seashepherd.org.au/news-and-media/2013/02/25/tensions-rise-in-clash-with-the-japanese-whalers-1504

Tester, Keith and Walls, John (1996) 'The ideology and current activities of the Animal Liberation Front', *Contemporary Politics*, **2** (2), pp. 79–91

'The ALF unmasked – interview with David Barbarash', accessed 8 August 2015 at http://www.animallib.org.au/more_interviews/barbarash

'The bullshit politics of betrayal: commentary by Captain Paul Watson', 8 January 2012, accessed 10 September 2016 at http://www.seashepherd.org/commentary-and-editorials/2012/01/08/the-bullshit-politics-of-betrayal-503

'The early history of animal rights extremism, Animal Liberation Front', accessed 12 October 2015 at http://www.understandinganimalresearch.org.uk/policy/animal-rights-extremism/the-early-history-of-animal-rights-extremism/

The Economist (2011) 'A beastly business – peaceful protests against animal testing is on the rise', 22 October 2011, accessed 1 December 2015, http://www.economist.com/node/21533451

The United Nations Convention for the Suppression of Unlawful Acts Against the Safety of Maritime Navigation, March 10 1988, 1678 U.N.T.S. 201

Trujillo, H.R. (2005) 'The radical environmentalist movement', *Aptitude for Destruction*, **2**, pp. 141–78

'US court tells Sea Shepherd to stay away from Japan's whaling fleet in Southern Ocean', *MercoPress*, 19 December 2012, accessed 19 December 2012 at http://en.mercopress.com/2012/12/19/us-court-tells-sea-shepherd-to-stay-away-from-japan-s-whaling-fleet-in-southern-ocean

'US court order to prevent clashes between Japanese whalers and Sea Shepherd vessels', *The Australian*, 19 December 2012

Vanderheiden, S. (2005) 'Eco-terrorism or justified resistance? Radical environmentalism and the 'war on terror', *Politics and Society*, **33** (3), pp. 425–47

Vanderheiden, S. (2008) 'Radical environmentalism in the age of anti-terrorism,' *Environmental Politics*, **17** (2), pp. 299–318

Vaughan, Claudette (2010) 'Animal soldiers – a rare exclusive interview with Ronnie Lee', accessed 11 October 2015 at https://carmen4thepets.wordpress.com/2010/03/22/animal-soldiers-a-rare-and-exclusive-interview-with-ronnie-lee/

Verhovek, Sam Howe (2001) 'Radical animal rights groups step up protests', *New York Times*, 12 November

Vienna Convention on the Law of Treaties, 23 May 1969, 1155 U.N.T.S. 331

Wade, John (2006) 'Radical environmentalism: is there any other kind', in Steven Best and Anthony Nocella (eds), *Igniting a Revolution: Voices in Defence of the Earth*, Oakland: AK Press, pp. 280–3

Wall, Derek (1999) *Earth First! and the Anti-Roads Movement: Radical Environmentalism and Comparative Social Movements*, London and New York: Routledge

Wall, Derek (2000) 'Snowballs, elves and skimmingtons?: Genealogies of environmental direct action' in B. Seel, M. Paterson and B. Doherty (eds), *Direct Action in British Environmentalism*, London and New York: Routledge

Wallace, R. (2012) 'Japanese whalers return to port', *The Australian*, 10 March

Watson Paul, Alternative Radio, recorded in Alma, MI, accessed 8 October 2001 at http://www.alternativeradio.org/programs/WATP001.shtml

Watson, Paul (1982) *Sea Shepherd: My Fight for Whales and Seals*, New York and London: W.W. Norton and Company

Watson, Paul (1991) 'Sea Shepherd Defense Policy', *Earth Island Journal*, **6** (4), pp. 41–3

Watson, Paul (1993) 'Captain's Log', *Sea Shepherd Log*, third quarter

Watson, Paul (1993) *Earthforce!: An Earth Warrior's Guide to Strategy*, Los Angeles, CA: Chaco Press

Watson, Paul (1994) *Ocean Warrior: My Battle to End the Illegal Slaughter on the High Seas*, Toronto: Key Porter Books Ltd

Watson, Paul (2003) *Seal Wars: Twenty-Five Years on the Front Lines with the Harp Seals*, Buffalo, NY: Firefly Books

Watson, Paul (2004) 'ALF and ELF – terrorism is as terrorism does', in Steven Best and Anthony Nocella (eds), *Terrorists or Freedom Fighters: Reflections on the Liberation of Animals*, New York: Lantern Books

Watson, Paul (2011) 'Will this be the Sea Shepherd's last Antarctic campaign?', 28 January, accessed 10 September 2016 at https://www.seashepherd.org.au/news-and-commentary/commentary/will-this-be-sea-shepherd-s-last-antarctic-campaign.html accessed

Watson, Paul (2012) 'The law takes precedence over justice in Germany', accessed 29 May 2012 at http://www.seashepherd.org/commentary-and-editorials/2012/05/29/the-law-takes-precedence-over-justice-in-germany-540

Watson, Paul (2012) 'Tora! Tora! Tora!, *Earth Ethics*, 341–46

'Watson prepares defense in Costa Rica', *Tico Times* (Costa Rica), 16 May 2012

Weinberg, L.B. and Davis, P.B. (1989) *Introduction to Political Terrorism*, New York: McGraw-Hill

Westlake, A. (2012) 'Japan's whaling industry looks forward to arrest of Sea Shepherd's Watson', *The Japan Daily Press*, 5 November

Westlake, A. (2013) 'Paul Watson steps down as Sea Shepherd leader, Australian Greens' Bob Brown takes over', *The Japan Daily Press*, 8 January, accessed 8 January 2013 at http://japandailypress.com/paul-watson-steps-down-as-sea-shepherd-leader-australian-greens-bob-brown-takes-over-0821046

Westlake, A. (2013) 'Sea Shepherd claims early victory against Japan's whaling fleet', *The Japan Daily Press*, 31 January 2013, accessed 31 January 2013 at http://japandailypress.com/sea-shepherd-claims-early-victory-against-japans-whaling-fleet-3122399

Weyler, Rex (2004) *Greenpeace: An Insider's Account*, London: Rosdale International

Whale Wars, seasons 1–4, *Animal Planet*, 2009–13

'*Whaling in the Antarctic (Australia v Japan: New Zealand Intervening)* Judgment, I.C.J. Reports', pp. 226–379, available at http://www.icj-cij.org/docket/files/148/18136.pdf

'What did we accomplish in 1987?', *Sea Shepherd Log*, December 1987

White, Jonathan Randall (1991) *Terrorism: an introduction*, Pacific Grove, CA: Brooks/Cole Publishing Company

Willacy, M. (2010) 'Sea Shepherd's Watson on Interpol's wanted list', *Australian Broadcasting Company*, 27 June

Wolke, H. and Foreman, D. (September 1980) *Memorandum Regarding Earth First*, p. 1

World Charter for Nature, G.A. Res. 37/7, 455, U.N. Doc. A/RES/37/7, 28 October 1982

Yamaguchi, M. (2010) 'Japan court convicts NZ anti-whaling activist', *Associated Press*, 7 July

Young, A.J. and Valencia, M.J. (2003) 'Conflation of piracy and terrorism in Southeast Asia: rectitude and utility', *Contemporary Southeast Asia*, **25** (2), pp. 269–83

Young, Peter (2010) 'Egg farm denies raid by ALF', *Voice of the Voiceless*, blog, 7 April, accessed 10 September 2016 at http://animalliberationfrontline.com/egg-farm-denies-raid-by-the-alf/

Young, Peter (2011) 'Walter Bond receives minimum sentence in A.L.F. arson', *Voice of the Voiceless*, blog, 13 February 2011, accessed 10 September 2016 at http://animalliberationfrontline.com/walter-bond-receives-minimum-sentence-in-a-l-f-arson/

Young, Robert (1996) '"Monkeywrenching" and the processes of democracy', in Freya Mathews (ed.), *Ecology and Democracy*, London: Frank Cass

Young, R.L. (2004) 'A time series analysis of eco-terrorist violence in the United States: 1993–2003', PhD dissertation, Sam Houston State University, Huntsville, TX

Index